MILLER'S
Collectables
PRICE ◆ GUIDE
1991-92

(Volume III)

Compiled and Edited by
Judith and Martin Miller

General Editor: Robert Murfin.

GUILD PUBLISHING

LONDON · NEW YORK · SYDNEY · TORONTO

Four Confederate Cavalry troopers and
1 officer, No. 2055, mounted in original box.
£90-100   *WAL*

MILLER'S COLLECTABLES PRICE GUIDE 1991/92

Compiled, edited and designed by
M.J.M. Publishing Projects for
Millers Publications Limited
This edition published 1991 by
Book Club Associates
by arrangement with
Millers Publications

Compiled and edited by
Judith & Martin Miller

General Editor: Robert Murfin
Editorial co-ordinator: Sue Boyd
Artwork: Nigel O'Gorman, Chris Huggett
Photographic co-ordinator and advertising executive: Elizabeth Smith
Display Advertisements: Trudi Hinkley
Index compiled by DD Editorial Services, Beccles
Additional photography by Ian Booth and Robin Saker

Typeset by Ardek Photosetters, St Leonards-on-Sea
Printed and bound in England by William Clowes Ltd
Beccles and London

Introduction

In a year that has seen a very quiet time for the general art and antiques market, it is surprising to report an encouraging buoyancy in the field of collectables. Is this because the sums of money involved are, by comparison, often less than those required to obtain established antiques or is it that collectors are more fanatical and are prepared to sacrifice other things in order to spend their disposable income on their beloved collections? I welcome, as always, your comments.

Toys continue to show not only a dedicated following but also a steady increase in price; dolls (we have a good selection of dolls house furniture and accessories this year), soldiers and trains, as well as diecast cars and aeroplanes are perennial favourites.

Coffee making equipment has become a popular and fascinating area for both collectors and students of social history, as indeed has 40s and 50s Americana. Whilst on the subject, ceramics of that era are beginning to attract attention. As I always say, identify what you like, learn your subject and start looking; there is no time like the present and there has never been a better time to buy.

We have also seen greatly increased interest in wristwatches. Post First World War, famous named watches, and watches that perform a variety of functions are keenly sought. Large diving type watches and chronographs are selling well in Europe and those beautifully designed and sophisticated looking watches from between the wars are both collectable and usable.

Many other 20s, 30s and 40s accessories, shoes, clothes, handbags and luggage particularly, are also now highly prized. Any items that were well made from top quality materials, and preferably showing a fashionable label, will always be worth collecting, so don't be too quick to throw away your trendy designer goods from the 1980s!

19th and 20th century glass is another area worth considering; we have a good selection of night lights in this year's book, many of which are still in daily or nightly use. We would be delighted to hear of other collectables which you may have that are still used regularly.

Your comments and suggestions are welcome both on this new edition and on ideas for next year. Finally, good luck and good hunting.

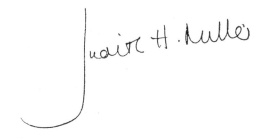

Key to Illustrations

Each illustration and descriptive caption is accompanied by a letter-code. By reference to the following list of Auctioneers (denoted by *) and Dealers (●), the source of any item may be immediately determined. In no way does this constitute or imply a contract or binding offer on the part of any of our contributors to supply or sell the goods illustrated, or similar articles, at the prices stated. Advertisers in this year's directory are denoted by †.

AAM †● Anything American (Chris Pearce), 33-35 Duddenhill Lane, London NW10. Tel: 081-451 0320

ABS ● Abstract, 58-60 Kensington Church Street, London W8. Tel: 071-376 2652

ACC †● Albert's, 113 London Road, Twickenham, Middx. Tel: 081-891 3067

AD ● Anne & Dolores, Victorian lace, linen and costume, Bartlett Street Antique Market, Bath. Tel: (0225) 330267

AG * Anderson & Garland, Marlborough House, Marlborough Crescent, Newcastle-upon-Tyne. Tel: 091-232 6278

AGM ● Alan & Gillian Meredith, Twist Knot House, Kyrle Street, Ross on Wye, Hereford and Worcester. Tel: (0989) 66089

AJ †● A.J. Partners, Alfies Stand F104, Church Street, Marylebone, NW8. Tel: 071-258 3602/723 5363

AL †● Ann Lingard, Ropewalk Antiques, Ropewalk, Rye, Sussex. Tel: (0797) 223486

ARC ● Architectural Antiques, West Ley, Alswear Old Road, South Molton, Devon. Tel: (07695) 3342

ASA ● AS Antiques & Decorative Arts, 26 Broad Street, Pendleton, Salford 6, Manchester. Tel: 061-737 5938

ASc ● Ascott Antiques, Narborough, Leics. Tel: (0533) 863190

BA ● Burman Antiques, 5A Chapel Street. Stratford-upon-Avon, Warks. Tel: (0789) 293917/295164

BBR ● British Bottle Review, 2 Strafford Avenue, Elsecar, Barnsley, S. Yorks. Tel: (0226) 745156/(0709) 879309

Bea * Bearnes, Rainbow, Avenue Road, Torquay, Devon. Tel: (0803) 26277

BEB ● Judy Bebber, Antique Dolls, L14 Grays Antique Market, 1-7 Davies Mews, London W1. Tel: 071-499 6600

BEV †● Beverley, 30 Church Street, London NW8. Tel: 071-262 1576

BLO †● Bloomsbury Antiques, 58-60 Kensington Church Street, London W8. Tel: 071-376 2810

Bon †* Bonhams, Montpelier Galleries, Montpelier Street, Knightsbridge, London SW7. Tel: 071-584 9161

BRE ● Brenin Porcelain & Pottery, Cowbridge, South Glamorgan

BRK ● Breck Antiques, 726 Mansfield Road, Nottingham. Tel: (0602) 605263

BS ● Below Stairs, 103 High Street, Hungerford, Berks. Tel: (0488) 682317

BY ● Bygones, Collectors Shop, 123 South Street, Lancing, Sussex. Tel: (0903) 750051/763470

An electrotype figure of a cricketer, 20in (50.5cm) high.
£800-1,400 *MSh*

C   *   Christie, Manson & Woods Ltd, 8 King Street, St James's, London SW1. Tel: 071-839 9060

CA   ●   Crafers Antiques, The Hill, Wickham Market, Suffolk. Tel: (0728) 747347

CAB   †●   Candlestick & Bakelite, PO Box 308, Orpington, Kent. Tel: 081-467 3743

CAC   ●   Cranbrook Antique Centre, High Street, Cranbrook, Kent. Tel: (0580) 712173

CAm   *   Christie's Amsterdam, Cornelis Schuystraat 57 1071 JG, Amsterdam, Holland. Tel: 020 64 20 11

CBA   ●   Chateaubriand Antiques Centre, High Street, Burwash, E. Sussex. Tel: (0435) 882535

CCC   †●   The Crested China Co, The Station House, Driffield, E. Yorks. Tel: (0377) 47042

CD   †●   The China Doll, 31 Walcot Street, Bath, Avon. Tel: (0225) 465849

Ced   ●   Cedar Antiques Studio, c/o Stamford Antiques Centre, Lincs.

CFA   ●   Cambridge Fine Art, Priesthouse, 33 Church Street, Little Shelford, Cambridge. Tel: (0223) 842866

CLH   †●   Clem Harwood, The Old Bakery, Keevil, Trowbridge, Wilts. Tel: (0380) 870463

CLI   ●   Cliffe Antiques, Warwick Antique Centre, 20 High Street, Warwick. Tel: (0926) 495704

CMon   *   Christie's Monaco, 98000 Park Palace, Monaco. Tel: 93 25 19 33

COB   †●   Cobwebs, 78 Northam Road, Southampton. Tel: (0703) 227458

COL   †●   Collectables, 335 High Street, Rochester, Kent. Tel: (0634) 293102

CNY   *   Christie, Manson & Woods International Inc, 502 Park Avenue, New York, NY 10022, USA. Tel: 212546 1000 (including Christie's East)

CS   †●   Christopher Sykes Antiques, The Old Parsonage, Woburn, Bucks. Tel: (0525) 290259/290467

C(S)   *   Christie's Scotland Ltd, 164-166 Bath Street, Glasgow. Tel: 041-332 8134

CSA   †●   Church Street Antiques, 15 Church Street, Godalming, Surrey. Tel: (0483) 860894

CSC   ●   The Chicago Sound Company, Northmoor House, Colesbrook, Gillingham, Dorset. Tel: (0747) 824338

CSK   †*   Christie's (South Kensington) Ltd, 85 Old Brompton Road, London SW7. Tel: 071-581 7611

CT   ●   Children's Treasures, 17 George Street, Hastings, E. Sussex. Tel: (0424) 444117/422758

DDM   *   Dickinson, Davy & Markham, Wrawby Street, Brigg, S. Humberside. Tel: (0652) 53666

DEN   *   Denham Associates, Horsham Auction Galleries, Warnham, Horsham, W. Sussex. Tel: (0403) 55699/53837

DH   †●   The Dog House, 309 Bloxwich Road, Walsall, W. Midlands. Tel: (0922) 30829

DIM   ●   Dimech, 248 Camden High Street, London NW1. Tel: 071-485 8072

DN   *   Dreweatt Neate, Donnington Priory, Donnington, Newbury, Berks. Tel: (0635) 31234

DOW   ●   Mrs M. Downworth, Great Western Antiques, Wednesday Market, Bartlett Street, Bath, Avon

DP   ●   David Payne, Bartlett Street Antiques Market, 9 Bartlett Street, Bath, Avon. Tel: (0225) 330267

EA   ●   Eleanor Antiques, Smith Street Antique Centre, Warwick. Tel: (0926) 497864

EAS   ●   Eastgate Antiques, Alfies Antique Market, 13-25 Church Street, London NW8. Tel: 071-724 5650

EHA   ●   Gloria Gibson, 2 Beaufort West, Bath, Avon. Tel: (0225) 446646

FA   ●   Frank Andrews, 10 Vincent Road, London N22. Tel: 081-881 0658

FAL   ●   Falstaff Antiques, 63-67 High Street, Rolvenden (Motor Museum), Kent. Tel: (0580) 241234

FEN   *   R. A. Fenner & Co, The Stannary Gallery, Drake Road, Tavistock, Devon. Tel: (0822) 617799

G&CC   †●   Goss and Crested China Ltd (Nicholas J. Pine), 62 Murray Road, Horndean, Hants. Tel: (0705) 597440

GH   *   Giles Haywood, The Auction House, St John's Road, Stourbridge, W. Midlands. Tel: (0384) 370891

GHA   ●   Garden House Antiques, 118 High Street, Tenterden, Kent. Tel: (05806) 3664

GIL   *   Gildings, Roman Way, Market Harborough, Leics. Tel: (0858) 410414

GIN   ●   Ray & Diane Ginns, PO Box 129, East Grinstead, W. Sussex. Tel: (0860) 294789

GKR   †●   GKR Bonds Ltd, PO Box 1, Kelvedon, Essex. Tel: (0376) 71711

GOL   †●   The Golf Gallery, Grays in the Mews B12, Davies Mews, London W1. Tel: 071-408 1239/081-452 7243

A silver plated and brown leather covered petrol burning table lighter, 8 day watch mounted on the front, 42½ by 32½in (108 by 82mm). **£300-400**   *CSK*

GSP * Graves, Son & Pilcher, 71 Church Road, Hove, E. Sussex. Tel: (0273) 735266

HAR ● Patricia Harbottle, 107 Portobello Road, Geoffrey Vann Arcade, London W11. Tel: 071-731 1972

HCH * Hobbs & Chambers, Market Place, Cirencester, Glos. Tel: (0285) 4736

HOW ● Howards Antiques, 73 Wyle Cop, Shrewsbury, Salop. Tel: (0743) 60737

HSS * Henry Spencer & Sons, 20 The Square, Retford, Notts. Tel: (0777) 708633

HUN ● Huntercombe Manor Barn, Henley on Thames, Oxon. Tel: (0491) 641349

IS †● Ian Sharp Antiques, 23 Front Street, Tynemouth. Tel: 091-296 0656

IW †● Islwyn Watkins, 1 High Street, 29 Market Street, Knighton, Powys. Tel: (0547) 520145/528940

J ● Jessop Classic Photogaphica, 67 Great Russell Street, London WC1. Tel: 071-831 3640

JAG ● J.A.G. Applied Arts, 248 Camden High Street, London NW1. Tel: 071-485 8072

JHo ● Jonathan Horne (Antiques) Ltd, 66B & C Kensington Church Street, London W8. Tel: 071-221 5658

JMG †● Jamie Maxtone Graham, Lyne Haugh, Lyne Station, Peebles, Scotland. Tel: (07214) 304

K †● Keith Gretton, 26 Honeywell Road, London SW11 and Unit 14, Northcote Road Antique Market, Battersea, London SW11. Tel: 071-228 0741

KEY ● Key Antiques, 11 Horse Fair, Chipping Norton, Oxon. Tel: (0608) 643777

KH ● The Keyhole, Dragonwyck, Far Back Lane, Farnfield, Newark, Notts. Tel: (0623) 882590

KOT ● Kotobuki (Stephen Joseph), Unit F100 Alfie's Antique Market, 13-25 Church Street, London NW8. Tel: 071-402 0723

LAY * David Lay ASVA, Auction House, Alverton, Penzance, Cornwall. Tel: (0736) 61414

LB †● The Lace Basket, 1a East Cross, Tenterden, Kent. Tel: (05806) 3923

LEW ● Jill Lewis, Geoffrey Vann Arcade, 107 Portobello Road, London W11. Tel: 071-221 1806 (Sats only)

LT * Louis Taylor, Percy Street, Hanley, Stoke-on-Trent, Staffs. Tel: (0782) 260222

MAN * F. C. Manser & Son Ltd, 53-54 Wyle Cop, Shrewsbury, Salop. Tel: (0743) 51120

MAT ● Christopher Matthews, Heathcote House, Forest Lane Head, Harrogate, N. Yorks. Tel: (0423) 887296/883215/885732

MB ● Mostly Boxes, 92 and 52b High Street, Eton. Tel: (0753) 858470

MCA †● Millers of Chelsea Antiques Ltd, Netherbrook House, 86 Christchurch Road, Ringwood, Hants. Tel: (0425) 472062

MIC ● Trevor Micklem, Frog Pool Farm, Moorwood, Oakhill, Bath. Tel: (0749) 840754

MIN †● Mint & Boxed, 110 High Street, Edgware, Middx. Tel: 081-952 2002

MIT ● Mervyn A. Mitton, 161 The Albany, Manor Road, Bournemouth

MN * Michael Newman, The Central Auction Rooms, Kinterbury House, St Andrew's Cross, Plymouth, Devon. Tel: (0752) 669298

MSh ● Manfred Schotten, The Crypt Antiques, 109 High Street, Burford, Oxon. Tel: (099382) 2302

NA ● Nostalgia Amusements, 73 Angus Close, Chessington, Surrey. Tel: 081-397 6867

Nor †● Sue Norman, L4 Antiquarius, 135 Kings Road, London SW3. Tel: 071-352 7217 and 081-870 4677

NP †● Neville Pundole, East Anglia 20th Century Antiques, 1 White House Lane, Attleborough, Norfolk. Tel: (0953) 454106

OD ● Offa's Dyke Antique Centre, 4 High Street, Knighton, Powys, Wales. Tel: (0547) 528635

ONS * Onslow's, Metro Store, Townmead Road, London SW6. Tel: 071-793 0240

OR ● The Originals, Alfies Antique Market, Stand 37, 13-25 Church Street, London NW8. Tel: 071-724 3439/7

P * Phillips, Blenstock House, 101 New Bond Street, London W1. Tel: 071-629 6602 and 10 Salem Road, London W2. Tel: 071-229 9090

PAR †● Park House Antiques, Park Street, Stow-on-the-Wold, Glos. Tel: (0451) 30159

PAT ● Patrician, 1st Floor, Georgian Village, Camden Passage, Islington, London N1. Tel: 071-359 4560/071-435 3159

PBA ● Pryce and Brise, 79 Moore Park Road, Fulham, London SW6. Tel: 071-736 1864

P(C) * Phillips, Cardiff, 9-10 Westgate Street, Cardiff. Tel: (0222) 396453

PC Private Collection

PCA ● Paul Cater Antiques, High Street, Moreton-in-Marsh, Glos. Tel: (0608) 51888

PCh * Peter Cheney, Western Road Auction Rooms, Western Road, Littlehampton, W. Sussex. Tel: (0903) 722264/713428

PGA ● Paul Gibbs Antiques, 25 Castle Street, Conwy, N. Wales. Tel: (0492) 593429

P(M) * Phillips, Manchester, Trinity House, 114 Northenden Road, Sale, Manchester. Tel: 061-962 9237

PO ● Pieter Oosthuizen. Tel: 071-352 1094/1493 (Business), 071-376 3069 (Home)

PVH ● Peter & Valerie Howkins, 39, 40 and 135 King Street, Gt Yarmouth, Norfolk. Tel: (0493) 844639

PW ● Philip Wilson, Stratford Antiques Arcade, 4 Sheep Street, Stratford-upon-Avon, Warks. Tel: (0789) 297249

RC †● Radio Crafts, 56 Main Street, Sedgebarrow, Evesham, Worcs. Tel: (0386) 881988

RdeR ● Rogers de Rin, 76 Hospital Road, Paradise Walk, London SW3. Tel: 071-352 9007

RFA ● Rochester Fine Arts, 86 High Street, Rochester, Kent. Tel: (0634) 814129

RG ● Rob Gee, The Fleamarket, Pierrepont Row, Camden Passage, London N1. Tel: 071-226 6627 (Wed & Sat)

RID * Riddetts of Bournemouth, 26 Richmond Hill, The Square, Bournemouth. Tel: (0202) 25686

RMC †● Romsey Medal Centre, 5 Bell Street, Romsey, Hants. Tel: (0794) 512069

RO ● Roswith, Stand F103, Alfies Antique Market, 13-25 Church Street, London NW8

RP ● Robert Pugh, 2 Beaufort Mews, St Saviour's Road, Larkhall, Bath. Tel: (0225) 314713

RPM ● Rosemary Antiques & Paper Moon Books, The Antiques Arcade, 4 Sheep Street, Stratford-on-Avon. Tel: (0789) 297249

RTT †● Rin Tin Tin, 34 North Road, Brighton. Tel: (0273) 672424/733689

RYA ● Robert Young Antiques, 68 Battersea Bridge Road, London SW11. Tel: 071-228 7847

S * Sotheby's, 34-35 New Bond Street, London W1. Tel: 071-493 8080

SAD ● Old Saddlers Antiques, Church Road, Goudhurst, Kent. Tel: (0580) 211458

SAI †● Sailor Ceramics, Camden Lock Antique Centre, 248 Camden High Street, London NW1. Tel: 081-981 1180

SBA ● South Bar Antiques, Digbeth Street, Stow-on-the-Wold, Glos. Tel: (0451) 30236

S(C) * Sotheby's Chester, Booth Mansion, 28-30 Watergate Street, Chester. Tel: (0244) 315531

SCR †● The Scripophily Shop, Britannia House, Grosvenor Square, London W1A 3AN. Tel: 071-495 0580

SHO ● Michael Shortall, 120 Marina, St Leonards-on-Sea, E. Sussex. Tel: (0424) 434854

SM †● Stephen Maitland, Now & Then Telephones, 7-9 West Crosscauseway, Edinburgh. Tel: (0592) 890235 and 031-668 2927

S(NY) * Sotheby's New York, 1334 York Avenue, New York NY 10021. Tel: 212 606 7000

Som ● Somervale Antiques, 6 Radstock Road, Midsomer Norton, Bath. Tel: (0761) 412686

SOP ● Shades of the Past, Unit 1, Northcote Road Antiques Market, London SW11. Tel: 071-228 6580

SP ● Sue Pearson, 13 Prince Albert Street, Brighton, E. Sussex. Tel: (0273) 29247

S(S) * Sotheby's Sussex, Summers Place, Billingshurst, W. Sussex. Tel: (0403) 783933

SSA ● Smith Street Antique Centre (E. Brook), 7 Smith Street, Warwick. Tel: (0926) 497864/400554

Sto ● Stockspring, 114 Kensington Church Street, London W8. Tel: 071-727 7995

SWa †● Stephen Watson, Alfies Antique Market, 13-25 Church Street, London NW8. Tel: 071-723 0678

SWN ● Swan Antiques, Stone Street, Cranbrook, Kent. Tel: (0580) 712720

SWO * Sworders, G. E. Sworder & Sons, 15 Northgate End, Bishops Stortford, Herts. Tel: (0279) 51388

TBC ● The Bramah Collection, PO Box 79, Eastleigh, Hants SO5 5YW

TED ● Teddy Bears of Witney, 99 High Street, Witney, Oxon. Tel: (0993) 702616

THA ● The Tudor House Antiques, 11 Tontine Hill, Ironbridge, Shropshire. Tel: (095) 2453783

TP †● Tom Power, The Collector, Alfies Antique Market, 13-25 Church Street, London NW8. Tel: 081-883 0024

TS ● Tim's Spot, Carnival Corner, Stratford-upon-Avon Antique Centre, Ely Street, Stratford, Warks. Tel: (0789) 297496

TVA ● Teme Valley Antiques, 1 The Bull Ring, Ludlow, Shropshire. Tel: (0584) 874686

UC ● Up Country, The Old Corn Stores, 68 St John's Road, Tunbridge Wells, Kent. Tel: (0892) 23341

VAG ● V.A.G. & Co, Possingworth Craft Centre, Brownings Farm, Blackboys, Uckfield, E. Sussex. Tel: (0323) 507488

VB ● Variety Box, 16 Chapel Place, Tunbridge Wells, Kent. Tel: (0892) 31868/21589

VH ● Valerie Howard, 131e Kensington Church Street, London W8. Tel: 071-792 9702

VS †* T. Vennett-Smith, 11 Nottingham Road, Gotham, Nottingham. Tel: (0602) 830541

Wai ● Wain Antiques, 7 Nantwich Road, Woore, Shropshire. Tel: (063 081) 7118

WAL * Wallis & Wallis, West Street Auction Galleries, Lewes, E. Sussex. Tel: (0273) 480208

WHA ● Wych House Antiques, Wych Hill, Woking, Surrey. Tel: (04862) 64636

WIL * Peter Wilson, Victoria Gallery, Market Street, Nantwich, Cheshire. Tel: (0270) 623878

WIN ● Winstone Stamp Co, Great Western Antique Market, Bartlett Street, Bath, Avon. Tel: (0225) 310388/445520

WO ● Woodville Antiques, The Street, Hamstreet, Ashford, Kent. Tel: (023373) 2981

WRe ● Walcot Reclamations, 108 Walcot Street, Bath, Avon. Tel: (0225) 66291/63245

WW * Woolley & Wallis, The Castle Auction Mart, Castle Street, Salisbury, Wilts. Tel: (0722) 21711

WHB * William H. Brown, Westgate Hall, Westgate, Grantham, Lincs. Tel: (0476) 68861

YON ● Yonna, B19 Grays Antique Market, 1-7 Davies Mews, London W1. Tel: 071-629 3644

Acknowledgements

The publishers would like to acknowledge the great assistance given by our consultants.

AERONAUTICA,
AUTOMOBILIA, RAILWAYS
& SHIPPING: **Patrick Bogue, John Jenkins,** *Onslow's, Metro Store, Townmead Road, London SW6.*

ART DECO: **Beverley,** *30 Church Street, London NW8.*
Eric Knowles, *Bonhams, Knightsbridge, London SW7.*

POTTERY: **Islwyn Watkins,** *1 High Street, Knighton, Powys.*

ROYAL DOULTON: **Tom Power,** *The Collector, Alfies Antique Market, 13-25 Church Street, London NW8.*

ART POTTERY: **Harry Lyon,** *Kensington Church Street Antique Centre, 58-60 Kensington Church Street, London W8.*

GOSS & CRESTED WARE: **Nicholas Pine,** *Goss & Crested China Ltd., 62 Murray Road, Horndean, Hants.*

MALING WARE: **Steven Moore,** *23 Front Street, Tynemouth.*
EPHEMERA: **Trevor Vennett-Smith, FRICS, FSVA, CAAV,** *11 Nottingham Road, Gotham, Nottingham.*

FISHING: **Jamie Maxtone Graham,** *Lyne Haugh, Lyne Station, Peebles, Scotland.*

MONART GLASS: **Frank Andrews,** *10 Vincent Road, Wood Green, London N22.*
MILITARIA: **Roy Butler,** *Wallis & Wallis, West Street Auction Galleries, Lewes, East Sussex.*

MEDALS, BUTTONS &
BADGES: **Jim Bullock,** *Romsey Medal Centre, 5 Bell Street, Romsey, Hants.*
ROCK & POP: **Sotheby's,** *34-35 New Bond Street, London W1*
JEWELLERY: **Valerie Howkins,** *39, 40 & 135 King Street, Gt. Yarmouth, Norfolk.*

COFFEE POTS: **Edward Bramah,** *PO Box 79, Eastleigh, Hants. SO5 5YW.*
NIGHT LIGHTS: **Raymond Slack,** *Tel: 081-651 5180.*

A 1940s microphone.
£25-30 *COB*

A Pepsi Cola fountain,
syrup and contents,
c1950, 9½in (24cm) high.
£15-18 *AAM*

A matching set of Willow
pattern salt, pepper and
vinegar pots, c1880, 5in
(12.5cm).
£350-400 *GIN*

A medical book, c1900.
£7-10 *COB*

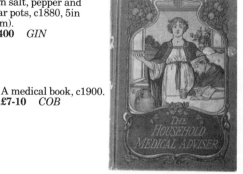

10

INDEX TO ADVERTISERS

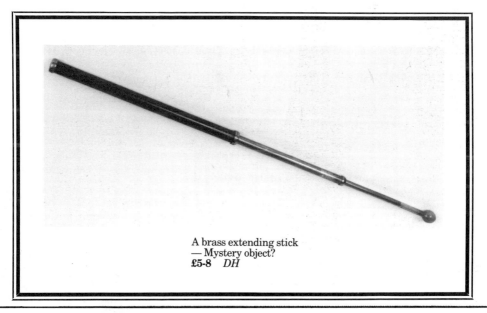

A brass extending stick
— Mystery object?
£5-8   *DH*

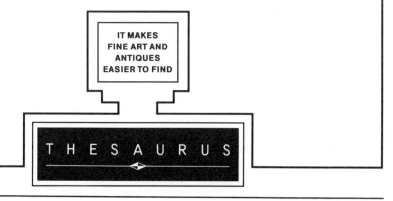

CONTENTS

Aeronautica

In the year celebrating the 50th Anniversary of the Battle of Britain it would be surprising if aeronautica did not increase. Uniforms, log books and ephemera from World War II are achieving very good prices. Modern aviation, particularly space travel look good areas to collect, but it will probably be some time before prices akin to 'Battle of Britain' period memorabilia are attained.

Ballooning

A Lambeth Delftware dish depicting a balloon in flight, c1784, 13in (33cm) diam.
£1,000-1,400   *JHo*

A panoramic photograph depicting a balloon meet, c1907, 10 by 45in (25 by 114cm), and 3 others.
£250-300   *C*

Books & Programmes

A selection of 21 books and works of aviation interest.
£450-500   *C*

A selection of aviation books and novels.
£20-45 each   *C*

A Bristol 'Bulldog' Mk IV original publicity booklet, and A.P. 1393, 1st Edition, 1930.
£100-150 *C*

Three rare Airspeed manufacturer's sales booklets.
£50-100 *C*

A World War II RAF fur-lined flying jacket, size 2, by D.G.L. London, with matching trousers, size 7, braces, helmet, oxygen mask and flying gloves, brown leather boots with durata soles, and a Mae West, on a display dummy.
£1,000-1,500 *C*

A book, by J. Leconnu, entitled La Navigation Aérienne, 6th edition, Paris 1913.
£100-150 *C*

Seventeen programmes for RAF Display, Hendon, from 1921-1937.
£200-250 *C*

A World War II period USAAF issue leather flying jacket, size 44, painted with the insignia of a B-29 with lightening flash on a yellow circle, the back decorated in nose art fashion, named 'Stardust'.
£1,000-1,500 *C*

Clothing

A Japanese fighter pilot's coat, c1942.
£450-500 *C*

A Royal Flying Corps pilot's No. 1 jacket, with label by Simpson & Son, pilot's wings, lapel badges, buttons and rank badges, forage cap by Castell & Son and Sam Browne belt.
£650-700 *C*

General

A laminated mahogany propeller, stamped M. Farman, 114in (290cm) diam.
£1,000-1,500   *C*

Part of a Zeppelin shot down at Lowestoft, April 1916.
£45-50   *COB*

A laminated mahogany propeller, stamped Monosoupape gnome, 94in (238cm) diam.
£1,000-1,500   *C*

Metal flying boat match striker, by Parker, c1930, 7in (18cm) wingspan.
£75-85   *COB*

An instrument panel from a Spitfire, with armoured windscreen, reflector gun sight and compass.
£1,500-2,000   *C*

A metal model of the 'Hindenburg', on black glass stand, 1936, 4in (10cm) long.
£75-95   *COB*

A Royal Flying Corps propeller blade photo frame, c1915, 36in (92cm) long.
£150-170   *COB*

An aluminium aeroplane
mascot, 7in (18cm)
wingspan.
£80-100   *ONS*

An aluminium model of a
de Havilland Tiger Moth,
1:36 scale, as flown by
James Capel, London-
Moscow 1989, 10in
(25cm) wingspan.
£1,000-1,500   *C*

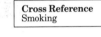

Cross Reference
Toys

A white metal model of
an inter-war period pilot
cigarette lighter, 11in
(28cm) high.
£450-500   *C*

A silver model of a de
Havilland Mosquito B
Mk IV, 1:72 scale, 9in
(23cm) wingspan.
£1,500-2,000   *C*

Cross Reference
Smoking

Walter L. Brock in
Bleriot cockpit, signed
and dated September
18th 1913.
£150-200   *ONS*

Two aluminium models,
by Doug Vaan, 1:72
scale, 6½in (16cm)
wingspan.
£1,000-2,500 each   *C*

Cross Reference
Autographs

Photographs

Marcus D. Manton in
Farman biplane, signed
and inscribed Hendon
and dated 13-9-13.
£100-150   *ONS*

Cross Reference
Photographs

Claude Grahame-White
seated in Bristol
monoplane, signed
Hendon July 1914.
£350-375   *ONS*

Posters

An Imperial Airways broadsheet showing the Handley Page Heracles, and brochures for the Fairey Gannet, Avro Vulcan, Hawker Hunter, Canberra, Concorde and F-16.
£200-250   *C*

German Airways, All the Year Round by Air, London-Berlin 5 hours, by Meerwald, 1936, 26 by 18in (67 by 46cm).
£450-500   *C*

KLM Amsterdam-Batavia, lithograph in colours, printed by L. Van Leer & Co. N.V., backed on linen, anonymous, 38½ by 25in (97 by 63cm).
£550-600   *C*

Fly TWA to Chicago, offset lithograph in colours, backed on linen, 40 by 25in (101 by 63cm).
£450-500   *C*

Exposition Internationale Nancy Mai-Octobre 1909, by Ludo, 52 by 30½in (132 by 77cm).
£50-100   *C*

Fly By Air Union and Get There First, C. Bellaigne, published January 1926, 15½ by 11½in (40 by 30cm).
£100-150   *ONS*

Imperial Airways Flying Boat, March 1939.
£500-550   *ONS*

Emporio, lithograph in colours, backed on linen, 43 by 30in (109 by 76cm).
£650-700   *C*

Paprika, French film poster, Marcel, published by Bauduin, 63 by 47½in (160 by 120cm).
£300-350 *ONS*

Fly to South Africa by BOAC and SAA.
£350-400 *ONS*

Jeunes Francais Pilote D'Avions, published July 1930, by H.T., on linen, 47½ by 31½in (120 by 80cm).
£1,000-1,500 *ONS*

Prints

Lone Spitfire, limited edition, colour reproduction, after Gerald Coulson, signed, 10½ by 35½in (26 by 90cm).
£750-800 *C*

Monoplane above an airfield, colour lithograph, Gamy, 17½ by 35in (44 by 89cm).
£400-450 *C*

A tribute to Sir Thomas Sopwith, limited edition colour reproduction, signed by Mr Tommy Sopwith, Dr Alan Watkins, Air Chief Marshal Sir Patrick Hine and others, Roderick Lovesey, 24 by 30in (61 by 76cm).
£400-450 *C*

Zeppelin, colour lithograph, E. Montaut, 17½ by 35in (44 by 89cm).
£300-350 *C*

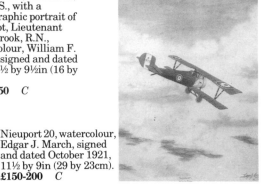

Bristol F2b (Felixstowe) R.N.A.S., with a photographic portrait of her pilot, Lieutenant T. H. Brook, R.N., watercolour, William F. Truby, signed and dated 1918, 6½ by 9½in (16 by 24cm).
£100-150 *C*

Nieuport 20, watercolour, Edgar J. March, signed and dated October 1921, 11½ by 9in (29 by 23cm).
£150-200 *C*

Mr L. R. Snook's Bonanza at Air Couriers, Croydon, watercolour, Douglas Ettridge, signed, 11 by 14in (28 by 36cm).
£100-150 *C*

Supermarine Southampton MKX flying boat 1930, pen and ink and watercolour, E. A. Wright, signed and dated 6.8.31, 6½ by 9in (16 by 23cm).
£50-100 *C*

1929 Schneider Trophy Supermarine Seaplane, signed, 12½ by 15½in (32 by 39cm).
£200-250 *ONS*

Sopwith Pup, in service with R.F.C., watercolour, Edgar J. March, signed and dated August 1921, 11½ by 9in (29 by 23cm).
£150-200 *C*

Messerschmitt Bf 109G, watercolour and gouache, Peter Endsleigh Castle, 3 by 9½in (8 by 24cm).
£50-150 *C*

Fokker D7, watercolour, Edgar J. March, signed and dated 1922, 11½ by 9in (29 by 23cm).
£150-200 *C*

FURTHER READING
History of British Aviation, Brett R. Dallas, 2 vols. 1908-14 and 1913-14.
British Flying Boats and Amphibians, G. R. Duval, 1909-52. London 1953.
The Fighters: The Men and Machines of the First Air War, Thomas R. Funderburk, London 1966.
The History of Aeronautics in Britain, J. E. Hodgson, 1924.
Janes All the World's Aircraft — published annually.
Airmails 1870-1970, James A. Mackay, London 1971.
Combat Aircraft of the World, F. C. Swanborough, London 1962.
Aeromodelling, R. H. Warring, London 1965.

Automobilia

Despite a levelling off of the prices for exotic supercars, the prices of collectable cars remains steady. This trend has been reflected in the automobilia field. Most items to do with veteran and vintage motoring have increased in value, but more so anything with a motor racing connection. Prints, photographs and motoring ephemera are worth noting for future increases.

An American motor cycle speedometer, c1934.
£35-45   *COB*

Accessories

An Etienne Teste 'Le Testophone' four note motoring horn, 26½in (67cm) long.
£400-450   *C*

A chrome and Bakelite taxi light, c1930.
£35-40   *COB*

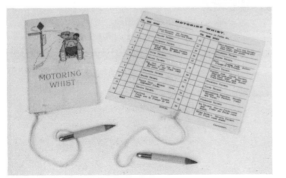

Motoring whist cards with pencils, c1930.
£3-5 each   *RTT*

Cross Reference
Games

Trophies

British Racing Drivers Club The 'Follett' Trophy, 30in (76cm) high.
£3,500-4,000   *ONS*

This trophy was presented to John Cobb as entrant of the V12 Sunbeam Tiger driven by Charles Brackenbury and Anthony Powys-Lybbe in the 1937 500km race at Brooklands.

Badges

Sunbeam Talbot, 4in (10cm) high.
£12-15 *BY*

A nickel plated Daimler Boyce motormeter.
£50-100 *ONS*

The Vespa Club of Great Britain, 3in (8cm).
£10-12 *BY*

Austin Ten, 4in (10cm) high.
£12-18 *BY*

A Brooklands 120mph, stamped Mrs E M Thomas, 29-9-28, won driving a Sunbeam.
£2,000-2,500 *ONS*

l. The London Douglas M.C.C., 3½in (8.5cm) high.
c. Alvis Owner Club, 4in (10cm) high.
£15-20 each
r. Humber, 3½in (8.5cm) high.
£10-12 *BY*

An AA car badge, 4in (10cm) high.
£28-30 *BY*

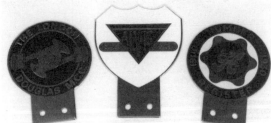

Vespa Club badges, 2½in (6cm) high.
£8-10 each
BY

Books & Brochures

An Aston Martin DB3S Competition Car, sales pamphlet, 1954.
£300-350   *CMon*

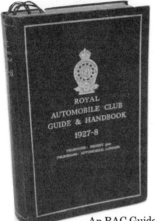

An RAC Guide and Handbook 1927-28.
£10-12   *RTT*

A sales list for the MG Magnette K Series.
£100-150
ONS

Sales brochures for Alvis Speed Twenty, 1932 and 1934.
£70-90 the pair   *ONS*

Practical Motorist magazine, September 1958.
£2-3   *RTT*

General

A road sign, 1930s-50s,
6in (15cm) diam.
£15-20 *COB*

Two shaped colour Shell
Motor Spirit advertising
leaflets, 1 a shell, the
other a wood case of
4 petrol cans, and an
unused invoice with
pictorial letterhead
Pratt's Motor Spirit.
£200-250 *ONS*

A bevelled glass and
wood limousine
compendium with
timepiece, 12in (31cm)
wide.
£100-150 *ONS*

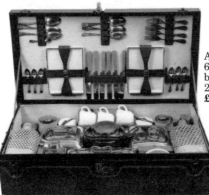

A picnic service for
6 settings, by Coracle, in
black vinyl covered case,
29in (74cm) long.
£1,500-2,000 *ONS*

A Continental silver
match case in the form of
an early Mercedes
radiator, 2in (5cm) wide.
£100-150 *C*

Schrader Tire Gauge
display cabinet, in the
form of a giant tyre
gauge printed tin, 15in
(38cm) high.
£200-250 *ONS*

Motoring subject ceramic
plates.
£300-350 each *ONS*

| Cross Reference |
| Ceramics |

Mercedes-Benz, white
metal enamelled pre-war
radiator badge.
£50-60 *ONS*

Petrol Cans

A Carburine petrol funnel.
£10-15 *FAL*

A Power Petroleum can.
£25-35 *FAL*

A Shell petrol can.
£25-35 *FAL*

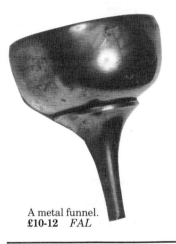

A brass and tin petrol can, 5in (13cm) high.
£22-25 *AL*

A metal funnel.
£10-12 *FAL*

Photographs

A National Benzole tin and brass petrol can, c1920, 12½in (32cm) high.
£20-25 *UC*

A Castrollo Upper Cylinder Lubricant, 1 pint can.
£15-20 *FAL*

Le Sport Automobile en 1905, published by Michelin, with illustrations of motor races and list of victories.
£1,500-2,000 *ONS*

Herbert J. Butler Motor Body Work, 1924.
£150-200 *ONS*

A collection of 18 black and white photographs of various racing scenes including a Jaguar D-Type at Sebring 1956.
£800-1,000 *C*

Posters

F. Bombled, Clement,
published by Moullot, on
linen, 37 by 50in (94 by 127cm).
£200-300   *ONS*

Two Hispano-Suiza
laminated showcards,
related to aero engines
and vehicles, each 12½
by 7in (32 by 18cm).
£200-250   *ONS*

Salon International de
L'Automobile et Du
Cycle Geneve, gouache,
on linen, 50 by 35in (127
by 90cm).
£300-350   *ONS*

Jack Le Breton, Fiat, The
Car of International
Reputation, A Classic
Achievement, The 17/50
Fiat, published by
McLay, 60 by 40½in (152
by 102cm).
£350-400   *ONS*

H. Behel, Georges
Richard Automobiles &
Cycles, published by
Camis, on linen, 73½ by
47½in (186 by 120cm).
£500-1,000   *ONS*

> **DID YOU KNOW?**
> Miller's Collectables
> Price Guide is
> designed to build up,
> year by year, into the
> most comprehensive
> reference system
> available.

Fifth International
British Empire Trophy
Race, Donington, 24 by
16½in (61 by 42cm).
£300-350   *C*

E. McKnight Kauffer,
Miles-Whitney Straight
Lubrication By Shell,
No. 477, 1937, on linen,
30 by 45in (76 by 114cm)
£1,500-2,000   *ONS*

'BP' Ethyl For Snappy
Engines, 1935.
£1,500-2,000 *ONS*

Crystal Palace Road
Circuit, published by
London Midland &
Scottish Railway, 40½ by
25in (102 by 64cm).
£550-600 *ONS*

Van Husen, XXVI
Internationales ADC
Eifelrennen, April 1963,
32½ by 23½in (83 by
60cm).
£300-350 *ONS*

Bogulund, General
Motors Den Store
Automobil Udstilling
Forum, April-May 1939,
published by Andreasen,
on linen, 33½ by 24½in
(85 by 62cm).
£450-500 *ONS*

Von Axster-Heudhab,
Berlin 1936, on linen, 39
by 24½in (99 by 63cm).
£550-600 *ONS*

G. Leygnac, 24 Heurs Du
Mans 1963, on linen, 22½
by 15½in (58 by 40cm).
£500-550 *ONS*

24 Heurs Du Mans 1966,
colour photograph, 22½
by 15½in (58 by 40cm).
£250-300 *ONS*

British Grand Prix
Silverstone, 10th July
1965, John Surtees in the
Ferrari.
£100-150 *ONS*

Drawings & Prints

Bryan De Grineau,
Mannin Moer, Isle of
Man, 1935, Raymond
Mays E.R.A. overtaking
Brian Lewis's Bugatti,
crayon and watercolour,
signed, 21 by 30½in (54
by 77cm).
£3,500-4,000   *C*

Bryan De Grineau,
Dieppe Grand Prix 1935,
P. J. Fairfield E.R.A.
passing Raymond Mays
at the Pits, crayon and
watercolour, signed, 21
by 30½in (54 by 77cm).
£2,000-2,500   *C*

Four 6C 2500
advertisements for
various models, 12 by
8½in (31 by 22cm).
£250-300   *C*

D Type at Le Mans,
charcoal, 16 by 19½in (41
by 50cm).
£200-250   *ONS*

Bugatti Type 35,
airbrush, signed with
initials, 12½ by 9in (32
by 23cm).
£400-450   *ONS*

Delage at speed on
straight road, 6 by 5in
(15 by 13cm).
£250-300   *ONS*

Observe Section Ends,
scraper board, and
2 saloon car studies.
£20-30   *ONS*

Delage cornering, charcoal heightened with white, signed and dated 1929, 6 by 9½in (16 by 24cm).
£350-400   *ONS*

Bentley 3 litre, artwork for Christmas card, 6 by 7in (15 by 18cm).
£250-300   *ONS*

Alfa Romeo Grand Prix Cars at speed, 6 by 9½in (15 by 14cm).
£200-250   *ONS*

Bugatti Type 35, charcoal heightened with white, pencil sketch on reverse, 9½ by 11½in (14 by 29cm).
£100-150   *ONS*

FURTHER READING
A-Z of Cars of the 1930s, and *A-Z of Cars 1945-1970,* Michael Sedgwick and Mark Gillies, Haymarket Publishing Ltd, 1986 and 1989. *Motoring Costume,* Shire Publications, Aylesbury, Bucks.

Nick, Terrot Cycles Motorcycles, published by Pertuy, Paris, on linen, 62½ by 47in (158 by 119cm).
£300-400   *ONS*

Motorcycling

Rudge 'It', poster on linen, 59 by 39½in (150 by 100cm).
£500-550   *ONS*

Geo Ham, Side-Car Cross et Motocross, on linen, 48 by 47in (123 by 119cm).
£150-250   *ONS*

Motor Cycle Magazine, May 1962.
£3-4   *RTT*

Art Deco

We have this year grouped a selection of everyday household and decorative items together, most of which were manufactured during the 1920s and 1930s, all of which reflect the Art Deco style. The Art Deco ceramics by factory/designer can be found in the Ceramics section.

The name Art Deco comes from the 1925 Paris Exhibition, 'L'Exposition Internationale des Arts Décoratifs et Industriels Modernes', and the style unites both arts with industry, incorporating geometric design and the machine age. Public buildings, lighting, furniture, household appliances, everything seemed to be influenced by the Art Deco style and just about everything today, especially chromeware and early plastics, are extremely collectable.

Household

A Heatmaster chrome and ceramic teapot, c1945, 7½in (19cm) high.
£20-30 *SAI*

Originally designed by Le Corbusier, an influential 20thC architect, renowned for clear lines and functional design.

A Hagenauer mirror, stamped, c1920, 13in (33cm).
£300-400 *DIM*

A silver plated salt, pepper and egg cup, by Christofle, Gallia series, c1925, 5in (13cm) wide.
£300-400 *ABS*

Box designed as a hen coop.

A plaster figure of a girl, c1935, 13in (33cm).
£35-50 *CLH*

An Art Deco green glass vase, 1930s, 10in (25cm) high.
£30-35 *COB*

Cross Reference
Glass

A chrome cruet.
£25-30 *SAI*

Lighting

Two Art Deco chrome
and resin lamps, 16½in
(41cm) high.
£45-70 each   *OR*

A pink Perspex lamp,
19in (48cm) high.
£45-70   *OR*

*Resin came in yellow,
green, red and blue only.*

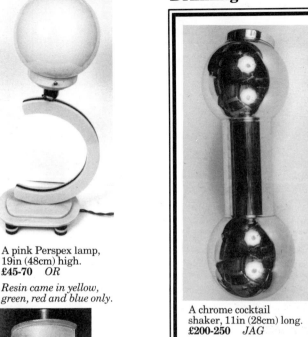

A pair of Perzel wall
lights, cylindrical shape
of gold flecked and acid
textured glass,
terminating in bronze
cones, 25in (64cm) long.
£500-1,000   *C*

Cross Reference
Bakelite

Drinking

A chrome cocktail
shaker, 11in (28cm) long.
£200-250   *JAG*

A silver plate champagne
bucket, c1930, 7½in
(18cm) high.
£150-200   *BEV*

A penguin glass
decanter, with chrome
head, glass eyes, and
black applied glass
wings, Austrian, c1930,
10½in (26cm) high.
£100-150   *JAG*

Cross Reference
Corkscrews

A chrome toaster, 1940s,
8in (20cm) high.
£20-25 *RTT*

A chrome cigarette
case/dispenser, c1930,
4in (10cm) square.
£20-25 *RTT*

A chrome frame, 4½in
(11cm) wide.
£20-30 *SAI*

Photo frames

A phenolic
frame, 10in
(25cm) wide.
£50-75 *SAI*

A marble frame, 7½in
(18cm) long.
£30-40 *SAI*

General

A green snakeskin
cigarette case.
£50-100 *SBA*

A Hagenauer polo
player, c1920, 5in (13cm)
diam.
£300-400 *DIM*

A cloud glass and chrome
ashtray, c1930, 7½in
(19cm) high.
£20-25 *CSA*

Bakelite

Bakelite is the best known trade name for phenol formaldehyde (phenolic) which was the first ever totally man-made plastic. The process involving the reaction between phenol and formaldehyde had been known about since the 1870s, but was worked on by Leo Baekeland in the USA who registered a patent for the resin Bakelite in 1907. These phenolic mouldings are the easiest of the early plastics to identify; the colours are very limited, dark shades of brown, blue, green and red, with the noticeable 'mottled' effect. These colours were often mixed to produce a distinctive swirling effect.

Bakelite, along with other early plastics, is now sought after by collectors, many of whom have moved on from the Art Deco ceramics areas, which are, at present, very expensive. As with all things, the condition is paramount, beware of cracking and crazing, particularly on the internal surfaces.

A Bakelite flask, made in England, 1920s, 9½in (24cm) high.
£10-15 *RTT*

A peach and black Bakelite cigarette box, 7 by 4in (18 by 10cm).
£40-50 *BEV*

A peach and black Bakelite table lamp, 14in (36cm) high.
£80-100 *BEV*

A Bakelite 'electric' battery operated cigarette lighter, c1950.
£15-20 *RTT*

A Bakelite flask, 11in (28cm) high.
£8-10 *RTT*

A green and pink Bakelite photo frame.
£40-50 *BEV*

A Bakelite Regentone
radio, 6½in (16cm) high.
£65-70   *RTT*

A chrome and Bakelite
cruet, 4½in (11cm) high.
£25-30   *BEV*

A Bakelite Premier
radio, c1948, 6½in
(16cm) high.
£70-80   *RTT*

Cross Reference
Radios

A Bakelite ashtray,
White Satin Gin, 5in
(13cm) wide.
£6-10   *RTT*

A Bakelite bottle pourer,
possibly American,
c1930, 5½in (14cm) long.
£40-50   *RTT*

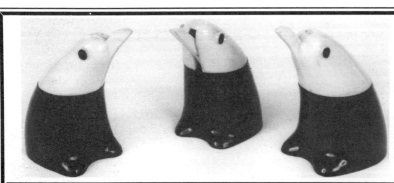

A Bakelite
penguin cruet
set, c1940,
3in (8cm) high.
£30-40   *RTT*

A pair Bakelite
compacts,
1920s, 5in (13cm).
£20-25   *CLH*

A Halex powder bowl,
4½in (11cm) diam.
£6-10   *RTT*

A Bakelite 'Siroma' hair
dryer, c1950, 9in (23cm)
long.
£10-20   *RTT*

An Austrian silver and
Bakelite candlestick,
marked, c1920, 7½in
(19cm) high.
£200-250   *DIM*

A Bakelite 'Dinkie' wave
dryer, with instructions,
c1930, 7½in (19cm) long.
£25-30   *RTT*

FURTHER READING
Early Plastics, Sylvia Katz, Shire Publications
Ltd, 1986.
Art Plastic, Andrea DiNoto, Abbeville Press,
1984.

A Bakelite table light,
17in (43cm) high.
£50-60   *RTT*

A Halex Bakelite tray,
powder bowl, comb and
nail buffer, c1930, tray
11 by 7½in (28 by 18cm).
£5-15 each   *RTT*

Bottle Collecting

Despite some increase in value of some of the more 'interesting' bottles, notably the rare colours, or amusing advertisements, bottle collecting has still to recover its earlier price levels. It remains, however, a cheap and extremely interesting hobby to pursue, both from the technical and social history point of view.

DID YOU KNOW?
The art of carbonising mineral water was discovered in 1772 by Joseph Priestley. This caused a major problem for bottle manufacturers as the gas seeped through earthenware. The manufacturers turned to glass containers but the pressure built up blowing the cork out.

Bottles

A Hoopers, London, bottle, 10in (25cm) long.
£5-6 *PC*

A Suprema bottle with marble inside, 9in (23cm) high.
£7-8 *PC*

An English water washed bottle, c1810, 9½in (24cm) high.
£45-50 *HAR*

An Allisons Common Room sealed bottle, c1790, 10½in (26cm) high.
£95-100 *HAR*

A French champagne bottle, c1850, 9½in (24cm) high.
£10-15 *HAR*

An English seal bottle, chip, 10½in (26cm) high.
£100-110 *HAR*

An LMS Hotels beer bottle, 7½in (19cm) high.
£12-15 *HAR*

A stoneware Seltzer gin bottle, c1830, 11½in (29cm) high.
£18-20 *HAR*

A Dutch pressed glass gin bottle, 19thC, 9½in (24cm) high.
£6-10 *HAR*

A Ryde Isle of Wight pure aerated water bottle, 9in (23cm) high.
£2-4 *HAR*

A Dutch wine cylinder, c1830, 9½in (24cm) high.
£20-25 *HAR*

A Dutch gin bottle, c1780, 10in (25cm) high.
£50-60 *HAR*

A Japanese papier mâché bottle holder, 19thC, 12½in (32cm) high.
£95-100 *HAR*

A stone bottle, T. Allcroft, 7½in (19cm) high.
£3-5 *PC*

A shoe whisky bottle, 7½in (19cm) wide.
£30-35 *OD*

A Mappin & Webb silver plate bottle stand.
£20-25
With Hamilton bottle.
£4-5 *HAR*

A Victorian vinegar
bottle, Champion & Slee
Ltd, 10½in (26cm) high.
£10-15   *PC*

A stoneware bottle, 'Jet
stain for leather'.
£3-5   *PC*

Three stoneware bottles
from Hastings, 7in
(17cm) high.
l. & r. **£10-20 each**
c. **£35-50**   *PC*

A Benbow's dog mixture
glass bottle with stopper,
6in (15cm) high.
£5-10   *PC*

If in dark brown £10-20.

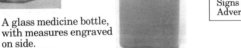

A Victorian aqua glass
bottle, initialled.
£5-10   *PC*

A stoneware ginger beer
bottle, c1905, 7in (17cm)
high.
£10-20   *PC*

A glass medicine bottle,
with measures engraved
on side.
£5-10   *PC*

Cross Reference
Signs
Advertising

Three stoneware ginger
beer bottles from Kent
and Sussex, 6 to 7in (15
to 17cm) high.
£10-25 each   *PC*

A collection of poison
bottles.
£1-5 each   *PC*

Boxes

An unusual glove box
with inlay in bark, 14in
(36cm) long.
£35-40 *HUN*

A Regency mahogany
sewing box, with drawer,
c1820, 11½in (29cm)
wide.
£550-600 *EHA*

A rosewood dressing
case, with original
fittings, c1860, 10in
(25cm) wide.
£200-250 *EHA*

A travel box, with
newspaper lining, c1878.
£40-50 *CAC*

*Beware — sometimes old
newspapers can be used
as drawer/furniture
linings to give a false
impression of age.*

A mahogany glove box,
with brass mounts,
c1880, 9in (23cm) wide.
£150-200 *EHA*

Wheelwright's grease boxes. **£15-25 each** *WO*

Buckles

A foreign
silver buckle,
3½in (9cm) wide.
£20-25 *VB*

A Chinese
silver buckle,
4½ by 2½in (11 by 6cm).
£50-60 *VB*

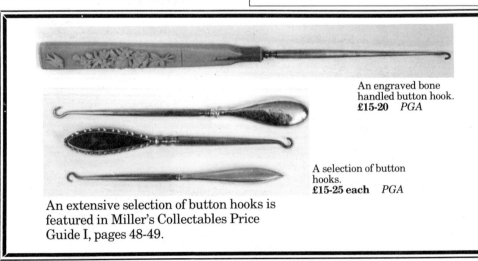

A foreign silver buckle of
Oriental design, 4in
(10cm) long.
£35-40 *VB*

A French silver gilt and
enamel buckle, 2in (5cm)
wide.
£25-30 *CA*

MAKE THE MOST OF MILLERS
Price ranges in this book reflect what one should
expect to *pay* for a similar example. When selling,
however, one should expect to receive a lower
figure. This will fluctuate according to a dealer's
stock, saleability at a particular time, etc. It is
always advisable, when selling, to approach a
reputable specialist dealer or an auction house
which has specialist sales.

Button Hooks

An engraved bone
handled button hook.
£15-20 *PGA*

A selection of button
hooks.
£15-25 each *PGA*

An extensive selection of button hooks is
featured in Miller's Collectables Price
Guide I, pages 48-49.

Buttons

t is very difficult to date buttons. If a
actory made a type of button which sold
vell they went on making it for ages and
iges. Some fashions came and went only
o return later, so you got very similar
ooking buttons but with differences in the
:onstruction as manufacturing techniques
vere improved.

Today we take buttons for granted, but
n Victorian times the ladies chose them
vith great care looking for quality and
•eauty of the button with the idea of using
hem again and again. These were
requently passed on in the family and
nake up the contents of old button boxes
vhich are such a joy to scrabble through.

Pierced, c1900.
£80-120 *AGM*

Pierced, c1900.
£80-120 *AGM*

3oxed Sets

Rose, thistle and
shamrock design, c1902.
£80-120 *AGM*

Art Nouveau lady,
1903, 1in (3cm).
80-120 *AGM*

Flowers, c1901.
£80-120 *AGM*

Geometric design, c1907.
£80-120 *AGM*

Art Nouveau style
flowers, c1901.
£80-120 *AGM*

Cherub, c1900.
£80-120 *AGM*

An ivory toothpick case,
with gold mounts, c1780,
3½in (9cm) long.
£70-80 *EHA*

Chrysanthemum design,
c1905.
£80-120 *AGM*

Musica, c1902.
£80-120 *AGM*

Roses, c1901.
£80-120 *AGM*

Liberty enamel and
silver, c1908.
£80-120 *AGM*

Daisy pattern, c1903.
£80-120 *AGM*

Georgian Buttons

Two silver buttons,
c1739, 3cm.
£15-30 each *AGM*

Two plain silver buttons,
2.5cm.
£15-30 each *AGM*

An oak leaf pattern
button, 2.5cm.
£15-30 *AGM*

DID YOU KNOW?
The name 'Copper Colonial' originates from the
American button collectors as the buttons date
from the time they were part of the British
colonies. Some English collectors call them 'old
coppers' as they are reminiscent of the old copper
pennies.

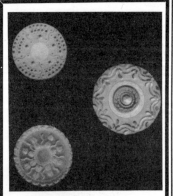

'Copper Colonial'
buttons.
£10-20 each *AGM*

'Copper Colonial' buttons. **£10-20** *AGM*

Picture buttons,
late 19thC.
£1-10 each
AGM

A papier mâché button,
with mother-of-pearl
flowers.
£5-10 *AGM*

A papier mâché fox head
button, 1in (3cm).
£5-10 *AGM*

A bridle button.
£1-10 *AGM*

*Some have company
insignia, i.e. railway,
breweries, etc., and some
have crests from large
households or town
liveries.*

Cross Reference
Horse Brasses and
Harness

An Iron Age button.
£5-20 *AGM*

A Basse Taille button,
with roses on a red
background, 2cm.
£1-10 *AGM*

Basse Taille buttons,
with blue centre and
white edge, 1cm.
£1-10 each *AGM*

Agate buttons.
£1-20 each *AGM*

A coral ball button.
£1-20 *AGM*

A pierced blue button,
1.5cm.
£1-5   *AGM*

A domed button, 1.5cm.
£1-5   *AGM*

A champlevé button,
2cm.
£1-5   *AGM*

A Dutch silver button,
2.5cm.
£5-20   *AGM*

Art Nouveau Lady
buttons, c1904, 4cm.
£5-20 each   *AGM*

A shield design button,
c1923, 4cm.
£5-20   *AGM*

General

A cloisonné button,
2.5cm.
£10-20   *AGM*

Two men drinking
button, c1903, 4cm.
£5-20   *AGM*

A William of Orange
button, c1901, 4cm.
£5-20   *AGM*

Mother and children
buttons, c1901, 2cm.
£5-20 each   *AGM*

Modern jeans buttons,
collectors items of the
future.
5-10p each   *AGM*

Modern craft buttons depicting cats, made with stencil/transfer.
50-75p each *AGM*

A selection of hotels buttons.
£1-5 each *AGM*

Modern enamel craft buttons.
50-75p each *AGM*

A selection of yacht clubs buttons.
£1-5 each *AGM*

A selection of public transport tramways buttons.
£1-5 each *AGM*

A selection of Brookes buttons, examples of craft buttons made in last 20 years, now collected as no longer made.
£1-1.50 each *AGM*

Hunt buttons.
£1-5 each *AGM*

Golf clubs buttons.
£1-10 each *AGM*

Royal household livery
buttons.
£1-10 each *AGM*

Livery buttons.
£1-5 each
AGM

Civic livery buttons.
£1-5 each *AGM*

Nobility livery buttons.
£1-5 each *AGM*

Continental silver plated
sporting buttons.
£5-15 each   *AGM*

Railways buttons, Taff
Vale, Brecon and
Merthyr, Bute Docks,
Rhymney Railway Co.
£10-20 each   *AGM*

Cross Reference
Railways

Police buttons.
£1-5 each   *AGM*

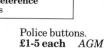

Livery buttons with
animals.
£1-5 each   *AGM*

Art Deco buttons.
50p-£2 each   *AGM*

Cross Reference
Art Deco

Livery buttons with
birds.
£1-5 each   *AGM*

FURTHER READING
The Complete Button Book, Lilian Smith Albert
and Cathryn Kent, London 1952.
The Collector's Encyclopedia of Buttons, Sally C.
Luscomb, New York 1967.
Buttons for the Collector, Primrose Peacock,
Newton Abbot 1972.
Buttons: A Guide for Collectors, Gwen Squire,
London 1972.

Cameras

A Concava S.A., Lugano, Switzerland, 35mm 'Tessina Automat' camera No. 463362.
£250-300 *CSK*

A Scovill Manufacturing Co, NY, USA, 5 by 4in (12.5 by 10cm) detective camera.
£400-450 *CSK*

A Thornton-Pickard quarter plate 'Duplex Ruby' reflex camera with Zeiss lens.
£150-200 *CSK*

An O. Berning, Germany, 35mm Robot Junior camera No. J 145375.
£100-150 *CSK*

A C. P. Goerz, Berlin, Germany, original box form, 3½ by 4½in (9 by 12cm) Anschutz camera No. 2.
£1,000-1,500 *CSK*

A Perken, Son and Rayment, London, quarter plate brass and mahogany field camera No. 5588.
£250-300 *CSK*

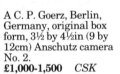

A Houghtons Ltd, London, Ticka watch camera with lens cap and swinging viewfinder.
£150-200 *CSK*

A Thornton-Pickard Ltd, Altrincham, quarter plate tropical reflex camera.
£750-800 *CSK*

An R. and J. Beck Ltd, London, early quarter plate Frena de luxe camera.
£500-1,000 *CSK*

A Folmer Graflex
Corporation, Rochester,
NY, USA, Cirkut outfit,
comprising a No. 6
Cirkut camera, c1932.
£1,000-1,500 *CSK*

A Graflex Inc, Rochester,
NY, USA, quarter plate
Speed Graphic technical
press camera, with Ektar
lens.
£350-400 *CSK*

*This camera was used by
the vendor to photograph
the Queen and Duke of
Edinburgh driving in an
open carriage through the
streets of Edinburgh
following their coronation
in 1953. The picture was
used on the front page of
the Scotsman and most
national newspapers.*

A Marion and Co,
London, 1½ by 2½in (4½
by 6cm) reflex camera,
with a Ross lens.
£350-400 *CSK*

A Linhof, Germany, 2½
by 3½in (6 by 8cm)
Technika Press camera
No. 8897, with a Carl
Zeiss Planar lens.
£750-800 *CSK*

A Hans Pock,
Munich,
Germany, 2½ by 3½in
(6 by 9cm) mahogany
bodied detective camera
No. 124, c1888.
£1,500-2,000 *CSK*

An Ihagee, Dresden,
Germany, 2½ by 2½in
(6 by 6cm) Exakta 66
camera No. 600390 with
a Tessar f2.8 80mm lens.
£500-1,000 *CSK*

A J. Fallowfield, London,
quarter plate 'Premier'
hand camera No. 76,
c1895.
£150-200 *CSK*

An Okam, Czechoslovakia, camera, c1935.
£300-350   *CSK*

A City, Sale and Exchange, London, quarter plate 'Salex Tropical Reflex' camera, with polished teak body.
£550-600   *CSK*

A Voigtlander, Braunschweig, Germany, 2½ by 3½in (6½ by 9cm) Bergheil de luxe camera No. D954299.
£150-200   *CSK*

A Kochmann, Germany, 'Korelle P' camera.
£200-250   *CSK*

A Houghton-Butcher Ltd, London, 'The Sanderson roll film' camera No. 11496, with original sales ticket.
£400-450   *CSK*

35mm Shanghai 58 camera No. 5873910.
£250-300   *CSK*

A Lumiere, Paris, 3 by 15in (8 by 38cm) 'Periphote' panoramic camera No. 114.
£11,000-12,000   *CSK*

The Lumiere Periphote camera was the subject of Swiss patent No. 23746 of 1901. The camera was worked by clockwork which moved the camera lens while the film stayed stationary, panoramas could be 180° or 360°.

A London Stereoscopic quarter plate Carlton twin lens reflex camera.
£150-200   *CSK*

A Franke and Heidecke, Braunschweig, Germany, 120 film Tele-'Rolleiflex' camera No. S 2301886.
£1,000-1,500   *CSK*

A Nagel, Stuttgart, Germany, 127 film Pupille camera No. 90809, c1932.
£600-650   *CSK*

A Butcher, 7 by 3½in (17 by 9cm) 'The stereo Cameo' camera No. 88734, c1912.
£150-200   *CSK*

An O.T.A.G., early Amourette camera No. 3598.
£250-300   *CSK*

The Amourette camera was made by the Osterreiche Telephon A.G. company and was based on a British patent issued to J. S. Singer on March 23, 1925. The camera was sold from 1926.

An I.S.O. Italy, 'Duplex Super 120' stereoscopic camera No. 4102, c1956.
£400-450   *CSK*

A Zeh, 120 roll film 'Zeca-Flex' twin lens reflex camera.
£700-750   *CSK*

A Franke and Heidecke, 'Heidoscop' stereo camera No. 7387.
£400-450   *CSK*

A Redding & Gyles, roll film 'Luzo' camera No. 1319, c1888.
£900-950 *CSK*

A Nikon 35mm chrome F2 camera No. 7324489.
£400-450 *CSK*

A Plaubel Makinette camera, c1932.
£550-600 *CSK*

A Houghtons 5 by 4in (12.5 by 10cm) tropical Hand and Stand camera, with polished teak body and brass binding strips, tropical double dark slides, in maker's fitted leather case.
£450-500 *CSK*

A Pignons 35mm Alpha Prisma Reflex III camera, lacking lens and hood.
£100-150 *CSK*

An Ernemann-Werke Klapp camera No. 752798.
£100-150 *CSK*

A Lizars quarter plate tropical Challenge hand and stand camera.
£250-300 *CSK*

A Lancaster & Son half plate brass and mahogany 'The Special Patent' tailboard camera.
£150-200 *CSK*

A Canadian Kodak, autographic Vest Pocket Kodak camera with a Tessar f4.9 9cm lens.
£200-300 *CSK*

The Zeiss lens dates to 1923 and a very small number of the camera were made.

Canon

A 35mm Canon IIB camera No. 26267.
£300-350 *CSK*

A 35mm Canon IV-S2 camera No. 181240, with accessories.
£350-400 *CSK*

A Canon IV SB camera.
£250-300 *CSK*

A green-chrome Leica Bundeseigentum M3 camera No. 927742, with a Leitz Elmar f4 135mm lens, c1959.
£2,000-3,000 *CSK*

A Leica 250 model FF Reporter camera No. 150105, c1935.
£6,000-7,000 *CSK*

From serial No. 150125 cameras were provided with shutter speeds from 1 second to 1/1000.

Leica viewfinders comprising a SFT00 Telyt 20cm sportsfinder, in maker's box, a VI00H finder No. 91803, a Rasuk/Ramet framefinder and a Rasuk framefinder.
£150-200 *CSK*

Leica

A Leica IIIb camera with a Leitz Summar 5cm f2 lens, and a Leicameter model 650.
£150-250 *CSK*

A Leitz Mikas device on an Ibsor shutter, in maker's original box.
£150-200 *CSK*

A Leitz Elmarit-R f2.8 135mm lens No. 2041079, in maker's plastic case.
£150-200 *CSK*

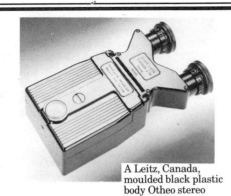

A Leitz, Canada, moulded black plastic body Otheo stereo viewer x5.
£550-650   *CSK*

A Leitz Stemar system outfit comprising a screw mount Stemar 3.3cm f3.5 stereo lens No. 1124378, a stereo 3.3cm Oidyo bright line viewfinder, Oimpo Stemar prism No. 1494, all contained in a Leitz fitted leather case.
£3,000-3,500   *CSK*

Commercial production of the Stemar system was undertaken in Canada after an initial production run in Wetzlar. Production was between 1954 and 1957. A special viewer Otheo was made to accompany the Stemar.

A 35mm Leica IIIg camera No. 943121.
£1,000-1,500   *CSK*

A 35mm Leica Ia camera No. 189, c1925.
£10,000-11,000   *CSK*

A 35mm Leicaflex camera No. 1082123, c1964.
£400-450   *CSK*

A Leica Ia camera No. 1672, a film cutting template, film cassette holder, supplementary lenses and accessories.
£2,000-3,000   *CSK*

A Leitz black Fofer longbase rangefinder and a chrome Wintu right angle finder.
£80-100   *CSK*

A Leitz, Aufsu waist level reflecting viewfinder.
£150-200   *CSK*

A Leitz, Canada, 35mm black Leica M4-2K camera No. K-4427, with delayed action control.
£2,000-3,000   *CSK*

A Leica IIIg camera No. 891046, lenses and various accessories.
£1,000-1,500 *CSK*

A Leitz double stroke Leica M3 camera, Leitz Summarit 5cm f1.5 lens and a Leica Meter.
£350-400 *CSK*

Zeiss

A tropical Adoro camera No. Q.97508.
£450-500 *CSK*

General

A 'Photoing on car' battery operated toy car with driver and passenger holding a camera with flashing flash unit, in maker's original box.
£100-150 *CSK*

Cross Reference
Toys

A Simplex-Ernoflex camera No. O.22696 with a Carl Zeiss Jena Tessar f4.5 8cm lens.
£500-550 *CSK*

A Contax-fit Stereotar C f4 3.5cm stereo lens No. W.26203, and Zeiss Ikon 543/30 stereo viewfinder.
£2,000-2,500 *CSK*

A 5 by 4in (13 by 10cm) wooden bodied magazine detective camera.
£200-250 *CSK*

A 'Demon' detective camera.
£650-750 *CSK*

The camera was made by W. Phillips of Birmingham for the American Camera Co. of London and was the subject of patent No. 10823 of July 26, 1888.

A Russian 35mm Horizont panoramic camera No. 7006284.
£250-350 *CSK*

A Franke and Heidecke 2½ by 5in (6 by 12.5cm) Heidoscop camera No. 6042.
£400-500 *CSK*

A 16mm 'John Player Special' spy camera No. C0227, with black painted metal body with 'JSP' logo and disguised cigarettes.
£750-800 *CSK*

This camera is reputed to have been made for Soviet espionage use, information about the camera is difficult to find. The camera design is based upon the Minolta 16 camera.

A biunial magic lantern, with chimney and electric illuminants, on mahogany base.
£750-850 *CSK*

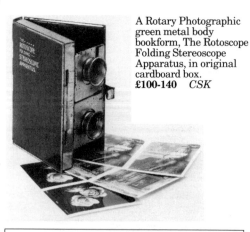

A Rotary Photographic green metal body bookform, The Rotoscope Folding Stereoscope Apparatus, in original cardboard box.
£100-140 *CSK*

A coloured ceramic statue of a photographer under a dark cloth with camera, 22in (56cm) high.
£350-450 *CSK*

A Czechoslovakian brownie figure, holding a box camera, c1930, 23in (59cm) high.
£100-200 *CSK*

FURTHER READING
An Age of Cameras, Edward Holmes, 1974.

Card Cases

For a comprehensive selection of card cases refer: Miller's Collectables Price Guide Vol. I, p.58, and Vol. II, p.42.

A mother-of-pearl card case, c1870, 4 by 3in (10 by 7.5cm).
£70-100   *EHA*

A mother-of-pearl card case, mounted in silver with cameo insert, c1845, 4 by 2½in (10 by 6cm).
£250-300   *CA*

A Dutch amboyna candlestick, 10½in (26cm) high.
£40-50   *SAD*

Candlesticks

A blue Kaiser Bill caricature candle holder, c1920, 5½in (14cm) high.
£45-75   *DIM*

A silver plate chamberstick, 3in (7.5cm) diam.
£20-30   *VB*

Various miniature candlesticks, tallest 4in (10cm).
£1-3 each   *DH*

Two pairs of miniature brass candlesticks, 2½in (6cm) and 3in (7cm) high.
£2-3 a pair   *DH*

A pair of candlesticks, 6in (15cm) one damaged, high.
£15-20   *DH*

FURTHER READING
Old Domestic Base Metal Candlesticks, R. F. Michaelis, Antique Collectors' Club, Woodbridge, Suffolk, 1978.

CERAMICS
Art Pottery

Art potters typified the spirit of the Arts and Crafts Movement which flourished during the late 19thC. It became a virtue to work with the hands instead of using machines. The designs were influenced by William Morris, Rossetti, Burne-Jones and others, and it gave artists and manufacturers a chance to break from the traditions of Victorian design.

The influence was far reaching in ceramics, from Doulton for instance, whose factories produced everyday household goods as well as superb art pieces to pure artistic examples by amateur potters.

Although these styles were produced into the 1920s and 30s, by 1925 the Great Exposition in Paris had occurred and the scene was set for Art Deco. We would refer you to the coverage of these potters in our two earlier volumes.

FURTHER READING
English Decorative Ceramics, John Bartlett, K.F. Publishing, London, 1989.

A pair of Eichwald vases, c1920, 9in (23cm) high.
£80-90   *BEV*

A Frederick Rhead Intarsio vase, c1900, 8½in (21cm) high.
£275-300   *CSA*

An Ault vase in green and brown, 8in (20cm) high.
£25-45   *BLO*

A Baron mauve and blue vase, 1920s, 3½in (8.5cm) high.
£30-50   *BLO*

A Minton Astra ware red vase, marked.
£45-60   *Ced*

A Frederick Rhead Foley Intarsio vase, 5½in (14cm) high.
£300-350   *BEV*

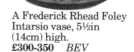

A Gouda vase, c1900, 13in (33cm) high.
£80-100   *BEV*

An Aller Vale pottery jug, c1880, 5in (13cm) high.
£45-60   *CA*

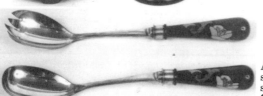

A pair of Foley Intarsio silver plated salad servers, 11in (28cm).
£100-200   *AJ*

A Frederick Rhead Foley Intarsio tobacco jar, 5in (13cm) high.
£200-250 *BEV*

An Ault vase, signed by Dresser, decorated by Clarissa Ault, 5½in (13cm) high.
£250-300 *BLO*

A Foley Intarsio stork vase, c1898, 14in (36cm) high.
£500-600 *AJ*

A Charlotte Rhead vase, c1930, 4½in (11cm) high.
£80-100 *BEV*

A Craven Dunhill red lustre vase, c1895, 5½in (14cm) high.
£150-170 *THA*

A Clement Massier ceramic vase, c1900, 13½in (34cm) high.
£350-375 *SAI*

A Frederick Rhead Foley Intarsio Toby Jug, Friar Tuck, 8½in (21cm) high.
£200-250 *BEV*

Cross Reference
Toby Jugs

59

A Frederick Rhead Foley Intarsio clock, 12in (30cm) high.
£800-1,200   *BEV*

A Moorcroft vase, Hibiscus pattern, c1955, 10in (25cm).
£200-230   *NP*

A Moorcroft two-handled vase, decorated with anemones, 1990, 13in (33cm).
£250-300   *NP*

A Moorcroft vase, Pomegranate pattern, c1913, 14in (35.5cm).
£600-650   *NP*

A Charlotte Rhead tankard, c1930, 7½in (19cm) high.
£200-250   *BEV*

A Moorcroft tyg, with green and gold Florian design, c1903, 5in (12.5cm).
£375-400   *NP*

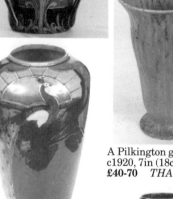

A Pilkington green vase, c1920, 7in (18cm) high.
£40-70   *THA*

A pair of Foresters Phoenix ware vases, c1910, 12½in (32cm) high.
£200-250   *SAI*

DID YOU KNOW?
Miller's Collectables Price Guide is designed to build up, year by year, into the most comprehensive reference system available.

A Charlotte Rhead vase, 8in (20cm) high.
£80-100   *BEV*

Brannam

The Brannam Pottery of Barnstaple, Devon, was started by Thomas Brannam, who exhibited pottery at the Great Exhibition of 1851. His son Charles, being unhappy with his father's work, produced the Barum Ware Art Pottery which has become so collectable during the past couple of years.

Using local red clay from Fremington, early Art pottery carried incised handwritten marks 'C.H. Brannam', 'Barum' and the date. (Barum is the Roman name for Barnstaple.) From about 1913 onwards the pottery was marked C. H. Brannam Ltd. Charles Brannam died in 1937 but the factory continues today.

FURTHER READING
A Family Business, The Story of a Pottery, by Peter Brannam, 1982.

Three Brannam vases with loop handles, decorated by James Dewdney, dated 1893, 18in (46cm) high.
£700-800 *BLO*

A Brannam candle holder/vase, 10½in (26cm) high.
£180-220 *BLO*

A Brannam posy holder, decorated by Thomas Liverton, dated 1895, 5½in (14cm) wide.
£110-120 *BLO*

Bretby

During the early 1880s William Tooth from the Linthorpe Art Pottery formed a partnership with William Ault in 1883, called the Bretby Art Pottery, at Woodville, near Burton-on-Trent, Derbyshire. The mark was as below, the word England was added from 1891. Their products were very similar to Linthorpe but were generally regarded as lower quality. William Ault did not stay long and in 1886 left to set up his own pottery. From the 1920s the firm advertised as 'Tooth and Co' and under different ownership is still in production.

A pair of Bretby vases, c1890, 14in (36cm) high.
£400-450   *BLO*

A Bretby vase, 5½in (14cm) high.
£20-40   *BLO*

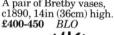

A Bretby heron vase, 12in (31cm) high.
£140-160   *BLO*

Rye Pottery

The Rye Pottery was founded in 1869 at Ferry Road, Rye, Sussex, when Frederick Mitchell took over and produced a series of decorative pottery. The marks were simple block letters 'SUSSEX WARE' and from 1869 S.R.W. RYE (Sussex Rustic Ware). From about 1920 S.A.W. RYE (Sussex Art Ware) was impressed or incised and the factory closed during the second world war. It was re-opened in 1947 by John and Walter Cole and all the printed or impressed marks used since then have the word RYE featured.

Two Rye pottery jugs, with hop design, 7in (18cm) high.
£200-250
2½in (6cm) high.
£60-65   *BLO*

A money box, c1904, 7in (18cm) high.
£200-250   *PC*

A unique item.

FURTHER READING
Sussex Pottery, John Manwaring Baines, Fisher Publications, 1980.

Cross Reference
Money Boxes

Two Rye pottery jugs,
l. 3½in (9cm) high.
£40-45
r. 5½in (14cm) high.
£60-65   *PC*

A hop design vase, 14in
(36cm) high.
£250-280   *PC*

Cross Reference
Jugs

Beswick

Beswick Ware was produced by J. Beswick
(Ltd) of Gold Street, Longton,
Staffordshire. The earliest wares were not
often marked, although some pre- and
post-war products were simply marked in
capital letters 'BESWICK ENGLAND'.
The printed mark used from 1936 onwards
is shown below. Beswick Ware is noted for
a variety of products, the most famous
being their flying birds, usually in threes,
sometimes fives, and most commonly
ducks, however, other birds like
kingfishers, pheasants and seagulls are
eagerly sought.

A Merry Wives of
Windsor tankard,
Falstaff, 1948-73, 4in
(10cm) high.
£25-30   *CSA*

A sugar sifter, c1935, 5in
(12.5cm) high.
£18-20   *CSA*

A jug, A Midsummer
Night's Dream, 1955-73,
8in (20cm) high.
£85-95   *CSA*

Beswick Ware.
MADE IN
ENGLAND

A jam pot and cover,
c1950, 4in (10cm) high.
£16-18   *CSA*

A double jam
dish, c1935,
5½in (14cm) diam.
£10-12   *CSA*

Burleigh

A basket, c1935, 10in
(25cm) wide.
£60-70 *CSA*

A sugar shaker, c1935,
6in (15cm) high.
£16-18 *CSA*

A hand painted jug,
c1930, 7½in (19cm) high.
£15-20 *OD*

Buckley

A black glazed brewing
jar, c1850, 18½in (47cm)
high.
£55-65 *IW*

For a further selection
of Buckley pottery see
Collectables Vol. II,
page 48.

Carlton Ware

Carlton Ware has been produced since
1890 at the Carlton Works, Stoke-on-
Trent. Very collectable Art Pottery was
produced during the 1920s and Art Deco
heavily influenced domestic china, all of a
very high quality.

The advertising figures, especially
Guinness, are extremely collectable at the
moment — see Drinking, Smoking and
Advertising sections. The company was
re-named Carlton Ware Limited in 1958.
Some marks, see below, feature the
previous name Wiltshaw and Robinson
Ltd.

Carlton Ware
MADE IN ENGLAND
"TRADE MARK"

A breakfast set in pink,
black with gilt trim, Deco
shape, c1920.
£280-300 *RO*

A sauceboat and stand,
Blackcurrant pattern,
c1935, 6in (15cm) wide.
£35-40 *CSA*

A bowl with Guinness toucans, 3½in (9cm) high.
£20-30 *RO*

A vase, Apple Blossom pattern, c1939, 3½in (9cm) high.
£35-40 *CSA*

A cruet, Foxglove pattern, c1939, 5in (13cm) diam.
£35-40 *CSA*

A set of 6 plates, 2 dishes, a bowl and servers, in green and orange, c1930, dish 9in (23cm).
£200-240 *RO*

A bowl, c1935, 9½in (24cm) long.
£60-70 *CSA*

An orange and green vase, 5½in (14cm) high.
£40-50 *THA*

A chocolate cup and cover, Apple Blossom pattern, c1939, 4½in (11cm) high.
£65-75
Without cover.
£35-40 *CSA*

65

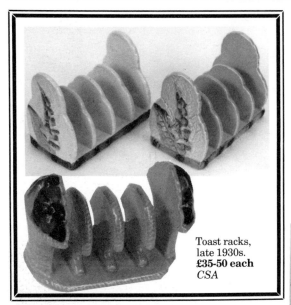

A mushroom cruet, 4in (10cm) diam.
£25-28 *CLH*

Toast racks, late 1930s.
£35-50 each
CSA

A salad bowl and servers, Foxglove pattern, c1939.
£75-85 *CSA*

l. A lemon squeezer and bowl. **£10-20**
r. A dish. **£30-40** *SAI*

A pair of handcraft vases, c1930, 8in (20cm) high.
£125-135
CSA

Clarice Cliff

For a further selection of Clarice Cliff designs see Collectables Vol. II, page 53.

A Clarice Cliff trio, Biarritz pattern, c1935.
£95-110 *CSA*

A cup and saucer, Foxglove pattern, c1939.
£35-40 *CSA*

An hors d'oeuvre dish, Buttercup pattern, 10in (25cm) long.
£45-50 *CSA*

A Clarice Cliff conical jug, Blue Chintz pattern, c1933, 4in (10cm) high.
£190-210   *CSA*

A Clarice Cliff teapot, daffodil shape with Honolulu design, c1933.
£500-600   *CSA*

A Clarice Cliff muffineer, Gibralter pattern, c1933.
£275-300   *CSA*

A Clarice Cliff sabot, orange Erin pattern, c1934, 6in (15cm) wide.
£300-325   *CSA*

A Clarice Cliff jug, Farmhouse design, c1931, 2½in (6cm) high.
£135-145   *CSA*

A Clarice Cliff mug in orange Secrets design, c1933, 3½in (9cm) high.
£180-200   *CSA*

A Clarice Cliff teapot, Athens shape, Summer house design, c1932, 7in (18cm) high.
£500-600 *CSA*

A Clarice Cliff biscuit barrel, painted in Autumn design, 5½in (14cm) high.
£550-600 *RO*

l. A Clarice Cliff geometric design jam pot and cover, c1928, 4½in (11cm) high.
£95-110
r. A Fern design pot, 3in (8cm) high.
£110-125 *CSA*

Cross Reference
Biscuit Barrels

A Clarice Cliff Patina Tree bowl, 5in (13cm) diam.
£165-175 *CLH*

A Clarice Cliff Rhodanthe bowl, 9½in (24cm) diam.
£350-400 *CLH*

Torquay

A Torquay pottery jug,
2in (5cm) high.
£6-10 *OD*

A Torquay pottery
candlestick, c1920, 4½in
(11cm) high.
£18-20 *CSA*

A Torquay pottery
pepper pot, 3in (8cm)
high.
£5-10 *OD*

A Torquay pottery jug,
4in (10cm) high.
£6-10 *OD*

Grays

A Grays silver lustre jug,
c1940, 5½in (13cm) high.
£50-60 *CSA*

Hancock

A Hancock Royal Corona
ware jardinière, Rosetta
pattern, c1915, 7in
(17.5cm) high.
£95-110 *CSA*

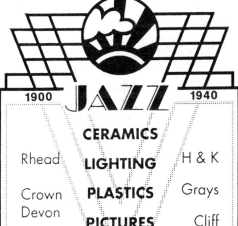

Crown Devon

A Crown Devon green
dog, filled with cement
for door stop, c1930, 9in
(23cm) high.
£30-40   *CA*

A Crown Devon vase,
c1935, 6½in (16cm) high.
£18-20   *CSA*

A Crown Devon vase,
c1939, 3in (8cm) high.
£16-18   *CSA*

A Crown Devon lustre
jug, c1940, 7in (18cm)
high.
£40-45
CSA

A Crown Devon dish,
c1939, 9½in (24cm) long.
£35-40   *CSA*

A pair of Crown Devon
vases, c1910, 8½in
(21cm) high.
£75-85   *CSA*

A Dartmouth pottery
jug, c1910, 4½in (11cm)
high.
£16-18   *CSA*

Dartmouth

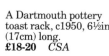

A Dartmouth pottery
teapot, c1930, 10in
(25cm) high.
£30-35   *CSA*

A Dartmouth pottery
toast rack, c1950, 6½in
(17cm) long.
£18-20   *CSA*

Doulton

A Doulton, Lambeth, stoneware tobacco jar, signed by Harry Simeon, c1915, 5in (13cm) high.
£130-160 *TP*

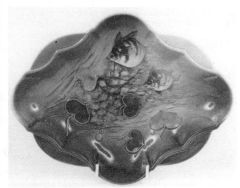

A Royal Doulton dish, 'The Old Wife' tropical fish, made for the Australian market in 1939, 9½in (24cm) wide.
£40-45 *CSA*

A Doulton ware jug in shape of Nelson's head, 7½in (19cm) high.
£250-300 *CAC*

A Royal Doulton Tony Weller teapot, c1940, 8in (20cm) high.
£900-1,100 *TP*

Tyneside Potteries

Maling Ware

1762-1815	Various wares produced at North Hylton, Nr. Sunderland. Unmarked.
1815-1859	Pottery moved to Newcastle. Creamware and lustre ware decorated by transfer printing with hand painting. Marks are rare but usually include the word Maling.
1859-1883	Relief moulded and simple transfer printed wares, mostly unmarked.
1883-1890	Hand coloured transfer printed wares. Good quality designs. Marks C.T.M. in a triangle, printed and impressed, various pattern names.
1890-c1915	Lithographs designed by C. J. Miguet. Good quality with tone and depth of colour. Emma Coppick employed as a gilder, producing fine work identified by the inclusion of a small shamrock-like leaf. Marks as before but with Cetem Ware from 1908.
1908-1922	Harry C. Toft became head of design department. Cetem Ware launched in 1908. High quality wares of a purely decorative nature produced for the first time. Marks Cetem Ware around a castle.
1922-1926	Charles N. Wright replaced Toft. Continued Cetem Ware production.

	Maling Ware launched in 1924. Production of lustre wares and lavish gold printed wares from 1925.
1926-1936	Lucien Emile Boullemier became designer, producing some of Maling's finest, and most collectable, designs.
1926-1936	Theodora (Theo) Maling began to design her own studio ceramics. Wares are rare and hand painted, some designs went into production. Unmarked or signed T. Maling.
1933-1963	Lucien George Boullemier joined his father as designer, eventually taking over from 1936. First design is Pastel. Introduced Regal dinner ware. Post War designs are simpler and mostly floral.
1936-1946	Norman Carling joined company as head modeller, designed ranges such as Blossom Time, Bambola and Flight. Experimented with figures, none of which made production, except Lady Nicotine.
1963	Factory Closed.

FURTHER READING
Maling, The Trade Mark of Excellence, Steven Moore, Tyne & Wear Museum Services, 1989.

An Exeter jug in the Rich Lady design with quart excise stamp, c1875, 7in (18cm) high. **£100-150** *IS*

A traveller's sample jug, decorated with a lithograph by C. J. Miguet, c1900, 15in (38cm) high. **£200-250** *IS*

A C. T. Maling ewer from a wash set, decorated with a lithograph by C. J. Miguet, c1903, 15in (38cm) high.
£100-150 *IS*

A Maling ware salad bowl, 1920-26, 8in (20cm) diam.
£50-60 *RO*

An ashtray in the Salmon Fly design after Theo. Maling, c1926, 3in (8cm) diam.
£60-80 *IS*

A Maling ware dish, embossed with lustre, 1920-26, 10½in (26cm) diam.
£100-120 *RO*

A plaque, with Lace border, c1937, 11in (28cm) diam.
£125-150 *CSA*

A footed bowl, with Primrose border, c1935, 9in (23cm) diam.
£100-125 *CSA*

A pierced dish, Peony design, c1935, 11in (28cm) wide.
£85-95 *CSA*

Maling ware kitchen items in cobblestone design
jug, 6in (15cm) high.
£55-65
pot 4in (10cm) high.
£25-35 *BEV*

This design was produced in blue, green and brown.

A Ripple ware vase by Norman Carling, c1936, 6in (15cm) high.
£100-150 *IS*

A No. 6 shape lamp base, with stand and cover, Prunus pattern, by H. C. Toft, coronet mark, c1930.
£150-200 *IS*

Part of a morning set, designed by L. E. Boullemier, c1934, teapot 4in (10cm) high.
£150-180 *IS*

A pair of plates in the Butterfly design by L. E. Boullemier, painted by Janet Taylor, c1930, 4in (10cm) diam.
£80-100 *IS*

An Empress shaped honey pot by L. E. Boullemier, c1930, 4in (10cm) high.
£100-120 *IS*

A plate, with embossed Iris design, c1930.
£150-200 *BEV*

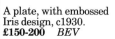

See also Lustre Ware from Tyneside Potteries, pages 107, 108 and 109.

Shelley

A 21-piece Shelley tea service, Oxford shape, Archway frames pattern, c1945.
£180-250   *AJ*

A Shelley 21-piece tea service, tall Queen Anne shape, Crabtree pattern, plate 6in (16cm) diam.
£350-400   *AJ*

A Shelley jelly mould, c1910, 5in (13cm) high.
£20-25   *CSA*

A Shelley Melody pattern tankard, c1935, 5in (12cm) high.
£55-65   *CSA*

A vase, c1930, 8in (20cm) high.
£35-45   *AJ*

A pair of Shelley Melody pattern vases, c1935, 5½in (14cm) high.
£75-85   *CSA*

The Shelley Group

The main aims of the Group are to promote and disseminate information on Shelley Potteries and to generally broaden the appreciation of Shelley wares.

Members receive quarterly newsletters and are able to research design and pattern details (through the Group).

Details from:
Linda Ellis
228 Croyland Road
Lower Edmonton
London N9 7BG

Minton

A saucer and 2 cups in
Minton Amherst Japan
pattern, c1840, saucer
6in (15cm) diam.
£60-70   *CSA*

A Minton Amherst
Japan slop bowl, c1840,
7in (18cm) diam.
£60-70   *CSA*

Radford Ware

A Radford ware tree
pattern vase, c1930,
5½in (14cm) high.
£50-60   *RO*

A Radford ware vase, 4in
(10cm) high.
£40-45   *RO*

Sweeney Mountain

A Sweeney Mountain
type pot, c1800, 8½in
(21cm) high.
£40-50   *IW*

A Sweeney Mountain
type commode pot,
18thC, 7½in (18cm) high.
£70-80   *IW*

Shorter Ware

The pottery of Shorter and Sons is becoming increasingly collectable. The tremendous variety of styles produced by this Staffordshire firm between the 1870s and 1970 provides a rich field for collectors of ceramics. It includes early traditional majolica ware, the characteristic fish and shell sets, striking Art Deco designs and a series influenced by ethnic pottery. Table ware in embossed floral and fruit designs, a wide range of novelties and literally dozens of character jugs were also part of the imaginative output of this small factory.

A Pompadour majolica style, hand painted butter dish, late 1920s 5in (13cm) wide.
£25-30   *PC*

A set of 3 Shorter Ware yachts, mid-1930s, 6 to 9in (15 to 23cm).
£65-75   *PC*

Three matt glazed wall pockets,
l. & r. Art Deco style, c1930, 5½in (14cm) high and c. c1950, 7in (18cm) high.
£20-25 each   *PC*

A Wan-Li sgraffito and hand painted wall plaque, c1939, 12in (31cm) diam.
£70-90   *PC*

A bulb trough, c1935, 8in (20cm) wide.
£10-15   *CSA*

77

A hand painted
kingfisher wall
decoration, mid-1930s,
5in (13cm) long.
£20-30 *PC*

A pair of hand painted
flying swans wall
decoration, mid-1930s,
11½ and 17½in (29 and
44cm) long.
£55-60 *PC*

A hand painted free
standing seagull,
mid-1930s, 13in (33cm)
wingspan.
£50-60 *PC*

A hand painted flying
seagull wall decoration,
mid-1930s, 13½in (34cm)
long.
£30-40 *PC*

Jugs

A hand painted Yacht
Ware jug, mid-1930s, 8in
(20cm) high.
£33-45 *PC*

Two sgraffito and hand
painted Khimara jugs,
designed by Mabel
Leigh, c1930,
6in (15cm) high.
£40-45
7½in (19cm) high.
£55-65 *PC*

A hand painted
Kandahar jug, mid-
1930s, 8½in (21cm) high.
£45-55 *PC*

A hand painted majolica
Oceanic jug, late 1920s,
7in (18cm) high.
£65-75 *PC*

A hand painted Daffodil
design jug, c1940, 9½in
(24cm) high.
£35-40 *PC*

Tableware

An Anemone teapot, c1935, 7in (18cm) high.
£85-95 *CSA*

> **Cross Reference**
> Teapots

Figures

Shorter Ware 'Modern Salad' Art Deco tableware, c1930, double dish, 7½in (19cm) long.
£15-25
bowl, 10in (25cm) wide.
£25-30
sauce boat and stand, 8in (20cm) wide.
£15-25 *PC*

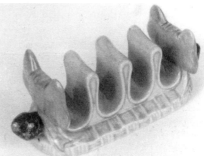

A Toby jug, The Cavalier, c1940, 7in (18cm) high.
£30-35 *CSA*

A toast rack, c1950, 7in (18cm) long.
£25-30 *CSA*

Shorter Ware hand painted character figures, late 1930s, Lovers with umbrella, 6½in (16cm) high and Mother Goose, 5½in (14cm) high.
£35-40 each *PC*

A character study of The Duke of Plaza Toro, 10in (25cm) high.
£45-55 *RID*

Produced for the D'oyly Carte Opera Co.

Vases

An art glazed vase,
c1950, 11in (28cm) long.
£25-35 *PC*

A pair of Khimara
sgraffito and hand
painted vases, designed
by Mabel Leigh, c1930,
7in (18cm) high.
£110-130 *PC*

A Khimara sgraffito and
hand painted ewer,
designed by Mabel
Leigh, c1930, 4½in
(11cm) high.
£40-45 *PC*

A Khimara
sgraffito and
hand painted vase,
designed by Mabel
Leigh, c1930, 4½in
(11cm) high.
£40-45 *PC*

Susie Cooper

Susie Cooper originally decorated china
for A. E. Gray & Co., but in the 1930s left
to form Susie Cooper Pottery (Ltd)., at
Burslem, Staffordshire. The Company
was re-named Susie Cooper Ltd., in the
early 1960s, and it is worth remembering
that the words 'Crown Works' do not
feature on the marks before 1932. All
Susie Cooper is collectable now, especially
the marvellous range of Art Deco shapes
and designs.

A matt glazed vase,
c1950, 12in (30.5cm)
high.
£35-45 *PC*

A coffee cup and saucer,
c1950, saucer 5in
(12.5cm) diam.
£8-10 *CSA*

A Malaga sgraffito and
hand painted vase,
mid-1930s, 12in (30.5cm)
high.
£80-100 *PC*

A coffee cup and saucer,
Talisman pattern, saucer
5½in (13.5cm) diam.
£8-10 *CSA*

A pair of Nosegay
pattern cups and saucers,
c1935.
£18-20 each   *CSA*

Susie Cooper
CROWN WORKS
BURSLEM
ENGLAND

A plate, c1940, 9in
(23cm).
£14-16   *CSA*

A Kestrel shape tureen,
with Dresden spray on
the lid which lifts to
make a separate serving
dish, c1935, 9½in (24cm)
diam.
£35-40   *CSA*

A tureen, c1948, 9½in
(24cm) diam.
£20-25   *CSA*

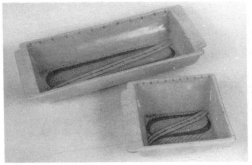

Hors d'oeuvre dishes,
c1932, 10 and 5in (25 and
12.5cm).
£10-20 each   *CSA*

A Kestrel shape cream
jug, c1935, 3in (7.5cm)
high.
£18-20   *CSA*

Wade

A lustre jam pot with
Bramble design, c1950.
£18-20 *CSA*

A Wade Heath teapot,
c1935, 6½in (16cm) high.
£45-50 *CSA*

Cross Reference
Teapots

A Wade Heath cheese
dish, c1935.
£40-45 *CSA*

A jug with acorn design,
c1950, 5½in (13.5cm)
high.
£20-25 *CSA*

A 'Sunshine' figure, with
cellulose paint, c1939,
7in (17.5cm) high.
£50-60 *CSA*

*The cellulose paint is
often in poor condition.*

Wemyss

Two Wemyss lids, 4in
(10cm) diam.
£15-20 each *SBA*

A jam pot with
blackcurrant design, 5in
(12.5cm) high.
£550-600 *SBA*

A Thomas Gordon dish,
impressed mark, 7in
(17.5cm) square.
£550-600 *SBA*

A vase with thistle
design, 7½in (19cm) high.
£550-600   *SBA*

A pin tray, 5in (12.5cm)
wide.
£140-160   *SBA*

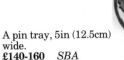

A mug with apple
pattern, 3½in (8.5cm)
high.
£300-350   *SBA*

Royal Worcester

A majolica figure,
impressed mark, c1865,
5in (12.5cm).
£180-200   *TVA*

Limited editions of
horses:
Arkle, 9½in (24cm) high.
£500-550
Stroller and Marion
Coakes and Nijinsky,
10in (25cm) high.
£240-260 each   *GSP*

Barge Ware

'Forget Me Not' teapot,
13½in (34cm) high.
£140-180 *PC*

'Home Sweet Home' tea
jug, 7in (17.5cm) high.
£50-80 *PC*

A teapot, with rare
vignette of a cricketer,
some restoration, 8½in
(21cm) high.
£350-400 *Sto*

DID YOU KNOW?
Miller's Collectables
Price Guide is
designed to build up,
year by year, into the
most comprehensive
reference system
available.

'Love at Home' teapot,
13½in (34.5cm) high.
£150-200 *PC*

No inscription, 12in
(30.5cm) high.
£70-80

A selection of Barge ware
teapots, all badly
damaged, to illustrate
price variations.

'Home Sweet Home',
8½in (21cm).
£50-60

With inscription, 1892,
11in (28cm).
£80-100 *HUN*

Biscuit Barrels

A Maling Ware biscuit
barrel, with peony rose
pattern, c1950, 7½in
(19cm).
£95-120   *CSA*

A Clarice Cliff biscuit
barrel, My Garden
pattern, c1934, 8½in
(21cm).
£250-300   *CSA*

A Clarice Cliff biscuit
barrel with Crocus
pattern, 8in (20cm).
£270-280   *CLH*

A Clarice Cliff biscuit
barrel, Secrets pattern,
replacement lid, c1934,
7½in (18.5cm).
£300-400   *CSA*

Shorter Ware biscuit
barrels, with chrome lids
and handles, 7in (18cm)
high.
Above. c1935. **£65-75**
Below. c1950. **£30-35**
CSA

A Clarice Cliff biscuit
barrel with Melons
pattern, c1932, 7½in
(18.5cm).
£500-600   *CSA*

A Royal Winton biscuit
barrel, c1930, 7in
(17.5cm).
£45-50   *CSA*

Children's Ceramics

A jug, c1840, 3½in
(8.5cm) high.
£45-50 *IW*

An S. Keeling & Co., cup
and saucer, printed in
red with Corinthian
Arch pattern, 1840s,
saucer 4½in (11cm) diam.
£25-30 *IW*

Cross Reference
Dolls House Furniture

A selection of blue and
white doll's plates and a
bowl, each with named
view, c1840.
£40-50 each *CA*

A pair of cream teacups,
with brown transfer
pattern, 19thC.
£20-25 *SWN*

A Staffordshire child's
creamware tea service,
decorated in brown with
a leaf border, c1810.
£100-150 *CSK*

Mugs

A Victorian Staffordshire
mug, with green transfer.
£15-20 *SWN*

A child's mug with brown
transfer, very stained.
£15-20 *SWN*

*In perfect condition –
£50-60.*

A child's mug depicting
Mr. Pickwick, c1860,
2½in (6cm).
£45-50 *IW*

A child's mug with racing scene, c1860, 2in (5cm).
£40-60 *IW*

Two mugs, 1820s, badly damaged.
£10-15 each *SWN*

This is an excellent way to start any collection, as these damaged examples are very good value.

A mug depicting 'Spring', 3in (7.5cm).
£40-60 *IW*

> **Cross Reference**
> Transfer printed ware

A transfer printed mug, mid-19thC, 2½in (6cm) high.
£25-30 *CAC*

'H' alphabet mugs, c1850, 3in (7.5cm).
£45-55 each
l. *SWN*
Above. *HOW*

Named children's mugs,
2½in (6cm) high.
£60-90 each *SWN*

A Staffordshire mug,
with red transfer c1850.
£35-45 *SWN*

A mug, with
lithophane
of Beatrix Potter as a
child in the base, 3in
(7.5cm) high.
£100-125 *CA*

'A Present for Robert',
black transfer printed,
c1820, 3in (7cm) high.
£100-120 *SWN*

A child's mug with puce
transfer print of 'Mother
Goose', c1860, 2½in
(6cm).
£60-80 *IW*

MAKE THE MOST OF MILLERS
Price ranges in this book reflect what one should
expect to *pay* for a similar example. When selling,
however, one should expect to receive a lower
figure. This will fluctuate according to a dealer's
stock, saleability at a particular time, etc. It is
always advisable, when selling, to approach a
reputable specialist dealer or an auction house
which has specialist sales.

Plates

A child's plate with enamelled decoration, 1820, 6½in (16.5cm).
£60-80   *IW*

A humorous hand coloured transfer printed plate, c1840.
£90-100   *SWN*

A Staffordshire plate in 4 colours, with inscription 'Want of cash does us more damage than want of knowledge'.   **£70-80**   *SWN*

A hand painted plate, mid-19thC.
£100-120   *SWN*

Two Swansea plates, l. c1840, very damaged.
£60-65 if perfect
r. c1830s.
£80-90   *CA*

A black printed embossed plate, c1850.
£80-90   *SWN*

Cups & Saucers

An extensive selection of cups and saucers is featured in Miller's Collectables Price Guide Vol. II, pages 95-97.

A Victorian Welsh cup and saucer.
£12-18   *OD*

A Midgham Parish Jubilee mug, 1887, 3½in (8.5cm).
£20-25   *CAC*

Commemorative

A Coalport blue and white plate, 10in (25cm).
£115-130   *CA*

A Royal Doulton two-handled tyg, 5in (12.5cm).
£150-200   *CA*

A lustre jug, 3in (7.5cm).
£50-60   *CA*

Royalty

A Staffordshire plate, with black transfer, 1851.
£50-70   *SWN*

A German commemorative vase, Coronation of Queen Mary, 1911, 6½in (16cm).
£30-35   *CSA*

A Queen Victoria's Jubilee mug, c1887, 3in (7.5cm).
£60-70   *CSA*

A Shelley match striker, c1900, 5in (12.5cm).
£20-25 *CSA*

An Albion relief moulded jug, Edward and Alexandra wedding, 1863, 6½in (16cm).
£100-130 *CA*

A lustre ware black transfer printed cup and saucer, Death of Princess Charlotte, c1817.
£85-95 *CSA*

A Paragon ware loving cup, Prince Andrew and Miss Sarah Ferguson's wedding, 1986.
£18-20 *CSA*

A lithophane mug, Coronation of Queen Alexandra, 1902, 3in (7.5cm).
£80-90 *CSA*

A Queen Victoria's Jubilee plate, 1887, 9½in (24cm).
£50-60 *CSA*

A Tuscan ware sepia print plaque, with gold rim, Queen Elizabeth's Coronation, 1953, 3½in (8.5cm) high.
£18-20 *CSA*

A Staffordshire pottery jug, with transfer of Queen Victoria and Prince Albert, c1840, 8in (20cm) high.
£350-400 *Bon*

A pair of Staffordshire portrait figures, modelled as Queen Victoria and Prince Albert, c1845, 6½in (17cm) high.
£400-600 *Bon*

Cross Reference
Staffordshire

A Coalport armorial plate, c1850, 10in (25cm) diam.
£800-1,000 *Bon*

A Staffordshire pearlware miniature bust of The Duke of York, restored, c1827, 6½in (17cm) high.
£150-200 *Bon*

A Staffordshire plate, the centre printed 'Victoria and Albert, Married Feb 10. 1840', 5in (13cm) diam.
£100-150 *Bon*

A Staffordshire pottery child's plate, printed and overpainted with a full portrait of Queen Victoria, c1837, 7in (18cm) diam.
£100-150 *Bon*

A Staffordshire alphabet plate, the centre printed with named half portraits of Queen Victoria and Prince Albert, 5in (13cm) diam.
£350-400 *Bon*

An English porcelain mug, 'In Memory of Caroline of Brunswick', 4½in (11cm) high.
£1,500-2,000 *Bon*

A German commemorative mug, Queen Victoria's Jubilee, 1887, 4½in (11cm).
£50-55   *CSA*

A Royal Crown Derby bone china loving cup, commemorating the Coronation of King George V, 5½in (14cm) high.
£400-450   *Bon*

A Copeland 'subscribers copy' loving cup, commemorating the Transvaal War of 1899-1900, 5½in (14cm) high.
£1,000-1,500   *Bon*

A Staffordshire pottery plate, commemorating Prince Alfred's visit to the West Indies, c1861, 9in (23cm) diam.
£750-850   *Bon*

A Royal Lancastrian pottery plaque, decorated by W. S. Mycock, to commemorate the Coronation of King George VI, 9½in (24cm) diam.
£50-100   *Bon*

An English bone china mug, to commemorate the 80th birthday of Queen Elizabeth The Queen Mother in 1980, 3in (8cm) high.
£50-100   *Bon*

A Copeland Spode pottery jug, to commemorate The Diamond Jubilee of Queen Victoria, 6in (15cm) high.
£150-200   *Bon*

A Staffordshire pottery mug, in memory of Queen Victoria, dated 1901, 4in (10cm) high.
£100-150   *Bon*

l. & r. A pair of Staffordshire portrait figures, modelled as Prince Alfred and The Prince of Wales, c1858, 8½in (21cm) high.
£350-450
c. A portrait of Queen Victoria, c1855, 11½in (29cm) high.
£250-350   *Bon*

Fairings

Three little girls, 2in (5cm) wide.
£15-20 *THA*

Who is coming?
£120-140 *BRK*

Twelve months after marriage.
£70-90 *BRK*

The wedding night.
£60-85 *BRK*

Lor Three Legs I'll Charge 2d.
£100-120 *BRK*

Caught, match holder
£80-100 *BRK*

Misses is Master.
£70-90 *BRK*

Returning at one o'clock in the morning.
£60-80 *BRK*

Fresh Chestnuts Sir?
£70-80 *BRK*

Pin Trays

Girl and dog.
£40-50   *BRK*

Turk reading, 4½in
(11cm) high.
£80-90   *BRK*

King.
£70-90   *BRK*

Bedtime.
£50-60   *BRK*

Wishing well.
£60-80   *BRK*

Tea set, 4in (10cm) high.
£50-60   *BRK*

A music group.
£70-80   *BRK*

Three graces.
£60-70   *BRK*

FURTHER READING
Victorian China Fairings, W. S. Bristowe,
London 1971.
Antique China and Glass under £5, Geoffrey
Godden, London 1965.

Figures

Victorian figures of children, 4in (10cm) high.
£45-55 *CA*

A Goldscheider Madonna, 10½in (26cm) high.
£210-225 *CLH*

A pair of Alton china figures of the King and Queen of Clubs, c1940, 4½in (12cm) high.
£30-35 *CSA*

Royal Doulton figures

An orange vendor, HN 72.
£250-300 *LT*

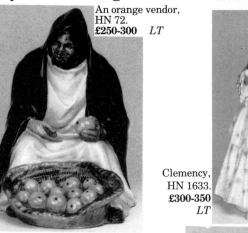

Clemency, HN 1633.
£300-350
LT

Georgina, HN 2093.
£450-500 *LT*

A Victorian match holder, 5½in (14cm) high.
£20-25 *CA*

Grandma, HN 2052.
£150-200
LT

Goss China

Goss Sulgrave Manor,
Northamptonshire.
£900 *G&CC*

Shakespeare's house, 5in
(13cm) wide.
£70-80 *SBA*

Military badges.
£35-65 each
G&CC

London Stone.
£135 *G&CC*

Italian krater,
International
League,
1922.
£85
G&CC

FURTHER READING

*The Concise Encyclopedia and Price Guide to
Goss China* and *The Price Guide to Arms and
Decorations on Goss China*, Nicholas Pine
(Milestone Publications), 62 Murray Road,
Horndean, Hants.
*William Henry Goss, The Story of the
Staffordshire Family of Potters Who Invented
Heraldic Porcelain*, Lynda and Nicholas Pine.

Nightlight.
£300 *G&CC*

Shakespeare's house
nightlight, half length,
with separate base.
£100 *G&CC*

St. Columb Major Cross,
brown version.
£125 *G&CC*

Named models
with
ecclesiastical
arms.
£7-10 each
G&CC

Hythe Cromwellian
mortar.
£9   *G&CC*

Three Chichester Arms
on matching models of
Chichester urn.
£20 each   *G&CC*

Stirling pint measure.
£8   *G&CC*

German sausage plate.
£100   *G&CC*

Seagull transfers on
cream jug.
£30   *G&CC*

Third period, Babies on
Ashtray.
£65   *G&CC*

Brass pipe rack.
£100   *G&CC*

Norwegian bucket.
£10   *G&CC*

Winchester pot with
matching College arms.
£25   *G&CC*

A selection of domestic
items.
£10-40 each *G&CC*

A selection with verses.
£20-55 each *G&CC*

Winchester Castle
Warden's horn.
£175 *G&CC*

Models with foreign
crests.
£7-10 each *G&CC*

Dartmouth Sack
bottle with
matching arms.
£14 *G&CC*

Nautilus shell.
£100 *G&CC*

Figurines:
l. Lady holding a kid.
r. Leda and the Swan,
coloured.
£750 each *G&CC*

Crested China

Ever popular characters.
£25-150 each
G&CC

Carlton John Citizen.
£100   *G&CC*

Arcadian Scottish
Soldier.
£130   *G&CC*

Arcadian 'Isn't this
rabbit a duck'
dual model.
£20   *G&CC*

WWI selection.
£10-50 each   *G&CC*

Carlton film
star Jackie
Coogan.
£30   *G&CC*

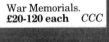

War Memorials.
£20-120 each   *CCC*

FURTHER READING
Crested China, Sandy Andrews.
The 1991 Price Guide to Crested China, Nicholas
Pine (Milestone Publications), 62 Murray Road,
Horndean, Hants.

Cats from various
factories.
£12-45 each
CCC

Coloured buildings,
various factories.
£65-200 each   *CCC*

Musical instruments,
Arcadian piano.
£14
Willow banjo. **£10**
Arcadian harp.
£7 *G&CC*

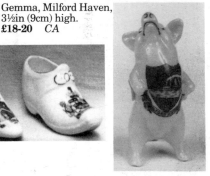

Gemma, Milford Haven,
3½in (9cm) high.
£18-20   *CA*

Florentine
lady's shoe,
18thC.
£7
and Arcadian Lancashire
clog.
£5   *G&CC*

Westcliff-on-Sea clog, 4in
(10cm) wide.
£4   *CA*

Arcadian map of Blighty
with verse.
£50   *G&CC*

Willow open 2-seater car.
£35   *G&CC*

Buildings, various
factories.
£45-120 each
CCC

The Cheshire Cat
Always Smiling, 3½in
(9cm) high.
£12   *CA*

Carlton Wembley
Stadium.
£50 *G&CC*

Carlton Pit Head.
£75 *G&CC*

Macintyre paper weight/
desk tidy, c1870, 3in
(8cm) high.
£15 *CA*

Assorted chairs.
£5-10 each
G&CC

Bathing Beauty trinket
tray by Carlton.
£50 *G&CC*

Crested buildings,
various manufacturers.
£15-30 each
G&CC

Hats by assorted
factories.
£20-30 each
G&CC

Teapots.
£8-18 each *CCC*

Teapots from various
factories.
£10-20 each *CCC*

Cross Reference
Teapots

French Faience

A platter,
c1930, 13½in
(34cm) diam.
£80-90 *MCA*

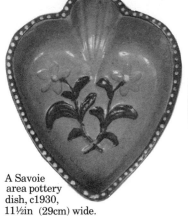

A Savoie
area pottery
dish, c1930,
11½in (29cm) wide.
£50-80 *MCA*

A pottery jug, c1880, 3in
(8cm) high.
£40-45 *MCA*

A water jug, c1880, 6in
(15cm) high.
£50-55 *MCA*

Ironstone

A Mason's Ironstone
67-piece dinner service,
with Imari pattern
decoration in blue and
iron red, with pagodas
and river scenes, 19thC.
£1,000-1,500 *P(M)*

A Mason's conical cover,
in Japan pattern, 8in
(20cm) high.
£40-60 *VH*

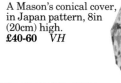

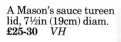

A Mason's tureen cover,
10in (25cm) diam.
£20-30 *VH*

A Mason's sauce tureen
lid, 7½in (19cm) diam.
£25-30 *VH*

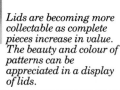

A garniture of 3 Mason's
Ironstone vases, tallest
9in (23cm).
£650-750 *SBA*

*Lids are becoming more
collectable as complete
pieces increase in value.
The beauty and colour of
patterns can be
appreciated in a display
of lids.*

Jugs

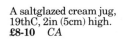

A saltglazed cream jug,
19thC, 2in (5cm) high.
£8-10   *CA*

A Jackfield painted jug,
damaged, c1750, 7in
(18cm) high.
£5-8
If perfect.
£15-20   *THA*

A Ridgeways moulded
jug, c1850, 8in (20cm)
high.
£85-95   *CSA*

An early Victorian Pratt
type moulded and
decorated jug.
£80-100   *SWN*

A copper lustre jug, The
Little Jockey, c1840,
4½in (11cm) high.
£100-120   *HOW*

A painted chintz jug,
mid-19thC.
£80-100   *SWN*

A Swansea cottage jug,
c1840, 7in (18cm) high.
£130-150   *HOW*

A Jackfield jug, c1750,
4½in (11cm) high.
£90-110   *THA*

A Ewenny jug, c1920,
1½in (4cm) high.
£15-25   *IW*

A Myott jug, c1930, 9in
(23cm) high.
£40-45   *CSA*

A Welsh lady cream jug,
4in (10cm) high.
£40-45   *OD*

A Staffordshire jug
decorated with a floral
sheet pattern, mid-
19thC.
£80-100   *SWN*

A Victorian lustre jug,
3½in (9cm) high.
£10-12   *CA*

A copper lustre jug with
yellow band, c1840, 3½in
(9cm) high.
£120-130   *HOW*

A Crown Devon jug,
c1930, 7in (18cm) high.
£15-20   *CSA*

DID YOU KNOW?
Miller's Collectables
Price Guide is
designed to build up,
year by year, into the
most comprehensive
reference system
available.

A pair of Falconware
green Deco jugs.
£45-55   *CLH*

Toby Jugs

A Shorter Ware guardsman Toby jug, 6½in (16cm) high.
£55-65 *CLH*

Cross Reference
Staffordshire Toby jugs

A Toby jug with B. J. C. Cameers, printed mark, 7½in (19cm) high.
£15-20 *CAC*

A Royal Doulton Toby jug, designed by Harry Fenton, marked 8337, c1939-69, 7in (18cm) high.
£90-130 *PC*

A Yorkshire Toby jug, 19thC, 9½in (24cm).
£80-100 *Wai*

Lustre Ware

Apart from the better known pink and orange lustre wares, most people do not realise the quality or the quantity of pottery produced on the rivers Tyne and Wear during the 18th and 19thC. A lot of so called 'Sunderland' ware was produced at Newcastle and at the many other Tyneside potteries. It is safe to say that the North East potteries produced everything that the Staffordshire potteries produced. Recently discovered information, as well as shards have shown that at least one pottery, John Carr of North Shields, produced 'Staffordshire'-type figures. Newcastle factories such as Sewell and Fell produced good quality creamware, many unmarked examples of which are attributed to Yorkshire factories. Most North East factories were small and many wares are unmarked.

A Tyneside lustre jug, with a view of Sunderland bridge, 1825-30, 8in (20cm) high.
£280-300 *IS*

A Sunderland creamware Masonic tankard, marked J. Phillips & Co., c1815, 5½in (14cm) high.
£300-330 *IS*

A Newcastle pottery relief moulded plaque, depicting St. Mark, by Thomas Fell, c1820, 7 by 5½in (18 by 14cm).
£450-500 *IS*

A Newcastle tea bowl and saucer, by Sewell & Donkin, c1825, saucer 4in (10cm) diam.
£40-45 *IS*

An animal spout milk jug, hand painted over a sheet transfer, c1850.
£80-100 *SWN*

A Tyneside pink lustre jug, c1840, 6in (15cm) high.
£120-150   *IS*

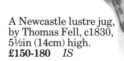

A Newcastle lustre bowl, with view of the bridge which opened in 1849, 3½in (9cm) high.
£85-95   *IS*

Two circular plaques, l. Sunderland, 'Prepare to meet thy God', and r. Tyneside, 'God is Love', c1820, 7 and 6in (18 and 15cm) diam.
£100-130 each   *IS*

A Newcastle lustre jug, by Thomas Fell, c1830, 5½in (14cm) high.
£150-180   *IS*

A Tyneside lustre mug, 'The Mariner's Compass', with toad inside, 5in (13cm) high.
£250-280   *IS*

A Sunderland lustre jug, by Dixon & Co., c1840, 9½in (24cm) high.
£250-300   *IS*

A Tyneside or Wearside, creamware Masonic tankard, with moulded frog inside, c1830, 5in (12.5cm) high.
£200-250   *IS*

A Sunderland lustre plaque, by Dixon & Co., c1840, 8 by 7in (20 by 18cm).
£100-120   IS

A Sunderland lustre mug, with moulded frog inside, by Scott & Son.
£180-200   IS

A Newcastle mug, with moulded frog inside and view of Tynemouth Haven, c1820, 5in (13cm) high.
£250-280   IS

A Sunderland pottery Paisley ware jug by Scott Bros., c1850, 7½in (19cm) high.
£300-350   IS

A Sunderland footed bowl, Dixon & Co., after 1859, 5½in (14cm) high.
£220-250   IS

A Sunderland pottery mug by Ball Bros., c1900, 3½in (9cm) high.
£40-45   IS

A Tyneside orange lustre jug, by John Carr, c1860, 4in (10cm) high.
£40-45   IS

A Tyneside lustre bowl, John Carr & Son, Low Lights Pottery, 8in (20cm) diam.
£150-180   IS

A Newcastle lustre bowl, Galloway & Atkinson, Albion Pottery, c1863, 4in (10cm) high.
£100-150   IS

A copper lustre jug and basin set, c1880, jug 2½in (6cm) high.
£35-40 *CSA*

A Sunderland orange lustre jug, by Ball Bros., Deptford Pottery, 1870s, 8in (20cm) high.
£150-170 *IS*

A lustre ware tea stand, with Lady Peace standing over British and Boer soldiers.
£60-80 *PO*

A Sunderland lustre plaque, with overglaze transfer, by Scott Bros., c1870, 8 by 8½in (20 by 21cm).
£180-200 *IS*

A Newcastle pottery bowl, Joseph Sewell, St. Anthony's Pottery, 11½in (29cm) diam.
£200-250 *IS*

Two copper lustre jugs, c1860:   l. 5½in (14cm).   r. 7in (19cm).
                                  £50-60   **£45-50**   *CSA*

A Newcastle pottery ewer, by C. T. Maling, c1850, 10½in (26cm) high.
£150-200 *IS*

Mugs

A pair of blue and grey banded mugs, c1870, 3½in (9cm) high.
£70-80 *IW*

A Worcester hand painted mug, c1899, 1½in (4cm) high.
£50-60 *THA*

A Mocha ware pint mug, 5in (13cm) high.
£45-50 *CAC*

An Arthur Wood cider mug, 5in (12cm) high.
£15-20 *CAC*

A Victorian hunting mug, c1840, 4½in (11cm) high.
£65-75 *CA*

A Staffordshire loving cup, printed in brown and painted with cricketing scenes, 6in (15cm) high.
£330-350 *WHB*

A pottery mug, 3in (8cm) high.
£25-30 *CAC*

A lustre ale mug, c1880, 4½in (11cm) high.
£35-40 *CAC*

A Dartmouth whistle mug, 4in (10cm) high.
£25-30 *CA*

MAKE THE MOST OF MILLERS
Condition is absolutely vital when assessing the value of any item. Damaged pieces appreciate much less than perfect examples. However, a rare, desirable piece may command a high price even when damaged.

Plates

For further spongeware items see Miller's Collectables Vol. II, page 78.

A spongeware platter,
20thC.
£80-85 *SWN*

A Staffordshire plate,
mid-19thC.
£70-80 *SWN*

A Geo. Jones plate, hand
painted by William
Burbeck, 9in (23cm)
diam.
£55-65 *CA*

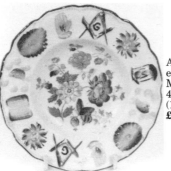

A Staffordshire deckle
edged plate, with
Masonic symbols in
4 colours, mid-19thC, 6in
(15cm) diam.
£60-70 *SWN*

A Bristol delftware
polychrome plate, c1720.
£400-450 *JHo*

Two Victorian
Sarreguemines plates,
c1870, 8in (20cm) diam.
£35-45 *CA*

An embossed plate,
bordered with animals,
mid-19thC.
£70-80   *SWN*

A Staffordshire named
plate, painted in
4 colours.
£120-130   *SWN*

Cross Reference
Children's Ceramics

A painted plate, 'The
flower basket'.
£80-90   *SWN*

A Staffordshire plate,
'The Favourite', black
transfer, mid-19thC.
£50-60   *SWN*

A black transfer printed
and painted plate, 'Little
Flora', mid-19thC, 5in
(13cm) diam.
£100-110   *SWN*

A Staffordshire embossed
black transfer printed
plate, 'My Brother',
mid-19thC.
£50-60   *SWN*

A Staffordshire marriage
plate, 1870s, 6½in
(16cm) diam.
£40-45   *IS*

DID YOU KNOW?
Miller's Collectables
Price Guide is
designed to build up,
year by year, into the
most comprehensive
reference system
available.

Printed Pot Lids

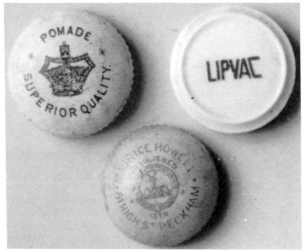

A selection of printed pot lids. **£1-3 each** *PC*

Shaving cream lids.
£30-35 each *PC*

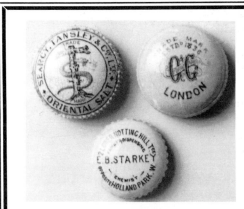

A selection of black and white lids and caps.
£2-10 each *PC*

Normally classified under black and white pot lids.

Atkinson's Rose Cold Cream.
£10-15 *PC*

Finigan's Nutritive Cream.
£30-40 *PC*

About 400 pot lid designs have been identified. These have been documented and numbered by A. Ball in his invaluable reference work *Price Guide to Pot Lids* which all collectors should possess. The listing which follows contains a representative selection of the pot lids most likely to be encountered by the general collector. The number refers to the listing system devised by Mr Ball in his book.

No. Description

1. Alas! Poor Bruin.
   £80-100
2. Bear attacked by Dogs.
   £500-700
3. Bear's Grease Manufacturer, lettering on marbled border.
   £2,000-3,000
4. Bear Hunting.
   £150-200
5. Bears Reading Newspapers.
   £600-700
6. The Bear Pit.
   £65-85
9. Bears at School.
   £80-100
11. Bear with Valentines.
    £1,800-2,400
13. Shooting Bears
    £25-30
15. The Ins.
    £100-150
16. The Outs.
    £100-150
17. Arctic Expedition.
    £400-500
18. Polar Bears.
    £100-140
20. All but Trapped.
    £1,000-1,400
21. Pegwell Bay.
    £600-800
23. Pegwell Bay.
    £600-800
24. Lobster Fishing, damaged.
    £80-120
25. Pegwell Bay, Lobster Fishing.
    £100-120
26. Pegwell Bay – Four Shrimpers.
    £30-40
27. Belle Vue Tavern.
    £200-230
29. Belle Vue Tavern.
    £220-250
30. Belle Vue without bay window.
    £70-100
31. Shrimpers, damaged.
    £60-80
33. Shrimping.
    £60-80
34. The Dutch Fisherman.
    £1,000-1,200
35. Still Life – Game.
    £100-120
37. Ramsgate, Farmyard Scene.
    £60-80
41. Royal Harbour.
    £50-60
42. Royal Harbour, Ramsgate.
    £40-50

Cold Cream.
l. & r.
£15-20
each
PC

l. **£15-20**   r. **£20-40**   *PC*

An Oriental printed lid.
£10-20   *PC*

Cold cream lids,   r. badly crazed.
l. **£25-30**   **£5-10** *PC*

Mint condition.   l. **£10-20**
£10-20   r. **£10-15**   *PC*

A selection of 'no name' cold cream pot lids.
£10-15 each   *PC*

Edward Cook's Tooth Soap.
£20-30   *PC*

Marbrero Tooth Paste.
£25-35 *PC*

No. Description

43. Nelson Crescent, Ramsgate.
£80-100
45. Walmer Castle.
£50-60
47. Walmer Castle.
£150-180
48. Pretty Kettle of Fish.
£75-95
49. Lobster Sauce.
£40-50
52B. Shell.
£45-55
53. Examining the Nets.
£50-60
55. Landing the Catch.
£30-40
57. The Fish Market.
£35-45
58. The Fish Barrow.
£45-55
60. The Net-Maker.
£200-250
62. Foreign River Scene.
£50-60
63. The Shrimpers.
£40-60
64. Sea Nymph and Trident.
£200-250
65. Swiss Riverside Scene.
£60-90
66. Dutch River Scene.
£100-120
70. Jar – Mending The Nets.
£70-80
78. Fall of Sebastopol.
£120-140
97. The Bride.
£120-150
98. An Eastern Repast.
£100-120
101. The Mirror.
£100-120
104. Reflections in Mirror.
£350-400
106. Lady with Hawk.
£90-100
107. Lady with Guitar.
£60-70
110. Lady Fastening Shoe.
£150-200
111. Lady Brushing Hair.
£160-200
114. The Matador.
£350-450
116. Jenny Lind.
£1,200-1,500
118. The Trysting Place.
£70-100
119. The Lovers.
£60-90
123. Musical Trio.
£80-100
134. Exhibition Buildings 1851.
Large with Acorn Border.
£250-300
135. Grand Exhibition 1851.
£40-50
137. The Crystal Palace.
£150-180

Toothpaste

Cherry Tooth Paste lids.   r. £15-20
l. £4-8

l. & r. £20-30 each   PC

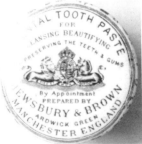

Areca Nut
Tooth Paste
pot lids.
£10-30 each   PC

Commans Areca Nut,
and Cracroft's Areca Nut.
£10-15 each   PC

Oriental Tooth Paste.
£10-15   PC

Cherry Tooth Paste.
£30-50   PC

Woods Areca Nut.
1920-24. £10-15   PC

No.	Description
139.	Crystal Palace, interior. **£260-300**
143.	Dublin Industrial Exhibition 1853. **£90-110**
144.	International Exhibition 1862. **£150-180**
145.	L'Exposition Universelle de 1867. **£75-100**
149.	England's Pride. **£125-155**
153.	The Late Prince Consort. **£75-85**
159.	Wellington with Cocked Hat. **£1,500-2,500**
160A.	Wellington with clasped hands. **£100-140**
164.	Tria Juncta in Uno. **£250-300**
166.	Balaklava, Inkerman, Alma. **£250-300**
167A.	Admiral Sir Charles Napier C.B. **£220-250**
168.	The Allied Generals. **£90-100**
170.	Sir Robert Peel. **£200-230**
171.	Peabody. **£80-120**
172.	Harriet Beecher Stowe. **£700-1,100**
174.	The Blue Boy. **£80-100**
175.	Dr. Johnson. **£30-50**
176.	Buckingham Palace. **£90-120**
179.	Drayton Manor. **£50-80**
180.	Windsor Park, Returning from Stag Hunting. **£120-150**
181.	Sandringham. **£60-80**
182.	Osborne House. **£50-80**
188.	Strathfieldsaye. **£70-110**
189.	Westminster Abbey. **£200-250**
190.	Albert Memorial. **£100-120**
192.	St. Paul's Cathedral. **£150-200**
193.	Charing Cross. **£80-100**
195.	New Houses of Parliament. **£100-150**
201.	Trafalgar Square. **£40-60**
202.	Holborn Viaduct. **£60-80**
203.	New St. Thomas's Hospital. **£50-60**
204.	Golden Horn. **£60-85**
205.	The Thirsty Soldier. **£60-80**
206.	Embarking for the East. **£60-80**

Foodstuffs

Various stoppers and caps.
£1-3 each *PC*

Fortnum & Mason's Mushroom Savoury sepia printed lid.
£50-75 *PC*

Similar design for Beales, £60-80.

Arthur's Young & Co., Yarmouth Herrings.
£100-200 *PC*

A very rare lid.

Harrod's Anchovy Paste.
£20-25 *PC*

Anchovy Paste.
£15-20 *PC*

Staffordshire Pot Lids

No. Description
209. Sebastopol.
    £60-75
210. The Battle of the Nile.
    £55-75
214. The Volunteers.
    £90-120
216. The Redoubt.
    £500-600
219. War.
    £35-45
220. Peace.
    £40-50
221. Harbour of Hong Kong.
    £50-60
222. Ning Po River.
    £80-100
223. Rifle Contest, Wimbledon 1864.
    £50-60
224. Wimbledon, July 1860.
    £45-55
226. Shakespeare's Birthplace – exterior.
    £40-50
227. Shakespeare's Birthplace – interior.
    £30-60
228. Anne Hathaway's Cottage.
    £50-60
229. Holy Trinity Church.
    £80-100
233. May Day Dancers at the Swan Inn.
    £30-50
236. The Parish Beadle.
    £90-110
237. The Children of Flora.
    £70-80
238. 'Christmas Eve'.
    £120-140
240. The Village Wedding.
    £20-30
241. Our Home.
    £100-150
244. The Bullfight, late issue.
    £35-45
245. The Enthusiast.
    £40-50
246. Blind Man's Buff.
    £100-150
247. Master of the Hounds.
    £30-40
249. Dangerous Skating.
    £50-70
250. Fair Sportswoman.
    £40-60
251. A False Move.
    £150-200
252. A Pair.
    £40-50
253. Snapdragon.
    £70-90
254. The Best Card.
    £25-30
255. Hide and Seek.
    £25-35
256. A Fix.
    £35-45
257. A Race or Derby Day.
    £30-50
258. The Skaters.
    £70-90
259. The Game Bag.
    £40-50

Derby Day,
4½in (11cm).
£60-70   BRK

Commemorative framed
pot lids.
Albert and Victoria and
The Late Prince Consort.
£100-110 each   CA

Transplanting Rice.
£70-85   BRK

Cries of London, Fine
Black Cherries, 4½in
(11cm).
£65-75   SBA

Printed Ware

A George Jones Abbey
ware blue and white milk
jug and hot water jug,
c1910, 3 and 6in (7.5 and
15cm).
Milk jug. **£18-20**
Hot water jug.
£35-40   *CSA*

A plate, Taylor Bros,
Leeds, c1881, 7½in
(18.5cm).
£80-90   *IW*

Copeland Spode blue and
white transfer printed
ware, c1850, footbath
19in (48cm) wide, jug
12½in (32cm), bowl 10in
(25cm) diam and ewer
8½in (21cm).
£2,000-2,500   *IS*

A blue and white
transfer printed mug,
1850s.
£85-95   *CA*

DID YOU KNOW?
Miller's Collectables
Price Guide is
designed to build up,
year by year, into the
most comprehensive
reference system
available.

A Ridgway's platter,
20½in (52cm) wide.
£280-320 *CA*

A Davenport plate,
Fisherman series, c1810,
7in (17.5cm).
£90-100 *IS*

A Pountney of Bristol
dessert plate, Drama
Series, c1830.
£70-80 *Nor*

A Watermill pattern
plate, Monk's Rock
series, maker unknown,
c1820, 10in (25cm).
£75-85 *Nor*

Two plates, makers
unknown, c1820, 10in
(25cm).
Grazing Rabbits pattern.
£85-95
Piping Shepherd.
£65-75 *Nor*

FURTHER READING
Blue and White Transfer Printed Pottery, Robert
Copeland, Shire Publications.

Staffordshire Pottery

Figures

l. & r. A pair of peacocks, lightly coloured, impressed T.H. Sandland, 11½in (29cm).
£120-150
c. A figure of a piper, 14in (35.5cm).
£65-85   *WHB*

A pair of figures of a fisherman and his companion, 11in (28cm).
£100-120   *WHB*

A portrait of Lady Hester Stanhope and Dr. Meryon, c1850, 7in (18cm).
£280-300   *Bon*

Turkey, England, France, 8½in (21cm).
£250-270   *BRK*

A pair of cow groups, one with a dairymaid in attendance carrying a pail, the other with a herdsman carrying a whip, on coloured gilt lined bases, c1850, 8½in (21cm).
£200-300   *Bon*

A Staffordshire figure, c1860, 4½in (11cm).
£140-160   *HOW*

Wesley, 11½in (29cm).
£160-180   *BRK*

T. P. Cooke, 7½in (18.5cm).
£150-170   *BRK*

A double-sided figure.
£150-170   *BRK*

A pair of putti,
c1800, 4in
(10cm).
£120-130 *CA*

Nelly Chapman, 11in
28cm).
£100-120 *BRK*

A Staffordshire umbrella
group, c1855, 7½in
(18.5cm).
£160-180 *HOW*

A seated figure, 4in
(10cm).
£100-125 *CA*

A figure of a lady with a
cat , c1800, 7in
(17.5cm).
£100-200 *CA*

Jacqueline Oosthuizen

A figure, 4½in (11cm).
£35-40 *CA*

A flower girl, impressed
Hall, 6in (15cm).
£260-300 *BRK*

Toby Jugs

A selection of Toby jugs,
10in (25cm).
£20-50 each   *WHB*

Cross Reference
Toby jugs

A Toby jug, 19thC, 10in
(25cm).
£65-85   *MN*

Three miniature Toby
jugs, c1820-40, 4½in
(11cm) high.
£125-145 each   *GIN*

Snuff Lady, c1880, 10in
(25cm) high.
£320-350   *GIN*

A Toby jug, with caryatid
handle, c1870, 10in
(25cm).
£175-200   *GIN*

Two Toby jugs, c1830
10in (25cm):
l. Plain face.
£280-300
r. Collier type, made
2 moulds and joined
down the centre, so
cheaper to produce.
£380-420   *GIN*

Paul Pry, c1830, 6in
(15cm).
£300-350   *GIN*

Three miniature Toby
jugs, c1820, 3 to 3½in
(7.5 to 9cm) high.
£110-130 each   *GIN*

Spill Vases

A swan spill vase, 4½in
(11cm).
£120-150 *BRK*

A shepherd, 9in (23cm).
£100-160 *BRK*

Cottages

A house
with orange
walls.
£50-100
Bea

A turreted
castle, 11in
(28cm) high.
£140-160
WHB

Staffordshire Peppers

An embossed pastille
burner, 5½in (13.3cm).
£120-130 *Bea*

Three policemen peppers,
6 to 6½in (15 to 16cm)
high.
l. & r. **£80-85 each**
c. **£140-150** *GIN*

A pepper
and a vinegar.
**£100-110
each** *GIN*

Teapots

A Burlington ware cottage teapot, 7in (18cm) high.
£25-30   *THA*

A Royal Doulton self-pouring teapot, with pump action designed to pour just one cup of tea, by J. J. Royal.
£80-120   *PC*

This teapot was very expensive to produce and apparently Queen Victoria was given one.

A creamware teapot, hand decorated by Robinson & Rhodes, Leeds, damage to spout, c1780, 7in (18cm) high.
£180-300   *CA*

Cross Reference
Golfing

A Copeland Spode golfing teapot.
£320-350   *GIL*

A Little Old Lady green teapot, c1930, 9in (23cm) high.
£35-45   *CAC*

A 'chintz' teapot and jug, teapot 4½in (11cm).
£40-50   *CAC*

A teapot, probably Bow, 18thC.
£230-250   *GIL*

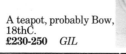

A Minton majolica teapot.
£350-400   *GIL*

Vases

A pair of Crown Ducal vases, c1910, 10in (25cm) high.
£85-95 *CSA*

An Arcadian ware vase, Barker Bros., 12in (31cm) high.
£155-175 *BEV*

A Derby hand painted vase, c1820, 3½in (9cm) high.
£55-65 *CA*

A Chameleon ware vase, 9in (23cm) high.
£70-80 *BEV*

A Moorcroft Pomegranate pattern vase, c1920, 9in (23cm) high.
£400-450 *CSA*

A plaited basket, Sewell & Donkin, c1830, 10½in (26cm) wide.
£240-260 *IS*

Cross Reference
Art Pottery

A Chameleon ware vase, Clews & Co., c1930, 12½in (31cm) high.
£165-185 *BEV*

General

A Wedgwood cane ware preserve jar, c1780, 3½in (9cm) high.
£200-300 *Wai*

An Italian Deruta dry drug jar, c1640, 7½in (19cm) high.
£700-800 *Wai*

A Pratt ware flask.
£400-450 *LT*

A George Jones majolica squirrel nut bowl.
£260-280 *GIL*

A dog clock, 6in (15cm).
£90-120 *CLH*

A Bailey's bed warmer, marked Heaton Mersey, c1900, 9½in (24cm) long.
£20-25 *IW*

A pearlware pink lustre heart shaped plume holder, late 18thC, 4in (10cm).
£150-200 *DN*

A Scottish treacle glazed planter, with reliefs of the 4 Apostles, c1870, 8in (20cm) high.
£70-80 *IS*

A pair of Staffordshire seated spaniels, with baskets of flowers in their jaws, 8in (20cm) high.
£100-150 *CSK*

Coca-Cola

A celluloid and metal shop display, 1950s, 12in (30.5cm) high.
£25-30 *COB*

A large tin, 1980s
£6-7 *COB*

A metal clock, 1960s, 6in (15cm).
£25-30 *COB*

A selection of metal and enamel brooches, 1980s.
£3-5 each *COB*

A metal tray, 1970s, 24in (61cm) wide.
£10-12 *COB*

Cross Reference
Drinking glasses

A selection of glasses, 1960-80.
£2-5 each *COB*

A Christmas plate and a set of coasters, 1980s.
Plate. **£8-10**
Coasters. **£6-7** *COB*

A truck, 1970s, 12in (30.5cm).
£5-10 *COB*

Pencil sharpeners, 1980s.
£2-3 each *COB*

Miniature bottles in crates, 1970s.
£3-5 each *COB*

A battery operated radio, c1960.
£30-40 *RTT*

A selection of ceramic and metal magnets, 1970s and 1980s.
£3-5 each *COB*

Coca Cola

Transformers, 1980s.
£3-5 each   *COB*

Various bottles, 1980s.
50p-£1   *COB*

A Ghostbusters can,
1989.
£2-3   *COB*

A 'T' shirt, 1980s.
£3-5   *COB*

A selection of Coke cans
1963-89.
£1-10 each   *COB*

Cross Reference
Bottles
Advertising

A selection of stickers,
1980s.
50p-£1 each   *COB*

A metal thermometer
1980s, 24in (61cm).
£15-20   *COB*

A selection of diecast
vans, 1980s.
£3-4 each   *COB*

Cross Reference
Diecast toys

An Aero Club du Rhone et du Sud-Est 13eme, Grand Prix 1924, lithograph, 63in (160cm) high. **£1,500-2,000** *C*

A Vickers Supermarine Spitfire Mark IX, oil on canvas, by Gerald Coulson, signed, 29 by 39in (73.5 by 99cm). **£6,000-8,000** *C*

A Continental silver cigarette case, signed Fokker, dated Berlin Jan 1919, decorated in coloured enamels with a Fokker Triplane, in original pouch, 4in (10cm) long. **£3,000-3,500** *C*

A bottle mounted on a radiator cap. **£250-300** *CMon*

Dawn Flight, a section of Spitfires above clouds, oil on board, by Wing Cdr. G. C. Olive, 23½ by 25in (60 by 64cm). **£500-800** *C*

A Dudley Burnside poster, acrylic, signed, 30 by 20in (76 by 51cm). **£200-250** *C*

l. A Butlins Car Club mascot, 5½in (14cm) high. **£35-50** *BY*

l. A Hispano-Suiza stork petrol cap, signed F. Bazin. **£750-1,000** *CMon*

A mascot for Type 41 'Royale', by Rembrandt Bugatti, 8in (20cm) high. **£3,000-4,000** *CMon*

A Sports Car in the Clouds radiator cap. **£550-600** *CMon*

A BARC enamelled car badge showing 2 racing cars at Brooklands. **£600-700** *CMon*

l. A mythological figure travelling in a wheel, signed Cottin, mounted on a radiator cap, 6in (15cm). **£700-1,000** *CMon*

129

E. Ruprecht, Grand Prix d'Europe Autos Bern 3-4 Juli 1948. **£2,000-2,500**   *ONS* l. Rene Lorenzi XVIIIe Grand Prix Monaco 29 Mai 1960. Est. **£3,500-4,500**   *ONS*

A collection of 9 original colour posters. **£2,500-3,000**   *CMon*

l. I Bolidi, 1961 film poster showing a Maserati sportscar followed by a 375 MM Ferrari, 56 by 39½in (142 by 99cm). **£1,700-2,000**   *CMon*

A Geo Ham Grand Prix de Pau poster, c1953, 24 by 16in (61 by 40.5cm). **£750-1,000**   *CMon*

A Max Huber 36° Gran Premio d'Italia, Monza 1965, poster linen mounted, 40 by 28in (101 by 71cm). **£750-1,000**   *CMon*

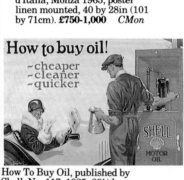

A May Grand Prix de Monaco 1964 poster, 24 by 16in (61 by 40.5cm). **£1,500-2,500**   *CMon*

How To Buy Oil, published by Shell, No. 117, 1925, 29½ by 45in (75 by 114cm). **£1,500-2,000**   *ONS*

A collection of Ferrari Yearbooks from 1949 to 1970, Italian text. **£2,800-3,500**   *CMon*

A Bompiani Gran Premio Cidonio, Circuito di Collemaggio, L'Aguila, poster. **£3,600-4,000** *CMon*

The Fuller Brush Magazine featuring 'Phil Hill, a young man in . . . A Race to Fame', with illustrations of Phil Hill driving and viewing Ferraris, c1959. **£500-600** *CMon*

A Gran Premio d'Italia, 8-9-1935, official race programme, the cover showing Codoguato's poster. **£500-800** *CMon*

l. A Michael Watson watercolour of the Monaco Grand Prix 1934. **£1,500-2,000** *CMon*

r. A Guy Lipscombe watercolour, The Bluebird at Brooklands, heightened with white, signed, 11½ by 17½in (29 by 45cm). **£5,500-6,000** *ONS*

l. A Nicholas Watts gouache of the Monaco Grand Prix 1931. **£3,000-4,000** *CMon*

A cloisonné box with cockerel on the lid, c1880, 9in (23cm) wide. **£575-600** *EHA*

An inlaid walnut sewing box, fully fitted in excellent condition, c1850, 10in (25cm). **£225-250** *EHA*

l. A Nicholas Watts gouache of the winning W125 Mercedes in the Monaco Grand Prix 1937, leading Carraciola in a similar Mercedes, signed, 31 by 29in (79 by 74cm). **£2,500-3,000** *CMon*

A cribbage box, the brass mounted lid being the board, c1880, 11in (28cm) wide. **£180-250** *EHA*

A French leather stationery
box, c1880, 10in (25cm) wide.
£225-250   *EHA*

A French jewellery box, c1820,
7½in (18.5cm) wide.
£150-175   *EHA*

A Victorian burr walnut
workbox, with mother-of-
pearl inlay, c1860.
£350-400   *BRK*

l. A Tunbridge ware
stationery box, c1870, 7in
(17.5cm) wide.
£520-560   *EHA*

A shell and brass snuff box, 19thC,
3½in (9cm) long.
£140-160   *EHA*

l. An oak tea
caddy, in the
form of a
settle, c1880,
11in (28cm)
wide.
£450-500   *EHA*

Two tortoiseshell patch boxes,
c1840, 2½in (6cm) wide.
£75-100 each   *EHA*

A tortoiseshell
card case,
c1860, 4in
(10cm) high.
£80-100   *EHA*

An Austrian glove case, containing
original unworn kid gloves with
stretchers, c1870, 15½in (39cm) wide.
£80-100   *EHA*

Above l. A gilt metal pin
box, c1850, 3in (7.5cm)
wide. **£65-85**   *EHA*

l. A papier mâché patch
box, c1820, 3in (7.5cm).
£80-100   *EHA*
r. A rosewood scissor box,
inlaid with satinwood,
c1820. **£75-85**   *EHA*

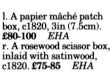

GRAYS

London's most important centre for Antiques.

Over 200 Specialist Dealers
Open Monday to Friday
10 am to 6 pm

58 Davies Street W1
1 - 7 Davies Mews W1
Tel: 071-629 7034/7036

A selection of papier mâché cheroot cases, 5½in (14cm) wide. **£150-350 each** *EHA*

Two Coca-Cola refrigerated vending machines, Cavalier Co., and Jacobs Co. **£900-1,500 each** *CAm*

Tortoiseshell or pressed horn buttons, inlaid with gold and pearl, 2.5cm diam **£10-20 each** *AGM*

A boxed set of Liberty silver buttons. **£80-120** *AGM*

r. A button with early lithograph applied to a coated metal base, c1800. **£10-30** *AGM*

l. A card of buttons, bugs and butterflies. **£10-20 each** *AGM*

A card of linen buttons, c1930. **£5-10** *RTT*

A selection of enamel buttons. **£5-15 each** *AGM* r. A Wedgwood button with copper surround, late 18thC. **£5-10** *AGM*

Two children's plates, c1830, 7in (17.5cm) diam. **£40-50 each** *IW* *OD*

A Stockton pottery plate, with inscription, 6½in (16cm). **£35-40** *IS*

A late Victorian plate, with risqué print, 6½in (16cm). **£20-30** *OD*

A pair of Staffordshire figures, Prince Albert and Queen Victoria, 4½in (11cm) high. **£120-150** *CA*

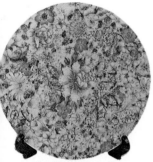

A pair of 'famille rose' mille fleurs plaques, c1850, 8in (20cm). **£350-400** *KOT*

A Reform teacup, Earl Grey, c1832, 2in (5cm) high. **£80-90** *OD*

A Bovey Tracey mess bowl and plate. **£80-100 each** *SWN*

A serving dish, Colossal Sarcophagus near Castle Rosso, c1815. **£180-220** *Nor*

r. A transfer printed teapot, c1820, 7in (17.5cm) high. **£70-90** *OD*

l. A pair of Coalport hand painted scent bottles, c1825, 4½in (11cm) high. **£225-250** *CA*
r. A Victorian hand painted porcelain egg. **£35-45** *CA*

l. A Wemyss goblet, Queen Victoria's Jubilee, 6in (15cm) high. **£300-400** *RdeR*
r. John Peel, a Staffordshire figure, 7in (17.5cm). **£150-170** *BRK*

135

Staffordshire figures.
Dick Turpin and Tom King, 7½in
(18cm) high. **£250-270** *BRK*
r. Widow, 9½in (24cm).
£350-380 *BRK*

Toby pepper pots,
English or Scottish.
£85-90 each *Nor*

A pot lid, Examining the Nets,
4½in (11.5cm) diam.
£70-85 *BRK*

A pot lid, Victor Emmanuel and
Garibaldi. **£70-85** *BRK*

A pot lid, Lobster Sauce.
£70-85 *BRK*

l. A pot lid, The Ning Po
River. **£70-85** *BRK*

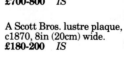

A lustre portrait plaque,
probably Ball Bros, c1860.
£130-150 *IS*

A mounted pot lid, Anne
Hathaway's Cottage.
£85-95 *BA*
l. A set of Seasons, Dixon
Austin & Co., c1825.
£700-800 *IS*

A Scott Bros. lustre plaque,
c1870, 8in (20cm) wide.
£180-200 *IS*

l. A Sunderland pottery Paisley ware basket, c1850, 11½in (29cm) wide. **£250-300** *IS*
r. A Sunderland lustre plaque, Dixon & Co., c1840, 9in (23cm) wide. **£130-140** *IS*

A Sunderland lustre plaque, Dixon & Co., c1840, 8in (20cm) wide. **£135-150** *IS*

A Sunderland lustre plaque, with Eastern scene, Dixon & Co., c1830. **£160-180** *IS*

A Sunderland lustre jug, Dixon & Co., c1820, 9in (23cm) high. **£250-280** *IS*

A Tyneside lustre jug, c1825, 7in (17.5cm) high. **£200-250** *IS*

A Tyneside Oddfellows jug, c1846, 5in (12.5cm). **£230-280** *IS*
r. A shaving mug, possibly Ewenny, c1890. **£60-70** *IW*

A Sunderland lustre jug, Dixon & Co., c1815, 7in (17.5cm). **£180-200** *IS*

A lustre ware jug. **£100-150** *SWN*
r. A Tyneside lustre tankard, c1825, 5in (12.5cm) high. **£120-150** *IS*

Wedgwood lustre miniature bowls, c1920. **£40-60 each** *CSA*
l. A Mason's Ironstone jug, 4½in (11cm). **£80-120** *PC*

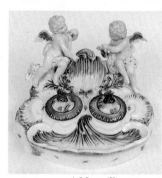

A Staffordshire cradle, early 19thC.
£120-140 *SWN*
l. A pair of Maling vases, designed
by C. J. Miguet, 1906, 10in (25cm).
£400-500 *IS*

A Marseilles
inkwell, by
Robert, c1790.
£350-400 *BRK*
A fairing, Every
vehicle driven
by a horse mule
or ass 2d.
£400-500 *BRK*

l. A fairing pin tray,
Rock me to sleep Mother.
£60-80 *BRK*

A fairing, Papa's new hat.
£80-100 *BRK*

A fairing pin tray, The
Artist.
£70-80 *BRK*

A fairing, The Power of
Love.
£70-80 *BRK*

A fairing, The
last in bed to
put out the
light.
£50-60 *BRK*

A fairing, To Epsom.
£700-750 *BRK*

Ceramic pigs in a holdall,
unmarked, 4in (10cm) wide.
£65-75 *LEW*
l. A Victorian ceramic
cradle box, restored,
7in (17.5cm) wide.
£150-200 *SP*

A fairing, Now they'll
blame me for this.
£120-160 *BRK*

A French Mosanic
pug, with glass
eyes, c1900.
£400-500 *RdeR*

138

A German figure of an actress, printed KPM mark in blue, c1910, 8½in (21cm) wide.
£350-400 *TVA*

r. Goldscheider figure, The Listening Lady, 13½in (34cm) high.
£950-1,000 *BEV*

A Goldscheider figure, 14½in (37cm) high.
£750-1,000 *BEV*

A Burleigh jug, c1930, 8in (20cm) high.
£100-120 *RO*
r. A flower holder, possibly Burmantofts.
£80-90 *CSA*

If marked £150-200

r. A Clarice Cliff Fantasque biscuit barrel.
£300-350 *SWO*

A Clarice Cliff Fantasque vase, Farmhouse pattern.
£1,600-2,000 *MN*

l. A selection of Clarice Cliff Fantasque Bizarre pottery.
£150-250 each *MN*

A rare Clarice Cliff jug, Blue Firs design, c1933, 6in (15cm) high.
£650-750 *CSA*
l. A selection of Clarice Cliff Bizarre pottery.
£100-1,200 each *MN*

A Clarice Cliff sugar sifter, c1932.
£600-700 *CSA*

139

A Clarice Cliff Red Roof pattern vase, c1931, 8in (20cm).
£800-900   *CSA*

A Carlton Ware teapot, c1930, 6½in (16cm) high.
£85-95   *CSA*
r. A Carlton Ware Spring Time jug, c1935, 8in (20cm). **£75-85**   *CSA*

l. A selection of Royal Doulton Sairey Gamp items, character jug. **£35-45** Teapot. **£900-950** *TP*

Carlton Ware napkin holders, c1935.
£25-30 each   *CSA*

A Maling ware bowl, c1929.
£200-225   *CSA*
l. A Hancock ivory ware jug, c1930.
£35-40   *CSA*

An Eichwald pottery vase, c1920, 10½in (26cm).
£100-150   *BEV*

A Gallé Great Dane, signed, c1950, 5in (12.5cm).
£50-60   *CA*

A Maling ware double inkstand, c1929, 9in (23cm). **£250-300**   *CSA*
r. A Maling ware ginger jar, c1936, 8½in (21cm) high.
£200-225   *CSA*

r. A Maling ware lustre vase, Azalea pattern, 12½in (32cm).
£200-250   *RO*

ENGLAND'S BIGGEST PERMANENT COLLECTORS MARKET

The Pen Box Stand S012   Selection of pens 1917-1990

A. J. Partners Stand G113/4 Foley 'Intarsio' stick stand, 25"

Alvin Ross Stand G009/10/11 English & German tinplate toys

International Antiques Stand F127/140 Bean slicer   c. 1880. Bread board c. 1920

The Originals Stand G049   RCA Victor Radio

Cliff Latford Stand G006 Sanderson hand and stand camera

Final Whistle Stand S061/3   Singapore No 3 Football shirt c. 1940

A selection of Shorter ware hand painted Pagoda pattern items, c1930, Teapot **£70-80**, Biscuit Barrel **£50-60**, Butter Dish **£25-35**   *PC*

A selection of Shorter ware sgraffito and hand painted jugs, mid-1930s. **£30-40**   *PC*

A Shorter ware hand painted Narcissus pattern bowl and plate, mid-1930s. **£30-40 each**   *PC*

A selection of Shorter ware hand painted Kashan pattern. **£40-60 each**   *PC*

A Shorter ware Medina sgraffito and hand painted jug, designed by Mabel Leigh, c1930, 8in (20cm) high. **£55-70**   *PC*

A Shorter ware hand painted majolica pattern jug and hall boy, late 1920s. **£50-65 each**   *PC*

A Shorter ware Moresque sgraffito and hand painted jug, designed by Mabel Leigh, c1930, 8½in (21cm) high. **£55-65**   *PC*

A pottery plate, early 19thC. **£140-160**   *RYA*

A hand painted and sponged pottery plate, early 19thC. **£200-220**   *RYA*

A Torquay pottery jug, 2½in (6cm) high. **£14-16**   *CSA*

l. A Shorter ware Mecca sgraffito and hand painted plaque. **£110-130**   *PC*

A Minton Secessionist vase, c1900, 10in (25cm) high. **£200-250** *CSA*

A Minton Secessionist vase, c1900. **£300-350** *CSA*

A Moorcroft Pansies vase, c1918. **£500-600** *CSA*

A Shorter ware Jardinière pattern jug and bowl, c1930. **£110-130** *PC*

l. A Shelley butter dish, c1935. **£75-85** *CSA*

l. A Shorter ware majolica jug, late 1920s. **£55-70** *PC*

r. A Shorter ware Basra sgraffito jug, by Mabel Leigh, c1930. **£50-60** *PC*

A Shorter ware Scratched Dragon sgraffito design wall plaque. **£100-120** *PC*

Three Shorter ware hand painted character jugs, c1950. **£30-40 each** *PC*

Three Shorter ware hand painted character jugs, c1940. **£20-60 each** *PC*

A Shorter ware Medina sgraffito plaque, designed by Mabel Leigh, c1930, 12in (31cm) diam. **£60-70** *PC*
r. A selection of Shorter ware in hand painted Pagoda pattern, c1930. **£25-40 each** *PC*

A hand painted metal cigarette case, 'Hands Up', 1920s, 3½in (8.5cm) high.
£90-120 *CLH*

A clown powder bowl, 6in (15cm).
£35-40 *CLH*

A French Art Nouveau aventurine powder bowl.
£150-175 *CLH*

A pair of clown powder bowls, 6in (15cm). **£35-40 each** *CLH*

Edwardian silk flowers in a glass dome.
£180-220 *CLH*

A ceramic teapot, dancing figures, 8in (20cm) high.
£50-60 *CLH*

An Eichwald comport, 13½in (34cm) high.
£175-185 *CLH*
r. An Egyptian scent bottle, 1930s, 3½in (9cm).
£55-65 *CLH*

A Kestner shoulder headed doll. **£425-500** *DOW*
Two Susie Cooper jugs and sugar bowl.
£145-155 *CLH*

A Simon and Halbig doll, 17in (43cm) high.
£620-700 *DOW*

A Wileman Intarsio
two-handled vase, by
Frederick Rhead, c1895.
£200-225   *CSA*

A Wileman Pastello design pot, by
Frederick Rhead, 4½in (11cm) high.
£325-350   *CSA*

A Villeroy & Boch vase,
1880-1920, 9in (23cm)
high.
£150-200   *BEV*

A Wade Heath biscuit
barrel, c1930, 6½in
(16cm) high.
£50-60   *CSA*

A Shelley
lustreware vase,
by Walter Slater,
facsimile
signature,
c1920.
£200-225   *CSA*

A Shelley
Intarsio vase,
by Walter
Slater, c1910.
£200-225   *CSA*

A pair of Villeroy & Boch
vases, drilled for use as
lamps, c1890, 12in (31cm)
high. **£200-300**   *CSA*

A Wemyss heart shaped tray,
painted by Nekola.
£400-600   *RdeR*

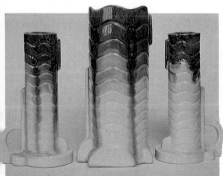

A Shorter ware art glazed vase and
2 matching candlesticks, c1930,
vase **£35-45**,
candlesticks **£40-50**   *PC*

A Wemyss, Bovey
Tracey, black
and white cat,
12½in (32cm).
£2-2,500   *RdeR*
r. An Arthur
Wood sunflower
bowl, 1930s.
£30-35   *CSA*

145

A Wileman Foley cabaret service, c1880. **£350-450**   *AJ*

l. A Royal Winton breakfast set, c1930. **£250-300**   *RO*

A Maling ashtray, made for the Newcastle Pageant, 1931, 4in (10cm) diam. **£100-150**   *IS*

A Maling ware tea caddy, c1937. **£45-50**   *CSA*

A Paragon George V and Queen Mary silver Jubilee cup and saucer, c1935. **£45-50**   *CSA*

A Maling ware bowl in the fruit design by L. E. Boullemier, damaged, c1926. **£80-120**   *IS*

A Maling ware vase, by Norman Carling, decorated by L. G. Boullemier, c1936. **£100-150**   *IS*

A Paragon commemorative cup and saucer, c1937. **£45-50**   *CSA*

A Theo Maling Bouncing Balls design jar, signed, c1932. **£150-180**   *IS*

A Maling ware stirrup cup, formed as a fox's head, c1930. **£350-450**   *IS*

A hand painted porcelain menu holder, 5in (12.5cm) high. **£40-50**   *CA*

A Maling ware plate, Apple Harvesters design, c1885. **£100-150**   *IS*

A Maling ware traveller's sample in the Tulip pattern, with original label on the base, 8in (20cm) high, c1933. **£250-300** *IS*

A fan with Snow White illustration, c1940. **£5-6** *CSA*

Mickey, Minnie and Pluto squeaker figures, 7½in (19cm) high. **£12-15 each** *RTT*

A Bru bisque headed bébé, with kid body, wooden lower legs and bisque lower arms, damaged. **£6,000-7,000** *CNY*

A pressed bisque headed bébé, with jointed fixed wrists, wood and composition body, damage, 18in (47cm). **£13,000-15,000** *C*

A German enamel striped corkscrew, 3in (8cm) high. **£300-400** *LEW*

Dolls house furniture and food, table 6in (15cm) long. **£35-40** Food **£2-20** *CD*

A Harrods delivery bicycle, 6in (15cm) long. **£40-60** *CD*

A selection of Eric Hornes wooden dolls, the largest 3in (8cm) high. **£12-18 each** *CD*

A dolls house baby carriage. **£250-300** *LEW*

Three painted chests, German, Hungarian and Austrian, 3in (7.5cm) wide. **£50-70 each** *CD*

Two dolls house post boxes,
5in (13cm) high.
£30-40 each   *CD*

A dolls house wardrobe, painted in
Alsatian pattern, 7in (18cm) high.
£240-260   *CD*

A dolls house dresser,
painted in Transylvania
pattern, 6in (15cm) high.
£160-180   *CD*

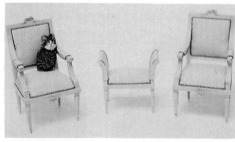

A painted dolls
house chair,
3in (8cm) high.
£40-60   *CD*

A selection of dolls house
books, leather bound and hand
coloured, by Lilliput Press,
1½in (4cm).   **£30-40 each**   *CD*

A pair of Louis XVI dolls
house chairs, 3½in (8.5cm)
high. **£70-80 each**
and a window seat.
£45-55   *CD*

A selection of dolls house
earthenware plates and
jugs, largest 2in (5cm)
high.
£2-15 each   *CD*

A Guinness table lamp
with penguin.
£150-180   *RO*

A Victorian birthday
card.
50-75p   *BEB*

*These cards represent
remarkable value for
money at the moment.
Refer to page 208.*

A German humorous card,
5½ by 3in (14 by 8cm).
£3-5   *BEB*

l. An Easter card, c1909.
£1-2 *BEB*

An Easter card.
£2-3 *BEB*

A Merry Christmas.

A Christmas card, c1870,
4 by 3in (10 by 8cm).
£1-2 *BEB*

A Christmas
card. £2-3 *BEB*

A teddy card,
with squeaker,
post war.
£5-10 *SP*

A Valentine card, c1865,
9½ by 8in (24 by 20cm).
£60-70 *BEB*

A Victorian
Valentine, 8in
(20cm) high.
£15-25 *SP*

I'M THINKING OF YOU

l. I'm Thinking of You.
£2-6 *PC*

A Victorian
Valentine, 8in
(20cm) high.
£15-25 *SP*

A set of prints by Longmans Green & Co., entitled
Golliwog's Circus, c1899. £50-80 *BEB*
l. To my dear mother. £2-6 *PC*

With the Season's Greetings To My Dear Mother.
£2-6 *PC*

A silk postcard.
£10-15 *PC*

*Refer to page 356 for
a further selection.*

A Men Only magazine, 1940.
£3-4 *RTT*

An American
Needlecraft
magazine,
Feb 1928.
£3-5 *RTT*

An American Vogue Pattern
Book, 1933. **£10-15** *RTT*

Above l. A Horse Show poster,
printed by J. Weiner.
£800-1,000 *ONS*
Above r. A Barclay's poster,
published by Publicity Arts
Ltd. **£350-400** *ONS*

l. A copy of the only existing
card dropped from a balloon
flight on Manchester Lifeboat
Saturday, 20th September 1902.
£2,800-3,000 *VS*
r. The Children's Paradise,
a poster, printed by
Dangerfield, 40 by 50in
(101.5 by 127cm).
£2,500-3,000 *ONS*

An Austin Reed's
double crown
poster.
£950-1,000 *ONS*

An Austin Reed poster,
60 by 40in (152 by 101.5cm).
£3,000-3,500 *ONS*

A Fry's
Chocolate
Sandwich poster,
2ozs 2d.
£350-400 *ONS*

A Yardley powder
poster, Orchis
2/–, printed
by J. Weiner.
£350-400 *ONS*

A poster, East Coast, printed
by Haycock Cadle & Graham.
£1,000-1,500 *ONS*

An East Coast Frolics
travel poster.
£400-600 *ONS*

An Edwards'
Desiccated
Soups poster,
printed by The
Avenue Press,
1922.
£400-600 *ONS*

An LNER travel
poster, by John
Waddington,
40 by 50in
(101.5 by 127cm).
£1,300-1,500 *ONS*
l. The
Adventuress,
printed by J. G.
Hudson.
£2,000-2,500 *ONS*

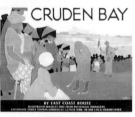

A Dangerfield poster.
£2,500-3,500 *ONS*

A Barclay
Perkins poster,
published by
Publicity Arts
Ltd.
£350-400 *ONS*
l. An East Coast
by LNER
poster, printed
by Baynard Press.
£5,000-6,000 *ONS*

A poster, printed by Haycock
Press. **£1,000-1,500** *ONS*

A set of 4,
Goat Cart.
£90-100   *CFA*

A selection of early Victorian colour engravings by J. H. Kronheim of London to the Baxter patent oil printing process.

A set of 4
Victorian Comedy.
£110-130   *CFA*

Goat Cart.

A set of 4, The Virtues, 6 by 5in (15 by 12.5cm).
£110-130   *CFA*

Goat Cart.

Goat Cart.

A set of 4, The Faithful Dog, 5½ by 4in (13.5 by 10cm).
£110-130   *CFA*

A set of 4, Romance, 4 by 3in (10 by 7.5cm).
£15-20 each   *CFA*

A set of 4,
The Reading Lesson.
£110-130   *CFA*

A set of 4, After the Hare, 3 by 4½in (7.5 by 11.5cm).
£15-20 each   *CFA*

152

Coffee Making

Coffee drinking first became fashionable 300 years ago. Coffee houses and the brewing equipment, e.g. roasters, grinders and coffee makers offer a treasure trail of art, craftsmanship and ingenuity, hidden behind three centuries of coffee trading.

Forty years ago the consumption of coffee in the UK was so low as to be negligible. In 1952, however, interest was revived with the coffee bar craze, and since 1956 with instant coffee being advertised relentlessly, we are now a nation of coffee drinkers.

Every generation and most countries in the western world have made individual contributions to the brewing of coffee, the quaint spirit heated cafetieres of England and the Continent, the electric percolators once beloved by the Americans, and the Italian steam pressure machines both big and small all provide a rich and varied field for collectors.

Siphons

A silver plated siphon, with screw fitting, late 19thC.
£1,500-2,000   *TBC*

A silver plated siphon, with cork fitting, late 19thC.
£1,000-1,250   *TBC*

An early Napier, English, mid-19thC.
£220-250   *TBC*

A Napierian silver plated siphon, with match holder, late 19thC.
£1,500-2,500   *TBC*

A Napierian silver plated siphon, Willow pattern, late 19thC.
£1,700-2,500   *TBC*

FURTHER READING
Coffee Makers – 300 Years of Art and Design,
E. & J. Bramah, P.O. Box 79, Eastleigh, Hants.
SO5 5YW.

Balancing Siphons

A French balancing siphon, similar to Preterre, with counterpoise weight replaced with round spring, late 19thC.
£1,000-1,300
TBC

A balancing siphon, patented by Preterre for the English market, mid-19thC.
£1,000-1,500   *TBC*

A French decorative balancing siphon, late 19thC.
£1,200-1,500   *TBC*

Push & Pull

A silver plated balancing siphon, patent of Louis Gabet, 1844, late 19thC.
£2,000-3,000   *TBC*

A Toselli ceramic locomotive balancing siphon, patented c1860.
£1,100-1,500   *TBC*

A Bearts machine replica, patented 1838.
Original **£500-800**
TBC

Hydrostatic

A Brains suction pump replica, patented 1835.
Original **£1,000-1,500**
TBC

A Ward Andrews replica, patented 1840.
Original **£500-800**
TBC

A Loysel hydrostatic plated machine, late 19thC.
£250-280   *TBC*

American

An Old Dominion coffee pot, patented 1856. Original **£300-500** *TBC*

A Bencini pot replica, for boiling coffee but preserving aroma by condensation, mid-19thC. Original **£300-500** *TBC*

Early Electric

A French Femoka maker, mid-20thC. **£60-80** *TBC*

Single Cup Filters

A French filter, with strainer and lid, early 20thC. **£10-20** *TBC*

A French silver plated one cup filter, early 20thC. **£25-50** *TBC*

An Italian Simerac pressure maker, mid-20thC. **£70-90** *TBC*

A silver plated single cup filter, early 20thC. **£50-60** *TBC*

A French electric pressure maker, mid-20thC. **£50-60** *TBC*

A French one cup glass filter, mid-20thC. **£80-100** *TBC*

Steam Pressure

A Darru locomotive replica. Original of 1839.
£1,000-1,300 *TBC*

A Le Brun's pressure pot, patented 1840.
£300-350 *TBC*

A Viennese Incomparable, late 19thC.
£100-120 *TBC*

Vacuum

A Raparlier type, late 19thC.
£100-130 *TBC*

An English copper, late 19thC.
£100-130 *TBC*

A self-extinguishing Eicke machine, c1878.
£200-230 *TBC*

Early Percolators

An American copper percolator, 20thC.
£80-100 *TBC*

An English copper percolator, 20thC.
£80-100 *TBC*

A Vardy & Platow, patented 1840.
£300-350 *TBC*

Urns & Infusers

An English silver plate coffee and tea machine, 1795.
£7,000-8,000   *TBC*

A copper urn, mid-19thC.
£300-350   *TBC*

An Old Sheffield plate coffee machine, c1795.
£5,000-5,500   *TBC*

Biggins

A copper biggin, late 19thC.
£120-140   *TBC*

An English silver biggin, Paul Storr, 1809.
£6,000-6,500   *TBC*

Catering Models

A Portuguese gas coffee urn, mid-20thC.
£400-500   *TBC*

An Espresso machine, c1955.
£400-500   *TBC*

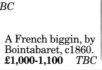

A French biggin, by Bointabaret, c1860.
£1,000-1,100   *TBC*

Popular 20thC Models

A Continental brass
Wika DRP, early 20thC.
£150-200   *TBC*

A Caffeta, by H. Weinet,
early 20thC.
£80-100   *TBC*

An Italian 'Atomic' coffee
maker, patented 1946
Milan, marketed in
London by Sassoon.
£20-25   *TBC*

*This coffee maker, heated
on an oven range or gas
ring, was a product of
post-war austerity. Steam
pressure forced the heated
water up the column; it
then passed through the
coffee in the loading
device fitted with metal
filters and a handle.*

Drip Filters

A Swan Brand
percolator, mid-20thC,
mint condition.
£45-65   *TBC*

A French
tinplate filter
pot, 19thC.
£80-100   *TBC*

The Bialetti, late 20thC.
£10-20   *TBC*

An early Cona vacuum
method, c1915.
£100-150   *TBC*

The Infusion pot, La
Cafetiere, mid-20thC.
£20-50   *TBC*

A reversible drip filter,
19thC.
£100-120   *TBC*

DID YOU KNOW?
Miller's Collectables
Price Guide is
designed to build up,
year by year, into the
most comprehensive
reference system
available.

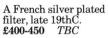

A French silver plated
filter, late 19thC.
£400-450   *TBC*

A copper drip filter pot,
19thC.
£200-220   *TBC*

A copper filter urn, late
19thC.
£200-230   *TBC*

A French lacquered
tinplate urn, early 19thC.
£350-450   *TBC*

A Dutch copper and brass
urn, with 3 taps, late
18thC.
£900-1,000   *TBC*

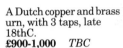

A silver plated
travelling
drip pot,
early 19thC.
£200-300   *TBC*

A Danish brass drip
filter, c1840.
£1,500-2,000   *TBC*

A Dutch pewter urn,
late 18thC.
£800-900   *TBC*

A French brass pot, with
bone handle, c1760.
£800-900   *TBC*

A Dutch brass urn, c1780.
£600-700   *TBC*

A General Hutchinson's
filter, late 19thC.
£100-130 *TBC*

A Staffordshire
creamware pot, c1785.
£500-600 *TBC*

A George III Sheffield
plate pot, 1760.
£600-650 *TBC*

An English copper and
brass filter pot, 19thC.
£80-100 *TBC*

A Worcester coffee pot,
The Milkmaids by
Robert Hancock, c1765.
£500-600 *TBC*

A copper pot, with
infusing bag, c1840.
£250-300 *TBC*

Coffee Pots

A pewter pot, E. Stacey,
mid-19thC.
£85-100 *TBC*

A St. Amand Nord pot,
mid-19thC.
£400-500 *TBC*

A pewter pot, James
Dixon, mid-19thC.
£85-100 *TBC*

An Elkington
centrepiece, c1858.
Silver. **£5,000-6,000**

Silver plate.
£2,000-2,500   *TBC*

*Camel caravans or camel
trains were also known as
'Ships of the Desert' and
were used extensively for
carrying coffee through
the desert terrain to
shipping ports such as
Aden and Hodeina in
Arabia.*

A George II coffee pot,
1743.
£3,500-4,000   *TBC*

An English copper pot,
c1820.
£200-250   *TBC*

A Turkish Ibrik set,
modern.
£80-100   *TBC*

A Baghdad boiler,
modern.
£30-90   *TBC*

An Ethiopian Jabena,
late 20thC.
£50-70   *TBC*

A George III
copper pot,
c1760.
£200-250   *TBC*

**MAKE THE MOST
OF MILLERS**
Condition is
absolutely vital when
assessing the value of
any item. Damaged
pieces appreciate
much less than
perfect examples.
However, a rare,
desirable piece may
command a high
price even when
damaged.

Two Scandinavian
copper boilers, c1880.
£150-250 each   *TBC*

A George III pot, 1764.
£3,000-4,000 *TBC*

A saltglazed coffee pot,
mid-18thC, 6in (15cm).
£1,000-1,200 *DN*

Roasters

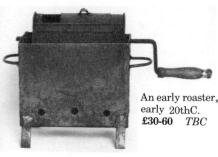

An early roaster,
early 20thC.
£30-60 *TBC*

A French long handled
roaster, early 20thC.
£80-110 *TBC*

Grinders

A French metal coffee
grinder, early 20thC.
£150-250 *TBC*

A large grinder, Savage
& Co., Eastcheap, early
20thC.
£400-450 *TBC*

A large roaster, Sheffield,
early 20thC.
£220-260 *TBC*

A basic iron hand
grinder, early 20thC.
£55-95 *TBC*

A large table grinder,
Parnall & Sons, Brisol,
early 20thC.
£200-250 *TBC*

An electric grinder, Japy
Frères, Paris, early
20thC.
£85-135 *TBC*

Corkscrews

Corkscrews are becoming increasingly popular and valuable, the selection is very large, from delicate ladies corkscrews to large bar counter attachments, from ingenious mechanical devices to simple metal objects given away as trade advertisements.

Some corkscrews have a number of gadgets, including glass cutters, tin openers and brushes, whilst others are found incorporated in various articles, umbrellas and walking sticks are an example. Corkscrews, like most other 'Drinking' collectables, are proving to be a very good investment.

| Cross Reference |
| Drinking |

A selection of miniature corkscrews.
£80-100 each *GSP*

A selection of Georgian silver sheathed corkscrews.
£100-400 each *GSP*

A 9ct gold mounted combined corkscrew, N.B.Ltd., Sheffield, 1921.
£110-120 *GSP*

A German mermaid Waiter's Friend.
£200-250 *GSP*

Three miniature mother-of-pearl penknives, all including corkscrews.
£15-20 each *GSP*

An American combined worm, bottle opener and blade, gold mounted, rolled gold loop.
£50-60 *GSP*

A selection of German corkscrews.
£130-400 each
GSP

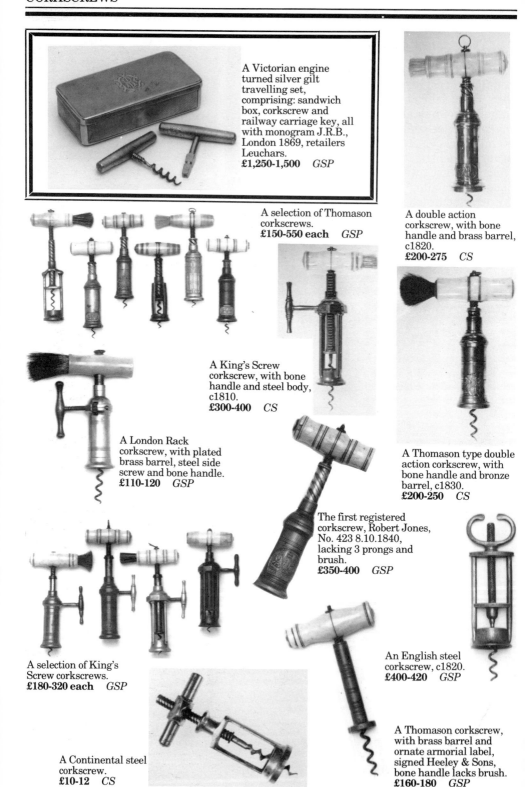

A Victorian engine turned silver gilt travelling set, comprising: sandwich box, corkscrew and railway carriage key, all with monogram J.R.B., London 1869, retailers Leuchars.
£1,250-1,500 *GSP*

A selection of Thomason corkscrews.
£150-550 each *GSP*

A double action corkscrew, with bone handle and brass barrel, c1820.
£200-275 *CS*

A King's Screw corkscrew, with bone handle and steel body, c1810.
£300-400 *CS*

A London Rack corkscrew, with plated brass barrel, steel side screw and bone handle.
£110-120 *GSP*

A Thomason type double action corkscrew, with bone handle and bronze barrel, c1830.
£200-250 *CS*

The first registered corkscrew, Robert Jones, No. 423 8.10.1840, lacking 3 prongs and brush.
£350-400 *GSP*

A selection of King's Screw corkscrews.
£180-320 each *GSP*

An English steel corkscrew, c1820.
£400-420 *GSP*

A Continental steel corkscrew.
£10-12 *CS*

A Thomason corkscrew, with brass barrel and ornate armorial label, signed Heeley & Sons, bone handle lacks brush.
£160-180 *GSP*

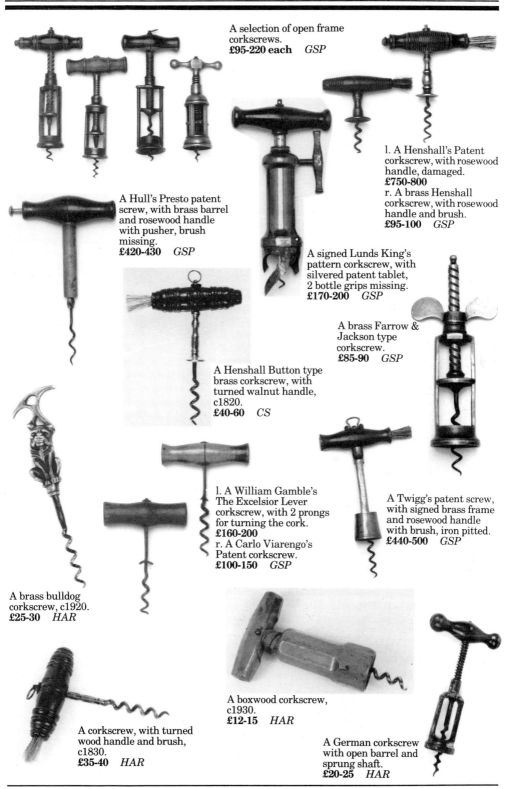

A selection of open frame corkscrews.
£95-220 each *GSP*

l. A Henshall's Patent corkscrew, with rosewood handle, damaged.
£750-800
r. A brass Henshall corkscrew, with rosewood handle and brush.
£95-100 *GSP*

A Hull's Presto patent screw, with brass barrel and rosewood handle with pusher, brush missing.
£420-430 *GSP*

A signed Lunds King's pattern corkscrew, with silvered patent tablet, 2 bottle grips missing.
£170-200 *GSP*

A brass Farrow & Jackson type corkscrew.
£85-90 *GSP*

A Henshall Button type brass corkscrew, with turned walnut handle, c1820.
£40-60 *CS*

l. A William Gamble's The Excelsior Lever corkscrew, with 2 prongs for turning the cork.
£160-200
r. A Carlo Viarengo's Patent corkscrew.
£100-150 *GSP*

A Twigg's patent screw, with signed brass frame and rosewood handle with brush, iron pitted.
£440-500 *GSP*

A brass bulldog corkscrew, c1920.
£25-30 *HAR*

A boxwood corkscrew, c1930.
£12-15 *HAR*

A corkscrew, with turned wood handle and brush, c1830.
£35-40 *HAR*

A German corkscrew with open barrel and sprung shaft.
£20-25 *HAR*

Sir Frances Drake brass corkscrew, c1920.
£25-30   HAR

Shakespeare brass corkscrew, 20thC.
£15-25   HAR

A corkscrew, with cigar shaped wood handle and brush, c1870.
£35-40   HAR

A corkscrew, with bone handle, carrying ring and brush.
£70-80   HAR

A silver plated key corkscrew combined crown cap lifter.
£30-50   CS

A decorative brass key corkscrew.
£15-25   CS

A buffalo horn corkscrew with spike, c1860.
£35-40   HAR

A cast steel 4 finger pull corkscrew, c1870.
£25-35   HAR

A Perille marked Delice Deposé corkscrew.
£50-55   HAR

A bronze corkscrew in the shape of a door key, c1890.
£30-50   CS

A cast steel 4 finger pull corkscrew.
£15-25   CS

A Magic Lever cork drawer.
£65-75   HAR

An all metal corkscrew.
£10-15   HAR

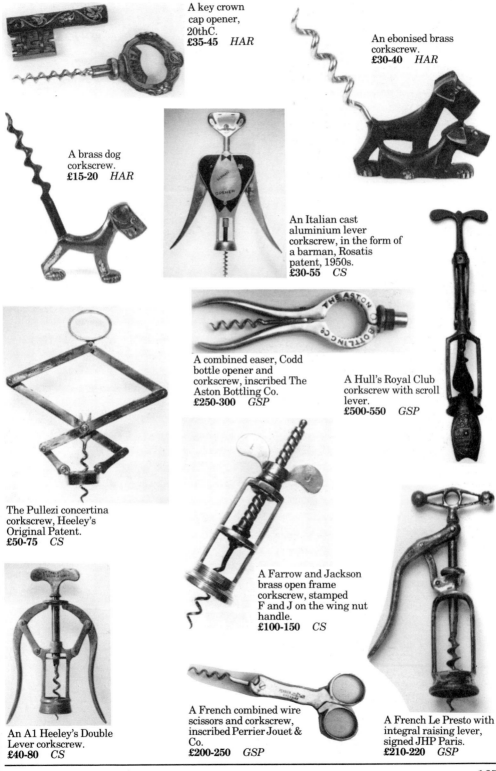

A key crown
cap opener,
20thC.
£35-45 *HAR*

An ebonised brass
corkscrew.
£30-40 *HAR*

A brass dog
corkscrew.
£15-20 *HAR*

An Italian cast
aluminium lever
corkscrew, in the form of
a barman, Rosatis
patent, 1950s.
£30-55 *CS*

A combined easer, Codd
bottle opener and
corkscrew, inscribed The
Aston Bottling Co.
£250-300 *GSP*

A Hull's Royal Club
corkscrew with scroll
lever.
£500-550 *GSP*

The Pullezi concertina
corkscrew, Heeley's
Original Patent.
£50-75 *CS*

A Farrow and Jackson
brass open frame
corkscrew, stamped
F and J on the wing nut
handle.
£100-150 *CS*

An A1 Heeley's Double
Lever corkscrew.
£40-80 *CS*

A French combined wire
scissors and corkscrew,
inscribed Perrier Jouet &
Co.
£200-250 *GSP*

A French Le Presto with
integral raising lever,
signed JHP Paris.
£210-220 *GSP*

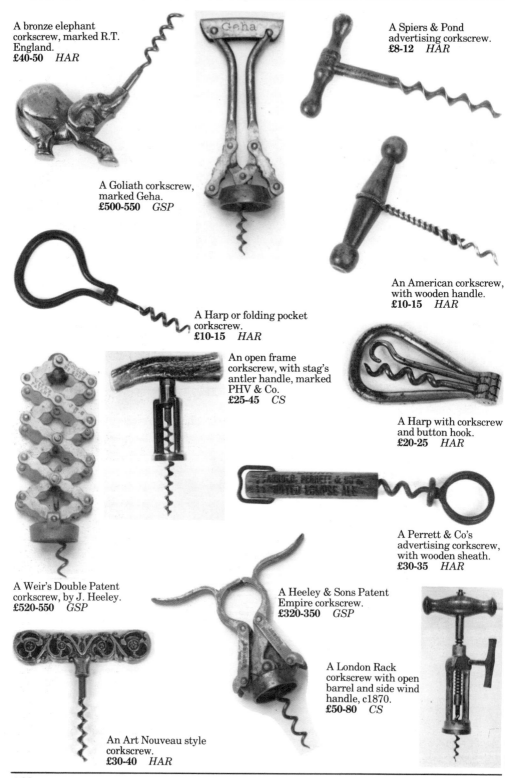

A bronze elephant corkscrew, marked R.T. England.
£40-50   *HAR*

A Goliath corkscrew, marked Geha.
£500-550   *GSP*

A Spiers & Pond advertising corkscrew.
£8-12   *HAR*

A Harp or folding pocket corkscrew.
£10-15   *HAR*

An American corkscrew, with wooden handle.
£10-15   *HAR*

An open frame corkscrew, with stag's antler handle, marked PHV & Co.
£25-45   *CS*

A Harp with corkscrew and button hook.
£20-25   *HAR*

A Perrett & Co's advertising corkscrew, with wooden sheath.
£30-35   *HAR*

A Weir's Double Patent corkscrew, by J. Heeley.
£520-550   *GSP*

A Heeley & Sons Patent Empire corkscrew.
£320-350   *GSP*

A London Rack corkscrew with open barrel and side wind handle, c1870.
£50-80   *CS*

An Art Nouveau style corkscrew.
£30-40   *HAR*

An English open framed corkscrew, with turned wooden handle, c1810.
£200-300 *CS*

An Italian brass lever corkscrew, 20thC.
£10-18 *CS*

A painted wooden novelty corkscrew.
£3-4 *DH*

A miniature penknife corkscrew.
£8-10 *HAR*

A miniature mother-of-pearl penknife incorporating corkscrew.
£30-40 *HAR*

An all steel corkscrew named The Joker, similar design to the French Perille type, c1980.
£20-45 *CS*

A bone handled penknife, incorporating corkscrew.
£10-15 *HAR*

A French Waiter's Friend corkscrew.
£10-18 *HAR*

A coachman's staghorn penknife, with 8 blades incorporating corkscrew, some damage.
£110-120 *GSP*

A bone multi-blade penknife, incorporating corkscrew and whistle.
£170-190 *GSP*

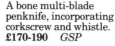

A corkscrew Codd bottle opener, with apple wood handle, c1875.
£35-40 *HAR*

A mother-of-pearl pistol knife, with corkscrew trigger.
£380-400 *GSP*

Cross Reference
Drinking

A pocket knife/tool by Loftus, incorporating corkscrew.
£230-250 *GSP*

A selection of concealed corkscrews, from Prohibition period.
£40-85 each   *GSP*

The Easi-Pull cork extractor, yellow plastic, with box, c1960.
£15-20   *HAR*

A bone handled walking stick, with silver collar and corkscrew, c1960.
£140-150   *HAR*

A Lunds lever corkscrew, with coat-of-arms, marked.
£50-60   *HAR*

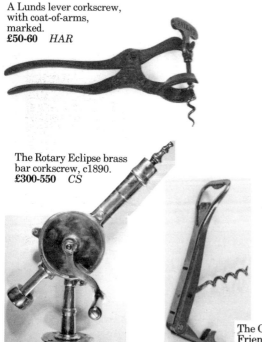

The Rotary Eclipse brass bar corkscrew, c1890.
£300-550   *CS*

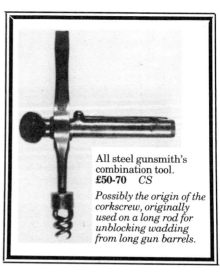

All steel gunsmith's combination tool.
£50-70   *CS*

Possibly the origin of the corkscrew, originally used on a long rod for unblocking wadding from long gun barrels.

The Casino Waiter's Friend.
£8-12   *HAR*

Cross Reference
Militaria

Dolls

The interest in dolls, dolls houses and furniture continues as strongly as ever. Dolls made before the First World War are eagerly sought. Original condition is extremely important, and clothes should be retained however poor the condition. Never repaint a doll.

Bisque

A bisque swivel headed doll, in provincial costume, right arm damaged, fingers chipped, 14½in (37cm) high.
£700-800 *C*

A bisque headed bébé, lower arms flaked, incised DEPOSE JUMEAU 9, 20in (51cm) high.
£4,000-4,500 *CNY*

A bisque shoulder headed doll, the stuffed body with bisque limbs, toe broken, c1865, 17½in (44.5cm) high.
£650-750 *C*

A French bisque socket head character doll, probably Jumeau, in pieces, 22in (56cm) high.
£500-600 *HSS*

A bisque swivel headed Parisienne, with kid body and individually stitched fingers, 14in (35.5cm) high.
£650-750 *CSK*

An all bisque child doll wearing contemporary dress, one arm missing, 6in (15cm) high.
£150-180 *C*

A Max Handwercke bisque doll, with jointed wood and composition body, head and one leg detached, c1900, 25in (64cm).
£370-400 *S(C)*

A bisque headed character child doll, with composition body and contemporary frock, coat, cape and beret, and with spare cotton frock, some damage, marked K * R 101 49, 19½in (49cm) high.
£4,000-4,500 *C*

A Melitta baby doll, 15in (38cm) high.
£350-450 *DOW*

A bisque headed character baby doll, with baby's body, eyes slightly slipping, hands restored, impressed SIMON & HALBIG 122 28, 11in (28cm) high.
£450-500 *C*

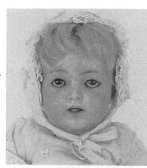

A Schoenau & Hoffmeister bisque character doll, with jointed wood and composition body, replaced black real hair wig, c1925, 29in (74cm) high.
£450-500 *S(C)*

A Jutta doll, with auburn wig and brown eyes, No. 1349, 32in (81cm) high.
£700-800 *DOW*

A French shoulder bisque swivel head fashion doll, with jointed kid body and bisque arms, and a small quantity of clothes, old hairline crack, late 19thC, 13in (33cm) high.
£700-750 *S(C)*

A Jules Steiner bisque doll, in original dress, stamped BEBE LE PARISIEN, c1880, 16½in (42cm) high.
£2,500-3,000 *S(S)*

An Armand Marseille character baby doll, No. 992 AM 12, 22in (55.5cm) high.
£650-750 *DOW*

A J. D. Kestner character bisque doll, impressed 211, c1912, 13½in (34cm) high.
£800-850 *S(S)*

A French swivel head shoulder bisque doll, in original dress, c1870, 10½in (27cm) high.
£500-550 *S(S)*

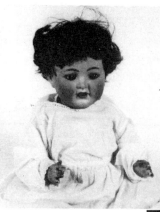

A Kammer & Reinhardt/
Simon & Halbig bisque
socket head girl doll,
with composition body
and bent limbs, 20in
(51cm) high.
£300-350   *HSS*

A bisque headed
character doll, with
closed pouty mouth,
jointed wood and
composition toddler
body, marked K * R
114 39, 15in (38cm) high.
£2,200-2,500   *CSK*

An Armand Marseille
bisque doll, with jointed
wood and composition
body, wig replaced,
c1900, 32in (81cm).
£550-600   *S(C)*

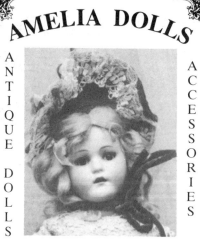
A bisque headed
character doll, with blue
eyes and jointed toddler
body, 21½in (54cm) high.
£450-500   *CSK*

A bisque headed child
doll, with jointed wood
and composition body,
marked Simon & Halbig
100, 40in (101.5cm) high.
£1,250-1,500   *CSK*

A Kestner domed bisque
shoulder headed doll,
with kid body and bisque
hands, 17in (43cm) high.
£1,300-1,500   *CSK*

A bisque headed character doll, with painted features and jointed composition toddler body, 10½in (26cm) high.
£850-950 *CSK*

An Edmund Edelmann bisque character doll, with chunky toddler composition body, impressed Melitta 14, c1922, 25in (64cm).
£350-400 *S(C)*

A Simon & Halbig shoulder bisque doll, with original blonde mohair wig, swivel head, original bead necklace, pink tinged kid body with bisque lower hands, in original chemise, No. 905, 11in (28cm) high.
£550-600 *S(C)*

A Jutta character bisque doll, with curved limb composition body, damage to hands, by Simon & Halbig for Cuno & Otto Dressel, c1914, 23in (59cm).
£450-500 *S(C)*

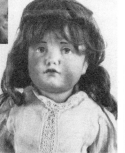

A bisque headed character doll, with composition body, dressed in original lace trimmed outfit, legs missing, marked K * R 114 34, the head 3½in (9cm) high.
£1,000-1,200 *CSK*

Papier Mâché

A papier mâché headed doll, the kid body with wooden limbs, c1830, 16in (41cm) high.
£400-450   *CSK*

Wax

A Pierotti-type poured wax shoulder doll, one arm damaged, one leg detached, English, c1880, 19in (48cm) high.
£450-500   *S(S)*

Miscellaneous

A pair of pottery book ends, 2 little girls under sunhats holding a camera and a rose, William Goebel crown mark, 6in (15cm) high.
£220-250   *CSK*

A porcelain doll brush, c1920, 8in (20cm) high.
£15-20   *CA*

FURTHER READING
The Ninth Blue Book of Dolls & Values, Jan Foulke, Hobby House Press.
The Price Guide to Dolls, Constance Eileen King, Woodbridge, Suffolk.

Dolls House Dolls

l. & r. A pair of bisque headed dolls house dolls, in contempory dresses, c. A composition headed dolls house doll, with wood body and painted arms and legs, c1860, 3in (7.5cm) high.
£350-400 *C*

A pair of Victorian dolls shoes, 2in (5cm) long.
£15-20 *SP*

A dolls house family, 4in (10cm) high.
£20-25 *CA*

A Victorian dolls house doll in native dress, all original, 3½in (9cm) high.
£80-100 *SP*

A Victorian Scotsman dolls house doll, all original, 3½in (9cm) high.
£80-100 *SP*

A Victorian bisque miniature doll with glass eyes, all original.
£80-100 *SP*

A bisque miniature Oriental doll, with glass eyes, 5in (12.5cm) high.
£80-100 *SP*

A dolls purse, 2in (5cm) long.
£60-70 *LEW*

A Victorian silver plate dolls purse.
£10-15 *SP*

177

Dolls House Ceramics

A tea set on silver tray, 2in (5cm) long.
£125-130 *CD*

A toilet set.
£20-30 *CD*

A Victorian plate, 3in (7.5cm) diam.
£6-10 *CA*

A Victorian hand painted miniature cup and saucer, cup 2in (5cm) high.
£25-30 *CA*

l. A jar and cover.
£15-20
r. A loving cup, 1in (2.5cm).
£5-6 *CD*

A teacup and saucer, teaspoon and plate.
£15-20 *CD*

A tea set on tray.
£55-65 *CD*

A jug and mug, jug 1in (2.5cm), mug ½in (1.5cm).
£20-30 each *LEW*

A porcelain jug and basin set.
£80-90 *LEW*

A tray with Bristol glass coffee set, c1830.
£240-260 *LEW*

l. A Victorian plate, 3in (7.5cm) diam.
£8-10
r. A blue and white plate.
£15-18 *CA*

Cross Reference
Miniature Ceramics

MAKE THE MOST OF MILLERS
Condition is absolutely vital when assessing the value of any item. Damaged pieces appreciate much less than perfect examples. However, a rare, desirable piece may command a high price even when damaged.

l. A gaudy Welsh miniature cup and saucer, 2½in (6.5cm) diam.
£30-35
r. A plate decorated in green, 2½in (6.5cm) diam.
£15-20 *CA*

Dolls House Provisions

Butter and lard.
£5-10 each *CD*

A cake and a pie.
£5-10 each *CD*

Smoked salmon.
£8-12 each *CD*

A selection of pastries.
£3-8 each *CD*

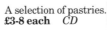

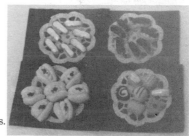

A butcher's block with meat, 5in (12.5cm).
£20-30 *CD*

A box of prunes and a box of apricots.
£8-10 each *CD*

Dolls House Furniture

An elm miniature ladderback open armchair, 10in (25cm) high, and a similar chair, mid-18thC style, 8in (20cm) high.
£300-350   *CSK*

A selection of carved and pierced bone furniture and opaque glass.
£280-320   *C*

A set of miniature oak dining room furniture, comprising refectory table, 6 chairs, 2 carvers and a twin tiered buffet, the table 2½in (6.5cm) high, probably by F. J. Early, c1920.
£500-600   *CSK*

A toilet mirror, 3½in (9cm) high.
£15-20   *SP*

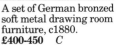

A Victorian chair.
£20-25   *SP*

A set of German bronzed soft metal drawing room furniture, c1880.
£400-450   *C*

A set of 3 Victorian cane chairs, 5in (12.5cm) high.
£30-50   *SP*

A Victorian bonheur du jour, 5in (12.5cm) high.
£80-120   *SP*

A crochet chair and settee, the chair 5in (12.5cm) high.
Chair. **£8-10**
Settee. **£12-15**   *OD*

An iron kitchen range,
5½in (14cm) wide.
£160-180
A selection of cast iron
pots and pans.
£2-8 each   *CD*

A pole screen, 17½in
(44.5cm) high.
£340-360   *LEW*

An iron bed with painted
back board, 6in (15cm)
high.
£40-60   *CD*

A Victorian shell
dressing table, 6in
(15cm) high.
£30-35   *CA*

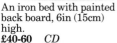

A set of 8 pieces of
furniture, 2½ to 3½in
(6 to 8.5cm) high.
£70-80   *AL*

A painted dresser, 5in
(12.5cm) high.
£18-20   *CA*

An Edwardian hand
painted dresser, 5in
(12.5cm) high.
£12-20   *SAD*

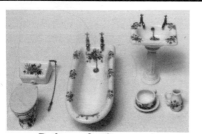

Bathroom furniture,
bath 5½in (14cm) long.
£90-110   *CD*

Dolls House Accessories

A baby carriage, 3in (7.5cm) high.
£240-260 *LEW*

A fire hydrant, 4½in (11.5cm) high.
£12-20 *CD*

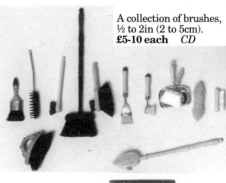

A collection of brushes, ½ to 2in (2 to 5cm).
£5-10 each *CD*

A hip bath, 3in (7.5cm) long.
£25-30 *CD*

A painted pewter Noah's Ark, 2in (5cm) long.
£20-25 *CD*

A selection of toys, 1in (2.5cm) high.
£7-15 each *CD*

A French toilet set, brush 4½in (11.5cm) long.
£50-70 *SP*

A baker's hand cart, 6in (15cm) high.
£55-65 *CD*

A child's toy till, 7in (17.5cm) high.
£12-20 *CAC*

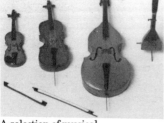

A selection of musical instruments, 3½ to 7in (8.5 to 17.5cm).
£20-40 each *CD*

A fireplace and implements.
£4-30 each *CD*

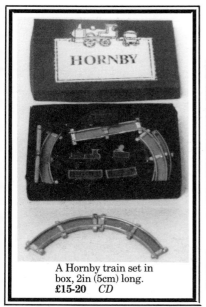

A Hornby train set in box, 2in (5cm) long.
£15-20   *CD*

A carpentry tool box, 6½in (16.5cm) high.
£70-90   *CD*

A bird with moving wings in a cage, ½in (1.5cm) high.
£50-70   *CD*

Cross Reference
Toys
Train sets

A costermonger's hand cart, 8in (20cm) long.
£45-55   *CD*

A Continental gilded wood sedan chair, with painted exterior, glazed hinged door and side panels, and lined interior, some damage, 19thC, 15in (38cm) high.
£150-180   *HSS*

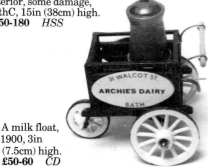

A milk float, 1900, 3in (7.5cm) high.
£50-60   *CD*

Dolls Houses

A late Georgian three-storey wooden carpenter-made dolls house, with central front door, 6 rooms with staircase and landings, the interior, window frames and glazing bars overpainted, c1830, 45in (114cm) high.
£2,000-2,500   *C*

A two-storey printed paper and wood dolls house, opening at the front, with 4 rooms, staircase and fireplaces, by G. & J. Lines Bros., c1924, 29in (74cm) wide.
£250-350   *CSK*

A late Georgian style three-storey painted wooden dolls house with 7 rooms, faded original papers, c1840, 46in (116.5cm) high.
£1,500-1,800   *C*

A three-storey wooden dolls house, with 6 rooms, all with original wall and floor papers, restored and overpainted exterior and overpainted interior doors, with Christian Hacker stamp on base, 33in (83.5cm) high.
£600-650   *C*

A dolls house front, painted in blue and brown, early 19thC, 24in (61.5cm) square.
£230-280   *SWN*

A two-storey painted wooden dolls house, with 6 rooms, late 19thC, 61in (155cm) high.
£450-500   *CSK*

Drinking

Advertising & Promotional

A Ben Truman sign, 16in (40.5cm) high.
£60-70 *CAC*

A rubber Bulmer's Cider sign, 8½in (21.5cm) high.
£10-15 *HUN*

Two Johnnie Walker figures, 9in (22.5cm) and 16in (40.5cm) high.
The smaller **£10-15**
The larger **£25-30** *HUN*

A ceramic Johnnie Walker clothes brush, c1950, 7in (17.5cm) long.
£10-15 *RTT*

A plastic White Horse Whisky sign, 6in (15cm) wide.
£10-15 *HUN*

Guinness

For a further selection of Guinness items refer to Collectables Volume II, page 127.

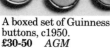

With the Compliments of GUINNESS

A boxed set of Guinness buttons, c1950.
£30-50 *AGM*

Cross Reference
Buttons

A Beswick Double Diamond figure, 8½in (21.5cm) high.
£130-160 *BEV*

An Arthur Bell & Sons Ltd ceramic jug, 5in (12.5cm) high.
£10-12 *RTT*

A plaster figure of Napoleon on horseback, on a plinth inscribed Courvoisier the Brandy of Napoleon, 13in (33cm) high.
£100-120 *Bon*

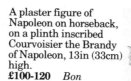

COURVOISIER
The Brandy of Napoleon

A beefeater in ceremonial dress on plinth, inscribed Beefeater Extra Dry Gin, 15in (38.5cm) high.
£60-80 *Bon*

A Mintons ceramic jug advertising Dewar's White Label Whisky, 3in (7.5cm) high.
£10-15 *RTT*

A Schweppes Ginger Ale plate, 4½in (11.5cm) diam.
£15-18 *CA*

A ceramic Beefeater Dry Gin jug, 5in (12.5cm) high.
£10-15 *RTT*

A Sandland Martell Brandy jug, c1950, 6½in (16.5cm) high.
£30-40 *RTT*

Bottle Openers

A brass bull bottle
opener, 4½in (11.5cm)
long.
£10-15 *HAR*

An Ind Coope bottle
opener, Italian, 7in
(18cm) long.
£5-10 *HAR*

A Blackpool Tower bottle
opener, 4½in (11cm) long.
£8-12 *HAR*

A Worthington bottle
opener, 1960s.
£2-3 *HAR*

| Cross Reference |
Corkscrews

A metal crown cork
opener, 3in (8cm) long.
£1-4 *HAR*

A metal crown cork
opener advertising the
Sheraton Hotel, 3½in
(9cm) long.
£2-3 *HAR*

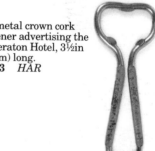

An iron knight's helmet
bottle opener, 5in (13cm)
long.
£5-8 *HAR*

A World War I bottle
opener, 5in (13cm) long.
£10-15 *HAR*

Cocktails

A bottle opener and case,
1950s, 5in (13cm) long.
£4-5 *HAR*

A crackle glass cocktail
shaker with chrome top,
c1930, 9in (23cm) high.
£20-25 *RTT*

General

A silver and mother-of-pearl fruit knife and travelling glass, in case, c1912, 4½ by 3in (11 by 8cm).
£50-60   *HAR*

A pewter and leather spirit drinking flask, c1900, 5½in (14cm) high.
£20-30   *HAR*

A 1 pint beer mug, 5in (13cm) high.
£8-10   *CAC*

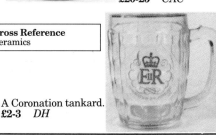

A transfer print cider mug, 3½in (9cm) high.
£20-25   *CAC*

A blue and white whisky jug, marked Fenton, 8in (20cm) high.
£40-50   *RG*

A silver spirit flask, Sheffield, marked J D & S, c1921, 5in (13cm) high.
£145-155   *HAR*

Cross Reference
Ceramics

A Coronation tankard.
£2-3   *DH*

Siphons

A jug of Sassolino Cucchi liqueur, sealed, 4½in (11cm) high.
£3-5   *CA*

A straw covered drinking flask with pewter top, 1920s, 5½in (14cm) high.
£18-20   *HAR*

A soda siphon, 14in (36cm) high.
£20-25   *AL*

A Schweppes soda siphon, 12in (31cm) high.
£10-15   *AL*

Wine Antiques

Labels

l. A label, Elizabeth Morley, London, c1804, 1in (2.5cm) high.
r. A label, Geo. Knight, London, c1818, 1in (2.5cm) high.
£85-90 each   *HAR*

A silver Rum label, Joseph Taylor, Birmingham, c1827, 2in (5cm) wide.
£45-55   *HAR*

A silver and mother-of-pearl Brandy cork, 19thC, 3in (8cm) long.
£15-25   *HAR*

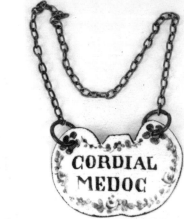

A French enamel Cordial Medoc label, c1830, 1½in (4cm) wide.
£35-45   *HAR*

A mother-of-pearl Brandy label, c1840, 1½in (4cm) wide.
£30-40   *HAR*

An Old Sheffield plate Gin label, 2in (5cm) wide.
£30-35   *HAR*

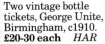

Two vintage bottle tickets, George Unite, Birmingham, c1910.
£20-30 each   *HAR*

A silver Port decanter label, Taylor & Perry, Birmingham, 1833, 2½in (6cm) wide.
£80-90   *HAR*

A set of 4 silver plate decanter labels, c1870.
£65-135 *CS*

A pair of French gilded porcelain wine labels, c1870, 2in (5cm) wide.
£110-120 *HAR*

A silver plated French wine label.
£10-20 *HAR*

Four white pottery wine cellar bin labels, with black enamel names, c1850.
£25-45 each *CS*

Champagne

A pair of Moet & Chandon champagne cork pliers, 6½in (16cm) long.
£15-20 *HAR*

A silver plated champagne tap, with ebonised handle, 6½in (16cm) long.
£45-55 *HAR*

A champagne tap, marked S. Maw & Son, London, with fleur de lys on/off turns.
£25-35 *CS*

A Victorian champagne tap with turned ebonised handle, c1880.
£35-45 *CS*

Champagne wire cutters, 4in (10cm) long.
£20-30 *HAR*

A metal champagne tap, marked C & G, 4½in (11cm) long.
£25-35 *HAR*

A champagne de-corker, shaped as a bottle, c1900, 7in (18cm) high.
£40-45 *CSA*

Goblets

A silver wine goblet, Hunt and Roskell, London, 1872.
£380-400 *CS*

A silver wine goblet, Edward Barnard and Sons, 1830.
£450-500 *CS*

A solid silver wine goblet, English, 1871.
£300-350 *CS*

Miscellaneous

A silver wine bottle stopper/cork, depicting a classical figure of a woman holding in her arms a cornucopia of flowers, Continental marks including .925 quality silver mark, 5in (12.5cm) high.
£180-200 *CS*

Three silver and whalebone toddy or punch ladles, c1780.
£150-250 each *CS*

A silver plate wine/port decanting cradle, decorated with vine branches, leaves and bunches of grapes, c1860.
£300-500 *CS*

A Sheffield plate coaster, 4in (10cm) diam.
£40-45 *HAR*

A Dutch dark green mallet shaped wine bottle, c1725.
£60-100 *CS*

A pair of lacquered coasters, with gilt acanthus and foliate decoration, 19thC, 5½in (14cm) diam.
£280-320 *HCH*

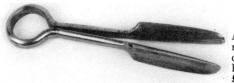

A cork reamer for removing crumbled port corks, c1870, 4in (10cm) long.
£30-40 *HAR*

Eggs

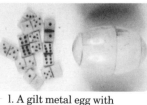

l. A gilt metal egg with thimble, 2in (5cm) long.
£40-45
c. An ivory domino holder.
£30-35
r. A wooden nutmeg grater.
£30-35 *CA*

A collection of miniature eggs, painted and polished wood, decorated ivory and marbled ceramic.
£20-30 each *CA*

A Victorian printed tin egg, child with a goat.
£25-30

Egg Cups

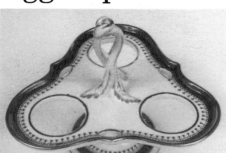

A nursery ware egg cup and beaker, beaker 3in (7.5cm) high.
Egg cup **£5-6**
Beaker **£18-20**
CSA

An early Victorian egg cup holder, 2½in (6.5cm) high.
£30-35 *CA*

Two Shelley egg cups, c1930.
£5-10 each *CSA*

A Dartmouth pottery egg cup, c1950, 3in (7.5cm) high.
£8-9 *CSA*

Two egg cups: l. Crown Ducal, c1930, and r. Crown Devon, c1950.
£4-10 each *CSA*

A Carlton Ware Apple Blossom egg cruet, c1939, 8½in (21.5cm) long.
£55-65 *CSA*

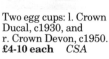

Cross Reference
Ceramics

Two egg cups, Barker Bros and unmarked floral.
£6-8 each *CSA*

A milk glass egg cup, early 19thC, 3in (8cm) high.
£18-22 *EA*

An Aldertons blue and white goose or double egg cup, c1910, 4in (10cm) high.
£12-14 *CSA*

Two Booth's blue and white egg cups, Old Willow pattern, c1920.
£8-10 each *CSA*

A Grays egg cup, 2in (5cm) high.
£4-5 *CSA*

A set of 4 Ruskin pottery egg cups and stand, stand 5½in (14cm) diam.
£40-50 *IW*

A blue and white egg cup, 2½in (6.5cm) high.
£4-5 *CSA*

A late Spode blue and white egg cup and saucer, egg cup 2in (5cm) high.
£12-20 *CAC*

Two Poole pottery egg cups, c1935.
£5-7 each *CSA*

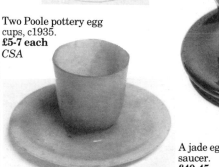

A pottery egg cup.
£5-6 *THA*

A jade egg cup and saucer.
£40-45 *HUN*

EPHEMERA
Autographs

Orville Wright, signed
first day cover, 1 July
1934, rare, VG.
£300-350 *VS*

Cross Reference
Aeronautica

Oliver North, at the Iran
Contra hearings, VG.
£30-50 *VS*

Andy Warhol, scarce,
VG.
£70-80 *VS*

Nazi, postcard of Udet,
Galland and Molders,
signed by latter 2 only,
rare, laid down, FR.
£60-70 *VS*

Eva Peron, signed,
colour, full signature,
Maria E. D. de Peron,
small tear to lower edge
and slight corner
creasing, FR to G.
£280-300 *VS*

Winston S. Churchill,
signed coloured
reproduction of the
painting by Frank O.
Salisbury, full signature,
slight edge wear, G.
£800-1,200 *VS*

Film & Theatre

Ingrid Bergman, signed,
with Michael Wilding,
slight crease, 1948, G.
£70-80 *VS*

A portrait photograph of
Bela Lugosi, signed and
inscribed.
£150-200 *CSK*

More if in pose of Dracula.

Dr. Josef Goebbels,
signed sepia postcard,
rare, EX.
£150-180 *VS*

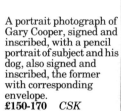

A portrait photograph of
Gary Cooper, signed and
inscribed, with a pencil
portrait of subject and his
dog, also signed and
inscribed, the former
with corresponding
envelope.
£150-170 *CSK*

Astaire and Rogers, in later years, VG.
£60-70 *VS*

Brigitte Bardot, signed, semi-naked, EX.
£35-45 *VS*

Basil Rathbone, signed postcard, first name a little weak, VG.
£150-160 *VS*

John Wayne, signed and inscribed, from True Grit, dated 1970, VG.
£50-60 *VS*

A publicity photograph of Laurel and Hardy, signed twice by each of them.
£320-350 *CSK*

Elizabeth Taylor, signed and inscribed postcard, Picturegoer No. W598, VG.
£60-70 *VS*

Helen Chandler, played in Dracula, signed postcard, Picturegoer 578, rare, VG.
£30-40 *VS*

A publicity photograph of Rudolph Valentino as Cossack Dubrovsky in The Eagle, United Artists, c1925, signed and inscribed.
£100-125 *CSK*

A film still of Humphrey Bogart, signed.
£550-600 *CSK*

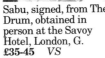

Sabu, signed, from The Drum, obtained in person at the Savoy Hotel, London, G.
£35-45 *VS*

A piece of paper signed and inscribed by Douglas Fairbanks Snr., with a machine print photograph of Douglas Fairbanks in the role of Don Quixote, framed.
£150-200 *CSK*

Leslie Howard, signed photograph, VG.
£80-90 *VS*

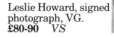

A portrait photograph of Noel Coward by Dorothy Wilding, signed and inscribed, mounted on tissue then card, signed by photographer on tissue.
£80-120 *CSK*

'Ginette' was probably Ginette Spanier, which also adds to the value.

Alan Ladd, signed and inscribed, EX.
£20-30 *VS*

Two portrait photographs, of Errol Flynn and Olivia de Havilland, by Elmer Fyer, each with photographer's stamp, signed and inscribed by subjects.
£140-150 *CSK*

EX	Excellent
FR	Fair
G	Good
MT	Mint
P	Poor
VG	Very Good

Casablanca, individual signed pieces, of Humphrey Bogart, Ingrid Bergman, Paul Henreid and Claude Rains, overmounted beneath a group shot from Casablanca, triple mount in silver, gold and ivory, framed and glazed, rare, VG.
£450-500 *VS*

A portrait photograph of Susan Hayward, signed and inscribed, window mounted, framed and glazed.
£80-100 *CSK*

Two portrait photographs of Laurence Olivier and Vivien Leigh, both signed by subjects.
£350-400 *CSK*

A publicity photograph of Ronald Reagan, signed and inscribed.
£100-110 *CSK*

Two portrait photographs of Laurence Olivier and Vivien Leigh, signed and inscribed.
£430-450 *CSK*

Laurence Olivier, signed with full signature, from Hamlet, EX.
£40-50 *VS*

Sporting

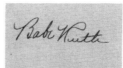

Babe Ruth, signed piece, rare, VG.
£300-320 *VS*

Maureen Connolly, Little Mo, signed, scarce, VG.
£55-65 *VS*

Two autographs of Vivien Leigh and Laurence Olivier, each signed on individual pages, in common mount with 3 film stills of subjects in famous roles including Vivien Leigh as Scarlett O'Hara.
£200-210 *CSK*

Joe Louis, World heavyweight champion, postcard in boxing pose, signed on reverse, slight creasing, G to VG.
£50-80 *VS*

EX	Excellent
FR	Fair
G	Good
MT	Mint
P	Poor
VG	Very Good

Laurence Olivier, colour, signed with full signature, from Sleuth, EX.
£35-45 *VS*

Cross Reference
Sport

A portrait photograph of Marilyn Monroe, by Cecil Beaton, mounted on card, signed and inscribed, with original envelope franked Beverly Hills Calif. March 9th 1960.
£2,300-2,500 *CSK*

Jack Hobbs, signed postcard, batting at the crease, laid down to album page, FR.
£40-50 *VS*

Literary

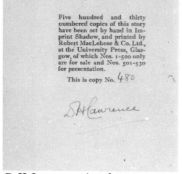

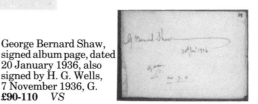

Rudyard Kipling, signed piece, attached to album page, also signed by Earl Beatty and Edward Evans, G.
£35-45   *VS*

Robert Browning, handwritten signed letter, dated 21 December 1888, agreeing to his correspondent dedicating a book of poems to Browning, rare, light foxing, G.
£250-300   *VS*

D. H. Lawrence, signed hardback edition of Rawdon's Roof, limited edition of 530, lacking dust jacket, G.
£180-200   *VS*

George Bernard Shaw, signed album page, dated 20 January 1936, also signed by H. G. Wells, 7 November 1936, G.
£90-110   *VS*

Musical

Elvis Presley, signed, colour, seated at press reception with, but not signed by, Priscilla Presley, on the occasion of their wedding, apparently obtained in person in New York in the 1970s, EX.
£20-30   *VS*

Arturo Toscanini, signed postcard, small photo inset, postal cancellation to image, early, G.
£60-70   *VS*

The Beatles monochrome postcard, depicting each of the 4 members, personalised on the reverse and autographed by John Lennon, Ringo Starr, Paul McCartney and George Harrison.
£140-160   *HSS*

It is probably prudent when considering an expensive addition to any collection of autographs to buy from reputable dealers and auctioneers. Not only are there many forgeries around, but also many documented instances of others signing on behalf of the stars; both Marilyn Monroe's dresser and her mother signed a lot of her publicity pictures, and the Beatles' roadies also signed pictures and even answered fan mail.

Cross Reference
Rock & Pop

Two publicity photographs of Louis Armstrong, signed and inscribed, with a supper menu from the Midland Hotel, Birmingham, also signed and inscribed.
£150-200   *CSK*

A portrait photograph of Enrico Caruso, signed and inscribed.
£80-90   *CSK*

A photograph of Fats Waller performing at the piano on stage, signed and inscribed, 1939.
£150-200   *CSK*

Elizabeth II, 2 pages, 22 June 1955, given at St. James's, being a remission document addressed to the Governor of Wormwood Scrubs, extending a pardon to David Frank King, convicted of an offence under the National Service Act, embossed paper seal, VG.
£150-200   *VS*

Royalty

H.R.H. Edward, Prince of Wales, a portrait photograph by Campbell Gray, signed and inscribed, mounted on card bearing photographer's printed credit, 1911.
£400-450   *CSK*

Prince Albert, 4 pages, 10 August 1841, to General Sir Francis Seymour, the Prince's Groom in Waiting, 2 tape stains to last page, affecting text but not signature, G.
£80-120   *VS*

H.R.H. Princess Mary, a portrait photograph by Campbell Gray, signed and inscribed, mounted on card bearing photographer's printed credit.
£50-60   *CSK*

H.R.H. Princess Mary and family, a portrait photograph by Alice Hughes of Princess Mary and her 3 eldest children, signed and inscribed by Princess Mary, mounted on card bearing photographer's printed credit, 1897.
£150-170   *CSK*

H.M. Queen Victoria, a print photograph by A. Bassano with photographer's credit, signed and inscribed, 1886.
£600-650   *CSK*

George VI, 2 pages, 11 July 1942, given at St. James's, being a remission document addressed to the Governor of Wormwood Scrubs, extending a pardon to Lawrence George Saunders, convicted of an offence under the National Service Act, blue paper seal, slight creasing, about VG.
£60-80   *VS*

Cigarette Cards

Antiques & History

Wills's set of 25, Old Furniture, 1923.
£60-120   *ACC*

Wills's set of 25, Old Silver, 1924.
£48-78   *ACC*

Wills's set of 50, Historic Events, 1912.
£36-72   *ACC*

Beauties

Kimball's Fancy Bathers, 50/50, 1889.
£200-250   *Bon*

Kinney's Surf Beauties, 50/50, 1889.
£300-350   *Bon*

Kimball's Beauties, playing card insets, 52/52, 1895.
£480-500   *Bon*

Kinney's National Dancers, 50/50, 1889.
£160-200   *Bon*

Dogs

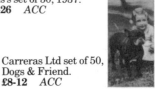

Wills's set of 50, 1937.
£16-26   *ACC*

Wills's set of 25, 1914.
£60-120   *ACC*

Carreras Ltd set of 50, Dogs & Friend.
£8-12   *ACC*

Engineering

Wills's set of 50, Mining, 1916.
£24-48 *ACC*

Wills's set of 50, Famous Inventors, 1915.
£30-60 *ACC*

Equestrian

Carreras set of 50, Tools and How to Use Them, 1925.
£30-50 *ACC*

Wills's set of 40, Racehorses & Jockeys, 1938.
£42-84 *ACC*

Kinney's Famous 25/25, Running Horses, 1890.
£85-95 *Bon*

Allen & Ginter's Racing Colours of the World, 50/50, 1888.
£250-300 *Bon*

Salmon & Gluckstein's set of 20, Owners & Jockeys, 1906.
£90-100 per card *ACC*

Lambert & Butler's set of 50, Horsemanship, framed, 1938.
£55-65 *ACC*

Flags & Heraldic

Wills's set of 50, Arms & Companies, 1913.
£22-44 *ACC*

Wills's set of 50, Arms of the British Empire, 1910.
£24-48 *ACC*

Allen & Ginter's, Flags of All Nations, 48/48, 1890.
£75-100 *Bon*

Fauna

Wills's set of 50, Wonders of the Sea, 1928.
£16-28 *ACC*

Wills's set of 50, The Sea-Shore, 1938.
£7-12 *ACC*

Wills's set of 48, Animalloys, 1934.
£8-16 *ACC*

Wills's set of 50, British Birds, 1917.
£35-70 *ACC*

Wills's set of 25, Animals and Their Furs, 1929.
£36-58 *ACC*

Kinney's Animals, 25/25, 1890.
£120-150 *Bon*

Wills's set of 50, British Butterflies, 1927.
£24-40 *ACC*

Flora

Wills's set of 50, Wild
Flowers, 1936.
£8-14   *ACC*

Wills's set of 50, Garden Flowers, 1933. **£15-25**

Military

Wills's set of
50, Military
Motors, 1916.
£45-90   *ACC*

Booklets set of 50, A
Short History of Gen.
N. P. Banks, W. Duke
& Sons, American,
issued 1888.
£750-1,500   *ACC*

Wills's set of 50, Allied
Army Leaders, 1917.
£50-100   *ACC*

Allen and Ginter's, The
World's Decorations,
50/50, 1890.
£130-180   *Bon*

Carreras set of 50,
History of Army
Uniforms, 1937.
£40-60   *ACC*

Naval & Shipping

Wills's set of 50, Naval dress and badges, 1909.

Kinney's Navy Vessels of
the World, 25/25, 1889.
£150-180   *Bon*

Carreras set of 50,
History of Naval
Uniforms, 1937.
£22-48   *ACC*

Wills's set of 50, Signalling, 1911. **£26-52**   *ACC*

Wills's set of 25, Rigs of
Ships, 1929.
£60-100   *ACC*

Wills's set of 50, Nelson
Series, 1905.
£100-200   *ACC*

Wills's set of 50,
Merchant
Ships of the
World, 1924.
£30-60   *ACC*

Railways

Wills's set of
50, Railway
Equipment, 1939.
£8-14   *ACC*

Wills's set of
50, Railway
Engines, 1936.
£30-50   *ACC*

Royalty

Wills's set of 50, 1908. **£40-80** *ACC*

Taddy's Coronation series, 30/30, 1902. **£170-200** *Bon*

Wills's set of 25, Cinema Stars, 1928. **£22-38** *ACC*

Show Business

Cora Tanner, Lady of France.

Duke's Portraits of Our Leading Actors and Actresses, series No. 2, 50/50, 1889. **£130-150** *Bon*

Wills's set of 50, Radio Celebrities, 1934. **£18-28** *ACC*

Josie Hall.

Abdulla & Co. Ltd., set of 40, Screen Stars, 1939. **£28-42** *ACC*

Ardath set of 50, Famous Film Stars, 1934. **£35-55** *ACC*

Mayo's American Actresses, Josie Hall, 1890. **£30-40 each** *ACC*

Ardath set of 50, Who is this?, 1936. **£40-70** *ACC*

Transport

Lambert & Butler's,
Motors, 25/25, 1908.
£240-300 *Bon*

Sporting

Cope Bros. & Co. Ltd. set
of 50, Copes Golfers,
1900.
£400-450 *CSK*

Godfrey Phillips & Sons,
General Interest, 1899.
£40-80 each *ACC*

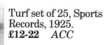

Turf set of 25, Sports
Records, 1925.
£12-22 *ACC*

Wills's set of 50, Safety First, 1934. **£20-32** *ACC*

Wills's set of 50,
Aviation, 1910.
£50-100 *ACC*

Wills's set of 48, Sporting Personalities, 1927. **£18-28** *ACC*

Wills's set of 50,
Cricketers, 1929.
£40-80 *ACC*

Wills's set of 50, Association Footballers, 1935.
£20-34 *ACC*

Ardath Cork set of 50, Cricket, Tennis & Golf
Celebrities, 1935. **£35-55** *ACC*

General

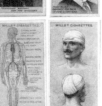

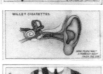

Wills's set of 50, First Aid, 1915.
£36-72 *ACC*

Wills's set of 50, Household Hints, 1936.
£6-10 *ACC*

Ardath set of 50, Stamps Rare and Interesting, 1939.
£45-68 *ACC*

Wills's set of 50, Romance of the Heavens, 1928. **£14-24** *ACC*

Ardath set of 50, Figures of Speech, 1936.
£30-45 *ACC*

Carreras set of 50, Notable MPs, 1929. **£24-38** *ACC*

Bocnal set of 25, Proverbs, 1938. **£36-54** *ACC*

FURTHER READING
Card Photographs, A Guide to their History and Value, Lou W. McCulloch, Millbank Books U.K.
The Guide to Cigarette Card Collecting, Albert's, London 1991.

Greetings Cards

I wish you would leave off that habit of smoking.
£20-30 *BEB*

Easter Greeting.
50p-£1 *BEB*

A cardboard easter egg with decorated transfer picture, with message inside An Easter Offering from a friend, c1900.
£25-35 *BEB*

A Joyous Eastertide.
£2-3 *BEB*

A Happy Easter, 1904.
£1-2 *BEB*

Wishing you a bright and glad New Year.
£2-3 *BEB*

A Christmas card.
£2-3 *BEB*

A Happy New Year.
£3-4 *BEB*

A Joyous Eastertide.

A New Year card.
£12-14 *BEB*

A Christmas card, Glad Times.
£1-2 *BEB*

A party invitation.
£2-3 *BEB*

A humorous card.
£6-7   *BEB*

A greetings card.
£4-5   *BEB*

Valentine Cards

Although the origins of the valentine card are lost in the mists of time the earliest known valentine, now in the British Museum, was sent by Charles, Duke of Orleans, in 1415 whilst he was imprisoned in the Tower of London.

At present, most Victorian greetings cards represent very good value for money and, of course, every one has its own story to tell.

A Victorian valentine, 8in (20cm) high.
£15-25   *SP*

Glad greetings to my Valentine I send.
£12-14   *BEB*

Cupid's Match Box.
£4-5   *BEB*

Two valentine cards, c1875, 9in (23cm) high.
£45-50 each   *BEB*

A valentine card.
£2-3   *BEB*

Magazines

Women of all Lands, with photographs by Hurrell, December 1938.
£4-5 *RTT*

The Dancing Times, 1915.
£2-3 *RTT*

The Playgoer and Society, 1911.
£3-4 *RTT*

Paris magazine, 1933.
£5-10 *RTT*

School Days, 1929.
£1-2 *RTT*

Leach's Berets and Scarves, 1930.
£3-4 *RTT*

Life, September 24, 1945.
£3-5 *RTT*

Vogue Knit, Smart Accessories, 1944.
£2-3 *RTT*

Span magazines, 1955-1956.
£3-4 each *RTT*

The Bazaar, May 1926
£4-5 *RTT*

Woman's Own, 1947.
£2-3 *RTT*

Colour & Health, 1928.
£1-2 *RTT*

The Tatler, September
1957.
£6-8 *RTT*

Topical Times, 1929.
£1-2 *RTT*

Home Chat, November
17, 1923.
£1-2 *RTT*

Illustrated, December
1947.
£3-4 *RTT*

Town & Country Homes,
1925.
£4-5 *RTT*

Look,
October 1945.
£5-8 *RTT*

Picturegoer,
May 1954.
£5-6 *RTT*

Seventy-five issues of
Lilliput.
£65-70 *ONS*

Six issues of Winter's Pie.
£30-35 *ONS*

Paris Music Hall, July 1936.
£6-10 *RTT*

Three issues of The Picture Show.
£30-40 *ONS*

Everybody's, September 1948.
£1-2 *RTT*

Eight hundred and ninety-eight issues of John O'Londons Weekly.
£20-25 *ONS*

A selection of Men Only magazines, 1940s.
£2-3 each *RTT*

Posters

J. Humbert Craig, Northern Ireland flax growing.
£450-500 *ONS*

East Coast Frolics No. 1.
£400-450 *ONS*

Carlton Studio, Finest New Zealand Cheese.
£50-60 *ONS*

East Coast Frolics No. 6.
£450-500 *ONS*

Three Nuns Tobacco.
£60-70 *ONS*

LNER Factory Sites.
£60-70 *ONS*

Tristram Hillier,
Jezreel's Temple,
Gillingham, Kent,
No. 469.
£400-450 *ONS*

Mods! published 1979.
£5-10 *BY*

> **Cross Reference**
> Rock & Pop

A letterpress poster,
1855.
£15-20 *COB*

A Civil
Defence poster,
early 1950s.
£2-3 *COB*

> **MAKE THE MOST OF MILLERS**
> Condition is absolutely vital when assessing the value of any item. Damaged pieces appreciate much less than perfect examples. However, a rare, desirable piece may command a high price even when damaged.

Wartime Posters

Care of Arms is Care of
Life, 15in (38cm) high.
£30-40 *ONS*

Rawls-Fougasse, Don't
Discuss Secrets on the
Telephone.
£80-90 *ONS*

N Y, She's in the Ranks
Too! Caring for Evacuees
is a National Service.
£40-50 *ONS*

Foss, Volunteer for Air
Crew Duties in the RAF.
£40-50 *ONS*

Bert Thomas, 'Ware Spies! Keep it Under Your Hat, damaged.
£60-70 *ONS*

Remember You Are on War Work, Over 1,000,000 tons of Axis Shipping Sunk in the North Sea and English Channel, Y'Entry Into the Navy and First Landing Operation Successfully Completed, letterpress.
£30-40 *ONS*

Keep Mum — she's not so dumb! Careless talk costs lives.
£40-50 *ONS*

We Must Have Exports, Dockers Back Up the Seamen, Speed the Turnround, Hit Back by Doing War Work and This is a Battlefield.
£30-50 *ONS*

E. Oliver, Metal for Salvage Means More Tanks.
£40-50 *ONS*

See How Your Salvage Helps a Bomber.
£60-70 *ONS*

Never was so Much Owed by so Many to so Few — The Prime Minister.
£250-300 *ONS*

Don't forget that walls have ears!
£250-270 *ONS*

Smash Japanese Aggression!
£60-70 *ONS*

Be careful what you say and where you say it!
£250-300 *ONS*

But of course
it mustn't
go any further!
£200-250   *ONS*

CARELESS TALK
COSTS LIVES

You never know who's
listening!
£250-300   *ONS*

CARELESS TALK
COSTS LIVES

Strictly between these
four walls!
£250-300   *ONS*

He did his duty, Will you
do yours?
£50-80   *ONS*

Coughs and Sneezes
Spread Diseases, trap the
germs by using your
handkerchief.
£150-450 each   *ONS*

*During the Second World
War H. M. Bateman
designed posters for the
Ministry of Power and
Ministry of Air
Production. This series
issued by the Ministry of
Health early in 1942
numbered 8 in total.*

Remember Belgium,
Enlist today.
£40-50   *ONS*

Help to Win by Getting
Into War Work.
£30-40   *ONS*

Lucy Kemp-Welsh,
Forward! Forward to
Victory, Enlist Now,
trimmed.
£250-300   *ONS*

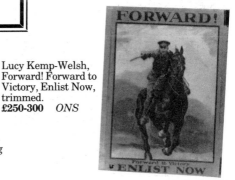

Theatre Programmes

Richard Burton, signed and inscribed theatre programme to inside cast list, The Boy With a Cart, at the Lyric Theatre, dated in another hand 19-1-1950, G to VG.
£15-25   *VS*

Programme for The First Mrs. Fraser with Henry Ainley, Marie Tempest and Ursula Jeans, c1920.
£2-3   *CSA*

Sybil Thorndyke as Joan of Arc programme, advertisement from back cover, 1920s.
£8-10   *CSA*

Programme for Sarah Bernhardt in An Actress's Romance, 1915.
£4-5   *CSA*

Nigel Bruce, signed theatre programme to back cover, also signed by Ann Todd and Celia Upton and 2 others to front cover, Point to Point at St. Martin's Theatre, dated in another hand 9-6-48, none of the signatories appear on the cast list, G to VG.
£50-60   *VS*

Graham Greene, signed theatre programme to front cover, also signed and inscribed by Dorothy Tutin and 1 other, The Living Room at Wyndham's Theatre, 16 April 1953, G to VG.
£20-30   *VS*

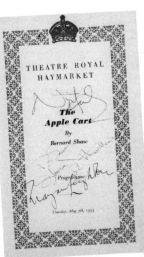

Noel Coward, signed theatre programme to front cover, also signed and inscribed by Olivia de Havilland and Margaret Leighton, The Apple Cart at the Theatre Royal, Haymarket, 7 May 1953, VG.
£30-40   *VS*

Winter Garden Theatre programme, Drury Lane, Tonight's the Night with Leslie Henson, 1924.
£3-4   *CSA*

The Birth of a Nation, motion picture souvenir programme, 1916.
£12-16 *CSA*

Motion picture programme, The House of Temperley, c1913.
£5-6 *CSA*

Cross Reference
Film Memorabilia

Graham Greene, signed theatre programme to front cover, The Potting Shed at the Globe Theatre, dated in another hand 5-2-58, VG.
£30-50 *VS*

General

Silver Jubilee sheet music, 1935.
£3-5 *COB*

Advertisement card Fine Wallpapers, Geo. J. Brennan, New York.
50p-£1 *BEB*

Cross Reference
Signs & Advertisements

A selection of Showcards.
£20-230 each *ONS*

Cross Reference
Adertising Postcards

R.S.P.C.A. Certificate of Merit, 1872.
£8-10 *COB*

Tucks Cut-Outs, The Window Garden series, VG.
£40-50 *VS*

A letterpress advertisement, 1849.
£8-10 *COB*

Ration books for a family of 5.
£7-8 *CA*

Fans

It was the early Portuguese explorers that first introduced fans to Europe from China during the 16thC. The range available to the collector is enormous, from beautifully crafted works of art to clever advertising devices from the 19thC. Original condition, boxes and cases are all plus points when assessing value.

A painted kid leaf marriage fan, with ivory sticks, early 18thC, 10in (25cm).
£900-1,000   *CSK*

It is possible that this fan commemorates the marriage of Princess Anne with the Prince of Orange in 1734, although it may be even earlier in date and a memorial to Queen Mary II.

A framed Roman fan leaf, the leaf c1690, 19in (48cm) wide, in a glazed frame, mid-18thC, 24in (61cm) wide.
£900-1,000   *CSK*

A silk leaf fan, painted with a blue urn of flowers and birds, the sticks lacquered in red and gold, worn, c1770, 11in (28cm).
£250-400   *CSK*

A Chinese painted silk fan, with ivory lacquered sticks, leaf damaged, early 18thC, 9in (23cm).
£100-200   *CSK*

A Northern European fan, with painted leaf and carved sticks, c1720, 10½in (26cm).
£650-750   *CSK*

A French miniature fan, with hand coloured etched leaf, horn sticks and metal gilt guardsticks, c1828, 4½in (11cm).
£450-550   *CSK*

A printed fan, the leaf a lithograph of cats dancing to a mouse band with wooden sticks, signed Aznar, repaired, c1840, 10in (25cm).
£200-300   *CSK*

A miniature gilt metal brisé fan, enclosing 8 photographs of Tom Thumb's wedding, c1870, 2in (5cm).
£250-350   *CSK*

A French painted fan, with silvered mother-of-pearl sticks, repaired, c1820, 8in (20cm).
£550-700   *CSK*

FURTHER READING
A Collector's History of Fans, Nancy Armstrong, London 1974.
Fan Leaves, Fan Guild, Boston 1961.

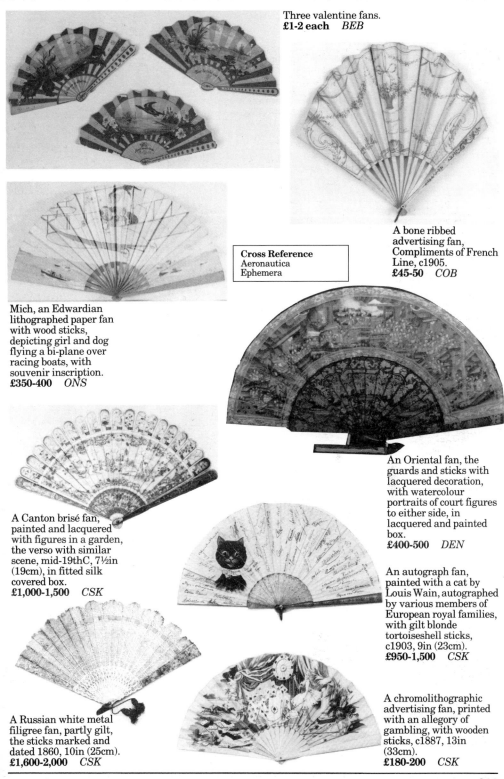

Three valentine fans.
£1-2 each *BEB*

Mich, an Edwardian
lithographed paper fan
with wood sticks,
depicting girl and dog
flying a bi-plane over
racing boats, with
souvenir inscription.
£350-400 *ONS*

Cross Reference
Aeronautica
Ephemera

A bone ribbed
advertising fan,
Compliments of French
Line, c1905.
£45-50 *COB*

A Canton brisé fan,
painted and lacquered
with figures in a garden,
the verso with similar
scene, mid-19thC, 7½in
(19cm), in fitted silk
covered box.
£1,000-1,500 *CSK*

An Oriental fan, the
guards and sticks with
lacquered decoration,
with watercolour
portraits of court figures
to either side, in
lacquered and painted
box.
£400-500 *DEN*

An autograph fan,
painted with a cat by
Louis Wain, autographed
by various members of
European royal families,
with gilt blonde
tortoiseshell sticks,
c1903, 9in (23cm).
£950-1,500 *CSK*

A Russian white metal
filigree fan, partly gilt,
the sticks marked and
dated 1860, 10in (25cm).
£1,600-2,000 *CSK*

A chromolithographic
advertising fan, printed
with an allegory of
gambling, with wooden
sticks, c1887, 13in
(33cm).
£180-200 *CSK*

Fishing

A Victorian wooden priest, very heavy.
£15-20
A Hardy corkscrew, brass rod-in-hand trademark.
£20-30
A pair of French scissors with several fishing devices for controlling the lead weights.
£15-20 *JMG*

A telescopic landing net, wood and brass, by C. Farlow & Co. Ltd., 191 The Strand, late 19thC, 51in (129.5cm) long.
£80-100 *GHA*

An Illingworth No. 4 spinning reel, enlarged for salmon spinning, 1930s.
£30-50
JMG

A turned wood priest, 19thC, 9½in (24cm) long.
£40-60 *GHA*

A stuffed and mounted chub in natural river bed setting, by J. Cooper, 28 Radnor Street, St. Luke, London, weighed 5lb., caught in the Thames at Eynsham by R. W. Hobden, 26 Dec. 1885, in bow fronted glass case, 14 by 27in (35.5 by 68.5cm).
£400-600 *GHA*

A brass telescopic gaff with cork handle, 15 to 27in (38 to 68.5cm) long.
£60-80 *GHA*

A black japanned tin for dry flies, with 15 compartments and celluloid spring lids, by G. Little & Co., Haymarket, London.
£60-80 *GHA*

A Hardy dry fly fishing rod, The Hollolight, split cane, unused, 102in (259cm) long.
£150-200 *GHA*

A carved wood fish model.
£2,000-3,000 *MSh*

A brass telescopic gaff with turned wooden handle, 17 to 28in (43 to 71cm) long.
£60-80 *GHA*

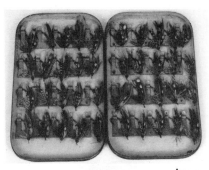

A Mallochs black japanned salmon fly box, with 40 salmon flies.
£80-100 *GHA*

A Hardy 'Neroda' Bakelite salmon fly box, with 40 clips and flies.
£100-120 *GHA*

An un-named short gaff, with turned black wood handle, c1890.
£15-20 *JMG*

A zinc live bait can, with lift-out perforated can for easy selection, 19thC.
£55-65 *GHA*

An English willow creel, late 19thC.
£80-100 *GHA*

Two cards of flies by Allcock of Redditch, made for the 1910 Grand Prix of Brussels, showing 6 flies.
£15-20 each *JMG*

A rosewood float and cast winder, with bone pillars, with compartment for shot and caps.
£40-60 *GHA*

An un-named line drier, with wooden handle.
£20-30 *GHA*

A rare Scottish vintage fishing tackle dealer, c1924, with a deep knowledge of old reels, grey beard, ruddy-ish patina, and a most generous nature towards owners of fine tackle; buys up to £300
JMG

Fishing Reels

A 3in fly reel, by Walter Dingley of Alnwick, with ivorine handle, telephone latch, red agate lineguard, c1920.
£25-35   *JMG*

A Carter & Co. 2½in aluminium trout reel, with ivorine handle.
£70-80   *GHA*

A 2½in Allcock & Co. brass reel, ratchet in working order, c1920.
£80-90   *BS*

A Swiss spinning reel, the Monti Super 2, post-war.
£15-20   *JMG*

A 5¼in Moscrop of Manchester brass reel, with unusual mechanism, c1900.
£50-75   *JMG*

A French multiplying reel, with line holder over the top, 1930s.
£30-50   *JMG*

A 3½in brass plate wind reel, with horn grip, original colour, 19thC.
£100-120   *BS*

A 4in brass plate wind reel, marked H & R 323B, 19thC.
£120-130   *BS*

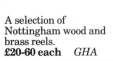

A 3¼in Mallochs patent reversible spool brass ratchet reel, c1900.
£200-230   *BS*

A selection of Nottingham wood and brass reels.
£20-60 each   *GHA*

Hardy Reels

A 3in Hardy wide-drum Perfect, desirable as it has the wartime Spitfire finish, just lacquer over the alloy, rare size.
£100-150 *JMG*

A 3³⁄₁₆in Hardy L R H lightweight trout reel.
£20-40 *GHA*

A Hardy fixed spool reel, The Altex, in original box.
£80-120 *GHA*

A 3³⁄₁₆in Hardy The Lightweight fly reel, first produced in 1936 with unusual internal check.
£60-100 *JMG*

A 2⅝in Hardy Uniqua fly reel, rare size, 1920s.
£50-80 *JMG*

A 3⅝in Hardy Perfect reel, in original box, in mint condition, post-war.
£80-90 *GHA*

A Hardy-Jock-Scott multiplying reel, for spinning, post-war.
£80-120 *JMG*

A 3⅞in Hardy Perfect check narrow drum reel, with ivorine handle, 1912.
£150-200 *GHA*

A 4½in Hardy Silex No. 2 spinning reel, extra wide model, with perforated drum core, rare, WW I.
£50-80 *JMG*

A 5¼in Hardy Ebona sea reel, spool made of dark brown ebonite, c1912, rare.
£30-50 *JMG*

FURTHER READING
Best of Hardy's Angler's Guides, Jamie Maxtone Graham, Scotland 1982.
To Catch a Fisherman, Jamie Maxtone Graham, Peebles, Scotland 1984.
Fishing Tackle of Yesterday, Jamie Maxtone Graham, Peebles, Scotland 1989.

GLASS
Carnival Glass

Carnival glass is moulded, iridescent glassware produced primarily in the U.S.A. between 1908 and 1928, see Miller's Collectables Vol. II, pages 197-200 for a detailed selection.

A Fenton Art Glass marigold holly pattern bowl.
£35-40 *TS*

A Dugan marigold posy bowl, 8½in (21cm) diam.
£30-35 *TS*

A Victorian bowl, 8in (20cm) diam.
£25-30 *OD*

A carnival glass marigold bowl, 4in (1cm) high.
£12-15 *OD*

An Imperial Glass marigold compote.
£25-30 *TS*

Cranberry Glass

A Fenton Art Glass green autumn acorns bowl.
£40-45 *TS*

A celery jar, 7½in (19cm) high.
£80-100 *BRK*

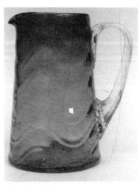

A milk jug, 6in (15cm) high.
£90-100 *BRK*

A cream jug, 4in (10cm) high.
£70-80 *BRK*

A bowl, 3in (8cm) high.
£80-95 *BRK*

A hyacinth vase, 6in (15cm) high.
£80-90 *BRK*

A cream jug, 4in (10cm) high.
£70-80 *BRK*

A baluster cream jug, 4½in (11cm) high.
£80-90 *BRK*

A trinket dish, 4½in (11cm) diam.
£75-85 *BRK*

A celery jar, 7in (18cm) high.
£80-100 *BRK*

An oil lamp, 20thC, 8½in (21cm) high.
£60-65 *PC*

DID YOU KNOW?
Miller's Collectables Price Guide is designed to build up, year by year, into the most comprehensive reference system available.

A decanter, 10in (25cm) high.
£150-170 *BRK*

Cross Reference
Lighting

Two salts, 4in (10cm) diam.
£50-60 *BRK*

Jobling Glass

A celery vase, 8in (20cm) high.
£80-100 *PC*

A bird ashtray, 1920s, 5in (13cm) high.
£60-80 *BEV*

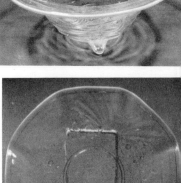

A plate, 12in (31cm) diam.
£80-100 *BEV*

A glass bowl with 3 feet, 11in (28cm) diam.
£120-150 *BEV*

A bowl, 6in (15cm) diam.
£30-35 *PC*

A glass vase, 1920s, 12in (31cm) high.
£100-150 *PC*

A glass plate, 10in (25cm) diam.
£55-65 *BEV*

A squirrel nut dish, 5in (13cm) diam.
£60-80 *BEV*

A glass dish, 10in (25cm) diam.
£55-65 *BEV*

A double-handled rose vase, 1920s, 8in (20cm) high.
£450-550 *BEV*

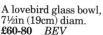

A lovebird glass bowl,
7½in (19cm) diam.
£60-80 BEV

A glass vase, 9½in
(24cm) high.
£100-150 BEV

A glass lovebird, 1920s,
4½in (11cm).
£100-120 BEV

Nailsea Glass

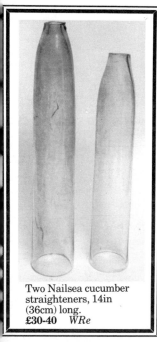

A green bottle glass jug
with opaque marvered
splashes, c1810, 5½in
(14cm) high.
£250-300 Som

A Nailsea type bell with
cranberry bowl, c1880,
11in (28cm) high.
£160-180 Som

Two Nailsea cucumber
straighteners, 14in
(36cm) long.
£30-40 WRe

Pressed Glass
Boots & Shoes

A pair of Sowerby brown,
amethyst and white
ornaments, marked,
c1880, 1½in (4cm) high.
£25-35 GH

A Sowerby marbleised
brown/amethyst and
white posy holder, trade
mark, c1880, 8in (20cm)
long.
£40-50 GH

A pair of Davidson amber tinted posy holders, unmarked, c1885, 5in (13cm) long.
£15-20 *GH*

Two Sowerby brown/amethyst and white posy vases, internal trade mark to one, c1880, 5in (13cm) long.
£25-30 each *GH*

A pair of Sowerby flint glass posy holders, unmarked, c1880, 5in (13cm) long.
£8-10 *GH*

Two Sowerby black opaque posy holders, internal trade mark to both, c1887, 5in (14cm) long.
£35-45 each *GH*

A Sowerby flint glass posy holder shoe, registration number 87058, 5in (13cm) long, and boot with simulated leather finish, unmarked, c1880, 3in (8cm).
£5-10 each *GH*

Commemorative

A Greener flint glass plate, registration mark for 1869, 8in (20cm) diam.
£25-30 *GH*

Two matching flint glass plates, unmarked, 1889, 5in (13cm) diam.
£4-6 each *GH*

A Greener flint glass saucer, inscribed George Peabody, marked, c1869, 5in (13cm) diam.
£20-25   *GH*

A pair of John Derbyshire translucent green figurines, Punch and Judy, both marked, c1875, 6½in (16cm) high.
£250-300   *GH*

A pair of translucent green busts, Gladstone and Disraeli, unmarked, c1880, 7in (18cm) high.
£300-350   *GH*

A Sowerby marigold jug, 5in (13cm) high.
£10-15   *TS*

A pair of J. J. & T. Derbyshire uranium coloured vases, both marked, 1871, 9in (23cm) high.
£100-150   *GH*

General

A Sowerby opaque white sugar bowl and cream jug, with moulded enamelled daisy and leaf pattern highlighted in red and green, both marked for 1879, both 3in (8cm) high.
£60-65   *GH*

Two Davidson flint glass plates, unmarked, c1885.
£20-25 each   *GH*

A Greener dark green glass tumbler, trade mark on base, c1880, 4in (10cm) high.
£12-15   *GH*

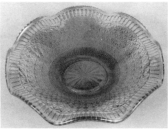

A Sowerby Ellison plate,
c1930, 8½in (21cm) diam.
£5-10 *TS*

A green pressed glass
dish, 8in (20cm) diam.
£5-10 *PC*

A Davidson blue pearline
tumbler, registration
number 130643 for 1899,
4½in (11cm) high.
£20-25 *GH*

A frosted flint glass
figurine bust of Our lady
of Lourdes, marked Cross
of Lorraine through S,
c1880, 7in (18cm) high.
£50-100 *GH*

A Davidson coral pink
pressed glass bowl, 1896,
8in (20cm) diam.
£24-30 *EAS*

A Molineaux Webb
frosted and clear flint
glass biscuit barrel, with
cover and stand, all with
diamond registration
marks for c1867, 8½in
(21cm) high.
£240-300 *GH*

A John Derbyshire
frosted and highlight
polished flint glass
figurine of Britannia,
trade mark and diamond
registration mark for
1874, 8in (20cm) high.
£210-250 *GH*

An opaque green/
turquoise sugar bowl,
attributed to Davidson,
unmarked, c1890, 2½in
(6cm) high.
£15-20 *GH*

A pair of Heppell opaque
white cream jugs,
marked for 1882, 5in
(12.5cm) high.
£40-50 *GH*

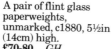

A pair of flint glass paperweights, unmarked, c1880, 5½in (14cm) high.
£70-80 *GH*

Three James Derbyshire flint glass stemmed goblets, all with diamond registration mark for 1866, 6in (15cm) high.
£25-30 each *GH*

A Davidson attributed marbleised blue and white cream jug, with coral handle, marked, c1885, 4in (10cm) high.
£25-30 *GH*

A Sowerby marbleised blue and white vase, with moulded decoration, unmarked, c1880, 4in (10cm) high.
£50-55 *GH*

A pair of marbleised blue and white vases, with moulded decoration, unmarked, c1880, 7in (18cm) high.
£80-90 *GH*

A Sowerby green malachite spill vase, unmarked, c1880, 4in (10cm) high.
£50-60 *GH*

A Davidson green malachite pomade pot with cover, unmarked, c1885, 4½in (11cm) high.
£140-150 *GH*

A Davidson marbleised brown/amethyst and white sweetmeat dish, with external moulded decoration, unmarked, c1885, 4½in (11cm) long.
£20-25 *GH*

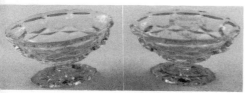

A pair of flint glass salts, unmarked, c1885, 3½in (9cm).
£20-25 *GH*

A marbleised turquoise and brown vase, with external moulded decoration, unmarked, c1875, 7in (18cm) high.
£170-200 *GH*

A Burtles Tate rose opalescent flower holder, registration No. 20086 for 1885, 7in (18cm) long.
£380-400 *GH*

A pair of marbleised brown/amethyst and white obelisks, unmarked, c1880, 8in (20cm) high.
£70-80 *GH*

A Sowerby Queen's ivory ware tea caddy and cover, with external moulded decoration, marked for 1879, 4in (10cm) high.
£250-300 *GH*

A Greener marbleised brown/amethyst and white teacup and saucer, both marked, c1880, saucer 6in (15cm) diam.
£65-70 *GH*

A Sowerby opaque white nine-piece dessert service comprising 2 small comports, a large comport and 6 plates, all marked, c1878.
£100-120 *GH*

A Sowerby aesthetic green plate, marked, c1880, 8in (20cm) diam.
£35-40 *GH*

A Heppell opaque white sugar bowl, with internal diamond registration mark, 1882, 5½in (14cm) high.
£45-50 *GH*

A Heppell opaque white butter dish and cover, both with internal diamond registration mark for 1882, 3½in (9cm) high.
£45-50 *GH*

An opaque white butter float and cover, with moulded leaf and berry decoration, unmarked, c1885, 7in (18cm) diam.
£35-40 *GH*

A Greener blue
opalescent comport
stand, unmarked, c1890,
5in (13cm) diam.
£15-20 *GH*

A Greener matching blue
opalescent lemonade jug
and goblet, registration
No. 217749 for 1893, jug
6in (15cm) high.
£30-40 *GH*

A black opaque
paperweight, unmarked,
c1885, 5½in (14cm) high.
£90-100 *GH*

A Burtles Tate yellow
opalescent flower holder,
registration No. 29106
for 1885, 6in (15cm) long.
£60-70 *GH*

A blue opaque vase with
external moulded
decoration, unmarked,
c1890, 8½in (21cm) high.
£35-40 *GH*

A Sowerby Queen's ivory
ware posy vase,
supported on 4 splayed
feet, marked for 1878,
3in (8cm) high.
£50-55 *GH*

A Sowerby Queen's ivory ware
'Venetian' blown jug,
with turquoise trailing to
neck rim, unmarked,
c1880, 2in (5cm) high.
£250-300 *GH*

A Sowerby Queen's ivory
ware posy vase,
supported on 4 splayed
feet, repaired, marked for
1878, 2½in (6cm) high.
£40-45 *GH*

A Greener white opaque sugar bowl, marked, c1880, 5½in (14cm) high.
£35-40   *GH*

A Greener blue opalescent domed night light cover, unmarked, c1890, 3in (8cm) high.
£22-30   *GH*

A Sowerby Queen's ivory ware spill vase, marked for 1879, 3½in (9cm) high.
£240-300   *GH*

l. A Sowerby turquoise opaque pin tray, with internal trade mark, c1876, 3in (8cm) diam.
£35-40   *GH*
r. A Davidson blue opaque spill vase, with external moulded shell and coral decoration, unmarked, c1890, 4in (10cm) high.
£20-25   *GH*

Vaseline Glass

A vaseline glass posy bowl, 3½in (9cm) high.
£20-25   *CAC*

A vaseline glass vase, 4in (10cm) high.
£15-20   *CAC*

A miniature vaseline glass tankard, 2in (7cm) high.
£2-3   *CAC*

A vaseline glass hanging vase, 8in (20cm) high.
£14-20   *CAC*

DID YOU KNOW?
Miller's Collectables Price Guide is designed to build up, year by year, into the most comprehensive reference system available.

20th Century Glass

A red glass wine cooler,
1930s, 12in (31cm).
£85-125   *CLH*

A Vasart glass posy bowl,
c1950, 8in (20cm) diam.
£40-45   *CSA*

A Vasart glass bowl,
c1950, 10in (25cm) diam.
£50-60   *CSA*

A Whitefriars trumpet
shaped vase, c1925, 11in
(28cm).
£100-120   *SWa*

A Stratbearn vase,
c1950, 4½in (11cm) high.
£16-18   *CSA*

A Whitefriars amethyst
vase, c1930, 8in (20cm)
high.
£65-75   *SWa*

See Miller's Collectables Volume II colour
section, pages 143-144 for larger selections
of these manufacturers.

Bottles & Flasks

A pair of glass flasks, amber and blue, 7½in (19cm) high.
£25-30 each   *CAC*

An engraved glass bottle, 4½in (11cm) high.
£3-5   *VB*

A green glass flask with pewter top, 7½in (19cm) high.
£38-40   *CAC*

Two flasks, c1860, 6½ and 8½in (16 and 21cm).
£90-100 each   *Som*

A Victorian glass smelling salts bottle, 2½in (6cm) high.
£30-35   *AD*

A Georgian cut glass toilet water bottle, 6in (15cm) high.
£80-100   *PC*

Custard Cups

Custard cups, 3 and 4in (8 and 10cm) high.
£4-6 each
VB

A Victorian custard cup, c1860, 3in (8cm) high.
£10-15   *VB*

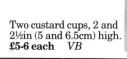

Two custard cups, 2 and 2½in (5 and 6.5cm) high.
£5-6 each   *VB*

Drinking Glasses

l. & r. A pair of bucket
rummers, c1830, 5in
(13cm) high.
£80-85
c. An ovoid rummer with
unusual terraced conical
foot, c1780, 5in (13cm)
high.
£85-90 *Som*

A pair of hollow stemmed
champagne flutes, 5in
(13cm) high.
£11-12 each *VB*

l. A pair of wine glasses,
c1810, 5in (12cm) high.
£50-55
Centre l. Two decorated
dram glasses, c1830,
2½in (6cm) high.
£35-40
Centre r. An engraved
tumbler, c1820, 3½in
(9cm) high.
£20-25
r. A plain tumbler with
flute cut base, 1830, 3in
(7.5cm) high.
£15-20 *Som*

A glass, c1840, 4½in
(11cm) high.
£15-20 *VB*

A pair of monogrammed
glasses, 4½in (11cm)
high.
£4-5 each *VB*

Four small wines, c1790,
4 to 5in (10.5 to 11.5cm)
high.
£25-30 each *Som*

A rummer,
c1850, 5in
(13cm) high.
£25-30 *VB*

A dram glass with red
spiral twist.
£125-130 *VB*

Two glasses with green
bowls, c1900, 5½in
(14cm) high.
£12-14 each *VB*

A firing glass,
4in (10cm) high.
£20-25 *VB*

Two pale green wine
glasses, 5in (13cm) high.
£5-6 each *VB*

DID YOU KNOW?
Firing glasses were manufactured to withstand
being used to gain people's attention by being
banged on a table, the noise sounding like a gun
going off.

A pair of Lalique daisy
liqueur glasses, c1930,
3in (8cm) high.
£50-70 pair *CSA*

An ale glass, c1740, 7in
(17cm) high.
£120-125 *VB*

A wine glass, c1800, 5in
(13cm) high.
£20-25 *VB*

A late 17thC ale glass
with tear drop in base,
8in (20cm) high.
£90-110 *VB*

l. A pair of wine glass
coolers with bridge fluted
bases, c1830, 4in (10cm)
high.
£60-70
r. A bell shaped jug with
plain foot, c1820, 4½in
(12cm) high.
£60-65 *Som*

Jelly Glasses

Five jelly glasses with rudimentary stems, trumpet bowls and plain conical feet, c1820, 4in (10cm) high.
£20-25 each

A pair of jelly glasses, c1780, 4in (10cm) high.
£70-75 *Som*

A jelly glass, 4in (10cm) high.
£15-20 *VB*

A pair of jelly glasses with prism and relief and small diamond cutting, c1830, 4½in (11cm) high.
£50-55 *Som*

Jugs

A Georgian cut glass cream jug, 4in (10cm) high.
£150-250 *PC*

A Continental gilt and enamel jug and bowl, c1920, jug 3in (8cm) high.
£40-50 *PC*

An engraved jug, 4in (10cm) high.
£16-18 *VB*

A square top jug, c1860, 5in (14cm) high.
£100-110 *PAR*

An engraved jug, 4in (10cm) high.
£9-10 *VB*

Perfume Bottles

Two scent bottles, in
amber and green, 5in
(13cm).
£40-50 each   *CLH*

A glass perfume flask,
6in (15cm) long.
£15-18   *PC*

l. An oblong fan cut scent
bottle with white metal
mount, c1830, 4in
(9.5cm) long.
r. An oblong scent bottle
with cut and gilt
decoration and white
metal mount, c1830,
3½in (9cm) long.
£90-95 each   *Som*

Three perfume bottles
with silver tops, ruby red
and green, c1880, 4 to 5in
(10 to 13cm) long.
£80-120   *PC*

A hobnail cut perfume
bottle, with silver plated
top, c1920, 4in (10cm)
high.
£25-30   *SA*

An Art Deco amber and
milk scent bottle, 3in
(8cm) high.
£35-45   *CLH*

Three 'throw away'
scents, Oxford lavenders,
with gilt decorations,
c1880.
£20-30 each   *Som*

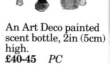

A pair of binocular/opera
glass type folding
double-ended scent
bottles, with silver tops,
c1870, 2½in (6cm) high.
£220-225   *PC*

An Art Deco painted
scent bottle, 2in (5cm)
high.
£40-45   *PC*

Two glass horn scent
bottles, top c1900, 4in
(10cm) long.
£80-100
and bottom, c1860, 2in
(5cm) long.
£150-170   *PC*

Two cut glass scent
bottles with silver tops,
late 19thC, 4in (10cm)
high.
£50-55 each   *PC*

A glass scent bottle with
gilt decoration, late
19thC, 3in (8cm) high.
£40-45   *PC*

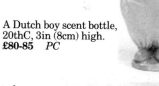

Two glass perfume
bottles with silver tops,
late 19thC/early 20thC,
l. 2½in (6cm) high.
£30-35
r. 3in (8cm) high.
£40-45   *PC*

A Dutch boy scent bottle,
20thC, 3in (8cm) high.
£80-85   *PC*

Two glass scent bottles,
20thC, l. 2½in (6cm) high
r. 2in (5cm) high.
£30-35 each   *PC*

l. An amethyst faceted
glass perfume bottle with
metal top, c1880, 3in
(8cm) long.
£150-160   *PC*
r. An amethyst faceted
glass perfume bottle with
embossed silver top,
c1860, 4in (10cm) long.
£200-210   *PC*

Two cut glass perfume
flasks, late 19thC,
l. with silver cap, 3in
(8cm) and
r. with brass top, 4½in
(11cm) high.
£30-35 each   *PC*

Two glass scent bottles
with silver tops, c1880,
2½ to 3in (6 to 8cm) high.
£120-130 each   *PC*

A blue glass perfume
flask with enamel
decoration and silver cap,
c1880, 5½in (14cm) long.
£75-80   *PC*

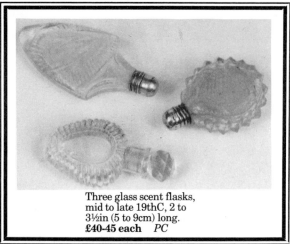

Three glass scent flasks,
mid to late 19thC, 2 to
3½in (5 to 9cm) long.
£40-45 each *PC*

A glass perfume bottle
with intaglio decoration
and silver top, early
20thC, 3½in (6cm) high.
£100-110 *PC*

l. A hand painted scent
bottle with brass top,
early 20thC, 2½in (6cm)
high.
£40-45
c. Milk glass scent bottle
with silver top, early
20thC, 3½in (9cm) high.
£60-65
r. Blue glass scent bottle
with brass top, early
20thC, 2½in (6cm) high.
£40-45 *PC*

A vaseline glass scent
bottle, c1900, 4in (10cm)
high.
£60-65 *PC*

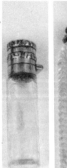

Three scent bottles, 2 to
2½in (5 to 7cm) high.
£40-50 each *PC*

A clear glass scent bottle
with gilt decoration,
c1900, 3½in (9cm) long.
£40-45 *PC*

Three glass
scent bottles,
3 to 3½in
(8 to 9cm)
long.
£30-40 each
PC

A cut glass scent bottle
with silver top, early
20thC, 3½in (9cm) high.
£50-55 *PC*

FURTHER READING
Commercial Perfume Bottles, Jacquelyne
Jones-North.
Perfume, Cologne and Scent Bottles, Jacquelyne
Jones-North, Millbank Books, U.K.

Measures

A measuring glass, 3in (8cm).
£2-3 *VB*

A measuring jug, 6in (15cm) high.
£4-5 *VB*

A glass measuring jug, 5in (12cm) high.
£8-9 *VB*

Salts

A cut glass shoe, part of a condiment set, 20thC, 3in (7.5cm) wide.
£15-20 *PC*

A ruby flashed salt cellar, 20thC, 2½in (6.5cm) diam.
£20-30 *PC*

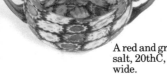

A red and green millefiori salt, 20thC, 4in (10cm) wide.
£20-25 *PC*

Pickle Jars

A pickle jar, 6½in (16.5cm) high.
£12-15 *VB*

A cut glass pickle jar, 6½in (16.5cm) high.
£12-15 *VB*

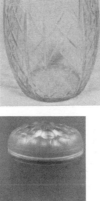

A Jobling pickle jar and lid, c1925, 5½in (14cm) high.
£40-60 *BEV*

A cut glass pickle jar, 6in (15cm) high.
£8-12 *VB*

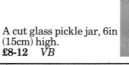

Vases

Opaline Glass Vases

A Victorian crackle glass vase, 8in (20cm) high.
£15-20 *OD*

An opaline glass vase, 9in (23cm) high.
£30-35 *EAS*

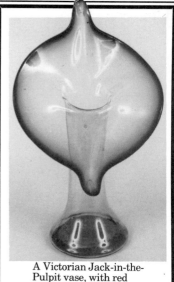

A Victorian Jack-in-the-Pulpit vase, with red decoration, 9½in (24cm) high.
£55-65 *TS*

An opaline cream glass vase, 8in (20cm) high.
£25-30 *EAS*

Two eau-de-nil satin glass vases, with enamel decoration.
£35-45 *EAS*

A bud vase with thorn ridges, 8½in (21cm) high.
£60-70 *PAR*

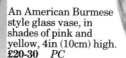

A green and white streaked glass vase, 20thC, 8in (20cm) high.
£20-25 *PC*

An American Burmese style glass vase, in shades of pink and yellow, 4in (10cm) high.
£20-30 *PC*

A green overlay glass cut and engraved toilet water vial, silver top missing, 6½in (16.5cm) high.
£100-120 *PC*

A turquoise blue satin vase, with enamel decoration, 8in (20cm) high.
£45-55 *EAS*

A Mary Gregory cranberry glass powder bowl, 19thC, 2½in (6.5cm) diam.
£100-150 *PC*

A cut glass toddy lifter, c1850, 6in (15cm) high.
£80-100 *PC*

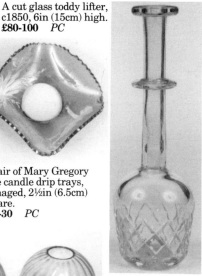

A pair of Mary Gregory blue candle drip trays, damaged, 2½in (6.5cm) square.
£25-30 *PC*

Three glass gas lampshades, 6in (15cm) high.
£8-15 each *WRe*

A pair of opaline glass vases, 12in (30.5cm) high.
£180-200 *EAS*

A cut glass night light holder, 4½in (11.5cm) high.
£45-50 *PC*

An amber cut glass dish, 4in (10cm) wide.
£15-20 *PC*

General

A pair of mugs, with gadrooned bases and strap handles, each decorated with floral engraving and monogram RK, the covers star cut with cut flat finials, 4½in (11cm) high.
£110-130 *Som*

Sand Pictures

A selection of sand pictures.
£2-7 each *VB*

A Latticinio bowl, 4in (10cm) diam.
£30-40 *PC*

A Victorian smoke bell.
£40-50 *BRK*

Used to hang over oil lamps to prevent smoke.

A glass lustre, 5in (12.5cm) high.
£50-60 *PC*

A glass fly trap, c1820, 7in (17.5cm) high.
£35-45 *IS*

Two French green glass boxes, with gilt fittings, 3½in (9cm) wide.
l. cut glass **£130-150**
r. opaline **£230-250** *PC*

A gilt, ormolu and green glass ornamental box, with lock and key, 3½in (8.5cm) high.
£250-300 *PC*

A pair of blue cloud glass candlesticks, 2½in (6cm) high.
£20-30 *PC*

A glass and silver match striker in the form of a sea urchin, with plain silver mount, Birmingham 1905.
£200-225 *WIL*

FURTHER READING
How to Identify English Drinking Glasses and Decanters, D. Ash, London 1962.
Eighteenth Century English Drinking Glasses, L. M. Bickerton, 1986.
The Arthur Negus Guide to British Glass, J. Brooks, 1981.
English Glass, R. J. Charleston, 1984.
English and Irish Antique Glass, D. C. Davis, 1964.
Glass and Glassmaking, R. Dodsworth, 1982.
Collector's Dictionary of Glass, E. M. Elville, 1961.
Masterpieces of Glass, D. B. Harden and Others, British Museum, 1968.
English Glass for the Collector, G. B. Hughes, 1958.
Old Glass, O. N. Wilkinson, 1968.
Country Life Pocket Book of Glass, G. Wills, 1966.

Hairdressing & Hatpins

A tortoiseshell hair slide,
2in (5cm) wide.
£10-20 *LEW*

For a further selection of hairdressing
items and hatpins, please refer to Miller's
Collectables Vol. I, p.208.

A collection of hatpins.
50p to £30 each *VB*

A tortoiseshell comb,
4½in (11.5cm) long.
£5-8 *LB*

DID YOU KNOW?
It was the ancient Egyptians who discovered that
hair could be made to curl by the application of
heated irons.

A tortoiseshell comb,
with paste decoration,
6in (15cm) long.
£18-25 *LB*

Hatpin holders.
£9-14 *VB*

Inkwells

A lead pen holder and
inkwell, 2in (5cm) high.
£20-25 *OD*

Cross Reference
Writing Accessories

A deer's foot inkwell, 4in
(10cm) high.
£40-50 *BRK*

A Victorian non-spill
inkwell, 2½in (6.5cm)
high.
£8-10 *CA*

247

A Wemyss inkstand, 7in (17.5cm) wide.
£250-300 *SBA*

An inkstand, 6½in (16.5cm) diam.
£50-55 *CA*

l. A screw top inkwell, c1900, 1½in (4cm) high.
£30-40
c. A crystal glass inkwell with brass top, 19thC, 2in (5cm) high.
£70-80
r. A cut glass inkwell with nickel plated top, c1920, 2in (5cm) high.
£30-40 *BS*

A glass inkwell, 5in (12.5cm) diam.
£60-70 *BRK*

A glass inkwell, 3½in (8.5cm) high.
£40-50 *BRK*

An early porcelain inkwell, unmarked, 3½in (9cm) wide.
£150-200 *SBA*

A selection of inkwells, c1900, 1½ to 2in (4 to 5cm) high.
£30-60 each *BS*

A Continental brass inkstand and pen rest, c1900, 8in (20cm) wide.
£220-240 *BS*

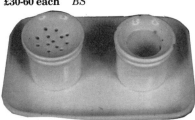

A white pottery inkstand, 8in (20cm) wide.
£10-15 *AL*

FURTHER READING
Writing Antiques, George Mell, Shire Publications Ltd.
Inkstands and Inkwells, Betty and Ted Rivera, Crown Publishers Inc, New York, 1973.
Writing Implements and Accessories, Joyce Irene Whalley, David and Charles, 1975.

A cranberry glass powder bowl, 3½in (9cm).
£140-160 *BRK*
l. A cranberry glass bulb grower, 5in (13cm) high.
£80-90 *BRK*

A highly decorative Mill vase, c1880, 6in (15.5cm) high.
£150-200 *Som*

A light green crown glass snuff jar, with turned over rim, c1810, 9in (23cm) high.
£130-150 *Som*

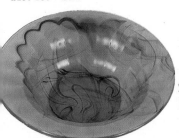

A cloud glass bowl, c1928, 9½in (24cm) diam.
£20-25 *CSA*

A carnival glass Good Luck bowl by Northwood, c1920, 9in (23cm) diam.
£50-60 *CSA*

An amethyst carnival glass flat comport, c1920.
£60-70 *CSA*

A green cloud glass dish, c1930, 14½in (37cm) long.
£35-40 *CSA*

l. An Art Nouveau Continental glass vase, with pewter handles, the scarlet body overlaid with globular peacock colours, probably Loetz.
£750-800 *MN*

A French opalescent vase with fish design, c1910.
£40-45 *CSA*

A crackle glass vase, 8in (20cm) high.
£50-80 *PC*

249

A pair of blue sauce bottles, with gilt labels and stoppers, c1790.
£550-600   *Som*

A Ketchup sauce bottle, c1790. **£130-150**
A pair of sauce bottles, c1810. **£400-450**   *Som*

A Newcastle blue glass rolling pin painted with enamels, c1820.
£80-100   *IS*

A Nailsea type crown glass carafe, with loop decoration, c1840, 7½in (19cm).
£240-260   *Som*

Three green wines, c1830, 4½in (12cm) high.
£50-75 each   *Som*

A pair of turquoise green wines and a pair of finger bowls, c1830.
£60-80 each   *Som*

A set of 8 hollow stem champagne glasses, with overlay facet cut stems, c1860, 5½in (13cm).
£250-300   *Som*

A pair of wines, with conical bowls, plain stems and shoulder collars, c1830.
£40-60 each   *Som*

A Nailsea crown glass storage jar, c1800.
£100-120   *Som*

A sugar basin and cream jug, c1780.
£150-180 each   *Som*

A Nailsea crown glass giant pestle, c1820, 35½in (90cm). **£50-70** and a Nailsea crown glass cream pan, 9in (23cm) diam. **£120-150**   *Som*

l. A carafe with inscription, c1852. **£120-150**
r. A glass boot, c1820, 4½in (11cm) high. **£180-200**   *Som*

Two egg cups, c1800, 3in (8cm).
£120-150 each   *Som*

250

A Davidson
pearline night
light on ceramic
base, 19thC.
£100-130   *PC*

Two vases by
Powell, both
with applied
decoration,
1920s.
£100-150   *FA*

A Bohemian
art glass vase,
c1930, 7in
(18cm) high.
£40-60   *FA*

A Bohemian
beaker, c1890.
£60-80   *Som*
r. A Bohemian
cut glass jug.
£85-95   *CSA*

A Vasart vase,
8in (20cm) high.
£50-70   *FA*

A Vasart table lamp
base, with millefiori
chips, 7in (18cm) high.
£60-75   *FA*

r. A Continental
jewelled candle top,
2½in (6cm) high.
£50-60   *PC*

A Monart vase decorated
with blue and white
'cloisonne', c1925.
£2,000-2,500   *FA*

A Vasart vase,
10in (25cm) high.
£70-80   *PC*

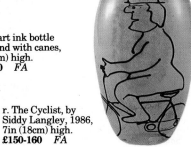

l. A Vasart ink bottle
red ground with canes,
4in (10cm) high.
£100-120   *FA*

r. The Cyclist, by
Siddy Langley, 1986,
7in (18cm) high.
£150-160   *FA*

A combed pattern glass
vase, c1880, 5½in (14cm)
high. **£80-100**   *PC*

251

A Webbs opaline biscuit barrel, with plated mount and lid, c1880. **£400-450** *Som*

An oval scent bottle with diamond and prism cutting, c1820. **£80-90** *Som* l. A gold plated chatelaine scent bottle, 3in (8cm) high. **£40-60** *AD*

A vaseline scent bottle, with silver top, c1860, 3in (8cm) high. **£150-160** *LEW*

Three perfume bottles: l. & r. With brass tops. **£70-80 each** c. With embossed silver top, 4½in (12cm) high. **£130-140** *PC*

Perfume bottles: l. With silver top, c1890, 3½in (9cm) high. **£50-55** c. Decorated red glass, early 20thC, 4½in (11cm) high. **£50-55** r. A glass barrel shape, c1880, 3in (8cm) high. **£80-85** *PC*

An amethyst cut glass scent bottle, with silver top, c1900, 5in (13cm) high. **£200-220** *PC*

A Mary Gregory perfume bottle with silver top, c1900, 4in (10cm) high. **£150-160** *PC* r. Cranberry glass scent bottles: l. 20thC. **£100-120** c. c1880. **£80-90** r. c1885. **£130-140** *PC*

Two hand painted miniature scent bottles, early 20thC. **£80-100 each** *PC*

A blue glass perfume bottle, with gilt decoration, c1900, 3in (8cm) high. **£150-160** *PC* l. A Continental jewelled top night light, 19thC. **£80-100** *PC*

A bronze and Siena marble giant watch stand, with 8-day silver mounted desk watch. **£2,000-2,500** *RFA*

A watchstand, c1880. **£90-100** *EHA*

r. A Palais Royale gold mounted mother-of-pearl writing set, c1830, 7½ by 10in (19 by 25cm). **£500-600** *CA*

A brass mounted and ebony T-framed octant with bone scale, the arc engraved with a 90 degree scale mounted with reflectors, signed Wilson of London, mid-18thC. **£300-350** *FEN*

r. A mahogany cigar dispenser, c1840, 10 by 7in (25 by 18cm). **£340-380** *EHA*

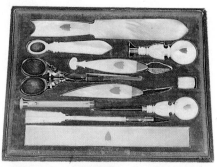

l. A selection of Victorian writing items. **£100-170 each** Seal. **£45-50** *CA*

A Minton & Holland tile, mounted in a pine candle box, 12in (31cm) high. **£35-40** *CA*
r. A binnacle deck compass, within brass casing, with window at the front and oil lighting unit at the side, on an octagonal teak base, by Wilhelm Ludolph of Bremen, c1905, 62in (157cm) high. **£500-550** *FEN*

A selection of 20thC fountain pens and pencils. **£400-700 each** except horizontal Mont Blanc safety pen. **£2,600-3,000** *Bon*
r. A tortoiseshell and enamel pen, by Cartier, in original fitted case. **£2,000-2,500** *C*

A pair of J & W Cary terrestrial and celestial globes, 3in (7.5cm) diam.
£4,000-4,500   *CSK*

Two terrestrial globes, each with maker's label, mid-19thC.
£2,000-2,500 each   *CSK*

A Cary brass transit telescope, No. 1966, 19½in (49.5cm) high.
£1,500-2,000   *CSK*

l. A lady miniature, by Simon Jacques Rochard, minor crack, 19thC, framed, 3in (7.5cm) high.
£1,400-1,600   *C*

A lacquered and silvered brass equinoctial dial, early 19thC, 4in (10cm) long.
£1,000-1,500   *CSK*

l. A gentleman miniature, attributed to Matthew Snelling, on vellum, in silver gilt frame, 17thC, 2½in (6cm) high.
£7,000-8,000   *C*

A lacquered brass Nairne-type chest microscope, in lined mahogany case, early 19thC, 11½in (29.5cm) wide.
£2,000-2,500   *CSK*

Miniatures, by P. L. Bouvier, signed, dated 1806.
£3,500-4,000   *C*

A miniature of Mrs. George Bankes and her 3 children, by Simon Jacques Rochard, signed dated 1828, 9in (22.5cm).
£5,000-5,500   *C*

A lady miniature, by François Theodore Rochard, in ormolu frame, signed and dated 1820, 3½in (9cm) high.
£1,000-1,200   *C*

A miniature of Louisa Plimer, the artist's daughter, by Andrew Plimer, in red leather case, 3½in (8.5cm) high.
£5,000-5,500   *C*

A miniature of a young girl, by John Smart, signed and dated 1804, 3in (7.5cm) high.
£8,000-8,500   *C*

A child's quilted cot cover.
£80-90   *AL*

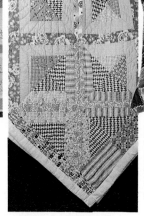

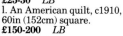

A crazy paving patchwork
cushion, made from Edwardian
velvets, 14 by 17in
(35.5 by 43cm).
£25-30   *LB*
l. An American quilt, c1910,
60in (152cm) square.
£150-200   *LB*

A cushion made from a hand woven
Paisley shawl, 19thC, 16 by 24in
(41 by 61cm).
£40-60   *LB*

An American Nashville
quilt, c1910, 75in
(190cm). **£80-90**   *LB*

A beadwork
cushion,
c1900.
£150-200   *LB*

A fine framed beadwork
sampler, c1900, 9in
(22.5cm) square overall.
£200-300   *LB*

A silk on linen
framed sampler,
c1846, 10½in
(26.5cm) square.
£80-100   *LB*

A wool on wool
netting sampler,
c1900, 13in
(33cm) square.
£40-50   *LB*
r. Various
bundles of silk
and velvet
flowers,
Victorian/
Edwardian.
£2-6 each   *LB*

An ivory 332
telephone,
1950s.
£200-250   *CAB*

A red 232 telephone,
c1955. **£350-400**   *CAB*

A green 232 telephone,
c1938. **£350-400**   *CAB*

The type 232 telephone was first produced in 1933.

255

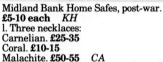

Midland Bank Home Safes, post-war.
£5-10 each *KH*
l. Three necklaces:
Carnelian. **£25-35**
Coral. **£10-15**
Malachite. **£50-55** *CA*

A metal Coronation
money box, 1953, in
its original box,
3½in (9cm) high.
£18-20 *BY*

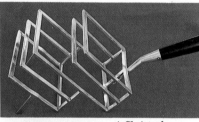

A Christopher
Dresser silver
plated toast
rack.
£18-22,000 *DEN*

A leather covered brass
counter box, with
original counters,
dated 1788, 2in (5cm)
high. **£135-150** *EHA*

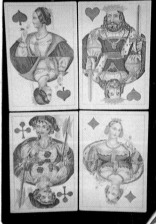

A pack of
playing
cards,
c1930.
£10-15 *RTT*

A W. H. Ell's
Patent Safe
Check, No. 22067
dated 1887.
£260-300 *FEN*
l. A papier
mâché crumb tray
and brush, c1910.
£75-95 *UC*

A part set of hand
painted court cards.
£140-150 *SHO*

l. Waddingtons
playing cards.
£10-12 *RTT*
r. A Carlton
Ware money box,
c1960. **£10-15** *PC*

A needlework and beadwork down filled cushion, 17in (43cm) square. **£90-110** *MAT*

A silk school cap, with tassel. **£40-70** *MSh*

A silk school cap, with tassel. **£40-70** *MSh*

A parrot's head tape measure, c1880. **£50-60** *CA*

A Cavalier Flake tin, one of Hignett's classic tins, c1912, 7in (18cm) wide. **£50-100** *K*

A Seidlitz Powders tin, c1930, 6in (15cm) wide. **£15-25** *K*

l. A fly spray tin, 1930s. **£15-20** *K*

A double sided enamel sign, Three Castles Cigarettes, by Wills, lettering only on reverse, c1925. **£150-200** *K*

An enamel sign, 1d. Monsters fizzy drink, c1900, 24in (61cm) wide. **£80-100** *K*

Mambo talcum powder tin with contents. **£10-15** *RTT*

Price's Piano Candles, in original box unopened, 9in (22.5cm) high. **£15-25** *BY*

A Hudson's Soap enamel sign, dated 2/25. **£60-80** *K*

l. Snake Charmer Cigarettes, a Salmon & Gluckstein tin, c1920, 4½in (12cm) high. **£15-25** *K*

l. Mackintosh's toffee tin, c1930, 10in (25cm) diam. **£20-25** *RTT*

Edmonds Baking Powder, New Zealand, c1930. **£20-25** *RTT*

A Macfarlane Lang trunk, 1913.
£90-110 *K*

A Tiger Lily cigarette tin, keenly
sought after, c1900.
£100-150 *K*

l. A small cut out tin sign, 1950s.
£50-75 *K*

A Stotherts Art Deco
string tin. **£40-50** *K*
r. A string tin, c1925.
£40-50 *K*

A tin box shop
display,
Edwardian.
£75-85 *K*
l. A Huntley &
Palmers biscuit
tin, 19thC.
£90-110 *K*

A Robertson's Toffee tin, shop counter type,
c1925. **£30-40** *K*

Victorian badges.
£10-25 each *K*

A Football Association metal
badge, 1932. **£20-30** *K*

A selection of pop pin buttons.
£1-5 each *K*

r. An Art Deco
plastic buckle,
handmade, c1930.
£35-55 *K*

258

A Union Jack Turns Into A
Bloody Cross.
£500-600 *CSK*

Guitar Turns Into A
Powerful Car, 11½ by 16½in
(29 by 42cm).
£250-350 *CSK*

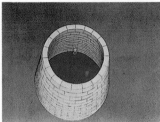

Pink Encircled By The Wall.
£700-800 *CSK*

A set of pencil drawings,
The Flowers In Sensual Embrace.
£1,200-1,400 *CSK*

Electric Guitar,
11½ by 16½in (29 by 42cm).
£450-550 *CSK*

The Teacher Turns Into A
Hammer.
£3,000-3,500 *CSK*

The Start Of Pink's
Metamorphis.
£250-350 *CSK*

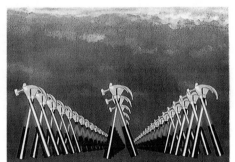

Ranks Of Hammers Marching In Formation,
11½ by 16½in (29 by 42cm).
£1,500-2,000 *CSK*

The Arrival
Of The
Schoolmaster.
£500-550 *CSK*

Machine-Gun Fire,
11½ by 16½in (29 by 42cm).
£300-400 *CSK*

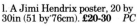

The Wall Begins To Close In Around
Pink. **£900-1,000** *CSK*
**A selection of Animation Art
Material, from Pink Floyd The Wall.**

Hypodermic Syringe,
11½ by 16½in (29 by 42cm).
£150-250 *CSK*

l. A Jimi Hendrix poster, 20 by
30in (51 by 76cm). **£20-30** *PC*

A Wurlitzer 2810 juke box,
Serial No. 605664, in wood
and metal case, with 100
record selection and
original coin mechanism.
£1,000-2,000 *CAm*

l. A Wurlitzer 2104 juke box, Serial No. 286547,
wood and chrome, with 104 record selection,
1957. **£2,000-3,000** *CAm*
c. A Rock-Ola 1426 juke box, Serial No. 101031,
in wooden case, with 20 record selection,
reconditioned, 1947. **£3,500-4,000** *CAm*
r. A Wurlitzer 1100 juke box, Serial No. 2107826,
1948. **£6,000-7,000** *CAm*

A Wurlitzer 1015
juke box, Serial
No. 1022010,
with 17 records,
American coins
and blank paper.
£9-10,000 *CAm*

A Wurlitzer 1015
juke box,
Serial No.
2065009,
renovated,
1948 style.
£7,500-8,500 *C*

A Wurlitzer 1015
juke box, Serial
No. 1017314, 24
record selection,
reconditioned,
1946.
£6,500-7,500 *CAm*

A Wurlitzer 1400
juke box, Serial
No. 18015, with
48 record
selection,
c1952.
£2,000-3,000 *CAm*

A Seeburg Envoy
juke box,
Serial No. 84924,
restored, 1938.
£2,000-3,000 *CAm*

A Rock-Ola 1428
juke box,
Serial No.
109968, 20
record
selection, 1948,
reconditioned.
£3,000-4,000 *CAm*

r. A Seeburg
Symphonola 1-48
juke box, 1948,
restored.
£3,000-4,000 *CAm*

A Wurlitzer 1250 juke box, Serial
No. 2327583, with 48 record selection,
1950. **£1,500-2,000** *CAm*
Above r. A Rock-Ola Monarch juke
box, Serial No. 34510, 1938.
£1,500-2,000 *CAm*

l. A Wurlitzer
42 Victory juke
box, 24 record
selection,
restored, c1945.
£11-12,000 *CAm*

An AMX-D juke
box, 40 record
selection,
1951.
£1,000-2,000 *CAm*

ANYTHING AMERICAN

INCORPORATING VINTAGE JUKEBOX

Specialists in Rare and Classic Jukeboxes
& American Collectibles

33-35 DUDDEN HILL LANE, LONDON NW10 2ES. TELEPHONE: 081-451 0320 FAX: 081-459 0044

A Steiff teddy bear, with hump and growler, some damage, c1907. **£3,000-4,000**   *C*

A Steiff teddy bear, 1930s. **£3,000-4,000**   *C*

l. A Steiff Petsy bear, with googlie eyes, 18in (46cm) high. **£2,000-3,000**   *C*

A teddy bear made by Merrythought for the Coronation in 1953. **£150-200**   *TED*

A Merrythought bear, with button in right ear, c1936. **£150-200**   *TED*

Pooh, Kanga, Tigger and Eeyore, made by Gund, c1964. **£200-250 the set**   *TED*

The Wedding Bears, c1938, 7½in (19cm) high. **£160-200**   *C*

An Ives clockwork Father Christmas, patent mark, 10in (25cm) high. **£5,000-5,500**   *CNY*

A Chiltern bear in silk clown outfit, 1950s, 11in (28cm). **£100-150**   *TED*

l. A Marconi 279AC transportable receiver, 1934. **£65-220**   *RC*

l. A Philips 310A radio, the perspex grille lights up when set is working, 1952. **£40-120**   *RC*

An Ekco AD65 radio, designed by Wells Coates, 1934. **£350-450**   *RC*

A Bing double garage with open Renault and Town Car, both clockwork powered, c1920. **£900-1,350** *MIN*

A Schuco fire engine with battery operated motor and adjustable steering, 1955. **£2,000-2,700** *MIN*

A Gunthermann open/closed 4 seater car, with clockwork mechanism, chauffeur and adjustable steering, c1928. **£2,000-2,400** *MIN*

A painted wooden Noah's Ark, with sliding side containing over 200 animals and 8 figures, Sonneberg 19thC, 27in (69cm) wide. **£6,000-6,500** *C*

A painted wooden toy butcher's shop, with marbleised slabs, stamped C H Schutzmarke, c1895. **£5,000-6,000** *C*

The Old Woman who lived in a Shoe with peg dolls, 8in (20cm) long. **£250-275** *LEW*

A collection of lead animals given away with Cadburys drinking chocolate and stamped Cadburys, c1930, 1 to 2in (3 to 5cm) high. **£130-150** *CA*

A wooden apple filled with skittles, 1930s, 3in (8cm) high. **£20-25** *CA*
r. A celluloid battery operated figure, The Waitress, Japanese, 1950s, 9in (23cm) high. **£125-150** *PC*

A set of circus figures, including an elephant standing on a drum, 1 to 5in (3 to 13cm) high. **£250-300** *CA*

l. A battery operated tinplate and plastic fork lift robot, movable legs, arms lifting platform, with box, by Horikawa, 1960s.
£550-600 *CAm*

A battery operated tinplate robot, with remote control, by Daiya, 1960s, 7½in (19cm) high.
£200-220 *CAm*

A clockwork robot, tinplate and plastic, by Yoshiya, 1960s. **£200-220** *CAm*

l. Lincoln International, Jaguar E Type.
£200-225 *MIN*
r. Victory Industries, Coles Ranger, Tower mounted crane.
£600-650 *MIN*

Palitoy Captain Zargon Action Man.
£30-35 *MIN*

Dinky 477, Parsley's Car.
£100-125 *MIN*

A Denys Fisher The Bionic Woman.
£15-25 *MIN*

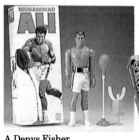

A Denys Fisher Muhammad Ali.
£15-25 *MIN*

J. Rosenthal (Toys) Ltd. Thunderbird 5.
£120-140 *MIN*
l. A Scalextric 65, Austin Healey 3000 and Mercedes 190 SL.
£400-500 *MIN*

l. A Japanese celluloid mechanical dancing doll, 1967. **£75-100**   *PC*

A Japanese celluloid Mickey on Pluto, by Masudaya, tinplate front wheel, keywind mechanism, in original box. **£6,000-6,500**   *CNY*

r. A Steiff Turkey, 6in (15cm) high. **£100-130**   *IS*

l. Two Dinky delivery vans, Heinz van with original box. **£1,500-3,000 each**   *CSK*

A rare Märklin 20-Volt 3-rail electric LMS E800 Compound locomotive and tender, with 3 trucks, some in original boxes, some track, 1938. **£22,000-25,000**   *C*

A French papier mâché growling bulldog. **£350-400**   *LT*

l. A rare Barney Google and Spark Plug scooter race, on 2 separate connected bases, c1924, 8in (20cm) long. **£5,000-5,500**   *CNY*

265

An Alps Japanese Lincoln Futura experimental car, 1956, 12in (31cm) long. **£3,000-3,800** *MIN*

A battery operated tinplate Batmobile with box, by Aoshin, Japanese, 1960s, 11½in (30cm) long. **£450-500** *CAm*

Goofy with wheelbarrow, with box, 5½in (14cm) long. **£40-50** *YON*
l. A Pink Panther car, with box, 8½in (21cm) long. **£35-45** *YON*

A Linemar Japanese tinplate Popeye in a rowboat, one oar missing. **£3,500-4,000** *CNY*

A Bestmaid mechanical Marionette Theatre, Japanese, c1938. **£2,800-3,000** *CNY*

A German Hessmobil with fly-wheel/friction mechanism, 1904. **£3,000-3,250** *MIN*

A Marusan model of the Mercedes Benz 300 SL, in its original box, Japanese, 1955. **£2,000-2,500** *MIN*

A Lionel Mickey Mouse handcar, in original box, 2 cracks on legs. **£1,500-2,000** *CNY*

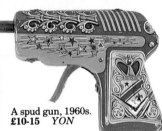

A spud gun, 1960s.
£10-15 *YON*

A Mettoy 8-cylinder, 4-door sports saloon, with clockwork motor and adjustable steering, c1935, 14½in (37cm) long. **£2,000-2,800** *MIN*

A Marx keywind Popeye The Champ, c1935.
£4,000-5,000 *CNY*

Two motor cycles, English and Japanese, 1950s.
£20-30 each *RTT*

A Cromato American Auto Spyder, battery and clockwork powered, with music box. **£1,000-1,750** *MIN*

A late Victorian rocking horse,
50in (125cm) high.
£1,500-2,000   *P(C)*

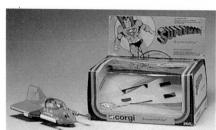

Corgi 265 Supermobile.
£25-35   *MIN*

J. Rosenthal (Toys) Ltd
Thunderbird I. **£100-150**   *MIN*

Yesteryear Y-2 1914 Prince Henry
Vauxhall. **£25-35**   *MIN*

Matchbox 21 Foden
Concrete Truck. **£15-25**   *MIN*

Yesteryear Y-6 1913 Cadillac.
£10-20   *MIN*

Dinky 27
Tramcar.
£800-900   *MIN*

Matchbox 46 Morris Minor 1000.
£65-75   *MIN*

Yesteryear Y-11 Aveling & Porter
Steam Roller. **£85-95**   *MIN*

Yesteryear Y-5 1907 Peugeot.
£10-20   *MIN*

l. Dinky Dublo
062 Singer
Roadster.
£75-85 *MIN*

r. Dinky 12D
Telegraph
Messengers.
£130-150 *MIN*

l. Hornby
Series 1
Luggage and
Trolley.
£320-370 *MIN*

r. Hornby
Series 21
Train Set.
£1,500-1,750 *MIN*

l. French Dinky
17 Train Set.
£1,000-1,100 *MIN*

r. Hornby
Series 3
Platform
Accessories.
£380-420 *MIN*

Dinky 3 Railway
Passengers.
£240-270 *MIN*

r. Dinky 3
Railway
Passengers.
£100-150 *MIN*

Dinky 13 Hall's Distemper
Advertisement. **£650-750** *MIN*

Corgi GS12
Chipperfield Circus
Crane Truck and Animal
Cage. **£165-195** *MIN*
l. Corgi 1143 American
La France Aerial Rescue
Truck. **£70-80** *MIN*

MINT & BOXED

ANTIQUE AND COLLECTABLE TOYS

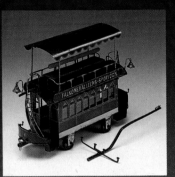

THE FINEST SELECTION OF ANTIQUE & COLLECTABLE TOYS

MINT & BOXED
ANTIQUE AND COLLECTABLE TOYS

l. Corgi 474 Walls Ice Cream Van. **£90-100**   *MIN*
r. Corgi 508 Commer Holiday Bus. **£55-65**   *MIN*

Dinky 280D Bisto Van. **£750-800**   *MIN*

Corgi 418 Austin FX4 Taxi.
£35-45   *MIN*

Corgi 246 Chrysler Imperial.
£55-65   *MIN*

l. Corgi 305 Triumph TR3 Sports. **£85-95**   *MIN*
r. Corgi 302 Hillman Hunter Rally Car. **£75-85**   *MIN*

l. Corgi 481 Chevrolet Police Car. **£50-55**   *MIN*
r. Corgi 439 Chevrolet Fire Chief. **£55-65**   *MIN*

Dinky 581 Horse Box, U.S.A. Issue. **£1,000-1,250**   *MIN*

French Dinky 512 Kart.
£55-65   *MIN*

French Dinky 1417 Matra Formula 1.
£35-45   *MIN*

l. Dinky 289 Routemaster Bus. **£65-75**   *MIN*
r. Dinky 300 Massey Harris Tractor. **£45-55**   *MIN*

A Rolex 18ct gold lady's
Oyster Perpetual
datejust wristwatch,
with gold Presidential
bracelet.
£1,500-2,000 *CSK*

A Piaget 18ct white gold
automatic wristwatch.
£900-1,000 *CSK*

A Piaget 18ct
white and
yellow gold
wristwatch.
£1,200-1,400
CSK

A Cartier gold steel
and diamond set
automatic wristwatch,
with steel flexible
bracelet.
£1,400-1,600 *CSK*

A Bulgari 18ct
gold wristwatch,
in original
case, 1988.
£1,000-1,200
CSK

l. A Concord Watch Co.
lady's wristwatch, 1930s.
£1,000-1,200 *CSK*
r. A Bulgari 18ct gold
quartz wristwatch, with
original leather strap.
£1,000-1,500 *CSK*

A Vacheron &
Constantin,
Geneve, Royal
Chronometer
automatic
wristwatch, in
original
packaging, with
guarantee dated
28th February
1986.
£2,500-2,800
CSK

A gentleman's Patek
Philippe gold and
diamond wristwatch.
£2,500-3,000 *CSK*

A gold Rolex
Oyster wrist-
watch, dial
cracked.
£1,200-1,500
CSK

A gold Rolex Oyster Precision wristwatch,
dial discoloured. **£350-450** *CSK*
r. A gold Rolex Oyster Perpetual Chronometer
wristwatch, with leather strap.
£1,400-1,600 *CSK*

A gold Rolex Oyster
Perpetual chronometer
wristwatch.
£950-1,000 *CSK*

l. A gold Rolex Oyster Perpetual chronometer wristwatch with bubble back. **£3,000-3,500** *CSK*
r. A gold Rolex Oyster Perpetual chronometer wristwatch in Bombay case. **£1,500-2,000** *CSK*

A pink gold Rolex Oyster Perpetual chronometer wristwatch, with bubble-back. **£2,000-2,500** *CSK*

A gold wristwatch by International Watch Company, Schaffhausen. **£1,000-1,500** *CSK*

A gold automatic wristwatch by Audemars Piguet, with 29 jewels. **£1,000-1,500** *CSK*

A gold curvex wristwatch, by Moeris, with signed gilt movement. **£800-1,000** *CSK*

r. A gold steel Rolex wristwatch with pink gold sides, maker's mark and signed movement. **£650-750** *CSK*

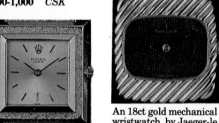

An 18ct gold mechanical wristwatch, by Jaeger-le Coultre. **£550-650** *CSK*

An 18ct gold Rolex wristwatch, in waterproof case. **£2,500-3,000** *CSK*

l. An automatic full calendar and moonphase wristwatch, by Jaeger-le Coultre. **£1,500-2,000** *CSK*
r. An 18ct gold alarm calendar wristwatch, by Jaeger-le Coultre, with original strap. **£1,500-2,000** *CSK*

A stainless steel Rolex Oyster Perpetual chronometer wristwatch with bubble-back. **£700-900** *CSK*

Horse Brasses

The earliest horse brasses were basic designs representing pagan and early religious symbols, i.e. moon, sun, stars and the cross.

By the 18thC many other subjects were featured, made from latten brass. These early brasses will all have hammer marks on the back; however, these are now reproduced but the marks are lighter and more shallow.

Horse brasses became very popular after the Napoleonic Wars and by 1835 cast brasses were beginning to appear, made from calamine brass, which has a coarse feel and is pitted.

By 1870 machine stamped horse brasses were appearing made from iron-rolled spelter brass.

All subject areas are highly collectable but pre-1815 examples are most desirable.

Brasses

A selection of 19thC horse brasses. **£10-25** *PCA*

A selection of 19thC horse brasses. **£10-25 each** Centre. **£70-80** *PCA*

A selection of pony and horse brasses, c1830. **£10-25 each** *PCA*

19thC horse brasses, with one Edward VII dated 1902. **£10-30** *PCA*

Six horse brasses, 4in (10cm) long. **£30-40 each** *BS*

Two horse brasses, 4in
(10cm) long,

l. Sheaf. **£80-90**
r. Acorn. **£60-70** *BS*

Two horse brasses,
3½in (8.5cm),

l. Griffin. **£60-70**
r. Star. **£70-80** *BS*

Commemorative Brasses

Two horse brasses,
Queen Victoria,
l. 3½in (8.5cm) diam.
£60-70
r. 2in (5cm) diam.
£35-45 *BS*

Two horse brasses,
Queen Victoria, 4in
(10cm) long.

l. **£150-160**
r. **£120-140** *BS*

Two horse brasses,
crowns, 4in (10cm) long.
£80-90 each *BS*

Two horse brasses,
Edward VII, 3½in
(8.5cm) diam.
l. **£60-70**
r. **£80-90** *BS*

A horse brass, Queen
Victoria's Golden
Jubilee, 3½in (8.5cm)
long.
£50-60 *BS*

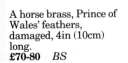

A horse brass, Prince of
Wales' feathers,
damaged, 4in (10cm)
long.
£70-80 *BS*

A City of Glasgow Police
headpiece, 5in (12.5cm)
long.
£80-90 *BS*

Face Plates

Martingales

l. An Edward VII martingale.
£120-140
r. A 19thC martingale.
£80-90   *PCA*

Three horse brasses on leather face plate, c1900, 20in (50.5cm) long.
£120-130   *BS*

DID YOU KNOW?
Miller's Collectables Price Guide is designed to build up, year by year, into the most comprehensive reference system available.

A heavy horse face plate, 19thC, 14½in (37cm) long.
£80-90   *BS*

A selection of martingales, l. Edward VII, the other 3 19thC.
£80-120 each   *PCA*

A selection of horse face pieces, 19thC.
£10-30 each   *PCA*

Horse Bits

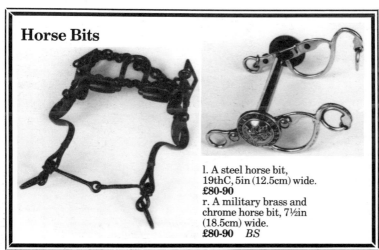

l. A steel horse bit, 19thC, 5in (12.5cm) wide.
£80-90
r. A military brass and chrome horse bit, 7½in (18.5cm) wide.
£80-90   *BS*

A two-brass martingale, 19thC, 11in (28cm) long.
£120-130   *BS*

Hame Plates

A commemorative brass hame, 6in (15cm) long.
£80-90 *BS*

A pair of hame plates, marked Thorn Saddler, Uffculm, 11in (28cm) wide.
£250-300 *BS*

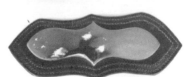

A hame plate, 8in (20cm) wide.
£60-70 *BS*

A named brass hame, 6in (15cm) wide.
£30-40 *BS*

Three brass hames, 5 to 6½in (12.5 to 16.5cm) wide.
Top. **£40-50**
Centre. **£35-45**
Bottom. **£25-35** *BS*

Two brass hames, top 6in (15cm) wide.
£50-60
Bottom, 5in (12.5cm) wide.
£80-90 *BS*

Straps

A pair of heavy horse leather straps, decorated with heart shaped brasses, 22in (55.5cm) long.
£120-140 *BS*

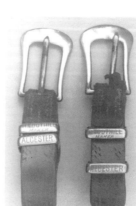

Two brass hames, 6in (15cm) and 7in (17.5cm) wide.
£80-90 each *BS*

DID YOU KNOW?
A hame is a curved bar holding the traces of the harness attached to the collar of a draught animal.

A pair of brass horse loop tugs, c1840.
£30-40 *PCA*

Swingers

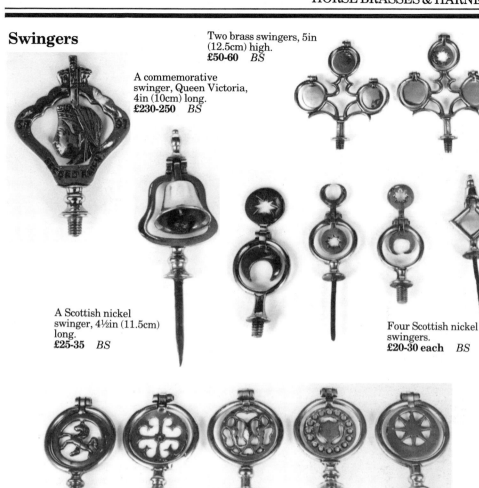

Two brass swingers, 5in (12.5cm) high.
£50-60 *BS*

A commemorative swinger, Queen Victoria, 4in (10cm) long.
£230-250 *BS*

A Scottish nickel swinger, 4½in (11.5cm) long.
£25-35 *BS*

Four Scottish nickel swingers.
£20-30 each *BS*

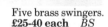

Five brass swingers.
£25-40 each *BS*

A Scottish nickel swinger, 5in (12.5cm) long.
£25-35 *BS*

MAKE THE MOST OF MILLERS
Price ranges in this book reflect what one should expect to *pay* for a similar example. When selling, however, one should expect to receive a lower figure. This will fluctuate according to a dealer's stock, saleability at a particular time, etc. It is always advisable, when selling, to approach a reputable specialist dealer or an auction house which has specialist sales.

A pair of Scottish nickel swingers, 4in (10cm) long.
£50-60 *BS*

Bells

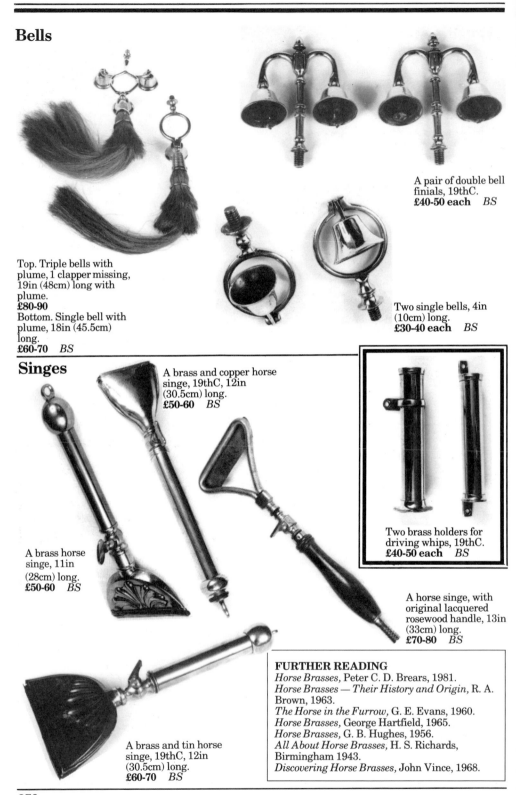

A pair of double bell finials, 19thC.
£40-50 each   *BS*

Top. Triple bells with plume, 1 clapper missing, 19in (48cm) long with plume.
£80-90
Bottom. Single bell with plume, 18in (45.5cm) long.
£60-70   *BS*

Two single bells, 4in (10cm) long.
£30-40 each   *BS*

Singes

A brass and copper horse singe, 19thC, 12in (30.5cm) long.
£50-60   *BS*

A brass horse singe, 11in (28cm) long.
£50-60   *BS*

Two brass holders for driving whips, 19thC.
£40-50 each   *BS*

A horse singe, with original lacquered rosewood handle, 13in (33cm) long.
£70-80   *BS*

A brass and tin horse singe, 19thC, 12in (30.5cm) long.
£60-70   *BS*

FURTHER READING
Horse Brasses, Peter C. D. Brears, 1981.
Horse Brasses — Their History and Origin, R. A. Brown, 1963.
The Horse in the Furrow, G. E. Evans, 1960.
Horse Brasses, George Hartfield, 1965.
Horse Brasses, G. B. Hughes, 1956.
All About Horse Brasses, H. S. Richards, Birmingham 1943.
Discovering Horse Brasses, John Vince, 1968.

Jewellery
Brooches

A Victorian gold circular boss brooch with central opal and diamond cluster, within a banding of blue enamel.
£300-400   *CSK*

A French silver brooch set with doublets, c1900.
£200-300   *ASA*

A 9ct gold and amber heart brooch, 1in (2.5cm) high.
£90-100   *CA*

A filigree and scroll work gold brooch with central solitaire garnet and half pearl border, one half pearl deficient, 19thC.
£200-250   *CSK*

A Christmas brooch, 1in (2.5cm) wide.
£15-25   *LEW*

An Art Deco brightly coloured enamelled brooch, 3½in (9cm).
£25-35   *ASA*

A Victorian gold, pearl and enamel brooch, 1½in (4cm) wide.
£110-120   *CA*

l. A silver and enamel figure brooch, c1912, 1in (2.5cm) long.
£8-10
r. A silver brooch with lighthouse, 1½in (4cm) wide.
£30-35   *CA*

A 9ct gold Baby brooch, Chester, 1907, 1in (2.5cm) wide.
£15-20   *CA*
A Victorian silver Baby brooch, 1½in (4cm) wide.
£25-35   *CA*

A selection of Victorian silver brooches, c1899.
£35-45 each   *CA*

A late Victorian English rose, Scottish thistle and Irish shamrock brooch.
£25-35 *PVH*

A Victorian silver love token brooch.
£25-35 *PVH*

An Edwardian base metal gilded Faith, Hope and Charity brooch.
£5-10 *PVH*

A late Victorian silver buckle and bow brooch.
£15-20 *PVH*

A silver and turquoise brooch, various marks.
£80-120 *ASA*

Various Victorian gold bar brooches.
£40-60 each *PVH*

A Victorian silver engraved scenic brooch, Chichester Cathedral.
£25-45 *PVH*

A silver gilt locket
surrounded by paste
stones, c1900.
£65-75   *PVH*

A Victorian cast silver
Diamond Jubilee
Masonic pendant set
with red, white and blue
pastes, 1897.
£40-50   *PVH*

A 9ct gold brooch.
£45-55   *SAD*

A Victoria Regina silver
commemorative brooch.
£15-20   *PVH*

Two silver and enamel
family crest brooches.
£20-40 each   *PVH*

A late Victorian base
metal, seed pearl and
enamel brooch.
£15-25   *PVH*

A selection of fly,
dragonfly and butterfly
brooches.
£5-20 each   *VB*

Bracelets

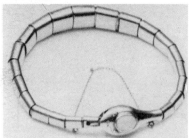

An articulated snake
bracelet, the head set
with an opal.
£300-400   *CSK*

A silver Art Nouveau
bracelet, c1900.
£40-60   *ASA*

A child's silver bracelet,
2in (5cm) diam.
£15-20   *LEW*

A Mexican silver
bracelet, c1930.
£80-150   *ASA*

A late Victorian Indian
silver bangle, with silver
coins engraved with
family names.
£25-35   *PVH*

Crosses

Three crosses, diamante,
gold metal and gold.
£12-30 each   *VB*

Four crosses, silver and
gold.
£10-15 each   *VB*

A mosaic cross, a
mother-of-pearl cross
and a pearl cross.
£6-15 each   *VB*

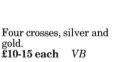

Three gold crosses, 1in
(2.5cm) high.
£10-15 each   *VB*

Mizpah

A gilded base metal brooch.
£5-15 *PVH*

A Victorian silver Mizpah brooch.
£25-35 *PVH*

A Victorian gold ring.
£50-75 *PVH*

A Victorian brooch in two-colour gold, with garnet and lucky bell.
£50-75 *PVH*

A mid Victorian vulcanite Mizpah locket.
£25-30 *PVH*

DID YOU KNOW?
MIZPAH is a Jewish word meaning 'The Lord watch between me and thee when we are absent from one another', taken from the Book of Genesis.

Necklaces

An enamel and Venetian glass scarab necklace, 1920s.
£120-140 *CLH*

A Danish silver pendant, c1930, by G. Jensen.
£100-150 *ASA*

A gold and cabochon garnet 5 stone cross pendant.
£200-250 *CSK*

A silver and enamel necklace, 1920s.
£60-70 *CLH*

MAKE THE MOST OF MILLERS
Condition is absolutely vital when assessing the value of any item. Damaged pieces appreciate much less than perfect examples. However, a rare, desirable piece may command a high price even when damaged.

Coin Holders

Three metal coin holders.
£10-20 each   *VB*

Two coin holders,
l. silver, 2in (5cm) wide,
r. brass, 1in (2.5cm)
diam.
£15-20 each   *VB*

Two coin holders, c1900.
£10-15 each   *VB*

A leather purse coin
holder.
£18-20   *VB*

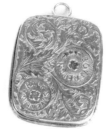

l. A brass coin holder,
r. A silver coin holder.
£10-15 each   *VB*

General

A collection of different
hearts on half a gold
Albert chain as a
bracelet, including
4 heart shaped glass
cases containing infants'
hair, with the names and
dates of birth.
£600-700   *PVH*

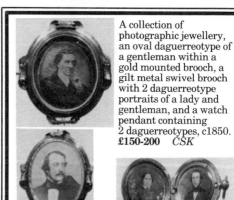

A collection of
photographic jewellery,
an oval daguerreotype of
a gentleman within a
gold mounted brooch, a
gilt metal swivel brooch
with 2 daguerreotype
portraits of a lady and
gentleman, and a watch
pendant containing
2 daguerreotypes, c1850.
£150-200   *CSK*

A set of bronze Finnish
jewellery, by
B. Weckstrom, c1970.
£175-185   *CLH*

FURTHER READING
All That Glitters, J. L. Lynnlee.
Costume Jewellery, the Fun of Collecting, Nancy
Schiffer.
The Power of Jewellery, Nancy Schiffer.
Costume Jewellery, the Great Pretenders,
Lyngerda Kelley and Nancy Schiffer.
Plastic Jewellery, Lyngerda Kelley and Nancy
Schiffer, Millbank Books, U.K.

Juke Boxes & Americana

A Buckley music box, c1940, 11½in (29.5cm) high.
£350-400   *AAM*

A Wurlitzer music box, late 1940, 12in (30.5cm) high.
£300-350   *AAM*

A Mills's Empress juke box, with 20 selector button, 5, 10 and 25 cent coin chute, stamped on back 12 43985, and inside 352A, c1939, 59in (150cm) high.
£2,000-2,500   *Bon*

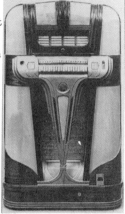

A Seeburg Select-O-Matic 200 Model 207, Serial No. 10413, with 200 selections, 53in (134.5cm) high.
£1,500-2,000   *CSK*

A Packard 'Butler' selector, late 1940s, 12in (30.5cm) high.
£150-200   *AAM*

A selector unit and loudspeaker for a telephone juke box system, 17in (43cm) high.
£400-450   *AAM*

A Wurlitzer 1250, juke box, c1950.
£3,500-5,000   *AAM*

An illuminated juke box loud speaker, by Aireon, designed by Raymond Loewy, c1946, 17in (43.5cm) square.
£500-550   *AAM*

A Coca-Cola customised wall box, originally metal or chrome, made by Seeburg, designed 1949, 13in (33cm) high.
£280-350   *AAM*

Cross Reference
Coca-Cola

Slot Machines

The Little A Bradshaw Stockbroker gaming machine, c1927.
£500-600   *Bon*

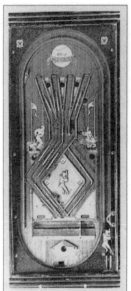

A Genco Official Baseball pintable.
£400-500 *Bon*

An American 'What the Butler Saw' peep show machine, with upright oak case, cast metal cabriole lion's paw feet, 50in (127cm) high.
£1,200-1,500 *Bon*

A Bally Fireball pinball table, with 5 ball play, 4 players, bonus and replay facilities, serial number 3811.
£420-450 *Bon*

A Cigaretto skill cigarette vending all win machine, with 1d. coin chute.
£300-400 *Bon*

A table top Test Your Strength machine, with 1d. coin chute below strength needle gauge.
£1,400-1,600 *Bon*

A Mill's High Top Cowboy one-arm bandit fruit machine, with 6d. coin chute, 72in (182.5cm) high.
£1,700-2,000 *Bon*

Americana

An Economy juicer, c1940, 7in (17.5cm) high.
£15-20 *AAM*

An American post box, c1910.
£350-400 *AAM*

DID YOU KNOW?
Miller's Collectables Price Guide is designed to build up, year by year, into the most comprehensive reference system available.

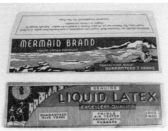

Two American condom
packets, guaranteed for
5 years, 1930s.
£4-5 each   *AAM*

An orange juice press,
c1940, 7½in (19cm) high.
£35-45   *AAM*

An American Coronet
toaster, 1940s, price
reflects design.
£50-60   *AAM*

A Jayne Mansfield hot
water bottle, produced in
America and England,
21in (53cm) high.
£100-120   *AAM*

A tin juicer,
c1935, 9in
(22.5cm) high.
£20-25   *AAM*

A cigarette trade
dispenser, a miniature
fruit machine, 12in
(30.5cm) high.
£480-520   *AAM*

A rocket bubble gum
dispenser, supplied free
to shops with the bubble
gum, in original box,
c1950.
£225-250   *AAM*

A Hamilton Juice citrus
press, c1930, 20in
(50.5cm) high.
£200-225   *AAM*

An American Ice-O-Mat
ice crusher, c1930, 9½in
(24cm) high.
£35-40   *AAM*

FURTHER READING
The Catalog of American Collectables,
Christopher Pearce, Mallard Press, New York.
*Fifties Source Book, A Visual Guide to the Style of
a Decade,* Christopher Pearce, Virgin.
Vintage Juke Boxes, Apple Tree Press, 1988.

KITCHENALIA
Advertising

Three white shoe
cleaners, c1930.
£1-5 each   *RTT*

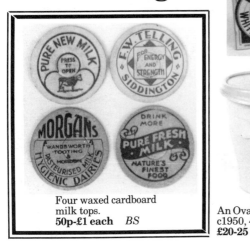

Four waxed cardboard
milk tops.
50p-£1 each   *BS*

An Ovaltine mug and lid,
c1950, 4in (10cm) high.
£20-25   *RTT*

An Odol glass beaker,
1930s, 3½in (8.5cm) high.
£10-15   *RTT*

Architectural
Fittings

Three loo pulls, 2 ceramic
and 1 ash.
£30-60 each   *BS*

Three loo pulls, c1900.
£45-75 each   *BS*

An upright soap holder,
6½in (16.5cm) high.
£5-10   *OD*

A Doulton loo pull on a
brass chain, late 19thC,
5in (12.5cm) long.
£130-140   *BS*

Three ceramic loo pulls.
£50-70 each   *BS*

Cooking Utensils

A copper bellied
saucepan and lid, with
mahogany handle, 6in
(15cm) high.
£210-230   *BS*

A cast iron kettle with
lid, c1900, 10½in
(26.5cm) high.
£70-80   *BS*

Trivets & Stands

An Edwardian copper kettle, 11½in (29.5cm) high.
£45-55 *AL*

A cast iron cauldron with lid, 7in (17.5cm) high.
£80-90 *BS*

A Scottish brass iron stand, 19thC, 10in (25cm) wide.
£70-80 *BS*

An iron trivet, 11½in (29.5cm) long.
£15-25 *AL*

A Clark & Co. patent cast cook pot with lid, ¾ pint capacity, 1878.
£125-135 *BS*

A cast iron stand, 19thC, 6in (15cm) wide, and a miniature cast iron stand, 2½in (6.5cm) wide.
£20-30 each *BS*

Kitchen Tools & Equipment

A Besney brass knife sharpener, c1900, 6in (15cm) wide.
£50-60 *BS*

A cast iron sugar cutter, by Bullock & Co., 1843, 14½in (37cm) wide.
£160-180 *BS*

Knife sharpeners, 5½ to 6½in (14 to 16cm) long.
£4-5 each *AL*

A Victorian or Edwardian sweet jar, with replacement lid, 11in (28cm) high.
£20-25 *CAB*

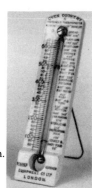

An oven cookery thermometer, patent 1927, 7in (17.5cm) high.
£40-50 *BS*

A miniature glass butter churn, c1920, 5in (12.5cm) high.
£60-70 *BS*

A fishing basket, 37in (94cm) long.
£20-25 *AL*

An enamel feeder cup, 2½in (6cm) high.
£8-10 *AL*

Two Blow butter churns, c1920.
£30-40 each *BS*

A French cutting board, c1900.
£45-50 *MCA*

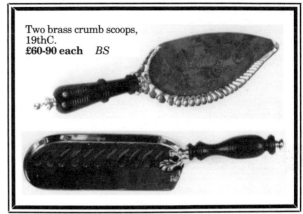

Two brass crumb scoops, 19thC.
£60-90 each *BS*

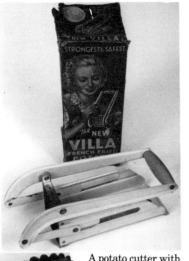

A potato cutter with original box.
£3-5 *WHA*

A French 17-piece blue on white enamel kitchen set, 1920.
£140-150 *MCA*

A boot spill holder, 7½in (18.5cm) high.
£5-10 *DH*

A plastic duck clothes brush holder, 11½in (29.5cm) high.
£15-20 *RTT*

Two egg timers, the Welsh lady 4in (10cm) high.
£12-15 each *AL*

Two decorated rolling pins.
£16-18 each *AL*

A lemon squeezer, 4½in (11.5cm) long.
£5-8 *OD*

A pressed glass butter dish, 7in (17.5cm) wide.
£30-35 *OD*

Domestic Ceramics

A jar with green and black decoration, c1930, 6½in (16.5cm) high.
£10-15 *AL*

A Propert's breeches and glove paste jar, 5in (12.5cm) high.
£20-25 *CA*

An Ovaltine jug mixer, c1930, 8in (20cm) high.
£15-20 *RTT*

A Cadbury's Drinking Chocolate jug, 6in (15cm) high.
£30-40 *BS*

A Govancroft foot warmer, c1927, 10in (25cm) high.
£60-70 *BS*

A hot water bottle/bed warmer, c1904, 9in (22.5cm) high.
£70-80 *BS*

A Sam Clarke's food warmer on stand, 12½in (31.5cm) high.
£220-240 *BS*

A Kents improved Monroes patent egg beater and batter mixer bowl, c1860, 8in (20cm) high.
£160-170 *BS*

A Doultons foot warmer, 10½in (26.5cm) long.
£30-40 *BS*

Domestic Machinery

A small spinning wheel, c1830, 22in (55cm) high.
£445-465 *MCA*

A cheese press, 19thC, 33in (83cm) high.
£250-260 *MCA*

Morton's Patent Household Whisk, 10in (25cm) high.
£25-30 *AL*

Larger sized machines of this type are in use in the finest bakeries in the world. The Morton Machine Co., Wishaw, Scotland, are the sole manufacturers.

An iron mangle with handle, 28in (71.5cm) wide.
£30-40 *AL*

Two waxed cream tubs, 2in (5cm) high.
£2-5 each *BS*

A Harrod's commercial knife sharpener.
£140-150 *COB*

A knife cleaner, 10in (25cm) wide.
£35-45 *AL*

Domestic Metalware

A Carson's Patent salting instrument, in original box with instructions, 19thC, 11in (28cm) long.
£220-240 *BS*

A copper gas pressure fire extinguisher, made by Read and Campbell, 75 Victoria St., London, 24in (61.5cm) high.
£35-40 *DH*

A Pyrene brass fire extinguisher, 14½in (37cm) high.
£6-10 *DH*

A spoon warmer.
£55-75 *MCA*

A toast rack, c1900.
£30-50 *PC*

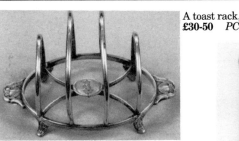

A wire egg whisk, 9in (22.5cm) long.
£1-2 *DH*

An adjustable bath rack.
£35-40 *AL*

A Demon beetle trap, 9in (23.5cm) diam.
£30-35 *AL*

Illustrated in the original Mrs. Beeton's.

A shop string tin, 12in (30.5cm) high.
£30-40 *AL*

The Queen's Pudding boiler, 6½in (16cm) diam.
£10-15 *AL*

A waffle iron, 30½in
(77.5cm) long.
£30-35 *AL*

A butcher's steel with
brass handle, 1875,
17½in (44.5cm) long.
£80-90 *BS*

Cross Reference
Coffee Making

A Kenrick York Minster
font cast coffee grinder,
in original finish, 7½in
(18.5cm) high.
£310-330 *BS*

A tin ale muller, 19thC,
8½in (21.5cm) high.
£30-40 *BS*

Irons

A Davis enamelled gas
iron and stand, 7in
(17.5cm) high.
£60-70 *BS*

A brass and iron tally
iron with poker,
W. Bullock & Co., 8½in
(21cm) wide.
£150-160 *BS*

An O K gas iron, c1920,
9in (22.5cm) long.
£50-60 *BS*

A triple steel tally iron,
early 19thC, 16in
(40.5cm) high.
£800-900 *BS*

A tally iron,
19thC, 6½in
(16.5cm) long.
£30-40 *BS*

A brass tally iron with
poker, early 19thC,
13½in (34.5cm) long.
£220-240 *BS*

A Salter '0000' iron, 4in
(10cm) long.
£65-75 *BS*

DID YOU KNOW?
A tally iron was used to press pleats and ruffles on
small linen garments.

A J. Keith & Blackman green enamelled gas iron, c1920, 6in (15cm) long.
£50-60 *BS*

An R. & A. Main gas iron, c1920, 6in (15cm) long.
£30-40 *BS*

A Fairy Prince enamelled gas iron with stand, c1935, 10in (25cm) wide.
£30-40 *BS*

A cast tally iron, 19thC, 8in (20cm) long.
£35-45 *BS*

A boudoir iron with methylated spirit tablet heater, 1926, 5½in (14cm) wide.
£20-30 *BS*

A Kenrick & Sons box iron with slug, 19thC.
£70-80 *BS*

A Fletcher Laurel gas iron, with enamelled finish, c1910.
£80-90 *BS*

A goffering iron, for pressing nurses' caps and collars.
£100-125 *AL*

A selection of flat irons.
£15-20 each *PC*

Moulds

A set of 4 chocolate
moulds, 1in (2.5cm) high.
£60-70 *BS*

Two miniature chocolate
moulds, c1876, 2 and 3in
(5 and 7.5cm) long.
£10-15 each *BS*

A cream cheese mould,
marked Wedgwood, 5in
(14cm) high.
£65-75 *AL*

Two traditional jelly
moulds, 3½ and 4½in
(9 and 11cm) wide.
£10-15 each *AL*

Six copper entrée moulds
made by Jones Bros., 2in
(5cm) diam.
£10-15 each *BS*

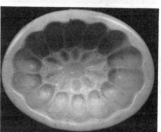

A jelly
mould, 3½in
(8.5cm) wide.
£16-20 *MAN*

A pair of miniature
copper chocolate moulds,
c1925, 4in (10cm) high.
£50-60 the pair *BS*

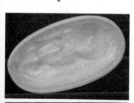

A Harrod's Ltd. copper
mould, 6in (15cm) diam.
£60-70 *BS*

A tin and copper jelly
mould, c1900, 7in
(17.5cm) wide.
£70-80 *BS*

Ceramic jelly moulds
with a dolphin and a
rabbit, 5½in (14cm) wide.
£15-20 each *AL*

FURTHER READING
*Cookie Cutters and Cookie Molds: Art in the
Kitchen,* Phyllis S. Wetherill.
Butter Prints and Molds, Paul E. Kindig,
Millbank Books, U.K.
Domestic Bygones, Jacqueline Fearn, Shire
Publications Ltd., 1977.

Lighting

A wrought iron rush nip, c1760, 6½in (16.5cm) high.
£120-160 *KEY*

A pewter chandelier with 6 removable branches, reproduction.
£270-290 *MIC*

A khaki painted carriage lamp, from a military horse drawn vehicle, with spring suspension and bearing plate with Government marking, C & M Birmingham 1918, 16in (41cm) high.
£50-70 *CSK*

A brass railway lamp, 8½in (21.5cm) high.
£40-50 *CBA*

A Fornasetti metal table lamp, mounted with metal fittings, printed with polychrome decoration, with paper label, Fornasetti, Milano, Made in Italy, 14in (36cm) high.
£300-320 *C*

A Welsh oak rush light nip, with original blue painted surface, c1740.
£360-380 *RYA*

A candle lamp, 9in (22.5cm) high.
£15-20 *WO*

A Patent oil lamp trimmer, c1830, 7in (17.5cm) wide.
£55-65 *HUN*

An 18thC style waxjack with a gadrooned and scroll pierced base with claw-and-ball feet and applied scroll handle, 5½in (14cm).
£150-170 *CSK*

A gilded Cupid figure, converted to table lamp, on circular marble plinth, late 19thC, 21in (53.5cm) high.
£90-120 *PCh*

Oil Lamps

A Corinthian column table oil lamp, with cut glass reservoir, contemporary shade, Sheffield mark 1903, 19in (48.5cm) high.
£750-850 *AG*

A Victorian satin glass oil lamp, 9in (22.5cm) high.
£100-120 *PC*

A gilt metal mounted cast iron lamp, made from a Prussian shell, with inscription, fitted for electricity, c1871, 18in (45.5cm).
£350-400 *C*

A Corinthian column oil lamp base, with cut glass reservoir, clear glass chimney and foliate etched shade, column 15in (38cm) high.
£300-350 *HSS*

An oil lamp on pottery base with cylindrical brass stem, opaque glass reservoir, brass mounts and milky glass shade, 26in (66cm) high.
£150-170 *DDM*

An American Fenton ABCO Nutmeg oil lamp in vaseline glass, 8in (20cm) high.
£100-120 *PC*

> ### Cross Reference
> Art Deco

An oil lamp with brass base, opaque glass reservoir, brass mounts and milky glass shade, 26in (66cm) high.
£85-100 *DDM*

A pair of of Art Nouveau lamps on ormolu bases, 17½in (44.5cm) high.
£600-800 *PC*

Locks & Keys
Locks

A round lock, Young's Patent, c1825, 9in (22.5cm) long.
£50-60 *KH*

A plate lock, with reproduction key, c1800.
£50-60 *KH*

A Chubb combination locking latch lock, with key and brass handle, c1835, 4½in (11.5cm) long.
£50-60 *KH*

A Russell and Erwin ornate cast iron drawer lock, locking latch with dead bolt, patented and registered 1878, with 2 keys, 3½in (8.5cm) long.
£50-60 *KH*

An early stamped Barron's lever lock in iron case, no key, c1780, 6in (15cm) long.
£60-75 *KH*

A double bolt, double throw deadlock, complete with original key, from a grille/metal door, c1830, 5in (12.5cm) long.
£60-75 *KH*

A warded plate lock with drop bar key with short shank, c1750.
£60-75 *KH*

Used in stables or store rooms so as not to damage the animal, e.g. horse in stable.

A chest lock with unusual key shape, c1500, 13in (33cm) long.
£150-200 *KH*

A 4-way lock by Branford Lock Works, 1865, 4in (10cm) wide, with original mineral knobs, patented 1851.
Lock without key.
£25-30
Knobs. **£15-20** *KH*

DID YOU KNOW?
Miller's Collectables Price Guide is designed to build up, year by year, into the most comprehensive reference system available.

An Irish lock and key, 18thC, 16½in (42cm) long.
£160-180 *PCA*

A double throw lock made by Thomas of Birmingham, with removable wards, complete with master key, c1820, 8in (20cm) long.
£100-125 *KH*

These were used in small police stations, if a key went missing and was not found within an hour, the lock had to be changed. This one required new ward and key instead of the entire lock.

A German chest lock, with engraved outer and inner plates, c1600, 9in (22.5cm) long.
£350-400 *KH*

Originally covered in leather.

A Chubb detector lock and key, c1850, 7in (17.5cm) long.
£75-85 *KH*

A Chubb Home Safe with key.
£5-10
and a Chubb tin money box for children.
£25-30 *KH*

A Banbury lock with key, c1750, 7in (17.5cm) long.
£50-60 *KH*

A Chubb keyhole cover, heavily chrome plated, c1920, 2in (5cm) diam.
£10-15 *KH*

A sectioned Chubb detector lock with 5 levers, 3 anti-picking devices, barrel and curtain false notches, and detector, with key, 5in (12.5cm) long.
£40-50 *KH*

These locks came with 4, 5 or 6 levers.

Keys

A double ended key, early 18thC, 15in (38cm) long.
£70-80   KH

The more levers cut into a key, the more difficult for a lock pick, but made the key weaker; therefore, many keys were damaged.

Two Bridgward keys, one Banbury type and one plate lock type, 5in (12.5cm) long.
Banbury. £15-20
Plate lock.
£10-15   KH

A George Price safe key, 6 lever, Cleveland Works, Wolverhampton, c1875, 3in (7.5cm) long.
£5-8   KH

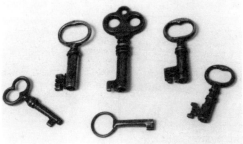

A selection of padlock keys, 17thC and 18thC, 2 to 3in (5 to 7.5cm) long.
£5-10 each   KH

A selection of Victorian jewel box and writing slope keys, 1 to 1½in (2.5 to 4cm) long.
£1-2 each   KH

Three Continental keys, 4 to 7in (10 to 17.5cm) long.
Small. £5-10 each
Large. £35-40   KH

Two brass key return tags, offering a reward, 1 and 1½in (2.5 and 4cm) long.
£5-10 each   KH

Three reproduction keys, display items only, made from traditional and original shapes, 8 to 9in (20 to 22.5cm) long.
£10-15 each   KH

A set of Chatwoods Invincible safe keys, 8 lever and 4 lever, marked Left and Right, all stamped, c1900.
£10-15   KH

A brass hotel key tag, c1900, 4½in (11.5cm) long.
£4-5   KH

A Victorian Chubb's pillar box key, 3½in (8.5cm) long.
£10-15 *KH*

A flat push-type padlock key, c1900, 2in (5cm) long.
£2-3 *KH*

Three keys by Cotterill, Chubb and Bramah, 19thC, 2 to 3in (5 to 7.5cm) long.
£5-10 each *KH*

Two keys, c1725, 3 and 4in (7.5 and 10cm) long.
£10-15 each *KH*

Two keys, the top one blacksmith made, 6in (15cm) long, the bottom one crudely made, 2½in (6.5cm) long, both c1400.
Top. **£45-50**
Bottom. **£15-20** *KH*

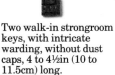

Two walk-in strongroom keys, with intricate warding, without dust caps, 4 to 4½in (10 to 11.5cm) long.
£75-100 each *KH*

Dust caps prevented dust accumulating inside the pipe, thus preventing the key from engaging the lock, Barron's Lever Patent.

Four keys, c1600, 2½ to 4in (6.5 to 10cm) long.
Large. **£50-85 each**
Small.
£20-30 each *KH*

Four keys, c1450, 3 to 3½in (7.5 to 8.5cm) long.
£15-25 each *KH*

Rarity and condition are reflected in the price.

A selection of O'Dell's latch or French latch lifters, O'Dells patented 1792, 1½ to 2½in (4 to 6cm) long.
£15-20 each *KH*

Two Miller's keys, c1900, 2½ and 3in (6.5 and 7.5cm) long.
£2-3 each *KH*

Padlocks

A Scandinavian type padlock, the shackle lifts out in one piece, 2½in (6cm) long.
£10-12   *KH*

These are often sold as paperweights because of their weight.

Two Gas Board padlocks, post-war, 2in (5cm) long.
£2-5 each   *KH*

There are many varieties from gas meters and they usually had non-standard keys to prevent people gaining access to them.

A Climax 6 Lever padlock, with flat push-type key, c1900, 2½in (6cm) long. Without key.
£5-10   *KH*

An early Yale padlock, c1880, 3in (7.5cm) long.
£5-10   *KH*

A letter combination padlock, c1900, 1½in (3.5cm) wide.
£10-15   *KH*

A kit bag padlock, used by threading straight bar through eyelets and bringing curved piece round before padlocking, c1914.
£5-10   *KH*

A bar padlock, with reproduction key, c1900, 8in (20cm) wide.
£10-15   *KH*

METALWARE
Brass

A brass hand clip, 4in (10cm) long.
£30-40   *CAC*

A brass door knocker and a cast iron door knocker, produced from the same mould, 8in (20cm) high.
Brass. **£110-130**
Iron. **£20-40**   *PC*

An early Victorian Barron's Lever padlock, complete with 2 keys, 4½in (11cm) long.
£30-40   *KH*

A brass plaque, early 19thC, 7in (17.5cm) long.
£50-70   *SWN*

Britannia Metal

A Victorian Britannia metal caster formed as a seated bear with raised paws, 4in (10cm) high.
£80-100   *C(S)*

A Britannia metal teapot, 7in (17.5cm) high.
£15-20   *PC*

A Britannia metal circular bodied teapot, 6½in (16.5cm) high.
£15-20   *PC*

Copper

Four 2-piece copper chocolate moulds, 3in (7.5cm) high.
£30-40 each   *BS*

An English replica copper percolator, by Mr. Jones of The Strand, c1840.
Value of original.
£500-800   *TBC*

A copper pot with lid, mid-19thC, 16in (40.5cm) diam.
£165-175   *MCA*

A copper jug, 13½in (34.5cm) high.
£110-130   *WO*

A French copper mixing bowl, 10in (25cm) diam.
£50-60   *CBA*

The chef would attach the bowl to his waist with the brass ring.

A Newlyn copper charger, the wide rim embossed with a continuous branch of fruiting medlars, impressed mark, 17in (43cm) diam.
£300-350   *LAY*

Two copper caddies, 4½ and 5in (11 and 12.5cm) high.
£12-20 each   *AL*

Pewter

A pair of candlesticks,
c1840, a beaker, c1850,
and a Continental
porringer, c1800.
Candlesticks. **£80-100**
Beaker. **£30-40**
Porringer.
£100-120   *KEY*

A Scottish crested tappit
hen, c1790, 11½in
(29.5cm) high.
£350-400   *KEY*

General

A pair of iron wedding
band hogscraper
candlesticks, c1800, 9in
(22.5cm) high.
£100-150   *KEY*

Cross Reference
Candlesticks

A set of 11 cylindrical
bell metal measures,
from standard bushel to
quarter gill, by Bate,
London.
£3,500-4,000   *AG*

Silver

A pair of sugar nippers,
with initials R.I.C.,
c1758, 5in (12.5cm) long.
£160-180   *SBA*

Two salts, Birmingham
1907, 2in (5cm), and
Chester 1897, 2in (5cm).
£20-30 each   *CAC*

A late Victorian dressing
table tray, Birmingham,
probably 1893, by S.
Walton-Smith, 10in
(25cm) wide, 248gr.
£150-180   *HSS*

**MAKE THE MOST
OF MILLERS**
Condition is
absolutely vital when
assessing the value of
any item. Damaged
pieces appreciate
much less than
perfect examples.
However, a rare,
desirable piece may
command a high
price even when
damaged.

A polished steel doorstop,
Britain's Pride, c1890,
11½in (29.5cm) high.
£60-80   *IS*

Cutlery

A horn handled butter knife, 7in (17.5cm) long.
£8-10   *CA*

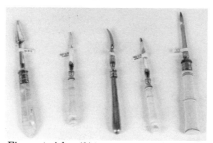

Five nut picks, 4½ to 5½in (11.5 to 13.5cm) long.
£7-12 each   *VB*

Three silver teaspoons.
£8-10 each   *MAN*

A bone handled fish knife, 17in (43cm) long.
£20-25   *HUN*

Five Regency table knives with inscribed ivory handles.
£100-120   *CSK*

Fruit Knives

Graters

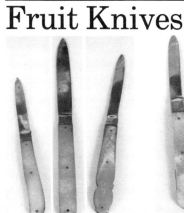

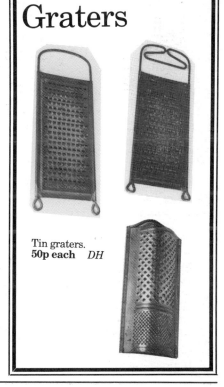

Silver and mother-of-pearl fruit knives, 4 to 5½in (10 to 14cm) long.
£20-25 each   *VB*

Two silver fruit knives, with mother-of-pearl and Art Nouveau handles.
£15-20 each   *VB*

Tin graters.
50p each   *DH*

Three silver fruit knives, with mother-of-pearl handles, 4in (10cm) long.
£15-20   *VB*

MILITARIA
Badges

An officer's forage cap badge of the Machine Gun Guards.
£90-100 *WAL*

An officer's silver glengarry badge of the 76th Regiment.
£120-140 *CSK*

The 76th did not receive the Nive honour until 1845; it later became the 2nd Bn. Duke of Wellington's (West Riding Regt.).

An other rank's brass and white metal cap badge of the 2nd Volunteer Battalion the Manchester Regiment.
£40-50 *WAL*

A scarce embroidered puggaree badge of the Motor Machine Gun Corps, on dark green patch, minor wear.
£60-70 *WAL*

An officer's silver bonnet badge of the Argyll and Sutherland Highlanders, Birmingham 1917.
£180-200 *WAL*

An other rank's brass and white metal glengarry of the 1st (the Royal) Regt., worn 1852-71, as 420 but scroll inscribed 'The Royal Regiment'.
£85-95 *WAL*

A Victorian other rank's white metal glengarry of the 43rd N. Durham Militia.
£160-180 *WAL*

A rare officer's gilt and silver plated 2nd pattern cap of the 21st (Empress of India's) Lancers, upright lances 795, very minor wear.
£320-350 *WAL*

An officer's silver badge of the 8th Punjab Regt., Birmingham 1939.
£90-100 *WAL*

A scarce Victorian white metal glengarry of the Glasgow Highlanders Cadet Corps, Blair Lodge.
£130-140 *WAL*

MAKE THE MOST OF MILLERS
Price ranges in this book reflect what one should expect to *pay* for a similar example. When selling, however, one should expect to receive a lower figure. This will fluctuate according to a dealer's stock, saleability at a particular time, etc. It is always advisable, when selling, to approach a reputable specialist dealer or an auction house which has specialist sales.

Belt Buckle

A Victorian other rank's glengarry badge of the 2nd R Tower Hamlets Militia, The Queen's Own Light Infantry.
£50-60 *WAL*

An officer's silver plated belt buckle of the First Royal Cheshire Militia.
£80-100 *WAL*

A scarce officer's silver plated cap badge of the West Riding Volunteers (1688).
£45-55 *WAL*

A rare officer's gilt and silver cap badge of the Tank Corps, 2nd Pattern, tank facing right (as 1921), and one collar.
£300-320 *WAL*

An officer's silver badge of the 8th Punjab Regt., Birmingham 1926, brooch pin.
£65-75 *WAL*

An other rank's white metal glengarry badge of the Royal E. Middlesex Militia.
£40-60 *WAL*

A Victorian other rank's white metal glengarry badge of the 2nd Volunteer Battalion The R. Warwickshire Regt.
£60-80 *WAL*

An officer's silver plated cap badge of the 6th Duke of Connaught's Bn. The Hampshire Regt., white, red and blue enamel centre.
£55-65 *WAL*

Shoulder Belt Plates

A Georgian silver coloured shoulder belt plate of the 15th (York East Riding) Regt. of Foot, with mounted 2-piece device, c1808.
£330-350 *WAL*

A Georgian officer's silver plated copper oval shoulder belt plate of the West Kent Militia, c1800.
£220-250 *WAL*

A Georgian officer's silver shoulder belt plate of the London and Westminster Light Horse Vols, London 1803.
£155-185 *WAL*

Helmet Plates

A post 1902 officer's helmet plate of the 1st Royal Jersey Light Infantry, gilt rubbed overall.
£160-200 *WAL*

A Victorian officer's white metal helmet plate of the 6th Lancashire, 1st Manchester, Rifle Vol. Corps.
£125-150 *WAL*

A helmet plate of the 3rd Volunteer Battalion, The Essex Regiment.
£210-250 *WAL*

A Victorian officer's silver plated helmet plate of the 4th West York Militia.
£200-250 *WAL*

A Victorian other rank's white metal helmet plate of the 4th Devonshire Rifle Volunteer Corps.
£70-80 *WAL*

A Victorian gilt and silver helmet plate of The South Staffordshire Regiment.
£130-200 *WAL*

An Imperial Russian Infantry shako plate with scroll, For Distinction, c1900.
£160-200 *CSK*

A Victorian officer's silver plated helmet plate of the 1st R. Tower Hamlets Militia, King's Own Light Infantry, some wear.
£160-200 *WAL*

Edged Weapons

A Victorian naval cutlass, with old black painted finish to iron guard and brass mounted leather scabbard.
£85-100 *WAL*

A Victorian 1821 pattern Light Cavalry officer's sword, leather covered scabbard, by F. T. Cater, 56 Pall Mall.
£80-90 *WAL*

A Persian shamshir, with ivory grips and leather scabbard.
£240-280 *Bon*

An American model 1860 Light Cavalry sabre, with brass guard and leather bound grip, stamped Chicopee Mass. & U.S. M.M. 1864.
£60-80 *Bon*

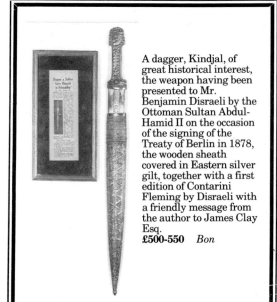

A dagger, Kindjal, of great historical interest, the weapon having been presented to Mr. Benjamin Disraeli by the Ottoman Sultan Abdul-Hamid II on the occasion of the signing of the Treaty of Berlin in 1878, the wooden sheath covered in Eastern silver gilt, together with a first edition of Contarini Fleming by Disraeli with a friendly message from the author to James Clay Esq.
£500-550 *Bon*

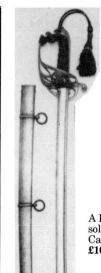

An officer's 1822 Infantry pattern sword, with crowned George IV cypher, with steel scabbard, by Andrews, Pall Mall.
£320-350 *CSK*

A Russian infantry soldier's hanger, Catherine II.
£100-120 *CSK*

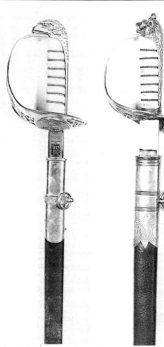

A Royal Navy officer's sword, with copper wire bound grip, lion's head pommel and leather scabbard, by Henry Wilkinson.
£200-220 *Bon*

This type of hanger was in use from about the time of Catherine's accession, 1762, until c1815, but the cypher indicates that this example was made no later than 1796.

A Japanese wakizachi, fully bound tsuka, plain metal tsuba, contained in its lacquered saya, complete with koduzka.
£100-120 *Bon*

An Elizabeth II Royal Air Force officer's sword, with black patent leather scabbard with brass mounts, by Wilkinson.
£300-350 *Bon*

An officer's silver mounted dirk of the Gordon Highlanders, retailed by Meyer and Mortimer, Edinburgh, 1918.
£550-600 *CSK*

DID YOU KNOW?
Miller's Collectables Price Guide is designed to build up, year by year, into the most comprehensive reference system available.

Headgear

A Victorian officer's chapka, 12th Lancers, lacks plume and chin chain.
£1,300-1,500 *Bon*

An officer's shako of the Cameronians, Scottish Rifles, of dark green cloth, trimmed with black braid, by Hawkes & Co., 14 Piccadilly.
£300-350 *CSK*

A Victorian officer's scarlet topped lance cap of the 12th, Prince of Wales's Royal, Lancers, with scarlet feather plume with gilt socket, A. Campbell, written on headband, purple silk lining bearing maker's name, Hawkes & Co.
£2,000-2,500 *CSK*

Presumably the Hon. Alexander Francis Henry Campbell, who was commissioned into the regiment in 1876 and later served in the Scots Guards.

An officer-quality pickelhaube, bearing gilt plate of standard Prussian line Infantry pattern.
£350-400 *CSK*

A French Cuirassier trooper's helmet, steel with brass crest, the skull stamped Godillot.
£300-350 *CSK*

An 1841 pattern Belgian Cuirassier/Dragoon helmet, plated white metal skull, marked 1851.
£450-500 *CSK*

A leather helmet of a Landwehr officer of Bavarian Artillery.
£500-550 *CSK*

An other rank's post 1952 Household Cavalry helmet of white metal with brass and white metal fittings, chin chain and red plume, also with a white plume and a rose boss.
£600-650 *CSK*

A blue-black velvet hat
of a Knight Grand Cross
of the Most Honourable
Order of the Bath.
£100-150 *CSK*

*Such hats were
occasionally worn before
1939, with large feather
plume, at certain
ceremonies of the Order.*

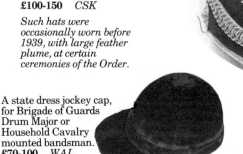

A Victorian officer's blue
cloth spiked helmet of
the 4th West Yorks.
Militia, with nameplate
H. Murray Esq. 4th West
York Mil.
£400-450 *WAL*

A state dress jockey cap,
for Brigade of Guards
Drum Major or
Household Cavalry
mounted bandsman.
£70-100 *WAL*

A post 1902 officer's
green cloth spiked
helmet of the
Somersetshire Light
Infantry, name inside
HHR Oakhill.
£450-500 *WAL*

A helmet probably made
for an officer of an Indian
Light Cavalry unit,
cream felt on a
composition base, with a
red cloth band, label
inside worded Garden &
Son, Army cap and
helmet makers, 200
Piccadilly, London:
officers' and cadets'
appointments.
£300-350 *CSK*

An officer's cap of the
Dorsetshire Regiment,
with box.
£80-90 *WAL*

A Georgian officer's
cocked hat of The Royal
Marines, black lace
bands and rosette.
£900-1,000 *WAL*

A post 1902 officer's blue
cloth spiked helmet of
The Royal Sussex Regt.,
in tin case with
nameplate RJPD
Aldridge, Royal Sussex
Regt.
£300-350 *WAL*

A Worcestershire
Regiment peaked forage
cap, c1890.
£250-300 *CSK*

Medals

Royal Navy Group with
The Order of the British
Empire.
£100-150 *WIN*

General Service Medal,
Army and R.A.F.
1918-62, with Iraq bar,
Pte H. H. Millward,
Duke of Cornwall's Light
Infantry.
£25-30 *RMC*

1914-18 Medal Trio with
Distinguished Service
Cross, Sub Lt. P. P.
Crawford R.N.R.
£400-450 *GIL*

Three medals to Capt.
B. J. Ellis, Royal Air
Force, Officer of the
Order of the British
Empire, British War
medal, and Defence
medal.
£40-70 *RMC*

Peace of Breda 1667,
Favente Deo, silver, in
original case.
£200-250 *WW*

Military Cross, George VI and group, Lt. D. F. Jenkins, Royal Fusiliers.
£300-400 *RMC*

I.G.S. 1936, 2 bars N.W. Front 1936-37, N.W. Front 1937-39 with M.I.D. oakleaf, 2 Lt. D. F. Gordon 2-7 Rajput.
£150-180 *WAL*

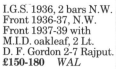

WWII group with Regular Army medal.
£45-55 *WIN*

Military Medal group, awarded in S.E. Asia, 1946, Naik Pinnu Khan, 121 Indian Company.
£350-400 *WIN*

WWII group.
£25-30 *WIN*

D.F.M. Geo. VI first type, 1939-45 Star, Air Crew Europe Star, Defence and War, Sgt. R. H. Burrows, R.A.F.
£300-350 *WAL*

Naval General Service, bar Yangtze 1949, H.M.S. London, Korea pair, Lt. G. C. Blatt, Royal Navy.
£450-600 *RMC*

1939-45 War Medal, Defence Medal (mounted in wrong order), G.S.M. bar Malaya, L.S. & G.C., Sgt. S. Harding, Royal Air Force.
£40-50 *RMC*

Pistols

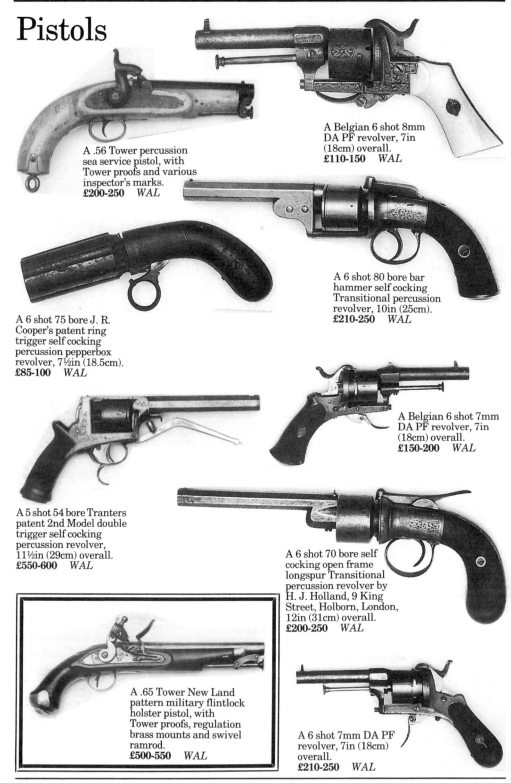

A .56 Tower percussion
sea service pistol, with
Tower proofs and various
inspector's marks.
£200-250 *WAL*

A Belgian 6 shot 8mm
DA PF revolver, 7in
(18cm) overall.
£110-150 *WAL*

A 6 shot 75 bore J. R.
Cooper's patent ring
trigger self cocking
percussion pepperbox
revolver, 7½in (18.5cm).
£85-100 *WAL*

A 6 shot 80 bore bar
hammer self cocking
Transitional percussion
revolver, 10in (25cm).
£210-250 *WAL*

A 5 shot 54 bore Tranters
patent 2nd Model double
trigger self cocking
percussion revolver,
11½in (29cm) overall.
£550-600 *WAL*

A Belgian 6 shot 7mm
DA PF revolver, 7in
(18cm) overall.
£150-200 *WAL*

A 6 shot 70 bore self
cocking open frame
longspur Transitional
percussion revolver by
H. J. Holland, 9 King
Street, Holborn, London,
12in (31cm) overall.
£200-250 *WAL*

A .65 Tower New Land
pattern military flintlock
holster pistol, with
Tower proofs, regulation
brass mounts and swivel
ramrod.
£500-550 *WAL*

A 6 shot 7mm DA PF
revolver, 7in (18cm)
overall.
£210-250 *WAL*

A 5 shot .31 Colt model 1849 pocket percussion revolver, 9½in (24cm) overall. **£360-400** *WAL*

A .455 British military Colt Government model 1911 semi-automatic pistol, 8½in (21cm) overall. **£500-600** *WAL*

A 9mm Luger P.08 semi-automatic pistol, the breech dated 1916, 8½in (21cm) overall. **£150-200** *WAL*

A 7.65mm German Railway Police FN Browning model 1922 semi-automatic pistol, 7in (18cm) overall. **£55-75** *WAL*

A 6 shot .44 Colt army SA percussion revolver No. 43739, 13½in (34cm). **£450-500** *WAL*

An Acvoke post-war air pistol. **£65-150** *VAG*

A 6 shot .455 Webley Mk VI DA service revolver with detachable shoulder stock, the frame dated 1917, 11½in (29cm) overall. **£300-350** *WAL*

A 30 bore percussion boxlock sidehammer belt pistol, engraved Hewson, London, No. 4681, 9in (23cm). **£140-160** *WAL*

A French 10 shot 6mm CF 'Le Protector' palm pistol, 4in (10cm). **£300-350** *WAL*

A 6 shot .44 Starr DA army percussion revolver, 12in (30.5cm). **£450-500** *WAL*

A 48 bore flintlock boxlock pocket pistol, by H. W. Mortimer, c1800, 6in (15cm). **£140-160** *WAL*

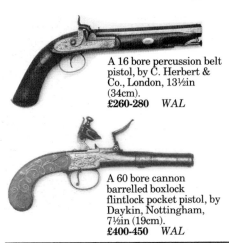

A 16 bore percussion belt pistol, by C. Herbert & Co., London, 13½in (34cm).
£260-280 *WAL*

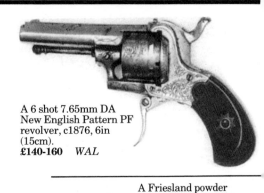

A 6 shot 7.65mm DA New English Pattern PF revolver, c1876, 6in (15cm).
£140-160 *WAL*

A 60 bore cannon barrelled boxlock flintlock pocket pistol, by Daykin, Nottingham, 7½in (19cm).
£400-450 *WAL*

A Friesland powder flask, early 19thC, 7in (18cm) long.
£80-90 *HAR*

Powder Flasks

A copper powder flask, spring broken and damaged measuring spout, 19thC, 8in (20cm) long.
£125-150 *BS*

A brass powder flask by G Roe, 19thC, 8in (20cm) long.
£165-200 *BS*

A copper powder flask by James Dixon & Son, in poor condition, 8in (20cm) long.
£50-60 *BS*

A copper powder flask by G & J W Hawksley, Sheffield, 19thC, 8½in (21cm) long.
£185-250 *BS*

A horn flask engraved with a crown, GR cypher, Hanoverian motto and a figure of a Grenadier with mitre cap.
£220-250 *CSK*

A copper powder flask embossed with 3 horses heads and stamped G & J W Hawksley Sheffield, 8in (20cm).
£35-45 *WAL*

A copper powder flask, spring broken, 5in (13cm) long.
£90-100 *BS*

Uniforms

The black silk mantle, of a Knight of Justice of The Most Venerable Order of St. John of Jerusalem in the British Realm.
£400-500 *CSK*

Sir Owen Cosby Philipps 1863-1937 was at various times Liberal M.P., Conservative M.P., Hon. Captain Royal Naval Reserve, Lord Lieutenant, and Vice-Admiral of North Wales.

A Major's khaki linen tunic of the 1st Chinese Regiment.
£100-150 *WAL*

A Captain's full dress scarlet doublet of The 92nd, Gordon Highlanders, Regiment, with yellow facings, c1875.
£160-200 *WAL*

The Victorian uniform of Major F. F. Hallett, 1st (Brighton) Sussex Rifle Volunteers.
£650-750 *WAL*

A post 1902 bandsman's full dress scarlet tunic of the 1st Volunteer Battalion The Royal West Kent Regiment, with issue stamps 1VWK.6068.
£100-150 *WAL*

A brown flying jacket of the Irvin thermally-insulated type.
£360-400 *CSK*

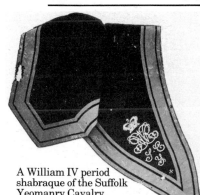

Cross Reference
Aeronautica

Accoutrements

A pair of officer's gilt scale epaulettes, probably Yeomanry, early 19thC.
£50-55 *CSK*

An officer's pouch flap of the 2nd Life Guards.
£75-85 *CSK*

A William IV period shabraque of the Suffolk Yeomanry Cavalry.
£1,200-1,500 *CSK*

This shabraque belonged to J. E. Polly who served in the Long Melford troop of the regiment.

A Household Cavalry trooper's cuirass.
£130-150 *CSK*

Above. A crimson and gold lace girdle with gilt toggles and heavy buckle, as worn by Lancer Officers up to 1840, 3½in (9cm) wide. Centre. A pair of gilt swan neck box spurs and a Lancer officer's red leather pouch with gilt VR cypher to the silver flap, H. & S. 1849. Bottom. A pouchbelt with only the slide, chain boss and picker plate, probably 12th Lancers.
£180-200 *CSK*

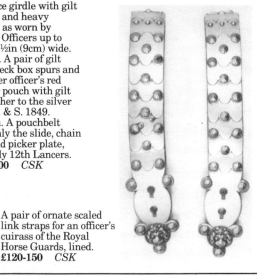

A pair of ornate scaled link straps for an officer's cuirass of the Royal Horse Guards, lined.
£120-150 *CSK*

A plain gold cord aiguillette, possibly that of an Extra Equerry to the King.
£60-80 *CSK*

General

A scarce painted wooden side drum of the 4th or West Regt. of Jersey Militia.
£600-650 *WAL*

A Chinese sword stand, inlaid with mother-of-pearl, 18thC, 22½in (57.5cm) high.
£550-600 *HUN*

A pair of World War II German Battery Commander's periscope binoculars, on extending oak tripod, 59in (149.5cm) high lowered.
£140-160 *CSK*

A double cavity .56 mould for Colt revolving rifle, with wooden handles and brass ferrules, minor wear, the sprue-cutter stamped Colts Patent, the body stamped .56″ over S, serial No. 16.
£180-220 *WAL*

A pair of German army field glasses, with original leather case, 1914-18.
£45-50 *COB*

A Georgian cut and polished steel belt hanger for a smallsword, curved for the hip, with cut and polished suspension chains and sprung swivel retaining clips.
£50-100 *WAL*

A Nationalist Chinese flag, 1940s.
£15-20 *COB*

A spontoon, with tapered head and raised central rib, on steel socket with raised turned reinforcer, long straps, on original wooden haft with stepped baluster brass socket at butt, c1700, head 10in (25cm).
£450-500 *WAL*

A heavy German cavalry trooper's breastplate, musket ball proof mark, lugs for strap fastening, short raised collar, edges pierced with holes for lining attachment, light rust, c1800.
£120-180 *WAL*

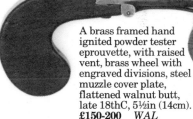

A brass framed hand ignited powder tester eprouvette, with raised vent, brass wheel with engraved divisions, steel muzzle cover plate, flattened walnut butt, late 18thC, 5½in (14cm).
£150-200 *WAL*

An E.I.C. gunner's brass rule, the steel tipped callipers with scales for measuring bore size and ball sizes, limbs engraved with scales entitled Guns and Shot, signed Crichton London, c1800, 7in (17.5cm).
£650-700 *WAL*

A Russian brass naval ammunition waist pouch, to be worn against the body, with 3 brass belt loops to back, front engraved, base stamped 1850 with anchor, 9½in (24cm) wide.
£200-220 *WAL*

An earthenware tank teapot, by Sadler & Co., c1930.
£85-95 *PGA*

A bronze figure of a private of The Grenadier Guards, on ebonised wooden plinth, base inscribed J. Boehm sc., c1820, 17½in (44cm) high.
£750-800 *CSK*

A Royal Doulton model of a bulldog.
£200-250 *LT*

Margaret Dovaston, Scene in the British Trenches following an Explosion, watercolour, monochrome, signed, 17½ by 10in (44.5 by 25cm), framed.
£180-220 *Bon*

A cast brass model of a mortar, 9in (22.5cm) long.
£60-80 *OD*

A model field cannon, in the style of the early 19thC, barrel 15in (38cm) long.
£180-200 *Bon*

A Royal Navy wooden rum measure, 1910, 6in (15cm) high.
£25-30 *COB*

A dagger brooch from Antwerp, 2in (5cm) long.
£12-18 *BY*

Miniatures

We have always had a fascination with miniature replicas of everyday articles. Collecting miniatures reached a peak during mid-Victorian times but still retains its popularity. Souvenirs are very popular as well as advertising packaging and romantic keepsakes. Most items shown here could be placed within other sections of the book, so they are not cross referenced.

A silver Mr. Punch sealing wax holder, 3in (7.5cm) high.
£140-160   *LEW*

A perfume or medicinal corkscrew, 1in (2.5cm) long.
£40-50   *LEW*

A horn cigar cutter, 2in (5cm) high.
£70-80   *LEW*

A gold and coral doll's rattle/whistle, 1in (2.5cm) long.
£230-270   *LEW*

An ivory vinaigrette, c1820, 1in (2.5cm) high.
£80-100   *LEW*

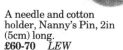

A needle and cotton holder, Nanny's Pin, 2in (5cm) long.
£60-70   *LEW*

A tartan ware brush, 3in (7.5cm) long.
£40-50   *LEW*

A silver and bone rattle, 1½in (3.5cm) diam.
£90-100   *LEW*

An ivory tape measure, 2in (5cm) high.
£80-100   *LEW*

A brass microscope, Ellis, Paignton, 2in (5cm) long.
£40-50   *LEW*

A tortoiseshell purse, c1840, 2in (5cm) long.
£90-100   *LEW*

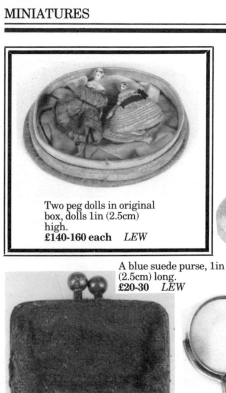

Two peg dolls in original box, dolls 1in (2.5cm) high.
£140-160 each *LEW*

A pin cushion commemorating the French Exposition, advertising Liebig, 2in (5cm) diam.
£20-30 *BY*

A mounted compass, 1in (2.5cm) high.
£20-30 *LEW*

A blue suede purse, 1in (2.5cm) long.
£20-30 *LEW*

A magnifying glass, 2in (5cm) long.
£240-260 *LEW*

A dolls house wishbone chair, 2in (5cm) high.
£6-10 *VB*

A cane three-piece lounge suite.
£40-50 *PCh*

An iron, 1in (2.5cm) long.
£20-30 *LEW*

A peg doll and clothes, c1860, doll 1in (2.5cm) high.
£340-360 *LEW*

A pair of spectacles in a brass container, inscribed 'Love is Blind', 1in (2.5cm) long.
£230-260 *LEW*

An ivory rolling pin, possibly a needle holder, 4in (10cm) long.
£40-50 *LEW*

Books

A Book of Common Prayer, Hymns Ancient and Modern, leather bound with ivory cover, 2in (5cm) high.
£40-50 *LEW*

A painted metal souvenir book, with London Katie 22.7.04 written inside.
£20-30 *LEW*

A bible in tartan ware box, inscribed Smallest Bible in the World, with Burns family register in the poet's handwriting, 2½in (6.5cm) high.
£240-260 *LEW*

A Prayer Book, leather bound with ivory cover, 2in (5cm) high.
£60-70 *LEW*

A red painted metal box, 1in (2.5cm) long.
£60-70 *LEW*

Boxes

A tortoiseshell cabin trunk 2½in (6.5cm) long.
£80-90 *LEW*

A mother-of-pearl box, 1½in (4cm) long.
£80-90 *LEW*

A papier mâché box, 1in (2.5cm) long.
£30-40 *LEW*

A pewter box, 1in (2.5cm) long.
£15-20 *LEW*

Figures & Animals

A selection of bronze animals, ½ to 1in (1.5 to 2.5cm) high.
£40-50 each   *LEW*

A pair of brass figures, 1½in (4cm) high.
£20-30 each   *LEW*

Notebooks & Pencils

A pug dog pencil in silver and gold, with garnet eyes, 2in (5cm) long.
£350-400   *LEW*

A note case and pencil with enamelled scene, 1½ by 1in (4 by 3cm).
£45-55   *LEW*

Tea Sets

A selection of Royal Worcester china, early 20thC.
£160-180   *PCh*

A steel note case and pencil with a view on the front, 2 by 1½in (5 by 4cm).
£65-75   *LEW*

A pencil in the shape of a barrel, 1½in (4cm) long.
£40-50   *LEW*

A Victorian green and white porcelain tea set, the teapot 3½in (9cm) high.
£120-190   *SBA*

Perfume Bottles

A Venetian glass
perfume bottle, 1½in
(4cm) high.
£65-75 *LEW*

A Venetian glass
perfume bottle, 1½in
(4cm) high.
£35-40 *LEW*

A Nailsea glass flask, 1in
(2.5cm) long.
£20-30 *LEW*

A Venetian glass
perfume bottle, 1½in
(4cm) high.
£35-40 *LEW*

Scissors

A pair of ivory and steel
travelling scissors, 2in
(5cm) long, folded.
£30-40 *LEW*

Silver scissors, shaped as
a bird, 2in (5cm) long.
£70-80 *LEW*

Toys & Games

A set of dominoes in
mahogany box with
sliding lid, 2in (5cm)
wide.
£25-35 *PCh*

A complete set of
Victorian playing cards,
1in (2.5cm) high.
£10-15 *CA*

An ivory box filled with
counters, 1in (2.5cm)
diam.
£65-75 *LEW*

A box containing
dominoes, 1½in (4cm)
high.
£20-30 *BY*

20thC Miniatures

A sterling silver penknife, 2in (5cm) long.
£30-40 *LEW*

A cast iron range with pots and pans, 9in (23cm).
£200-500 *WRe*

A gramophone, 4½in (11cm) high.
£230-270 *LEW*

A gilt and enamel perfume bottle, a souvenir from Margate, 1½in (4cm) long.
£40-50 *LEW*

Black & White whisky magnetic scottie dogs.
£20-30 *LEW*

A Scandinavian butter box, 3in (8cm) wide.
£18-20 *CA*

A Player's Digger tin, 2in (5cm) high.
£8-10 *BY*

A record and cover, supposedly the smallest record in the world, plays God Save the King, only 250 issued, 1in (2.5cm) diam.
£150-250 *BY*

A Ryvita packet, 1½in (4cm) long.
£3-6 *BY*

A pair of Guinness bottles, filled with Guinness, 3in (7.5cm) high.
£8-15 *BY*

A Butlin's Christmas mug, 1961, 2½in (6.5cm) high.
£8-12 *BY*

A figure of Mr. Creamy Sharpy, the Sharp's Toffee man.
£40-60 *BY*

Cross Reference
Drinking

A bottle of Mackeson stout, 2in (5cm) high.
£6-12 *BY*

A Players cigarette packet, 1in (2.5cm) high.
£8-12 *BY*

A silk covered guitar, 3in (7.5cm) long.
£90-100 *LEW*

Jack Dempsey's boxing gloves.
£15-25 *BY*

A tortoiseshell and ivory veneered mother-of-pearl inlaid mandolin, 5½in (14cm) long.
£80-90 *LEW*

A box of Eversharp red top square leads, 1½in (4cm) long.
£8-10 *LEW*

A Hohner mouth organ, in original box, 1½in (4cm) long.
£10-20 *BY*

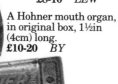

A tortoiseshell and mother-of-pearl inlaid guitar, 6in (15cm) long.
£60-70 *LEW*

Money Boxes

A Yorkshire pottery
money box, chipped,
c1850.
£120-130   *BRE*

A money box,
5in (13cm)
high.
£27-30   *YON*

A G.R. VI money box, 3in
(7.5cm) high.
£10-15   *RTT*

A Post Office Savings
money box, 4½in
(11.5cm) high.
£2-5   *CAC*

A tin Sharp's Toffee
money box, 4½in
(11.5cm) wide.
£25-35   *BY*

A wooden money box,
c1930.
£7-10   *RPM*

A Dr. Barnardo's money
box, c1950, 4½in (11.5cm)
high.
£10-15   *RTT*

A Butlin Beavers'
money box, 6in
(15cm) high.
£7-10
RTT

A brown glazed spaniel's
head money box, mid-
19thC.
£60-80   *SWN*

A dog money box, 5in
(13cm) high.
£35-40   *PW*

Home Safes

Post Office home safes, l. Introduced 1930, c. c1910, r. c1950.
£5-10 each *KH*

A Sheffield and Ecclesall Co-operative Society Ltd. home safe, produced from 1900 onwards, 3½in (8.5cm) wide.
£5-10 *KH*

These were for you to save your money for the Co-operative; they kept the key and credited the money to your account. They had an ingenious way of preventing people from picking the lock, i.e. a panel came across the money slot to prevent shaking the money out.

Three home safes, Union Bank of Manchester, Coventry Savings Bank and Northampton Town and Country Benefit Building Society, c1925.
£5-10 each *KH*

Two money boxes, Birmingham Municipal Bank and Williams Deacon's Bank.
£5-10 each *KH*

Two Midland Bank home safes, c1925.
£5-10 each *KH*

They were issued by various banks and building societies, with half size ones for children.

A National cash register, 17in (42.5cm) high.
£350-500 *NA*

Night Lights

Night lights, or fairy lights as they are
sometimes known, come in a multitude of
sizes, shapes and designs and were used,
not only as bedside night lights, but also as
table decorations.

This form of domestic lighting was
patented by Samuel Clarke in London in
1886. The Clarke 'Cricklite' featured glass
covers in a variety of colours, the bases
generally of pressed glass, often showing
the maker's name. Subsequent night
lights have been manufactured in many
different materials.

A point to note is that the covers and
bases have often become mis-matched,
thus affecting the value.

Blue and vaseline glass
night lights:
l. A Davidson base with
American top.
£25-30
r. American, 20thC.
£15-20   *PC*

A Victorian night light
holder on an 'orange'
base, 20thC, with
matched top, 5½in
(14cm) high.
£150-160   *PC*

A pink, crown shaped
night light, probably
American, 4½in
(11.5cm).
£60-70   *PC*

A pressed glass night
light, 20thC, 6in (15cm)
high.
£35-40   *PC*

A two-part glass night
light, top 20thC, base
19thC, 6in (15cm).
£50-60   *PC*

An owl night light, 4½in
(11cm) high.
£100-120   *PC*

A satin glass night light
and holder, 4in (10cm)
high.
£80-90   *PC*

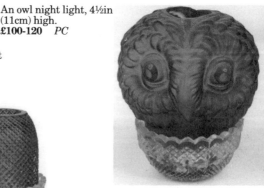

Three coloured night
lights, assorted tops and
bases, 4in (10cm) high.
£30-35   *PC*

A pineapple shaped
night light, English base,
American top, 4in (10cm)
high.
£45-50   *PC*

A green glass night light,
19thC, 4½in (11cm) high.
£80-100   *PC*

A beehive night light,
cranberry base and
raindrop design top,
probably American,
4½in (11cm) high.
£45-50   *PC*

A blue three-piece night
light, probably Greener,
5½in (14cm) high.
£100-120   *PC*

Two glass night lights,
pink and blue:
l. 20thC, 4½in (11cm)
high.
£15-20
r. 19thC, 4in (10cm) high.
£40-50   *PC*

A pink glass dovecote
night light holder,
probably German, late
19thC, 7½in (19cm) high.
£100-130   *PC*

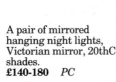

A turquoise blue night
light, 5in (12.5cm) high.
£45-50   *PC*

A ruby red swirl night
light, 4in (10cm) high.
£35-40   *PC*

A pair of mirrored
hanging night lights,
Victorian mirror, 20thC
shades.
£140-180   *PC*

A hanging mirrored
night light.
£120-130 *PC*

A moulded glass night
light on stand, with
Davidson top and
Baccarat candlestick
base, 12in (30.5cm) high.
£80-100
Candlestick alone.
£50-60 *PC*

A ruby night light on
yellow glass stand, top
possibly American, base
modern American, 9½in
(23.5cm) high.
£30-40 *PC*

A Continental moulded
glass stand with metal
and jewelled night light
holder, 12in (30.5cm)
high.
£60-70 *PC*

A Clarke's 'Cricklite'
stand with a moire glass
top, 14½in (37cm) high.
£80-100 *PC*

*This is not the correct top,
which should be a soft
fringed shade or a plain
glass shade.*

A Good Morning night
light, possibly German,
4in (10cm) high.
£140-150 *PC*

Two glass night lights on
stands:
l. 8in (20cm) high.
£45-50
r. 9in (22.5cm) high.
£30-40 *PC*

A child's night light in
the form of a glass bird on
a chrome base, c1925.
£20-30 *ASc*

A silver plate and
cranberry glass night
light, 19thC, 4in (10cm)
high.
£70-80 *PC*

A black boy night light, 4½in (11.5cm) high.
£100-130   *PC*

A Negro head night light, 4in (10cm) high.
£100-120   *PC*

A ruby red night light on ceramic base, 7in (17.5cm) high.
£100-130   *PC*

A Highland Terrier night light, 4in (10cm) high.
£100-150   *PC*

A Pyramid night light, c1865, 2in (5cm) diam, and a teaspoon measure, 1in (2.5cm) high.
£10-15 each   *CA*

A moulded glass night light holder, on stand with floral decoration, c1880, 6in (15cm) high.
£40-50   *PC*

A ceramic night light holder, probably for a coiled night light, c1930, 3in (7.5cm) high.
£40-50   *PC*

A nursery house night light, 3in (7.5cm) high.
£20-30   *PC*

Oriental
Ivory

A carved Indian ivory caparisoned elephant with 4 attendants, 4½in high.
£200-250   *PC*

Two Japanese carved ivory figures, 1½ and 4½in (4 and 11cm) high.
£80-150 each   *PC*

MAKE THE MOST OF MILLERS
Condition is absolutely vital when assessing the value of any item. Damaged pieces appreciate much less than perfect examples. However, a rare, desirable piece may command a high price even when damaged.

An Indian ivory carving of 4 elephants on wood base, 8in (20cm) long.
£120-150 *PC*

A Cantonese carved ivory needle case, 5in (13cm) high.
£55-65 *PC*

A carved ivory crab, 4in (10cm) wide.
£150-200 *PC*

A Chinese Devil's Work Ball on carved ivory stand, 7in (17.5cm) high.
£150-180 *PC*

Two Japanese carved ivory figures of a tradesmen, 2½in (6cm) high.
£120-150 each *PC*

A carved ivory figure of a stag, 3in (8cm) wide.
£70-90 *PC*

Scrimshaw ivory spoons.
£15-20 each *PC*

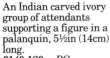

An Indian carved ivory group of attendants supporting a figure in a palanquin, 5½in (14cm) long.
£140-180 *PC*

A Chinese carved ivory hanging decoration with a Devil's Work Ball, 9in (23cm) long.
£70-90 *PC*

A Japanese carved ivory figure of a vegetable seller, signed, 10in (25cm).
£170-200 *DEN*

Two Japanese carved
ivory figures.
£40-60 each   *PC*

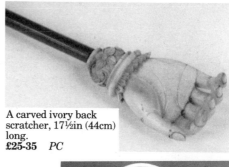

A carved ivory back
scratcher, 17½in (44cm)
long.
£25-35   *PC*

An ivory box and cover,
1½in (4cm) diam.
£20-30
and an ivory needle case,
3½in (9cm) long.
£20-25   *PC*

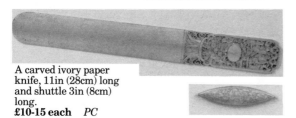

A carved ivory paper
knife, 11in (28cm) long
and shuttle 3in (8cm)
long.
£10-15 each   *PC*

Netsukes

Three ivory netsukes,
the figure with the tall
hat is Jurojin who is one
of the 7 Japanese Gods of
Good Fortune, 1½ to 2in
(4 to 5cm) high.
£70-120 each   *PC*

Three ivory netsukes,
1 to 1½in (3 to 4cm) high.
£80-140 each   *PC*

Two ivory netsukes, 1 to
1½in (3 to 4cm) high.
£80-120 each   *PC*

Snuff Bottles

An agate snuff bottle
with carving of a
bird on the front,
coral stopper,
c1830.
£300-350
Bon

An agate
snuff bottle,
19thC.
£75-100   *Bon*

A chalcedony snuff bottle, carved in the front with ochre inclusions in deep relief, c1830.
£180-200   *Bon*

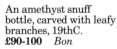

An amethyst snuff bottle, carved with leafy branches, 19thC.
£90-100   *Bon*

A carved chalcedony snuff bottle, c1850.
£220-250   *Bon*

General

A Canton decorated porcelain jar and cover, late 19thC, 2in (5cm) high.
£20-25   *PC*

A Chinese soapstone reticulated hexagonal spill vase, 4½in (11cm) high.
£50-75   *PC*

Bronzes

A Chinese bronze figure of a Buddhistic lion, originally 1 of a pair, 19thC, 6½in (16cm) high.
£100-150   *PC*

A Sino-Tibetan bronze figure of a Bodhisattva, 17th/18thC, 6in (15cm) high.
£200-300   *PC*

Two agate archer's rings, one with a carving of a boy and one with a cat and plant, using the natural inclusions of the stone, 19thC.
£75-90   *Bon*

Patch Boxes

A patch box lined with tortoiseshell, c1840.
£95-120   *EHA*

An extensive selection of patch boxes can be found in Miller's Collectables Price Guide Volume I, page 273.

Papier Mâché

A glove box, 12in (31cm) long.   **£20-25**   *CAC*

A spectacles case, 5½in (14cm) long.
£95-110   *SBA*

A hand painted tray,
12in (31cm) wide.
£15-20   *HUN*

A Victorian blotter, 9 by
6in (23 by 15cm).
£35-40   *CAC*

A further selection of papier mâché items
is included in Miller's Collectables Price
Guide Volume II pages 287 and 288.

Photographs

Old negatives and photographs have seen
a great increase in interest and as a result,
prices. Before 1870 the interest is mainly
the technical process, after then, the
photographer and subject matter are more
important. There has been a tremendous
interest in 20thC photographers during
the past year, examples of some of their
work are shown here.

J. H. Clarke and others,
the Muir family Indian
album, approximately
100 albumen prints and
1 salt print, c1870, 7½ by
10½in (19 by 27cm).
£200-300   *CSK*

*A note inside the album
states Sir Wm. Muir was
British Envoy to India,
oriental scholar and
President of the Royal
Asiatic Society. The
photographs include
colonial and Indian
portraits, amateur
theatrical scenes,
architectural and
topographical views and
a view of cricketers at
Nynee Tal.*

A framed gelatin silver
print, Pierrette from the
Triadic Ballet, attributed
to Oscar Schlemmer,
1925, 4 by 3in (10 by
8cm).
£2,500-3,000   *CNY*

Victor Guidalevitch, Je
Pense-donc Je Suis,
gelatin silver print,
c1930, 15½ by 12in (39 by
30.5cm).
£700-800   *CNY*

DID YOU KNOW?
Miller's Collectables
Price Guide is
designed to build up,
year by year, into the
most comprehensive
reference system
available.

Anon Burmese album
with 25 albumen prints,
1890s, 8 by 10½in (20 by
27cm).
£260-300   *CSK*

A Victorian tin type
photograph in frame.
£25-35   *J*

A papier mâché decorated photograph album, late 19thC, 6 by 4in (15 by 10cm).
£45-55 *CAC*

Twelve day/night views for use with a conical polyrama panoptique, with pin-pricked highlights and hidden scenes mostly showing Paris and London views, retailer's label A. Bouchet, 52 George Street, Portman Square, 4in (10cm) diam each.
£500-600 *CSK*

Cecil Beaton, Andy Warhol and Candy Darling, matted and framed, the photographer's name stamp on the reverse, 1969, 13 by 8in (33 by 20cm).
£2,000-2,300 *S(NY)*

Captain W. De W. Abney, Thebes and its Five Greater Temples, with 40 carbon prints, 1876, each 6 by 8in (15 by 20cm).
£400-500 *CSK*

V. Jíru, Chorus Line, a framed gelatin silver print, 1920s, 9½ by 7in (24 by 18cm).
£400-450 *CNY*

Mayer & Pierson, two portraits of a lady and a gentleman, hand coloured salt prints, 1860s, 8½in (21cm) high.
£260-300 *CSK*

Kusakabe Kimbei, Japanese costume studies, 50 hand tinted albumen prints, 1890s, 8 by 10½in (20 by 27cm).
£700-800 *CSK*

Gyula Halasz Brassai 1899-1984, Kiki surrounded with Men at the Cabaret des Fleurs, Rue de Montparnasse c1932, a framed gelatin silver print, 1960s, 11½ by 8½in (29 by 21cm).
£1,000-1,500 *CNY*

Margaret Bourke-White, Cement Factory – Novorossisk, On the Black Sea, USSR, a framed gelatin silver print, c1932, 13 by 9in (33 by 23cm).
£4,500-5,000 *CNY*

Weegee, Audience, the photographer's Weegee the Famous credit stamp and Arthur Weegee Fellig, 6526 Selma Avenue, Hollywood studio stamp on the reverse, 1940s, 10½ by 13in (27 by 33cm).
£1,200-1,400 *S(NY)*

Irving Penn, Deep Sea Diver, a framed multiple printed and hand coated platinum palladium print on aluminium, number 36/38, 1980, 19 by 15in (48 by 38cm).
£1,800-2,000 *CNY*

Robert Capa 1913-1954, Militarized Zone on the Bridge, outskirts of Barcelona, a gelatin silver print, titled in ink and stamped on reverse, 1936, 7 by 9½in (18 by 24cm).
£2,000-2,500 *CNY*

Margaret Bourke-White, U.S.S. Akron, World's Largest Airship, a framed gelatin silver print on textured paper, 1931, 17½ by 23in (44 by 59cm).
£5,000-5,500 *CNY*

Framed in duralumin used in girder construction of the United States airship Akron built by the Goodyear Zeppelin Corporation as noted on the frame.

Brett Weston, a plate from the White Sands portfolio, matted and framed 1946, printed c1949, one in an edition of 75, 7½ by 9½in (19 by 24cm).
£1,000-1,200 *S(NY)*

Aaron Siskind, Selected Images, 3 photographs, including Lima 224, Jalapa 4 and Uruapan, Mexico.
£1,000-1,200   *S(NY)*

Harold Leroy Harvey 1899-1971, Chesterfield Cigarettes advertisement, gelatin silver print, 1930s, 10½ by 13½in (26 by 34cm).
£1,200-1,400   *CNY*

Ansel Adams, Gerry Sharpe, Ouray, Colorado 1958, gelatin silver print from Portfolio VII, 1976, number 62/115, 19 by 15in (48 by 38cm).
£900-1,200   *CNY*

Harold Edgerton, Cutting the Playing Card Quickly, a gelatin silver print 1960, 14 by 18½in (36 by 47cm).
£1,700-2,000   *CNY*

In the execution of this study a .30 calibre bullet cut the card in less than a millionth of a second.

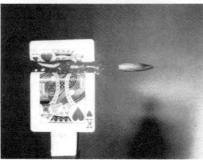

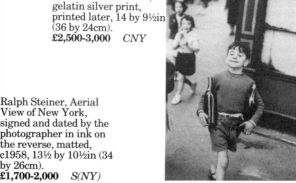

Richard Avedon, Carmen, Homage to Munkacsi, coat by Cardin, Place François-Preier, Paris 1957, a gelatin silver print from The Retrospective Portfolio, framed, signed and numbered 34/75, 1978, 18 by 14in (46 by 36cm).
£4,000-4,500   *CNY*

Henri Cartier-Bresson, Rue Mouffetard 1954, a gelatin silver print, printed later, 14 by 9½in (36 by 24cm).
£2,500-3,000   *CNY*

Ralph Steiner, Aerial View of New York, signed and dated by the photographer in ink on the reverse, matted, c1958, 13½ by 10½in (34 by 26cm).
£1,700-2,000   *S(NY)*

Ansel Adams, Aspens, New Mexico 1958, gelatin silver print 1972, 10½ by 13½in (26 by 34cm).
£4,000-5,000 *CNY*

This print is accompanied by correspondence between the owner and Adams which confirms the printing date of 1972.

Bill Brandt, Nude August 1953, framed gelatin silver print, 1970s, 13½in by 11½in (34 by 29cm).
£700-800 *CNY*

Elliott Erwitt, Selected Images 1946-78, 12 gelatin silver prints, printed later, each approx. 12 by 18in (31 by 46cm).
£2,800-3,500 *CNY*

Brett Weston, Garapata Beach 1954, gelatin silver print, printed later, 10½ by 13½in (26 by 34cm).
£950-1,000 *CNY*

Richard Avedon, The Chicago Seven: Lee Weiner, John Froines, Abbie Hoffman, Rennie Davis, Jerry Rubin, Tom Hayden, Dave Dellinger 1969, 3 gelatin silver prints mounted together, 10 by 24in (25 by 61cm) overall.
£1,800-2,000 *CNY*

William Wegman, A Sequence of Furniture Arrangement, 3 framed gelatin silver prints, 1972, 13 by 11in (33 by 28cm).
£2,000-2,500 *CNY*

> **DID YOU KNOW?**
> Miller's Collectables Price Guide is designed to build up, year by year, into the most comprehensive reference system available.

André Kertész, Wines and Liquors, Paris 1929, gelatin silver print, 1970s, 10 by 8in (25 by 20cm).
£800-900 *CNY*

Bill Brandt, Evening in Kew Gardens, London 1930s, gelatin silver print, printed later, 13 by 11½in (33 by 29cm).
£450-500 *CNY*

Frederick Sommer, Cut Paper, a framed gelatin silver print, signed, 1977, 9½ by 7½in (24 by 19cm).
£5,500-6,000   *CNY*

Sarah Charlesworth, Black Mask, a framed laminated cibachrome print, 1983, 39½ by 29½in (100 by 75cm).
£1,700-2,000   *CNY*

Michael Kenna, Covered Urn, Versailles, France 1987, two gelatin silver later prints, signed, dated and numbered from the edition of 25, 18½ by 15in (47 by 38cm).
£1,000-1,500   *CNY*

Shiela Metzner, Summer Fiesta Ware Bowls, a framed fresson print, initialled in pencil and embossed stamp in the margin, 1985, 16½ by 26in (42 by 66cm).
£1,200-1,500   *CNY*

Michael Spano, Portrait of a Man 1986, a framed solarized gelatin silver print, signed, dated and numbered 8/15, 1988, 34½ by 27½in (87 by 70cm).
£1,700-2,000   *CNY*

Minor White, Jupiter Portfolio 1947-71, Light Gallery New York 1975, 12 gelatin silver prints each signed, titled and dated in pencil with Princeton University Trustees stamp on the reverse and numbered 65 from an edition of 100, 10½ by 8½in (26 by 21cm).
£9,500-10,000   *CNY*

Josef Sudek, From the Window of My Atelier, 5 gelatin silver prints, 1950-65, varying sizes.
£2,700-3,000   *CNY*

A. Aubrey Bodine, Pennsylvania Train Yard, gelatin silver print, signed, 16 by 14in (41 by 35.5cm), framed.
£2,300-2,600   *CNY*

Robert Mapplethorpe, Larry and Bobby, a framed gelatin silver print, signed, dated and numbered 4/10, 1979, 14 by 14in (36 by 36cm).
£3,500-4,500   *CNY*

Joel-Peter Witkin, Melvin Burkhart, Human Oddity, a gelatin silver print, signed, titled, dated, and numbered 5/15, 15 by 15in (38 by 38cm).
£1,500-2,000   *CNY*

Robert Mapplethorpe, Tulips, a gelatin silver print, signed, dated and numbered 5/10, 1983, 15 by 15in (38 by 38cm).
£4,500-5,500   *CNY*

Kipton Kumler, A Portfolio of Plants, 10 platinum palladium prints, privately published in 1975 and 1977.
£1,600-1,800   *CNY*

Charles Hoff, Explosion of the Hindenburg, Lakehurst, N.J., gelatin silver print, 1937, 10 by 13in (25 by 33cm), framed.
£3,500-4,000   *CNY*

Robert Mapplethorpe, Orchid, a framed gelatin silver print, signed, dated and numbered 1/10, 1988, 19 by 19in (48 by 48cm).
£4,000-5,000   *CNY*

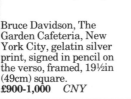

Bruce Davidson, The Garden Cafeteria, New York City, gelatin silver print, signed in pencil on the verso, framed, 19½in (49cm) square.
£900-1,000   *CNY*

Pincushion Dolls

Four pincushion dolls,
2 to 2½in (5 to 6.5cm)
high.
£15-20 each   *LB*

A pincushion doll, 1920s,
3½in (8.5cm) high.
£25-30   *LB*

A pair of Art Deco
ceramic figures, probably
German, 4in (10cm) high.
£150-160   *LB*

Two porcelain pincushion
dolls, 2½in (6.5cm) high.
£65-75 each   *SBA*

A further selection of pincushion dolls is
featured in Miller's Collectables Price
Guide Volume I, pages 280-281.

Playing Cards

Two packs
of advertising
playing cards.
£3-6 each   *BY*

Advertising playing
cards.

l. **£12-15**
r. **£6-10**   *BY*

A card box and contents,
11½ by 6in (29 by 15cm).
£25-30   *CAC*

Packs of playing cards,
c1935.
£5-6 each   *BY*

A pack of Happy Families.
£5-7 *BY*

Pin-up girl playing cards.
£5-7 each *BY*

Two packs of playing cards, l. Help Yourself, c1950 and r. Guinness, c1930.
£5-10 each *RTT*

Cross Reference
Drinking

DID YOU KNOW?
Miller's Collectables Price Guide is designed to build up, year by year, into the most comprehensive reference system available.

A pack of Esso playing cards, unused.
£8-10 *RTT*

A pack of transport playing cards.
£10-15 *BY*

A pack of French playing cards, Le Poker Politique.
£4-8 *BY*

A card case with 4 packs, c1930.
£18-20 *OD*

A deck of 52 playing cards, manufactured by Goodall and Son, London, c1882.
£300-350 *CSK*

Police

A collection of 5 tipstaffs, including one with a cast metal crown finial, the orb without the cross, and hollow brass shaft with unscrewing base cap and containing a City of London writ dated October 1814 regarding the delivery to the Keeper of Newgate of the body of Michael Stanley, charged with stealing one hogshead of the value of eight shillings, 9½in (24cm) long.
£550-600 *CSK*

For an extensive selection of Police collectables see Miller's Collectables Price Guide Volume I, pages 286 to 291 and Volume II, pages 293 to 295.

Lady Katharine Booker, by William Smith, signed on obverse, in gilt metal frame, c1776, 2in (5cm) high.
£150-200 *C*

Portrait Miniatures

Charlotte Branfill, signed with monogram JW, c1730, in gilt metal frame with ribbed border, 2in (5cm) high.
£520-550 *C*

Two children of the Hohenzollern family, in silver point heightened with colour by David Boudon, signed on obverse, dated 1790, with square gilt wood frames.
£500-600 *C*

Mrs William Russell, by Samuel Rickards, in gilt metal bracelet clasp frame with lock of hair on reverse oval, 2in (5cm) high.
£600-650 *C*

A child by Roger, signed on obverse, in gilt mounted metal frame, c1800, 3½in (9cm) high.
£300-400 *C*

An officer, in scarlet coatee of the 30th (Cambridge) Regiment of Foot, Scottish School c1816, with gilt metal mount, 2½in (6cm) high.
£450-500 *C*

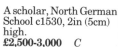

A scholar, North German School c1530, 2in (5cm) high.
£2,500-3,000 *C*

A lady, French School c1780, signed JC, with beaded gold mount in the lid of a tortoiseshell box, 2½in (7cm) high.
£750-850 *C*

A gentleman, believed to be John William, Elector Palatine of Neuburg, Swedish School c1700, on card with original crystal cut glass in silver gilt frame, 1½in (4cm) high.
£700-800 *C*

A gentleman, Dutch School c1650, oil on copper, contemporary gold locket with hinged cover, 2in (5cm) high.
£400-500 *C*

A mother seated holding her baby, Italian School c1830, in chased gilt metal frame with pierced scrolling foliate border, 2½in (7cm) high.
£400-450 *C*

A mother and child seated in a garden, French School c1780, with gold mount studded with pellets, 3½in (9cm) diam.
£550-600 *C*

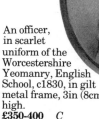

A lady, Scandinavian School c1790, with chased gold mount in the lid of a tortoiseshell lined ivory box with gold rim, 2in (5cm) diam.
£180-220 *C*

A gentleman, by Nathaniel Hone, R.A. 1718-84, signed with monogram on obverse and dated 1764, 1½in (4cm) high.
£450-500 *C*

An officer, in scarlet uniform of the Worcestershire Yeomanry, English School, c1830, in gilt metal frame, 3in (8cm) high.
£350-400 *C*

Postcards
Aviation

Four identical rare cards showing the Crawley & Crawley Special, a motor vehicle as an aeroplane for the Parade of the Coronation 1937, VG.
£90-100 *VS*

Only 8 of these cards were produced and given to the people who made the vehicle.

Airships, RP R.100 under construction at Howden, Yorks, G to VG.
£15-20 *VS*

Cross Reference
Aeronautica

Bournemouth, Graham White, Morane, published by Chandler 31.8.1910, G.
£20-25 *VS*

Balloons, France, Aero Club, with message referring to flight of 17th April 1901, possibly sent by one of the crew, FR.
£35-50 *VS*

The Mayfly airship coming out of hanger and referring to the launch, used May 22nd 1911, G.
£22-25 *VS*

Art Nouveau

Raphael Kirchner, girl with Aladdin's Lamp, No. 252, UB, slight album corner marks and scuffing, G.
£30-40 *VS*

Three girls heads with flowers, published by E.S.W., UB, slight album corner marks, G to VG.
£55-60 *VS*

Raphael Kirchner, Charms, UB, very slight album corner marks, VG.
£25-45 *VS*

Raphael Kirchner, girl with heart pendant, UB, slight album corner marks and scuffing, G.
£30-35 *VS*

Commonly used abbreviations — See Miller's Collectables Price Guide, Vol I, page 304.

Two Femmes Modernes, girls head in circular borders, UB, G.
£45-50 *VS*

Advertising Postcards

More Miles on Shell, No. 228, scarce, slight album corner marks, about VG.
£35-45 *VS*

Pickfords Removal through the Ages, complete, op, VG to EX.
£26-30 *VS*

Raphael Tuck, Fry's Five Boys Milk Chocolate, 1502, pu 1907, G.
£15-20 *VS*

Raphael Tuck, Celebrated Posters, Gilmour Thomson's Scotch Whisky, 1507, G to VG.
£60-70 *VS*

Fry's boy with toy train, by Pears, scarce, VG.
£13-18 *VS*

Shell, No. 273, scarce, VG.
£25-35 *VS*

Mansell, girl with cup, slight album corner marks, about VG.
£15-20 *VS*

Disasters

The Croydon-Sutton tram disaster, Easter Monday 1907, pu, G.
£25-30 *VS*

Airship RP, R101 crash with investigation team, scarce, slight corner crease, G.
£13-18 *VS*

Hand Drawn Postcards

'This beautiful landscape view was done (like the Irishman) in a hurry', 1923.
£4-5 *BEB*

'The idea of that girl bathing with that frightful costume on!', 1903.
£4-5 *BEB*

'A good gun', hand painted, 1906.
£3-5 *BEB*

'For gootness sake go back! Here kom der City Battalions', WWI.
£4-5 *BEB*

'Who ses Germans?', 1915.
£3-5 *BEB*

'Off to Philadelphia in the mornin'.
£4-5 *BEB*

'Mrs Grundy (from the country) Well I wouldn't show myself like that not for nothing. The compliments of the season to you both whatever it means', 1907.
£4-5 *BEB*

An original design framed with corresponding postcard, signed, watercolour, 5 by 10½in (13 by 26.5cm).
£600-650 *HSS*

'Oh my prophetic soul! My uncle!' Hamlet Act I, Scene 5, hand painted.
£3-5 *BEB*

'Me and my dog'.
£3-5 *BEB*

Donald McGill

The name of Donald McGill (1875-1962) summons up in the mind of most people all that is typical of the English Seaside. His fat ladies, silly parsons, hen-pecked husbands, cute children and above all his unashamed vulgarity, have become part of recent English social history.

No other postcard artist reached anywhere near his popularity or range of output. His first card was published in 1905 and for the next fifty years his sole occupation was the creation of postcard designs.

An original design framed with corresponding postcard, signed, watercolour, 8 by 6in (19.5cm by 14.5cm).
£900-1,000 *HSS*

This card was taken from a real life situation in which McGill had once found himself — he turned embarrassment into amusement.

An original design framed with corresponding postcard, signed, watercolour, 4½ by 9½in (12 by 24cm).
£450-475 *HSS*

"Well, I don't see much in that, do you, Rupert?"

A pair of original designs, the mount with printed caption attached, each signed, watercolours, each 8 by 6in (20 by 15cm).
£600-650 *HSS*

An original design framed with corresponding postcard, signed, watercolour, 7 by 5in (17.5 by 12.5cm).
£650-700 *HSS*

An unpublished original comic design, signed, watercolour, 5 by 10½in (12.5 by 25.5cm).
£450-500 *HSS*

An original design framed with corresponding postcard, signed, watercolour, 8 by 6in (20 by 15cm).
£450-475 *HSS*

An original design framed with corresponding postcard, signed, watercolour, 8 by 6in (20 by 15cm).
£500-550 *HSS*

An original comic postcard design, framed with corresponding postcard, signed, watercolour, 8½ by 6½in (21 by 15.5cm).
£450-475 *HSS*

An original design framed with corresponding postcard, signed, watercolour, 8 by 5½in (19.5 by 14cm).
£750-800 *HSS*

DID YOU KNOW?
Many of these originals were used as evidence in obscenity trials — and these tend to be the most desirable.

Silks

Woven red Pius XII
Vatican silk, C.S., slight
foxing to mount, G.
£30-40 *VS*

Allied flags embroidered
envelopes enclosing
cards, 5½ by 3½in (14 by
9cm).
£4-5 each *PC*

A Bright Birthday.
£5-6 *PC*

Royal Artillery badge
card.
£7-8 *PC*

World War I Silk Postcards

Two woven silk
postcards, Good News
From France.
£8-9
Forget Me Not.
£7-8 *THA*

An Allied flags
embroidered card, in
card mount, 5½ by 3½in
(14 by 8.5cm).
£3-4 *PC*

Right is Might, with
French and Allied Flags.
£3-4 *PC*

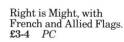

Cross Reference
Militaria

Royal Field Artillery.
£8-9 *PC*

An Australian Military
Forces card, quite rare.
£6-8 *PC*

General

A bear card.
£1-2   *CAC*

Waiting For The Feast.
25-50p   *CAC*

Rabbits cycling.
50p-£1   *CAC*

A galloping horse,
German, 1908.
£1-2   *CAC*

A German postcard,
1903.
£4-5   *CAC*

Horses, sent from
Selfridges roof garden.
£2-3   *CAC*

A Tuck postcard, 1921.
£1-2   *CAC*

'You And Me'.
50p-£1   *CAC*

From Davos, 1904.
50p-£1   *CAC*

Mrs Thatcher

Throughout history famous figures, especially politicians have been lampooned, Mrs Thatcher is no exception as the following set of modern postcards shows.

A Mrs Thatcher Don't 'donor' card!
30-35p *PC*

PREVENT STREET CRIME

A selection of Mrs Thatcher postcards.
30-35p each *IW*

As these cards are political and collectable the prices will rise over the years.

DID YOU KNOW?
Miller's Collectables Price Guide is designed to build up, year by year, into the most comprehensive reference system available.

General

Two birthday cards by Mabel Lucie Attwell.
£2-3 each *CAC*

'We are having a lovely time. Come and join us'.
30-40p *CAC*

With Best Wishes for Your Birthday, 1920.
£1-2 *CAC*

A card from Barmouth, 1905.
75p-£1 *CAC*

Sent from Margate, 1909.
50p-£1 *CAC*

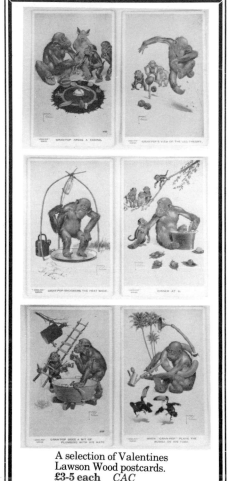

A selection of Valentines Lawson Wood postcards.
£3-5 each *CAC*

Puppies.
20-25p *CAC*

FURTHER READING
Discovering Picture Postcards, C. W. Hill, Aylesbury, Bucks 1978.
The Woven Silk Postcard, C. Radley, Barking 1978.
IPM Catalogue of Picture Postcards and Year Book 1989, J. H. D. Smith, Hove 1989.
Collecting Military Postcards, G. White, Bristol 1987.

Prints

George Baxter 1804-67, who was the son of a Lewes printer, perfected and patented in 1835 a colour printing process using oil colours. It is hard to imagine the impact that these colour reproductions had in the mid-18th Century when only monochrome prints were available. Several other printers employed the Baxter process, including J. M. Kronheim & Co., some of whose work is featured here. In 1850 Baxter licensed his pupil Robert Le Blond to produce a series of 32 oval shaped prints, we would refer you to Miller's Collectables Volume II, pages 307-309 for an extensive selection of these.

Moonlight, No. 111.
£80-120 *BEE*

Le Blond prints

Sunday Morning. No. 101.
£90-130
BEE

Learning to Ride, No. 104.
£90-130 *BEE*

The Wedding Day, No. 102.
£90-130 *BEE*

The Leisure Hour, No. 112.
£90-130 *BEE*

Baxter Prints

Le Retour de la Chasse.
£140-160 *CFA*

Victorian Comedy, set of 4.
£110-120 *CFA*

The Milkmaid and The Gleaner.
£110-120 pair *CFA*

The Farewell.
£110-120 pair   *CFA*

Harvesting, set of 4.
£110-120   *CFA*

The Fair Warrior, set
of 4.
£140-160   *CFA*

Woodcutters, set of 4.
£110-120   *CFA*

The Pleasures of the
Garden, set of 4.
£140-160   *CFA*

Picking Cherries, set of 4.
£140-160   *CFA*

At the Seaside, set of 4.
£90-110   *CFA*

Palais Royal, set of 4.
£110-120   *CFA*

Messengers, set of 4.
£110-120   *CFA*

Radios

A Sobell wireless, 1948.
£90-125 *CLH*

An Ivalek crystal set
with box, c1950.
£30-40 *RTT*

A Schuco Radio 4012, a
toy with a music box,
made in West Germany,
c1950, car 6in (15cm)
long.
£150-200 *RTT*

Cross Reference
Automobilia

A Japanese valve set, late 1950s,
6½in (16cm) wide. **£35-40** *RTT*

A Japanese battery
operated transistor radio
by Marc, 1950s, 9½in
(24cm) high.
£50-60 *RTT*

A comprehensive selection of early pre-
war and post-war radios is featured in
Miller's Collectables, Volume II pages
310-313. This year we have featured more
recent 'novelty' radios.

Railways

Coats-of-Arms

A transfer printed Great Western Railway shield on green ground.
£40-50 *CSK*

Four transfer printed coats-of-arms for Midland Railway Company, Furness Railway Company, London North Western Railway and the London Midland and Scottish Railway Company.
£14-16 each *CSK*

A transfer printed coat-of-arms for the Talyllyn Railway Company, 12in (30cm) high, a hand painted oval plaque for the Barry Railway Company, 1884, and an L.N.E.R. coat-of-arms on an oak shield.
£5-10 each *CSK*

A transfer printed coat-of-arms for the North London Railway, an N.L.R. embossed iron shield and another on board.
£70-75 each *CSK*

Three transfer printed coats-of-arms on board: Great Eastern, Lancashire and Yorkshire Railway and Great Northern Railway Board.
£18-20 each *CSK*

Buttons

Great Central, Metropolitan & Great Central, Chester & Holyhead, Great Northern and Great Eastern Railways.
£10-20 each *AGM*

> **Cross Reference**
> Buttons

Two transfer printed coats-of-arms on wooden shields for the Metropolitan Railway and Metropolitan Great Western Joint Stock, 18½in (47cm) wide.
£45-50 each *CSK*

London South Western, Great Western Police and Great Northern.
£10-20 each *AGM*

Cast Iron Signs

DORSET
ANY PERSON WILFULLY INJURING
ANY PART OF THIS COUNTY BRIDGE
WILL BE GUILTY OF FELONY AND
UPON CONVICTION LIABLE TO BE
TRANSPORTED FOR LIFE
BY THE COURT
7 & 8 GEO 4 C30 S15 T FOOKS

A London Midland
Scottish Railway,
Wolverton Works, switch
cover, 6 by 5in (15 by
13cm).
£14-18 *WIN*

A bridge sign, 18 by 24in
(46 by 61cm), pre-1930.
£150-170 *COB*

A railway sign, 1930s.
£40-45 *COB*

A Powell Duffryn plate,
7½ by 10½in (19 by
26cm).
£20-30 *WIN*

Nameplates

British Guiana axle
cover plate, 1927.
£50-175 *WIN*

Kinlet Hall, G.W.R.
No. 4936 ex Churchward
4–6–0 locomotive
nameplate.
£2,500-3,000 *CSK*

A Demerara Railway
nameplate, 1898, 6½ by
6½in (16 by 16cm).
£120-130 *WIN*

Westminster Hall,
G.W.R. No. 5197, cast
brass and steel
nameplate.
£3,500-4,000 *ONS*

A Lebanon Railway
heavy freight locomotive
plate, 20 by 4in (51 by
10cm).
£50-60 *WIN*

Princess Mary GCR
No. 510, L.N.E.R. 2664, a
cast brass locomotive
nameplate.
£2,600-3,600 *ONS*

Thomas Hardy,
Britannia 70034, a cast
brass locomotive
nameplate.
£4,500-5,000 *ONS*

MAKE THE MOST OF MILLERS
Price ranges in this book reflect what one should
expect to *pay* for a similar example. When selling,
however, one should expect to receive a lower
figure. This will fluctuate according to a dealer's
stock, saleability at a particular time, etc. It is
always advisable, when selling, to approach a
reputable specialist dealer or an auction house
which has specialist sales.

Railway Posters

Kenneth Shoesmith,
Brighton and Hove,
published by L.M.S.
£800-900 *ONS*

I'm taking an early
holiday, published by
S.R., 1936.
£450-500 *ONS*

Perry Barr, Birmingham,
LMS, a lithograph in
colours, printed by
James Cond Ltd.,
Birmingham, backed on
linen, minor tears and
repairs, 39½ by 25½in
(100 by 65cm).
£400-450 *CSK*

Magical Margate, a
lithograph in colours,
damaged, 40 by 25in
(101.5 by 64cm).
£330-400 *CSK*

Use Road-Rail
Containers, published by
G.W.R., L.M.S, L.N.E.R.,
and S.R.
£30-40 *ONS*

The Tarbet Hotel, Loch
Lomond, a lithograph in
colours printed by
McCorquodale and Co.
Ltd., Glasgow, damaged,
39½ by 29½in (100 by
75cm).
£70-75 *CSK*

L. Burleigh Bruhl,
Falmouth, published by
G.W.R.
£200-250 *ONS*

Torquay The English
Riviera, published by
G.W.R.
£240-300 *ONS*

L. Burleigh Bruhl,
Glorious Devon,
published by G.W.R.
£200-250 *ONS*

Scotland, LNER, a lithograph in colours, printed by Dangerfield Printing Co., damage and repairs, 40 by 25in (101.5 by 64cm).
£300-350 *CSK*

Karo, Holiday Fares Not Increased, coloured poster on card, 40 by 25in (101.5 by 64cm).
£10-15 *CSK*

Scarborough, lithograph in colours, printed by Chorley & Pickersgill, Leeds, backed on linen, some fold marks, 39 by 24in (99 by 61cm).
£400-450 *CSK*

Lovely Loch Earn, a lithograph in colours, printed by Dobson, Mole and Co., Edinburgh, some damage, 40 by 60in (101.5 by 152cm).
£150-200 *CSK*

Huveers, Thinking of a Holiday?, coloured poster on card, 40 by 25in (101.5 by 64cm).
£10-15 *CSK*

Loch Tay, CCR, a lithograph in colours, printed by Dobson Mole and Co., Edinburgh, some damage, 39 by 59in (99 by 149.5cm).
£110-150 *CSK*

P. Irwin Brown, The Royal Scot 10-0am, on linen, 1931, 120in (305cm) high.
£1,000-2,000 *ONS*

Sir William Russell Flint, R.A., Bamburgh, L.N.E.R., lithograph in colours, printed by The Avenue Press, London, damaged, 40 by 51in (101.5 by 129.5cm).
£400-500 *CSK*

Leslie Carr, Seaford, S.R., a lithograph in colours, printed by Waterlow and Sons Ltd., London, backed on linen, some damage, 1930, 39½ by 25in (100 by 64cm).
£400-500 *CSK*

Photographs & Ephemera

F. Moore, LB & SCR, No. 70 4–4–0 locomotive, overpainted photograph, 6½ by 9½in (16 by 24cm).
£200-250 *ONS*

A selection of railway Holiday Guides.
£7-8 each *COB*

Railway books, late 1940s.
£6-7 each *COB*

A booklet, 1950s.
£8-10 *COB*

An etching with aquatint, part printed in colours, Henschel, Kassel, possibly Georg Kroning, 26 by 20½in (66 by 52cm).
£200-250 *CSK*

A promotional railway brochure, 1927.
£15-18 *COB*

An Act of Parliament, to enable the Oswestry and Newtown Railway Company to construct additional lines of railway to Llanfyllin and Kerry in the County of Montgomery, May 1861.
£10-15 *CSK*

Vic Welch, Caledonian Railway, No. 141 4–4–0 locomotive, signed, gouache, 12 by 18in (31 by 45cm).
£100-150 *ONS*

General

A white metal cased pocket watch, the reverse embossed with a passenger train, in leather carrying case, 3½in (8.5cm) high.
£300-350   *CSK*

A limited edition plaque, with certificate, 1970s.
£40-45   *COB*

London and North West Railway, coffin bell.
£50-60   *WIN*

A cast iron British Automatic Co Ltd., platform ticket machine, with brass pull handle and enamelled B.T.C., 42½in (107cm) high.
£800-900   *CSK*

A handlamp, with brass plate NBR stamped Plains, with original burner.
£300-350   *ONS*

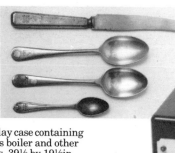

Silver plated cutlery, pre-war.
£3-6 each   *COB*

A display case containing various boiler and other fittings, 39½ by 19½in (100 by 49cm).
£300-400   *CSK*

An L.M.S. indicator, 1940s, 4in (10cm) high.
£40-45   *WIN*

The whistle from the SR West Country class 4–6–2 locomotive No. 34092, City of Wells, mounted, 15½in (39cm) high.
£120-150   *CSK*

A French silver presentation trowel, with carved ivory handle, c1848, 12½in (32cm).
£550-600   *CSK*

A G.W.R. insulator, 5in (13cm) high.
£4-6 *WIN*

A British Rail tilley lamp, 16in (41cm) high.
£30-40 *WIN*

A mahogany cased drop dial clock, engraved GWR 2744, 25in (64cm) high.
£450-500 *CSK*

Three whistles, various railways.
£35-65 each
ONS

A London & North Western Railway block and bell, 25in (64cm) high.
£140-150 *WIN*

A Midland Railway block instrument, 18in (46cm) high.
£110-120 *WIN*

A British Rail Western Region signal lamp, 8in (20cm) high.
£15-25 *WIN*

Royal Train Fittings

A revolving chair with green leather seat and back on modern base, from a Great Northern Railway Royal train.
£320-350 *ONS*

An ornate brass electric radiator, 19½in (50cm) high.
£220-250 *ONS*

A bergère armchair, on casters, with original green leather cushion, Great Northern Railway.
£850-950 *ONS*

Rock & Pop Memorabilia

The Beatles

A half-length gouache on celluloid of John Lennon, Yellow Submarine, 1968, 12½ by 16in (32 by 41cm).
£480-500 *CSK*

An EP record sleeve of Twist and Shout, signed on reverse, with record.
£1,000-1,500 *VS*

A fan magazine signed on the cover by the 4 Beatles in 3 different coloured inks, 1963.
£1,000-1,500 *CSK*

A publicity photograph of the Beatles playing at The Cavern in 1961, signed and inscribed on the reverse, 5 by 6½in (13 by 17cm).
£850-900 *CSK*

A black and white print of the Beatles during rehearsals for the Royal Variety Performance, November 4th 1963, with negative and copyright, 3½ by 3½in (9 by 9cm).
£600-700 *CSK*

A limited edition group photograph by Robert Freeman used on the album cover With The Beatles, signed by the photographer on front and reverse of mount, framed, 1963, 20 by 16in (51 by 41cm).
£550-650 *CSK*

General

A publicity postcard of Elvis Presley, signed in blue biro.
£350-400 *CSK*

Printed sheet music for the song Imagine, signed John Lennon, 1971, 12 by 9in (31 by 23cm).
£1,500-1,750 *CSK*

A Wings presentation gold disc, London Town, 19½ by 15½in (49 by 39cm).
£800-1,000 *CSK*

A bass drum with hand painted cover decorated with Gentle Giant logo, accompanied by a letter of authenticity from drummer Mike Smith, 23in (59cm) diam.
£550-600 *CSK*

According to the accompanying letter the drum also featured on 2 Gentle Giant albums, Gentle Giant and Acquiring The Taste.

A Prince presentation platinum disc, Sign Of The Times.
£750-1,000 *CSK*

Murray Levy was Prince's chauffeur.

Four rare psychedelic concert posters for cancelled performances, each 25 by 17in (64 by 43cm).
£350-400 *CSK*

A printed songbook, Bob Dylan At Budokan, Warner Bros. Inc., signed and inscribed on front cover, 1978.
£260-300 *CSK*

Two autographed albums Led Zeppelin and The Runes, both signed by Robert Plant, John Bonham, John Paul Jones and Jimmy Page.
£480-550 *CSK*

A silkscreen print, titled, numbered 5 from an edition limited to 250, signed and inscribed by subject Eric Clapton, and a certificate of authenticity, 1988, 23½ by 16½in (60 by 42cm).
£700-900 *CSK*

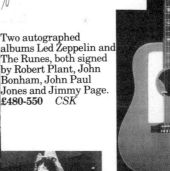

An imitation leather waistcoat, trimmed at the shoulders with imitation tiger skin, and a full length machine print photograph of Marc Bolan.
£1,000-1,500 *CSK*

A Gibson FJ-N acoustic guitar in rosewood with mother-of-pearl inlays, with certificate of authenticity from Elvis Presley Museum confirming Elvis owned and used the guitar, 40in (101.5cm) long.
£6,000-6,500 *CSK*

371

Film Memorabilia

A tiara of simulated diamonds and pearls set in white metal, worn by Ava Gardner as Empress Elizabeth of Austria-Hungary in the film 'Mayerling', 1968, and accompanied by an autographed photograph.
£330-400 *CSK*

A 1954 colour calendar photograph of Marilyn Monroe, the photograph taken May 27th 1949.
£110-120 *VS*

A Sergio Gargiulo original poster artwork, Clark Gable and Vivien Leigh in 'Gone with the Wind', signed and dated '44, pastel, 16½ by 12in (42 by 31cm).
£400-500 *CSK*

Scales & Balances

Avery red Post Office scales, 16½in (42cm) high.
£25-35 *CAB*

Kitchen scales, 17½in (44cm) high.
£20-25 *DH*

A brass postal balance, R. W. Winfield, dated 1840, 6½in (16cm) high.
£190-200 *BS*

A set of apothecary scales and weights, in oak case, 19thC, 6½ by 3in (16 by 8cm).
£75-85 *BS*

A set of money scales and weights, in mahogany case, 19thC, 8 by 3½in (20 by 9cm).
£85-95 *BS*

Weights

Cast iron weights, 1-7lb,
c1900.
£60-70 *BS*

Two ½oz brass weights.
£25-30 each *BS*

Two copper 2lb weights,
4 and 4½in (10 and
12cm) high.
£35-45 each *BS*

Two 1lb nickel weights,
3½in (9cm) high.
£5-10 each *BS*

A 7lb grocer's weight
made by Wedgwood,
19thC, 5½in (14cm)
diam.
£170-180 *BS*

A set of fancy cut
Kenrick weights,
1oz-4lb, 19thC.
£70-80 *BS*

Seven small brass
weights 1 and 2oz, 1½ to
2in (4 to 5cm) high.
£12-18 each *BS*

Three brass weights.
£10-15 each *BS*

Brass cup weights,
19thC.
£20-25 per set *BS*

A set of 7 bell metal
weights, in fitted case,
dated 1888.
£1,200-1,500 *AG*

Scientific Instruments

Globes

A 3in (7.5cm) terrestrial globe, the oceans with tracks of explorers and navigators, and a table of latitudes and longitudes, with label inscribed Cary's Pocket Globe, case hinge defective, late 18thC.
£1,500-1,700   *CSK*

A time globe, with gilt brass mounts and stand and enamelled numerals on the equatorial circle, unsigned, late 19thC, 8in (20cm) high.
£700-800   *CSK*

A 12in (30.5cm) celestial globe, with ebonised stand, early 19thC.
£1,200-1,400   *CSK*

A NASA moon globe, 1970, 24in (61.5cm) diam.
£35-40   *COB*

General

An ivory slide rule.
£80-100   *HUN*

A brass circumferentor, on tripod/staff mounting, signed on the horizontal circle J. Bennett London, 10in (25cm) diam.
£350-400   *CSK*

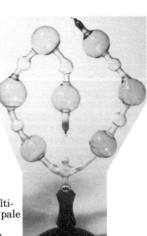

An Irish sundial plate, engraved with the names of many Irish towns and a correction table for foreign lands and cities, signed and James Farrell and dated, gnomon missing, 16in (40.5cm) long.
£150-200   *CSK*

A rare Crookes' multi-sphere tube, with 7 pale green spheres interconnected with 5 bulbs, on wood stand, 12in (30.5cm) high.
£150-200   *CSK*

An unusual bronze
protractor, dated 1826,
3in (8cm) radius.
£100-120 *CSK*

A brass horizontal
sundial, signed Chas.
Harrison, Limerick,
early 19thC, 14in
(35.5cm) diam.
£450-550 *CSK*

An iron Geryk glass
vacuum pump, by the
Pulsometer Engineering
Co. Ltd., 19thC, 30in
(50.5cm) high.
£70-100 *CSK*

A brass and iron
spectrometer, late 19thC,
16½in (42cm) diam.
£300-350 *CSK*

A wireless telegraphy
10in (25.5cm) induction
coil spark gap
transmitter, with ivorine
label of Newton and Co.
Opticians to the Queen,
and paper label under
the mahogany baseboard,
c1895.
£800-900 *FEN*

*As used by Marconi in
early marine
installations.*

Cross Reference
Radios

A pair of brass and iron
dividers, unsigned,
possibly French, with
stamped maker's mark II
over a fleur-de-lys, late
17thC, 6½in (16.5cm)
long.
£450-500 *CSK*

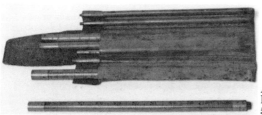

A measuring pole in
leather case.
£80-100 *HUN*

An oxydised brass
surveying level, by
Troughton & Simms,
London, engraved Port of
London Authority, 17in
(43cm) wide, with a
levelling staff.
£250-300 *CSK*

Optical Instruments

Binoculars

A pair of
ivory and brass
opera glasses, cased.
£100-120 *DP*

A pair of gentleman's
binoculars, Baker,
Opticians, 244 High
Holborn.
£14-20 *DH*

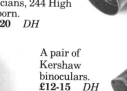

A pair of brass and
mother-of-pearl opera
glasses.
£70-80 *DP*

A pair of
Kershaw
binoculars.
£12-15 *DH*

A pair of chromium
plated opera glasses,
with pink enamel
decoration, c1920.
£5-10 *DH*

Spectacles

A pair of Blendex eye
protectors, auto goggles,
c1930, 5in (12.5cm) wide.
£10-15 *RTT*

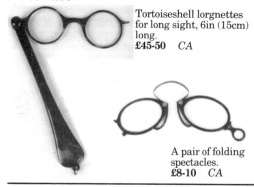

Tortoiseshell lorgnettes
for long sight, 6in (15cm)
long.
£45-50 *CA*

A pair of folding
spectacles.
£8-10 *CA*

Telescopes

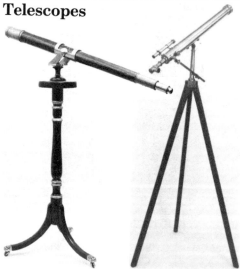

A refracting telescope on
stand, the tapering
leather covered body
tube signed H. Hughes &
Sons Ltd., 59 Fenchurch
Street, London, 57in
(144.5cm) long.
£550-600 *CSK*

A lacquered brass
refracting telescope,
signed on the eye-piece
backplate, W. Watson &
Sons, No. 1665, with
accessories in fitted
mahogany case, 44in
(112cm) long, and
associated tripod.
£1,000-1,200 *CSK*

Microscopes

A Ross type compound binocular microscope, signed on the Y-shaped stand Husbands Bristol, with many accessories arranged in a mahogany carrying case with 2 brass handles, 19thC, 21½in (54.5cm) high.
£800-1,000   *CSK*

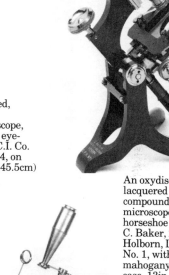

A black enamelled, nickel and brass travelling microscope, with micrometer eye-piece, engraved C.I. Co. Ltd., No. C316594, on iron stand, 18in (45.5cm) wide.
£100-120   *CSK*

An oxydised and lacquered brass compound monocular microscope, signed on the horseshoe stand C. Baker, 244 High Holborn, London D.P.H. No. 1, with accessories in mahogany fitted carrying case, 13in (33cm) high.
£300-350   *CSK*

A Japanese microscope, c1930.
£15-20   *DH*

A Jones's Most Improved type lacquered brass compound monocular microscope, signed on the folding stand Cary, London, with accessories in fitted mahogany case, early 19thC, 14in (35.5cm) wide.
£1,500-2,000   *CSK*

A lacquered brass Culpeper-type compound microscope, signed on the stage Dollond, London, with accessories in pyramid shaped case with a drawer, 17½in (44.5cm) high.
£700-750   *CSK*

A lacquered brass pocket aquatic microscope, unsigned, in mahogany case, 19thC, 4in (10cm) wide.
£350-400   *CSK*

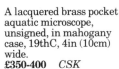

Medical Instruments

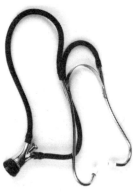

A binaural stethoscope, by Arnold and Son, c1900.
£80-90   *BS*

A horn handled reflex hammer, by P. Harris & Co., c1900, 9in (22.5cm) long.
£30-40   *BS*

A steel tooth key, with ivory handle and pivoting head, for pulling teeth, 18thC, 5½in (14cm) long.
£150-200   *BS*

A brass ear trumpet, 19thC, 12in (30.5cm) long.
£140-180   *BS*

A copper and brass ear trumpet, c1920, 5in (12.5cm) long.
£140-180   *BS*

A brass enema, c1880, 10in (25cm) high.
£120-150   *BS*

A tortoiseshell covered lancet, in original case, 19thC.
£50-60   *BS*

A mahogany cased enema, by Fannin & Co., Dublin, 19thC, 4½ by 10in (11.5 by 25cm).
£150-200   *BS*

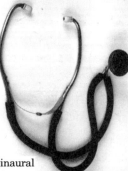

A 19thC binaural stethoscope.
£180-200   *BS*

A Celluloid simulated tortoiseshell ear trumpet, c1910, 10in (25cm) long.
£200-250   *BS*

A silver tongue depresser, 5in (12.5cm) long.
£40-50 *BS*

A laryngeal mirror, 6½in (16.5cm) long.
£15-20 *BS*

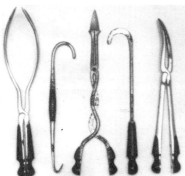

A pair of obstetric forceps, with ebony handles, by Aitken, a perforator, a blunt hook with crotchet, a pair of craniotomy forceps, and a Ramsbotham's pattern decapitator.
£400-450 *CSK*

A pair of brass single blade scarificators, in marbled paper embossed leather covered case, 18thC, 3in (7.5cm) long.
£800-850 *CSK*

A fine composition anatomical figure of the human male, coloured, late 19thC, 23½in (60cm) high.
£650-700 *CSK*

A cupping set with 16 blade scarificator, signed Savigny with 6 cupping glasses, in mahogany case, 10½in (26.5cm) wide.
£250-300 *CSK*

A collection of dental instruments, by J. Wood, York, in lined mahogany case, 14in (35.5cm) wide.
£250-300 *CSK*

An amputation knife and saw set, in brass bound box.
£150-160 *MB*

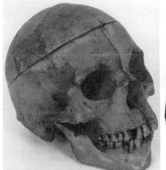

A human skull, 19thC.
£150-180 *SSA*

FURTHER READING
Antique Medical Instruments, Keith Wilbur, M.D., Millbank Books, Schiffer Publishing Ltd.

Scripophily

U.S.A.

Insull Utility
Investments Inc., dated
1930.
£30-50 *SCR*

Chicago and Alton
Railroad Company
$1,000 bond, printed in
green and black.
£15-25 *SCR*

State of Louisiana $500
bond, vignette of State
Capital at Baton Rouge,
1892.
£15-25 *GKR*

 The Mississippi Bonds
There are 2 types of
Mississippi bonds, those
issued by the Planters
Bank in denominations
of $1,000 and those
issued by the Union
Bank in denominations
of $2,000. Both were
guaranteed by the State.
In 1841 both types fell
into default, causing
considerable political
and financial upset over
the ensuing years.
Planters Bank $1,000
bond issued 1833.
£180-190
Union Bank $2,000 bond
issued 1838, yellow seal.
£220-240 *SCR*

Merchants Exchange of
St. Louis, dated 1882,
black/white.
£20-30 *SCR*

Pine Creek Railway
Company $1,000 bond, in
excellent condition but
hole cancelled, brown/
black, dated 1885.
£125-175 *SCR*

The New York & Harlem
Railroad, green/black,
dated 1943, and made
out to J. P. Morgan & Co.
£8-12 *SCR*

United States Lines,
modern share in U.S.
shipping line, dated
1962, 100 shares, orange.
£5-10 *SCR*

Chinese

Banque Industrielle De Chine share certificate printed in yellow, black and red.
£35-45 *SCR*

Chinese Imperial Railway, £100 bond issued in 1907 as part of the financing of the Canton-Kowloon Railway, finely engraved by Waterlow and printed in red and black.
£80-90 *SCR*

Honan Railway £100 bond in railway built under instruction of Pekin Syndicate, green/yellow, dated 1905.
£80-90 *SCR*

Tientsin-Pukow Railway £100 bonds, orange/black, 1908.
£65-75 *SCR*

Great Britain

Middleton & Tonge
Cotton Mill Ltd.
certificate, black/white,
dated 1875.
£35-45 *SCR*

Tal Y Drws Slate
Company Ltd, certificate
of £5 Preference shares,
black/white, 1868.
£20-30 *SCR*

The Holywell Level
Silver Lead Mining
Company, located in
Flintshire, black/white,
dated 1866.
£20-30 *SCR*

Bristol District Patent
Ramoneur Company
who devised a chimney
cleaning device, with
royal coat-of-arms,
black/white, dated 1847.
£25-35 *SCR*

The Lands Allotment
Company Ltd, share
certificate, printed black
on white and signed by
Jabez Spencer Balfour,
1877.
£25-30 *GKR*

Brinsop Hall Coal
Company Ltd, black/
white with pink
overprint 'fully paid',
dated 1874.
£15-20 *SCR*

The Altrincham Gas Company share
certificate, printed on buff paper
with an affixed yellow paper seal,
dated 1846. **£40-50** *SCR*

Kineton Gas Light, Coal
& Coke Co. Ltd.
certificate for one £2
share, only 750 issued,
printed black on white,
1863.
£15-20 *GKR*

Worldwide

Scindia Steam
Navigation Co. Ltd.,
brown/yellow, c1943.
£8-12 *GKR*

Brazil Railway Company
$40m warrant to bearer
for 1 preferred share,
red/black, 1910.
£15-25 *GKR*

The Dominion Copper
Co. share certificate,
red/black, dated c1906.
£10-14 *SCR*

City of St. Petersburg
bond of 187.50, 4½% loan
1901, yellow/green/blue.
£15-20 *GKR*

The Atlantic Quebec & Western Railway Company £100 bond, green/black, dated 1911.
£15-20   *SCR*

1912 4½% City of Moscow £20 bond, yellow/brown, 50,001 issued.
£15-20   *SCR*

The Manila Railway Company £100 bond, the company was liquidated in 1954, brown/black, 1907.
£10-20   *SCR*

Compagnie des Claridges Hotels share certificate, depicting a cruise ship and train, orange/yellow/black, dated 1921.
£60-70   *SCR*

The Malabar Forests & Rubber Company Limited certificate for 1 share, green/buff, 1921.
£10-14   *GKR*

A Fr500 bearer share certificate in the Port of Bruges, multi-coloured and dated 1906.
£200-250   *SCR*

Savana bearer share, brown, dated 1952.
£10-14   *SCR*

An industrial and financial company located in Pondichery India and registered in Bordeaux.

Lloyd Bank Hungary share certificate, black/white, dated 1923.
£130-140   *SCR*

FURTHER READING
Collecting Old Bonds and Shares, Robin Hendy, London 1978.

Chilean Government
4.5% Loan 1893, £100
bond, red/black with full
coupon sheet and crest of
Chile.
£90-100 *SCR*

*Although 4,800 were
originally issued the loan
was settled by Chile in
1982. No more than
32 examples remain
outstanding.*

Compania Carbonifera
Agujita Y Annexas
share, a Mexican coal
company, purple/black,
dated 1910.
£15-20 *SCR*

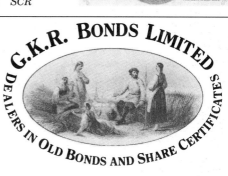

Société Coloniale
Agricole & Minière
bearer share, green/red,
dated 1938.
£10-20 *SCR*

Quebrachales
Paraguayos bearer
share, an Argentinian
registered company,
company dissolved in
1957, certificate dated
1911.
£10-20 *SCR*

*The company's principal
activities were cattle
raising and forest
exploration in Paraguay.*

1927 Republic of Estonia
7% bonds, blue/black,
1927.
£55-65 *SCR*

*As a result of 1969
repayment these bonds
are rare.*

Serviette Rings

A heavy silver serviette ring, c1900, 1½in (4cm) high.
£30-40 *VB*

A further selection of serviette rings can be found in Miller's Collectables Price Guide, Volume I, page 338.

A selection of pins, needles, cotton and a pencil, 'farthing change' goods produced between 1880-1939.
£4-8 each *PC*

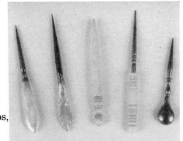

Sewing

General

A selection of stilettos, 1880-1930.
£6-9 each *PC*

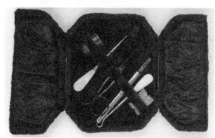

Victorian sewing case, 5in (13cm) high.
£25-30 *CA*

A Victorian sewing machine, by Jones, 15in (38cm) wide.
£100-120 *PAR*

A wooden box, covered in paper with various sized crochet hooks and one bone handle, early 19thC.
£15-20 *PC*

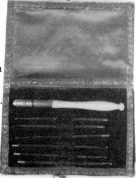

Three cards of linen buttons and one card of pearl from Marks and Spencer Penny Bazaar.
£3-5 each *PC*

Cross Reference
Buttons

A Bakelite holder for cottons, with a selection of reels, c1925.
£18-25 *PC*

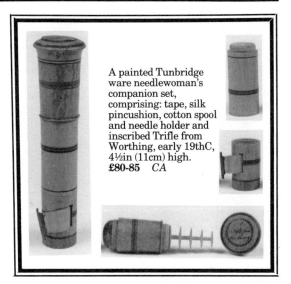

A painted Tunbridge ware needlewoman's companion set, comprising: tape, silk pincushion, cotton spool and needle holder and inscribed Trifle from Worthing, early 19thC, 4½in (11cm) high.
£80-85 *CA*

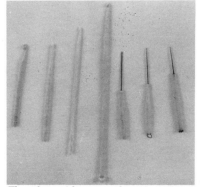

Three bone, 3 bone metal crochet hooks and one all bone hook for tricot crochet, 1900-20.
£4-8 each *PC*

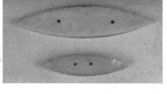

A selection of tatting shuttles in bone, shell and wood, late 19thC.
£4-8 each *PC*

A selection of aluminium advertising thimbles, Sainsbury's, Lyons Cakes, Mother Seigel's Syrup, Diploma Milk and Gas for Economy.
£6-12 each *PC*

Net making

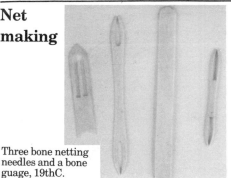

Three bone netting needles and a bone guage, 19thC.
£4-6 each *PC*

Nécessaires & Etui

An ivory and gilt metal egg-shaped nécessaire, 19thC, 3in (8cm) long.
£750-850 *LEW*

A tortoiseshell inlaid with silver egg-shaped nécessaire, 3in (8cm).
£180-200 *LEW*

A Victorian walnut nécessaire, 2½in (6cm).
£800-900 *LEW*

A plastic container for emergency repairs, 1930s onwards.
£6-8 *PC*

DID YOU KNOW?
An etui is a flattened, slightly tapering, cylinder with a deep hinged lid, to carry or hang on a chatelaine, slotted to hold personal trifles such as scissors and memo slip. Often delightfully decorative in jewelled precious metals, painted enamels, porcelain, ivory, etc.

A nécessaire serves the same purpose as the etui but is box-shaped for the dressing table.

A Victorian pin cushion, 3½in (9cm) wide.
£15-20 *CA*

Pin cushions

A Victorian pin cushion, 6in (15cm) square.
£18-25 *CA*

A gilt shoe pin cushion, Woolworth's, New York, 3in (8cm) high.
£50-60 *LEW*

Sewing Boxes

A tortoiseshell sewing box, with mirror in lid and 18ct gold accessories, c1840, 6½ by 4in (16 by 10cm).
£1,400-1,500 *CA*

A Victorian sewing box, with original mother-of-pearl fittings.
£400-450 *PC*

Rug Making

A selection of rug making tools, 20thC.
£4-6 each *PC*

The Home Rug Making Machine, 1900, 7in (18cm).
£10-15 *PC*

Scissors

A pair of silver folding scissors, 3in (8cm) wide when closed.
£30-40 *LEW*

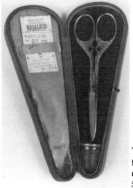

Victorian scissors, thimble and needles in a case, 6½in (16cm) long.
£18-20 *CA*

A pair of steel scissors, early 19thC, 4½in (11cm) long.
£15-20 *CA*

FURTHER READING
Needlework Tools and Accessories. A Collectables Guide, Molly G. Proctor, Batsford Pub.

Darners

Wooden glove darners, 1880-1930.
£3-8 each *PC*

Three patent darners for socks, c1920.
£6-15 each *PC*

A plastic box containing needles and threads, which converts into a darning mushroom, 1930-50.
£8-12 *PC*

Needles

A selection
of packets of
needles, pre-1920.
£3-5 each *PC*

A brass container for
packets of needles, by
W. Avery, late 19thC.
£20-25 *PC*

A collection of Avery's
needle holders, c1870.
£30-40 each
The large one 'The
Unique'.
£60-70 *CA*

Free gifts of pins and
needles, 1920-39.
£3-6 each *PC*

A wooden rolling pin
needle case, 3½in (8.5cm)
long.
£30-40 *LEW*

A shell needle
case, 3in
(7.5cm) long.
£20-30 *LEW*

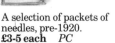

A selection of packets of
needles, pre-1920.
£3-5 each *PC*

Wood and ivory needle
holder parasols, 4in
(10cm) long.
£45-55 each *LEW*

Various packets of
needles, pre-1920.
£3-5 each *PC*

DID YOU KNOW?
No trade marks before 1840.
No fancy labels before 1860.
No needles stuck into piece of cloth or paper
before 1900.
No aperture to view the eyes before 1920.

Knitting

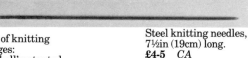

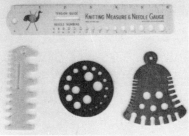

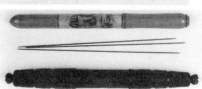

A selection of knitting needle gauges: Gilt metal 'bell' patented 1847, but many later copies. Painted metal disc, c1930, and two modern plastic items.
£3-8 each *PC*

Steel knitting needles, 7½in (19cm) long.
£4-5 *CA*

A Victorian Mauchline ware knitting needle holder, 9½in (24cm) long.
£30-35
A carved walnut needle holder, 10in (25.5cm) long.
£30-35 *CA*

DID YOU KNOW?
At one time knitting was not considered a suitable pastime for a genteel lady.

A selection of wooden knitting needle sheaths, two Welsh and one from Durham, 19thC, 7in (18cm).
£10-15 each *PC*

Tape Measures

A selection of advertising tape measures, c1900.
£35-40 each
Puritan soap.
£45-50 *CA*

Various tape measures.
£30-45 each *CA*

Tape Measures:
l. Brass.
l. centre. Celluloid.
r. centre. Mauchline.
r. Bone. **£30-45 each** *CA*

l. A Celluloid bird tape measure, 4in (10cm) high.
r. A brass and malachite hare tape measure, 2in (6.5cm) long.
£40-45 each *CA*

A clock tape measure, with moving handles, c1890, 3cm square.
£60-70 *CA*

Shipping Posters

Norman Keene, The Blue Funnel Line, 13½ by 19in (34 by 48cm), framed.
£45-55   *ONS*

Bibby Line, Short Sea Cruises.
£550-600   *ONS*

A French Line poster, 1930s.
£100-150   *COB*

A British Rail poster, 1958.
£20-25   *COB*

A P & O poster, 1970s.
£20-25   *COB*

Royal Mail, Britain's Fastest Service To South America, Alcantara, some damage.
£250-300   *ONS*

Leslie Carr, Southampton Docks, RMS Queen Mary and SS Normandie, 1936.
£550-600   *ONS*

A Post Office advertisement, 1907.
£15-20   *COB*

South America, Luxurious Travel By The Royal Mail Line.
£400-500   *ONS*

Norman Wilkinson, Ireland via Holyhead.
£200-250   *ONS*

Frank H. Mason, SS Arnhem, New Luxury Ship Harwich-Hook of Holland Service, published by LNER.
£100-200   *ONS*

Shipping Ephemera

A Cunard map and schedule.
£8-15 each   *COB*

A Cook's sailing list, 1909.
£25-30   *COB*

A model making book, 1906.
£10-12   *COB*

Cross Reference
Ephemera

A selection of ship's postcards, 1930-60.
£1-3 each   *COB*

A photograph album, 1938.
£15-20   *COB*

A naval book, WWI.
£6-10   *COB*

Adhesive luggage labels.
£2-3 each   *COB*

A Lloyds Register, 1956-57.
£10-15   *COB*

Ocean liners menus and brochures.
£5-15 each   *COB*

A magazine, 1898.
£15-20   *COB*

A selection of 1930s brochures.
£7-15 each *COB*

Postcards, 1930s.
£2-3 each *COB*

An Antilles booklet 1960s.
£8-10 *COB*

A menu cover from Royal Yacht, Victoria and Albert, in wooden frame
£15-20 *COB*

Menus from American ships, c1968.
£5-6 each
COB

GOING ABROAD VIA CUNARD AND ANCHOR LINES

Cunard Lines, 1933.
£25-30 *COB*

A limited edition print of 350 Titanic prints, signed by artist and a survivor, 1982.
£25-35 *COB*

Ocean Liner advertising brochures, 1930s.
£20-25 each *COB*

A selection of tie-on
luggage labels.
£2-3 each *COB*

French ships'
magazines,
1907.
£15-18 each
COB

A lithograph of SS Great
Britain, in original
frame, c1855.
£85-100 *COB*

Naval books, c1910.
£7-10 each *COB*

Shipping Models

A model of a Chinese junk in teak, origin unknown, c1880.
£100-150   *HUN*

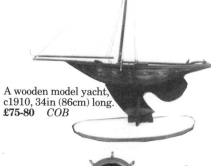

A wooden model yacht, c1910, 34in (86cm) long.
£75-80   *COB*

A plastic clockwork model of the HMS Pretunia Castle, 1960s.
£20-40   *COB*

A selection of badges from various shipping lines.
£5-10 each   *PC*

Cross Reference
Toys

A Dinky toy model, pre-war, in original box.
£25-30   *COB*

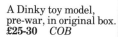

A 1:50 scale model of a two-masted schooner, The Scottish Maid, 25in (64cm) long, in glazed case.
£180-220   *WHB*

Various badges.
£2-4 each   *COB*

A ship in a bottle, c1920, 10½in (26cm) long.
£25-30   *OD*

General

An embroidered badge
made for the crew on the
French Titanic dive,
3½in (8.5cm) diam.
£35-40 *COB*

A medallion
commemorating the
Battle of Jutland, 1916.
£20-25 *COB*

United States Lines
unopened packs of
playing cards, in
presentation box.
£15-20 *BY*

A Titanic limited edition
plate, 1980s, 5in
(12.5cm).
£10-12 *COB*

> **DID YOU KNOW?**
> Miller's Collectables
> Price Guide is
> designed to build up,
> year by year, into the
> most comprehensive
> reference system
> available.

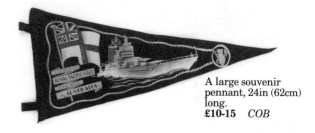

A large souvenir
pennant, 24in (62cm)
long.
£10-15 *COB*

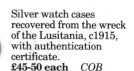

Silver watch cases
recovered from the wreck
of the Lusitania, c1915,
with authentication
certificate.
£45-50 each *COB*

The Lusitania medal to
commemorate its
sinking, German, in
original box.
£10-15 *COB*

An English green
painted ship's starboard
light, with brass fittings,
in working order, c1900,
13in (33cm).
£85-95 *UC*

A set of silver ingots depicting the history of ships, 1976, with casket.
£120-130   *COB*

A brass office nameplate.
£25-30
COB

A hardwood caulker, stamped with initials S.B., 19thC.
£50-60   *SWN*

A sailor's implement for sealing leaky decks.

A Royal Navy brass ashtray, 1950s.
£5-8   *COB*

A wooden sign from Southampton docks, 1950s, 18in (45.5cm) high.
£35-40   *COB*

A collection of wooden sailmaker's tools, late 18thC/early 19thC.
£30-40 each   *SWN*

These tools were often made aboard ship during slack periods.

A bone china Queen Mary souvenir plate, 1960s.
£10-15   *COB*

A brass bound serving mallet, c1850.
£60-70   *SWN*

A sailor's tool for rigging work.

A selection of brass and enamel badges, 1980s.
£3-10 each   *COB*

P & O wooden lifeboat name boards, c1950, 7in (17.5cm) long.
£15-18 each   *COB*

Signs & Advertising

Ceramics

Yardley's Old English Lavender, from a perfumier's or chemist's shop, marked, Dresden, c1880, 12in (30.5cm) high.
£240-280 *RG*

The Gourmet pie cup. **£2-6** *PC*

Potted meat pots, under-valued at present, most of these pots are pre-1930s.
£1-5 each *PC*

A Victorian ointment pot.
£10-20 *PC*

Robertson's gollies.
50p-£1
THA

A medicine spoon.
£5-10 *PC*

FURTHER READING
Antique Advertising Encyclopedia, Ray Klug, Millbank Books, Schiffer Publishing Ltd.

A Virol stoneware jar,
found in a wide range of
sizes, up to 14 or 28lb.
Small £4-6
Large £30-40   *PC*

Two ointment pots.
£20-25 each   *CA*

Cross Reference
Bottles

A pottery Dulux dog
figure, modelled by Mr.
Mortimer and made by
Beswick, 12in (30.5cm)
high.
£200-250   *BBR*

Enamel Signs

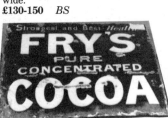

An original Fremlins
enamel advertisement,
c1910, 16in (40.5cm)
wide.
£130-150   *BS*

Fry's milk chocolate and
cocoa sign, signed Tom
B., by the famous
illustrator Tom Browne,
14in (35.5cm) high.
£400-600   *BBR*

Fry's Cocoa, metal and
enamel.
£25-35   *ARC*

Strike out Foreign
Competition by buying
England's Glory
Matches, original frame,
29½in (75cm) wide.
£600-700   *ONS*

Black Cat cigarettes,
36in (92cm) high.
£250-350   *ONS*

Senior Service, metal
and enamel sign.
£25-35   *ARC*

Puritan Soap.
£20-40   *ARC*

Stotherts Chest and
Lung Mixture, 36in
(91.5cm) wide.
£25-35   *ARC*

Glass & Mirrors

Colman's Mustard, framed mirror, 21½in (54cm) high.
£70-80 *ONS*

Wills's Gold Flake, framed mirror, 19in (48cm) high.
£45-55 *ONS*

A Waterman's Ideal Fountain Pen mirror, 44in (111.5cm) high.
£100-120 *AL*

An advertising mirror, 44in (111.5cm) high.
£100-120 *AL*

An advertising mirror, 70½in (178.5cm) wide.
£130-150 *AL*

ANTLER TRAVEL GOODS

An advertising panelled glass door with brass letter box and handles, 82in (208cm) high.
£250-300 *AL*

General

A Libby's tin piercer, 2½in (6.5cm) high.
£8-10   *CA*

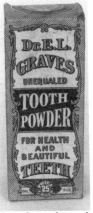

A tooth powder packet, 4in (10cm) high.
£3-5   *OD*

A Stephens' Inks advertising thermometer, 5in (12.5cm) high.
£175-225   *PC*

Advertising playing cards for beer: Carling, c1980. **£2-5** Hammerton, c1930. **£5-10** Mackeson, c1960. **£2-5** Ansell's, c1970. **£2-5**   *COL*

Canterbury Belts Ltd. rubber mould advertising figure, hand painted, c1925, 28½in (72cm) high.
£150-250   *K*

Advertising playing cards: Nivea, c1960. **£3-6** Rice Krispies, c1970. **£2-5**   *COL*

Three advertising playing cards for whisky: Grants, c1890. **£1-5** Claymore, c1950. **£5-10** Gilbey's, c1950. **£8-12**   *COL*

Advertising playing cards: T. Guntrip, bookmaker, c1950; Crestona, c1930; Boiler Setters & Erections Ltd., c1950. **£5-10 each**   *COL*

A cardboard advertising
poster, c1890, framed,
30in (76cm) high.
£75-80   *COB*

A plaster shop display
advertisement, 1950s,
18in (45.5cm).
£25-30   *COB*

Hudson's Soap, Liverpool
to York in 11 hours,
advertisement on linen,
29½in (75cm) high,
framed.
£250-300   *ONS*

An advertisement of the
Felt Hatters & Trimmers'
Unions of Great Britain,
9in (23cm) high.
£20-30   *ONS*

A paper advertisement,
with wooden frame, some
damage, 24in (61cm)
wide.
£15-20   *BBR*

Norman Wilkinson,
Players Medium, yacht
race Burnham.
£50-60   *ONS*

Stephens' Inks, For All
Temperatures,
thermometer, 33in
(84cm) high.
£100-150   *ONS*

Keating's Powder Kills
Bugs, Fleas, Beetles
Moths, 18in (46cm) high.
£200-220   *ONS*

Smoking
Advertising

An Idris ashtray,
Colclough mark, 5in
(12.5cm) diam.
£10-20 *BBR*

A signs of the Zodiac
globe cigarette holder,
11½in (29cm) high.
£15-20 *COL*

Bottles and Barrel
striker, circular pedestal
with ribbed striking
region, 5in (12.5cm)
diam.
£40-60 *BBR*

Three table lighters
advertising lager.
£2-5 each *COL*

A cigarette tin, 5 by 3in
(12.5 by 7.5cm).
£3-5 *OD*

Cross Reference
Tins

A Wills's Woodbines
ashtray, 4in (10cm)
square.
£8-10 *CA*

A pair of brass cannon
cigarette lighters, 7½in
(19cm) long.
£25-30 *PC*

*If Dunhill £500-550.
Ronson or other known
make £75-95.*

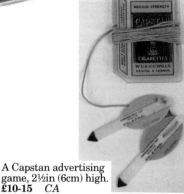

A Capstan advertising
game, 2½in (6cm) high.
£10-15 *CA*

For a further selection of Smoking, Pipes
and Lighters, refer to Miller's Collectables
Volume II, pages 350-361.

Two Dutch spelter table lighters.
£8-10   *COL*

A gold petrol burning cigarette lighter, containing a watch, 19in (48cm) high.
£400-500   *CSK*

Tobacco Jars

A saltglazed rustic tobacco jar, North Wales, 6½in (16.5cm) high.
£25-30   *IW*

Two cast iron tobacco boxes, with domed lids, 6in (15cm) high.
£50-70 each   *SBA*

General

A leather cigar case, dated 1848, 5in (12.5cm) high.
£90-100   *EHA*

A silver plated cigar box with sporting scenes, c1850, 6in (15cm) high.
£200-250   *EHA*

A selection of cigarette boxes.
£1-10 each   *RTT*

Art Deco pipe holders,
3in (7.5cm).
£8-12 each *CLH*

A snakeskin vesta case,
with silver mounts,
hallmarked London
1889, 2½in (6.5cm) high.
£60-70 *EHA*

A miniature matchbox,
'Now Stand a Drink You
Beggar', 'No More Burnt
Pockets', 'A Light With
Pleasure', 1in (2.5cm).
£15-20 *CA*

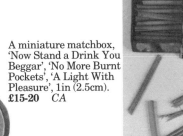

An Edwardian
Meerschaum pipe in the
shape of a bird's head,
6½in (16.5cm) long.
£230-250 *SBA*

Matchboxes.
£3-6 *PO*

A rare ash pipe, c1790,
27in (69cm) long.
£180-200 *HUN*

FURTHER READING
Complete Guide to Collecting Antique Pipes, Ben
Rappaport, Millbank Books, Schiffer Publishing
Ltd.

A tobacco cutter, c1820,
9in (22.5cm) long.
£65-75 *HUN*

A brass pig vesta case,
with match striker on
base.
£70-80 *LEW*

A brass ash can, 10½in
(26.5cm) diam.
£50-80 *AL*

Two brass ashtrays, 4in
(10cm) and 5½in (14cm)
diam.
£4-5 each *PC*

A cigarette pot, 4in (10cm) diam.
£20-30 *CAC*

A leather cased cigarette holder, c1880, 3in (7.5cm) long.
£25-35 *EHA*

An Asprey silver cigarette case, 1940s, 2½in (6.5cm) square.
£65-75 *CLH*

A metal cigarette case, souvenir from India.
£6-10 *COL*

An Art Deco bakelite and silver plate ashtray, 3in (7.5cm) high.
£10-20 *CAB*

> **Cross Reference**
> Art Deco

A pop-up cigarette case,

> **DID YOU KNOW?**
> Miller's Collectables Price Guide is designed to build up, year by year, into the most comprehensive reference system available.

Snuff Boxes

An ebony and ivory shoe snuff box, 3½in (8.5cm) long.
£140-160 *LEW*

A brass snuff box, 3in (7.5cm) wide.
£60-70 *SBA*

A silver mounted horn snuff box, 4in (10cm) wide.
£240-270 *SBA*

SPORT
Boxing

The Great Contest Between Sayers and Heenan, aquatint by J. R. Mackrell and J. B. Rowbotham, published by C. Roker, 19 by 24in (48.5 by 61.5cm).
£180-220 *CSK*

Rocky Marciano, undefeated World Heavyweight Champion 1952-56, signed in biro, rare.
£35-45 *VS*

A boxing bronze, 15in (38cm) high.
£1,500-2,500 *MSh*

A Continental coloured bisque figure of a boxer, 7½in (17.5cm) high.
£140-160 *CSK*

Max Schmeling, World Heavyweight Champion 1930-32, signed and inscribed postcard.
£40-50 *VS*

Jack London, British Heavyweight Champion 1944-45, signed postcard.
£80-90 *VS*

Eddie Paynter, an electroplated ashtray.
£900-1,000 *CSK*

Paynter, who played in 3 of the 5 Test matches of 1932-33, and finished the series with the top batting average of 61.33, was in fact a very heavy smoker.

Cricket

A pair of ceramic book ends, foreign, 4in (10cm) high.
£85-95 *AL*

A copper plaque, signed and dated, 6in (15cm) high.
£150-200 *MSh*

Cricketers, 1912, 50 F. & J. Smith cigarette cards.
£300-320 *CSK*

Cricketers, 1930, a complete set of 50 John Player cigarette cards, 38 signed across the image by the respective players including Bradman.
£400-450 *CSK*

> **Cross Reference**
> Cigarette Cards
> Autographs

A pair of Austrian cold painted bronze figures of batsmen, 19thC, 4½in (11cm) high.
£300-350 *CSK*

W. G. Grace at the Wicket, photogravure signed in pencil by both artist and subject, published by Manson, Swan and Morgan, May 1, 1891, after Archibald Stuart Wortley, 20in (50.5cm) high.
£550-600 *CSK*

A cricket bat commemorating the Triangular Test Tournament of 1912 signed by members of the South African, Australian and England teams, the back signed by the Australian and England teams of 1921 and various members of the South African and England teams of 1924, and further inscribed 'Record Score for Lords, 30.8.26 316, J. B. Hobbs' at centre.
£350-400 *CSK*

A Cadbury's Cocoa yellow glazed ceramic plate, 9in (22.5cm).
£100-150 *CSK*

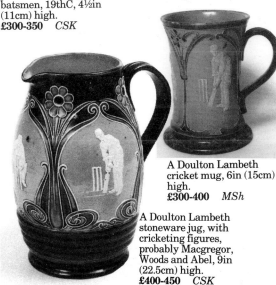

A Doulton Lambeth cricket mug, 6in (15cm) high.
£300-400 *MSh*

A Doulton Lambeth stoneware jug, with cricketing figures, probably Macgregor, Woods and Abel, 9in (22.5cm) high.
£400-450 *CSK*

Australian XI, 1905, a team photograph by J. Herbert Wilson, Leicester, signed on the mount by all the team members, 8½ by 11in (21.5 by 28cm).
£800-850 *CSK*

Golf
Clubs

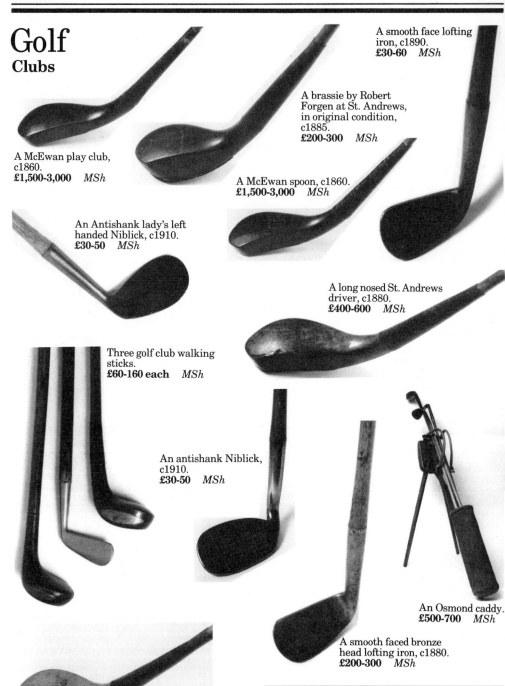

A smooth face lofting iron, c1890.
£30-60 *MSh*

A brassie by Robert Forgen at St. Andrews, in original condition, c1885.
£200-300 *MSh*

A McEwan play club, c1860.
£1,500-3,000 *MSh*

A McEwan spoon, c1860.
£1,500-3,000 *MSh*

An Antishank lady's left handed Niblick, c1910.
£30-50 *MSh*

A long nosed St. Andrews driver, c1880.
£400-600 *MSh*

Three golf club walking sticks.
£60-160 each *MSh*

An antishank Niblick, c1910.
£30-50 *MSh*

An Osmond caddy.
£500-700 *MSh*

A smooth faced bronze head lofting iron, c1880.
£200-300 *MSh*

An R. Forgan transitional head driver, c1890.
£300-400 *MSh*

FURTHER READING
Golf, The Golden Years, Sarah Baddiel.
Encyclopaedia of Golf Collectibles, Morten and John Olman.
The Sourcebook of Golf, Don Kennington.
Golf and the Printed Word, R. Donavan and J S. F. Murdoch.

General

A pair of spelter book ends.
£600-800 *MSh*

A silver match striker.
£220-250 *GOL*

Golf car mascots, both with clubs missing, 4in (10cm) and 5½in (14cm) high.
£90-150 each *MSh*

A plated golf inkwell.
£500-800
MSh

A silver spoon.
£35-45 *GOL*

A plated golf ball and clubs inkwell.
£200-300 *MSh*

A plated golf plaque, 1908, 15in (38cm) high.
£200-300 *MSh*

A spelter golf figure, 9½in (24cm) high.
£250-350 *MSh*

A French handpainted papier mâché bonbon box.
£250-300 *GOL*

411

A set of 8 Hassall prints.
£800-1,400 *MSh*

Prices vary on condition of prints.

A Dartmouth mug, 5½in (14cm) high.
£40-60 *MSh*

A Royal Doulton dish with Charles Crombie caricatures, 9½in (24cm).
£200-300 *MSh*

A Royal Doulton jug, 9in (23cm) high.
£300-450 *MSh*

A Copeland Spode mug, 7in (18cm) high.
£150-250 *MSh*

A Doulton Lambeth mug, 5in (13cm) high.
£500-700 *MSh*

Polo

AN INTRODUCTION TO POLO

The Mountbatten polo book collection of over 200 books and bound magazines, with related works on horsemanship formed by Lord Louis Mountbatten.
£22,000-25,000 *CSK*

A framed and glazed photograph of the future Edward VIII as Prince of Wales by W. W. Rouch & Co, 11 by 9½in (28 by 24cm).
£170-200 *CSK*

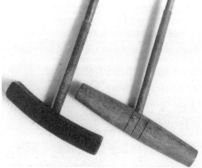

Polo mallets.
£30-70 each *MSh*

Tennis

A mahogany tennis press.
£80-130 *MSh*

A bronze figure of a tennis player inscribed P.H. Kittler, Nürnberg, 10½in (26cm) high.
£1,100-1,500 *CSK*

A plated tennis trophy, c1880, 18in (46cm) high.
£2,000-3,000 *MSh*

A lawn tennis racket by F. H. Ayres, c1885.
£100-200 *MSh*

A Birmal all metal racket.
£80-150 *MSh*

A lawn tennis racket by Benetfink, London, c1880.
£300-500 *MSh*

A fishtail racket, c1910.
£60-90 *MSh*

A real tennis racket, c1890.
£200-300 *MSh*

A fishtail racket, c1895.
£80-120 *MSh*

Two Malins lawn tennis rackets, c1875.
£400-700 each *MSh*

A child's racket, c1885.
£60-80 *MSh*

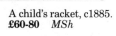

A tennis racket, c1925.
£20-30 *MSh*

413

Soccer

A pair of football boots.
£20-40 *MSh*

Mementoes of the 1982
World Cup Football in
Spain.
Spanish Orange. **£10-12**
Toy rattle. **£2-4** *COL*

A large Victorian leather
bound and gilt tooled
scrap album containing a
collection of
approximately 1,100
football cards, printed by
J. Baines, Manningham,
W. N. Sharpe, Bradford
and others.
£950-1,000 *C(S)*

*Football cards were a
craze of the late 19th and
early 20thC. J. Baines, in*
*his publicity, claimed to
have produced 888,888
different designs. This
perhaps explains many of
the rather obscure
selections, covering both
Association and Rugby
football clubs. The cards
were retailed in packets
costing ½d and prizes
were offered for the
largest number of empty
bags returned each week.*

A 1982 World Cup
Official Programme.
£1-2 *COL*

A football used in the
Scottish Cup Final of
1904-5 at New Hampden,
painted alternatively
maroon and white.
£520-600 *C(S)*

A Victorian black
painted brass umbrella
and stick stand, the back
cast with a figure of a
footballer holding a ball,
inscribed above, and
2 removable trays to
base, 34in (86cm) high.
£500-600 *C(S)*

A programme for the
1961 Football
Association Cup Tie,
Leicester City v
Tottenham Hotspur.
£4-6 *COL*

A Stanley Matthews
badge, 1950.
£3-5 *COL*

General

A table tennis net and turned wooden posts.
£20-40   *MSh*

Three caps.
£40-90 each   *MSh*

A Harlem Globetrotters programme, 1968.
£1-2   *COL*

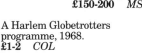

A cycling plaque.
£150-200   *MSh*

A Doulton Lambeth cycling jug, 7½in (19cm) high.
£200-300   *MSh*

FURTHER READING
Baseball Collectables, Peter Capano, Millbank Books, Schiffer Publishing Ltd.

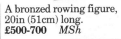

A bronzed rowing figure, 20in (51cm) long.
£500-700   *MSh*

An archery target.
£30-50   *MSh*

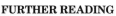

A Peterborough Speedway programme 1972.
50p-£1   *COL*

FURTHER READING
Tennis, Squash and Badminton Bygones, Gerald N. Gurney, Shire Publications Ltd, Aylesbury.
Billiards and Snooker Bygones, Norman Clare, Shire Publications Ltd, Aylesbury.

Two Olympic medals, London 1908, 1in (3cm) diam.
£45-55 each   *BY*

Stevengraphs

The Present Time 60 miles an Hour, Lord Howe and 2 carriages woven in silk, in original Oxford frame.
£50-100 *CSK*

DID YOU KNOW?
Originally Stevengraphs were available in the standard size of 6 by 2in (15 by 5cm) and unframed at a cost of one shilling. However for 2/6d (12½ new pence) they could be purchased in a gilded 'Oxford' frame.

Wellington & Blucher, a framed and glazed Stevengraph, 11 by 8in (28 by 20cm).
£90-100 *VS*

Taxidermy

A stuffed turtle.
£50-55 *COB*

A barn owl, 19thC, 17 by 14½in (43 by 37cm).
£150-200 *PC*

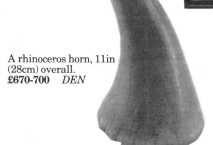

A rhinoceros horn, 11in (28cm) overall.
£670-700 *DEN*

A pair of kingfishers mounted in a glazed cabinet, 19thC.
£150-230 *BS*

A mounted tawny owl in glazed cabinet, 19thC.
£150-200 *BS*

A barn owl in glazed case, 19thC.
£150-200 *BS*

Telephones

The invention of the telephone is credited to Alexander Graham Bell in Boston, Massachusetts, in 1876. The system was demonstrated to Queen Victoria at Osborne House in 1878 and a year later the first telephone exchange was opened in London at 36 Coleman Street.

Many of the telephones shown here actually work and are sought after by those who just want a different telephone in their homes as well as collectors.

A No. 162 ivory coloured telephone, c1930.
£250-280 *CAB*

A copper and wooden extension telephone, c1920.
£60-70 *COB*

A 150 candlestick telephone with bell, set No. 1, 1920s.
£250-300 *CAB*

A wooden wall telephone, 121 type with back board and writing shelf, c1925.
£475-500 *CAB*

A No. 332 telephone, c1938.
£70-80 *CAB*

A No. 232 telephone, c1937.
£70-80 *CAB*

A wooden telephone, c1919.
£75-85 *COB*

A World War II scrambler telephone, identified by green hand set.
£150-160 *CAB*

A Post Office candlestick telephone with early solid back transmitter, 1920s.
£100-250 *SM*

A Post Office candlestick wall telephone with back board and writing slope, 1920s.
£120-280 *SM*

A demonstration model telephone, made for the Festival of Britain Exhibition 1951.
£1,000+ *PC*

A single station from a house telephone system, c1905.
£50-120 *SM*

An Antwerp telephone, made in England, but used extensively on the Continent, c1930s.
£100-120 *CAB*

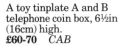

A No. 332 ivory coloured telephone with drawer, c1950.
£200-250 *CAB*

A toy tinplate A and B telephone coin box, 6½in (16cm) high.
£60-70 *CAB*

A Standard Telephone & Cables, London, Bakelite intercommunication wall telephone, 1930s.
£80-120 *SM*

An Ericsson intercommunication telephone, 1920s.
£80-120 *SM*

A Dutch telephone, with brass carrying handle, designed in the 1940s.
£60-70 *CAB*

This design was also produced in a copper finish.

A G.P.O. chromium plated trimphone 712, with original coloured wiring, c1965.
£80-100 *CAB*

An A and B coin box used in the old G.P.O. telephone boxes, introduced in the 1930s, decimalised in the early 1970s, but unused.
£300-350 *CAB*

An Ericsson metal fiddle back magneto telephone with writing slope, c1915.
£180-300 *SM*

An APT monophone, manufactured by the Automatic Telephone Manufacturing Co., 1930s.
£90-150 *SM*

FURTHER READING
Britains Public Payphones, M. Goss, British Telecom, 1984.
Introduction to Telephony & Telegraphy, E. J. Jolley, Pitman, 1968.

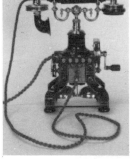

A Kjøbenhavns Telefon Aktieselskab Ericsson skeleton magneto telephone, c1900.
£300-600 *SM*

CANDLESTICK & BAKELITE

TELEPHONES FROM THE 1920's to 1960's

Catalogue available from
P.O. Box 308, Orpington, Kent, BR5 1TB
Telephone 081-467-3743

A No. 710 transparent demonstration model telephone, c1965.
£100-150 *CAB*

TEXTILES
Costume

A Victorian lawn dress with lace inserts.
£200-300 *LB*

A printed cotton dress, c1860.
£100-150 *LB*

A Victorian wedding slip in an assortment of laces.
£150-200 *LB*

A silk chiffon jacket with beadwork, 1920s.
£100-150 *LB*

A Victorian needlepoint lace wedding veil, 96in (243.5cm) square.
£150-250 *LB*

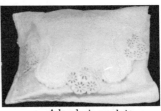

A broderie anglais nightdress case, c1910, 16in (41cm) wide.
£15-20 *LB*

An Edwardian embroidered silk on net blouse.
£60-100 *LB*

A bridal veil, 1920s, 96in (243.5cm) square.
£60-80 *LB*

MAKE THE MOST OF MILLER'S
Condition is absolutely vital when assessing the value of any item. Damaged pieces appreciate much less than perfect examples. However, a rare, desirable piece may command a high price even when damaged.

Children's Costume

A Victorian silk christening gown with slip needlepoint and Valencia lace.
£60-100 *LB*

A baby's christening gown, voile edged in Irish crochet work, with Irish crochet bonnet.
£40-50 *LB*

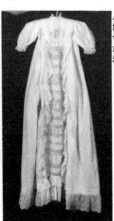

A christening gown, in fine lawn and white work with threaded blue satin ribbon, c1880.
£150-300 *LB*

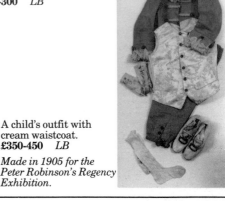

A child's outfit with cream waistcoat.
£350-450 *LB*

Made in 1905 for the Peter Robinson's Regency Exhibition.

An Edwardian hand worked child's dress.
£60-70 *LB*

Doilies

A crochet edged doily, 12in (31cm) diam.
£3-5 *LB*

An Irish crochet work doily, 10in (25cm) diam.
£5-10 *LB*

A tape work doily, 10in (25cm) diam.
£5-10 *LB*

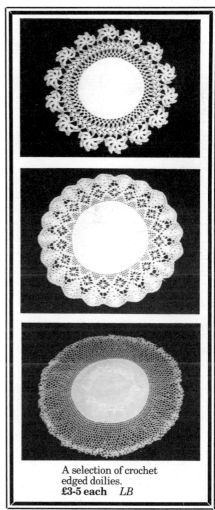

A selection of crochet edged doilies.
£3-5 each *LB*

Gloves

A pair of cream kid
gloves with pearl
buttons, c1900.
£5-10 *LB*

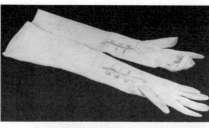

A pair of black suede and
green leather gloves,
made in Paris, 1920s.
£8-10 *LB*

A pair of white crochet
gloves, c1910.
£5-9 *LB*

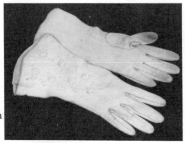

A pair of white leather
gloves embroidered with
flowers, c1930.
£10-15 *LB*

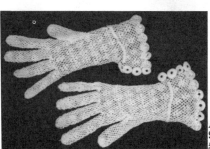

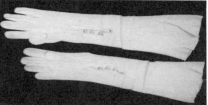

A pair of crochet gloves,
9in (23cm) long.
£5-8 *PC*

A pair of suede gloves
with pearl buttons,
17½in (44cm) long.
£5-8 *PC*

Hats & Bonnets

A Victorian straw hat
with velvet trim.
£80-90 *LB*

A child's blue striped hat
box, c1910, 8in (20cm)
diam.
£12-20 *LB*

An oyster silk poke
bonnet, by Bradleys,
4 Royal Colonnade,
Brighton.
£150-250 *PC*

*This bonnet belonged to
Princess Alice.*

A child's straw hat,
c1920.
£30-45 *LB*

A baby's bonnet with silk
ribbon.
£18-20 *LB*

A Victorian silk and
straw hat, maker's name
Jabez Chack, The
Colonnade, Tenterden.
£60-90 *LB*

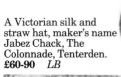

An embroidered smoking
cap, c1910.
£30-50 *LB*

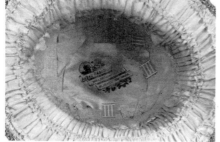

A silk bonnet etched in
lace and ribbon work,
c1910.
£20-30 *LB*

A Victorian hat stuffed
with horse hair and
trimmed with silk.
£80-100 *LB*

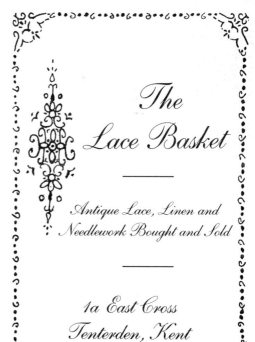

Household Linens

A hand embroidered linen tray cloth, 1930s.
£8-10 *LB*

A hand embroidered linen tea cloth, 1930s, 50in (127cm) square.
£20-30 *LB*

A hand embroidered linen tea cloth, 1930s, 40in (101.5cm) square.
£15-20 *LB*

A hand embroidered crochet edged linen tea cloth, 1930s, 50in (127cm) square.
£20-25 *LB*

A Continental crochet and linen pillow case, c1910, 28in (71cm) square.
£20-25 *LB*

A pair of Continental crochet and linen pillow cases, c1910, 28in (71cm) square.
£45-55 *LB*

A silk embroidered handkerchief, Souvenir de France.
£8-10 *LB*

A floral Durham quilt, pink and white, c1900, 76in (193cm) square.
£100-120 *LB*

Cross Reference
Silk Postcards

Two prisoner of war silk embroidered handkerchiefs, Royal Army Service Corps, 1914.
£6-8 each   *LB*

A lace edged nightdress case, c1910, 20in (51cm) wide.
£15-20   *LB*

A Victorian beadwork cushion, 15in (38cm) wide.
£150-260   *LB*

Parasols

A chintz parasol, 1920s, 33in (84cm) long.
£18-25   *LB*

An Edwardian cream lace parasol, 35in (89cm) long.
£60-70   *LB*

An Edwardian blue silk parasol, decorated in black lace and jet, 29½in (75cm) long.
£60-75   *LB*

Pictorial & Samplers

A Victorian woolwork picture, 16in (41cm) diam.
£250-300 *LB*

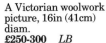

A Victorian silkwork picture, 17in (43cm) high.
£150-200 *LB*

A rosewood stand, early 19thC, 9½in (24cm) square.
£35-45 *CA*

An embroidered picture, 17½in (44cm) square.
£150-200 *PC*

A framed sampler in red and blue wool, 1924, 13 by 11in (33 by 28cm).
£40-50 *LB*

A sampler by Mary Swiney aged 12, 1815, worn, 15 by 13in (38 by 33cm).
£250-300 *CSK*

Purses & Handbags

A Regency tray inlaid with brass, the embroidered silk panel with centre pen and ink drawing, metal thread work and sequins.
£200-250 *LB*

A silk grosgrain evening bag, with Continental silver clasp, unmarked.
£75-85 *LB*

A chain purse, 1930s, 6in (15cm) long.
£25-35 *BY*

A Turkish purse, made from red velvet with gold thread trim, c1830, 3 by 2in (8 by 5cm).
£60-70 *LEW*

A silk and metal threadwork bag, 1900, 7½in (19cm) long.
£35-40 *LB*

A 1930s grosgrain evening bag, 8in (20cm) wide.
£10-15 *LB*

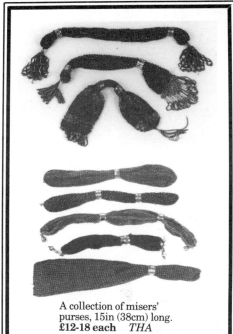

A collection of misers' purses, 15in (38cm) long.
£12-18 each *THA*

Shawls

A zebra shawl, mid-19thC, 70 by 68in (177.5 by 172.5cm).
£250-300 *CSK*

A paisley shawl with floral motifs, with an indistinct signature, 136 by 62in (346 by 157cm).
£800-900 *CSK*

A printed silk paisley shawl, green and violet on cream ground, c1910, 52in (132cm) square.
£50-70 *LB*

A woven paisley shawl, 132 by 60in (335.5 by 152cm), c1860.
£700-800   *LB*

A woven paisley shawl with cream centre, c1840, 66in (167.5cm) square.
£300-400   *LB*

Shoes

A pair of stiffened leather baby's shoes.
£30-50   *LB*

A pair of Victorian cream silk shoes.
£40-60   *LB*

A pair of lavender silk shoes, with diamanté decorated heels, c1900.
£50-80   *LB*

A pair of black and pink satin and silk shoes, made in Paris, c1920.
£50-80   *LB*

A pair of Chinese silk slippers, c1900.
£20-30   *LB*

A pair of Victorian black leather shoes with beadwork and jet trim, very narrow, 10in (25cm) long.
£100-150   *LB*

Tiles

Three Wedgwood
Months of the Year tiles,
August, September and
October, c1870.
£50-60 each *Nor*

A set of 6 Minton tiles,
6 by 6in (15 by 15cm)
each.
£180-200 *ARC*

A pair of green tiles by
Gibbons Hinton & Co.,
Stonebridge, 18 by 6in
(46 by 15cm).
£180-200 *ARC*

Two Minton tiles
designed by Moyr Smith
from Morte d'Arthur
series, c1890, 6 by 6in (15
by 15cm) each.
£30-40 each *CSA*

Reproduction tiles taken
from an original old
design and framed.
£80-90 *THA*

FURTHER READING
The Decorated Tile, J. and B. Austwick, The
Pitman House 1980.
Victorian Ceramic Tiles, Julian Barnard,
London 1972.
Tiles, A General History, Anne Berendson,
London 1967.
English Delftware, F. H. Garner and M. Archer,
London 1972.
A Catalogue of English Delftware Tiles, J. Horne,
London 1980.
Dutch Tiles, C. H. de Jonge, Pall Mall Press 1971.
Dutch Tiles, D. Korf, New York 1964.
*Guide to the Collection of Tiles: Victoria and
Albert Museum,* Arthur Lane, London 1960.
English Delftware Tiles, Anthony Ray, Faber,
London 1972.

A pair of tiles, green lady,
6 by 6in (15 by 15cm).
£12-18 each *ARC*

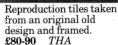

Tins

A Boer War chocolate tin with contents and history of the owner.
£50-55 *COB*

A Bemax cardboard and tin container, c1930, 7in (18cm) high.
£8-10 *COL*

A vesta tin of pigeon reviver pills.
£30-35 *CA*

A biscuit tin of neo-classical design, 10 by 7in (25 by 18cm).
£25-30 *HUN*

A Beecham's Pills box, with pills, 1½in (4cm) diam.
£2-3 *OD*

A pair of sealed tins of snuff, 2 by 1½in (5 by 4cm) each.
£5-6 *BY*

A tin matchbox cover.
£4-8 *OD*

A collection of gramophone needle tins.
£12-18 *BY*

A Moss Rimmington H.R.H. Princess of Wales mustard tin, c1897.
£100-150 *K*

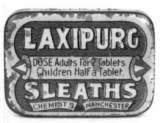

A chemist's tin, 1½ by 1in (4 by 3cm).
£2-4 *OD*

A Pascall's Home Sweets tin, 6½ by 4in (16 by 10cm), 1940.
£4-6 *RTT*

A Huntley & Palmers Rye Bread papier mâché box, c1930, 6½in (16cm) high.
£10-14 *COL*

A canister of Secto, kills bugs and beetles, 3in (8cm) high.
£3-4 *CA*

A Betterwear floor polish tin, 4½in (11cm) diam.
£6-7 *COL*

A Moss Rimmington & Co., Tennyson commemorative mustard tin, anti-rheumatic mustard oil for rheumatism and neuralgia, 4in (10cm) square.
£20-25 *RTT*

A miniature sample tea tin, c1920.
£5-8 *COB*

A Pascall's fruit bonbon tin, c1930, 8½in (21cm) high.
£20-25 *RTT*

A Kodak portrait attachment tin, 1½in (4cm) diam.
£5-6 *COL*

FURTHER READING
Decorated Biscuit Tins, American, English and European, Peter Hornsby, Millbank Books, Schiffer Publishing Ltd.

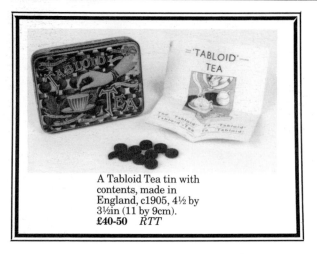

A Tabloid Tea tin with contents, made in England, c1905, 4½ by 3½in (11 by 9cm).
£40-50   *RTT*

A tin of Minerva varnish, 1940s, 4½in (11cm) high.
£9-10   *COL*

L'onglex nail polish and Myone cold cream. Nail polish, 1in (3cm) diam. **£3-4** Cold cream, 2in (6cm) diam.
£6-7   *COL*

A post box tin, 3in (8cm) high.
£7-8   *OD*

> **Cross Reference**
> Money boxes

A Huntley & Palmers biscuit tin with original paper label, 7½in (19cm) wide.
£10-15   *RTT*

> **FURTHER READING**
> *Advertising Collectables,* Keith and Penny Gretton, BBR Publishing, Barnsley 1989.

Cigarette Tins

A Prince Albert cigarette tobacco tin, 4½in (11cm) high.
£12-18   *BY*

A Churchman's Silver Wreath tin, c1915, 3½ by 3in (9 by 8cm).
£50-60   *RTT*

> **Cross Reference**
> Signs & Advertising

A Muratti's tin, c1930, 3½ by 3in (9 by 8cm).
£30-40   *RTT*

Oxo Tins

An Oxo tin filled with animal cut outs, 2in (5cm) high.
£55-65 *BY*

Three Oxo tins.
£3-5 each *OD*

A painted Oxo cube tin, 2½ by 2in (6 by 5cm).
£20-30 *LEW*

Toiletries

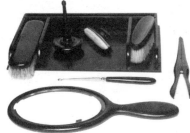

An ebony dressing table set.
£40-60 *HUN*

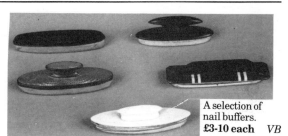

A selection of nail buffers.
£3-10 each *VB*

Wardonia Barrel-Hole Blade, 2in (5cm) wide.
£5-6 *CA*

An American Ever Ready safety razor and box, c1915, 4 by 2½in (10 by 6cm).
£10-15 *RTT*

A swan's down and silk powder puff, c1920.
£5-10 *LB*

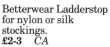

Betterwear Ladderstop for nylon or silk stockings.
£2-3 *CA*

A Cutex manicure set,
original box, c1939.
£20-25   *PAT*

An Imperial
stropping
machine.
£8-10   *CA*

Silver lidded dressing
table boxes, Birmingham
1904.
£125-150 each   *CLI*

A selection of Victorian
glass toilet jars, with
scroll engraved and
monogrammed silver
lids.
£30-50 each   *GSP*

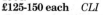

A swan's down powder
puff, c1930, 7in (18cm)
square.
£10-15   *LB*

A selection of silver nail
buffers, 4 to 5in (10 to
12.5cm) long.
£14-18 each   *VB*

Three cardboard boxes
for Roger & Gallet soaps,
Monarch Brand cotton
and Creme Thais
perfume.
£5-10 each   *RTT*

4711 Eau de Cologne in
original box, 5in (13cm)
high.
£2-5   *CA*

Two silver nail buffers,
3in (8cm) and 3½in (9cm)
long.
£12-18 each   *VB*

Gardening Tools

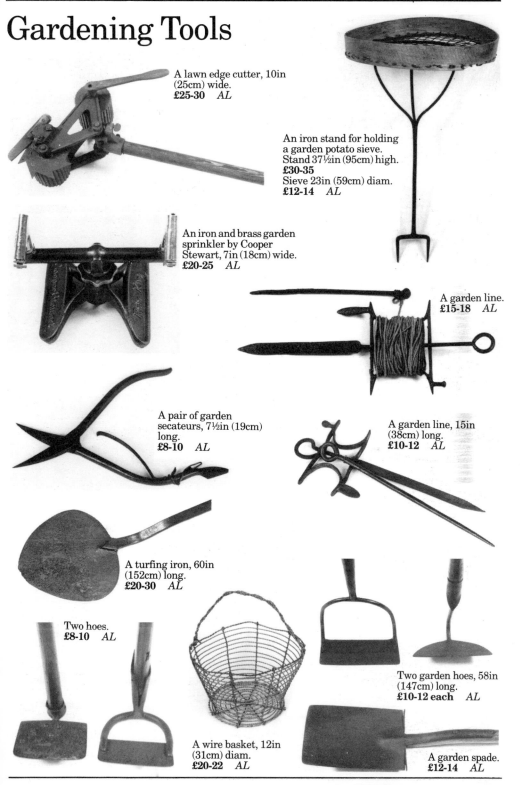

A lawn edge cutter, 10in (25cm) wide.
£25-30 *AL*

An iron stand for holding a garden potato sieve. Stand 37½in (95cm) high.
£30-35
Sieve 23in (59cm) diam.
£12-14 *AL*

An iron and brass garden sprinkler by Cooper Stewart, 7in (18cm) wide.
£20-25 *AL*

A garden line.
£15-18 *AL*

A pair of garden secateurs, 7½in (19cm) long.
£8-10 *AL*

A garden line, 15in (38cm) long.
£10-12 *AL*

A turfing iron, 60in (152cm) long.
£20-30 *AL*

Two hoes.
£8-10 *AL*

Two garden hoes, 58in (147cm) long.
£10-12 each *AL*

A wire basket, 12in (31cm) diam.
£20-22 *AL*

A garden spade.
£12-14 *AL*

A lawn edge cutter, 26in (66cm) long.
£8-10   *AL*

A pump bucket with leather non-return valve, 46in (116.5cm) long.
£35-40   *WO*

A potato fork, 15in (38cm) long.
£25-30   *AL*

A garden hand rake, 13½in (34cm) long.
£5-10   *AL*

A daisy grubber, 3½in (9cm) long.
£8-10   *AL*

Two garden dibbers, 8 and 14in (20 and 36cm) long.
£6-8 each   *AL*

Two garden cultivators.
£12-14 each   *AL*

A large garden cultivator.
£14-18   *AL*

Two hoppers, now used for flowers.
£12-14 each   *AL*

Two garden rakes:
Small. **£10-12**
Large, damaged.
£8-10   *AL*

Two brass garden sprays, 20in (51cm) long.
£12-14 each   *AL*

A wooden hand chopper.
£10-12   *AL*

A boot cleaner.
£65-80   *WO*

A lady's gardening fork and a standard fork.
£14-18 each   *AL*

Tools

A combination tool kit,
with 6 tools in boxwood
handle, 19thC, 8½in
(21cm) long.
£50-60   *BS*

A boxwood ring size, 10in
(25cm) long.
£35-45   *BS*

A pair of brass and steel
tailor's shears,
T. Wilkinson, Sheffield,
c1920, 14in (36cm) long.
£145-155   *BS*

A brass measure, 3½in
(9cm) wide.
£25-35   *BS*

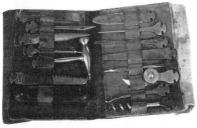

A travelling tool kit in
leather case by Bonsa,
c1900, 11in (28cm) long
open.
£240-250   *BS*

A part set of
watchmaker's tools with
fruitwood handles, set in
4 trays inside a gilt
tooled leather carrying
case, 19thC, 9½in (24cm)
wide.
£550-600   *CSK*

A set of Kenrick cast iron
revolving nail cups, from
a cobblers, c1900, 8½in
(21cm) diam.
£110-120   *BS*

A moulding plane by
Cogdel, mid-18thC, 10in
(25cm).
£60-75   *WO*

A birch handled carpet
stretcher, c1900, 26in
(66cm) long.
£50-60   *BS*

An un-named moulding
plane, early 18thC, 10in
(25cm).
£20-30   *WO*

A set of plumber's
boxwood bobbins,
14in (35cm) long.
£12-15   *WO*

Rules

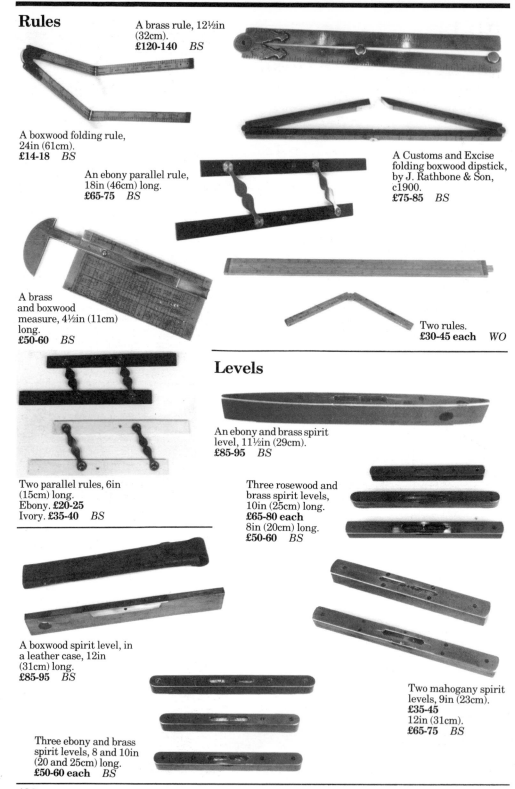

A brass rule, 12½in (32cm).
£120-140 *BS*

A boxwood folding rule, 24in (61cm).
£14-18 *BS*

An ebony parallel rule, 18in (46cm) long.
£65-75 *BS*

A Customs and Excise folding boxwood dipstick, by J. Rathbone & Son, c1900.
£75-85 *BS*

A brass and boxwood measure, 4½in (11cm) long.
£50-60 *BS*

Two rules.
£30-45 each *WO*

Levels

An ebony and brass spirit level, 11½in (29cm).
£85-95 *BS*

Three rosewood and brass spirit levels, 10in (25cm) long.
£65-80 each
8in (20cm) long.
£50-60 *BS*

Two parallel rules, 6in (15cm) long.
Ebony. **£20-25**
Ivory. **£35-40** *BS*

A boxwood spirit level, in a leather case, 12in (31cm) long.
£85-95 *BS*

Two mahogany spirit levels, 9in (23cm).
£35-45
12in (31cm).
£65-75 *BS*

Three ebony and brass spirit levels, 8 and 10in (20 and 25cm) long.
£50-60 each *BS*

TOYS

This year we have featured two very important and desirable areas of toy collectables: Disney and Teddy Bears. Both have increased noticeably in popularity and therefore in value. Diecast and tinplate toys have been featured in greater detail in the two previous editions of Miller's Collectables, as specified in the Cross Reference boxes.

Diecast
Dinky

Dinky 701 Shetland flying boat.
£850-900   *MIN*

French Dinky 804 Nord 2501 Noratlas.
£250-300   *MIN*

Dinky 60R Empire flying boat.
£400-450   *MIN*

Dinky 717 Boeing 737 Airliner.
£35-45   *MIN*

Dinky 62P Armstrong Whitworth Ensign airliner.
£325-375   *MIN*

A Dinky gift set No. 699 Military Vehicles (1), comprising Austin Champ, 1-Ton Truck, APC and 3-Ton Wagon, in original box.
£500-550   *C*

A Dinky gift set No. 2, Commercial Vehicles, comprising red and cream 25m Bedford End Tipper, brown 27d Land Rover, yellow and green 30m Farm Produce Wagon, 30pb Esso Tanker and blue and light blue 30s Austin Covered Wagon, in original box, c1952.
£1,400-1,600   *C*

Dinky 728 R.A.F. Dominie jet fighter.
£35-45   *MIN*

Dinky 179 Studebaker President sedan.
£115-125 *MIN*

A Dinky gift set No. 149, Sports Cars, comprising 108 M.G. Midget 28, 109 Austin Healey 21, 107 Sunbeam Alpine 34, 110 Aston Martin 22 and 111 TR2 29, in original box.
£700-800 *C*

Dinky 401 Coventry Climax forklift.
£45-55 *MIN*

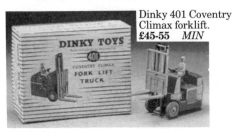

Dinky 188 Jensen FF Interceptor.
£55-65 *MIN*

Dinky 918 Guy Ever Ready van.
£500-550 *MIN*

Dinky 252 Bedford refuse wagon.
£125-145 *MIN*

Dinky 953 Continental touring coach.
£525-575 *MIN*

Corgi

Corgi 480 Chevrolet taxi cab. **£55-65** *MIN*

Corgi 851 Magic Roundabout train. **£300-350** *MIN*

Corgi 207M Standard Vanguard III. **£60-70** *MIN*

Novelty, Cinema & Television Related Toys

Novelty toys first appeared during the latter half of the 19thC, but became very popular with the advent of cinema and television.

Probably the first example was the Buck Rogers Spacecraft produced by Tootsietoy in 1937.

The first Corgi T.V.-related item was the James Bond Aston Martin made in 1965. All of these toys are extremely sought after, current favourites are Thunderbirds, Captain Scarlet and The Beatles' Yellow Submarine.

Corgi 290 Kojak Buick.
£25-35 *MIN*

Corgi Chipperfield's
Circus, set of 5 vehicles,
in original boxes.
£300-350 *CSK*

Corgi GS19
Chipperfield's Land
Rover and trailer.
£145-165 *MIN*

Corgi 404 Bedford
Dormobile.
£45-55 *MIN*

Corgi 436 Citroën Safari.
£75-85 *MIN*

Corgi gift set No. 38 1965
Monte Carlo Rally, in
original box, with
packing card.
£400-450 *CSK*

Corgi 218 Aston Martin
DB4.
£85-95 *MIN*

Corgi 206 Hillman
Husky.
£45-55 *MIN*

Corgi 209 Riley
Pathfinder.
£85-95 *MIN*

Corgi 330 Porsche
Carrera 6.
£45-55 *MIN*

General

Triang Minic MO12
Vanwall racing car.
£330-350 *MIN*

NFIC AEC
Routemaster
bus.
£20-25 *MIN*

Solido 241
Hanomag
half-track.
£10-15 *MIN*

Matchbox

Matchbox 52 BRM
racing car.
£20-25 *MIN*

Yesteryear Y-9 Fowler
showman's engine.
£85-95 *MIN*

FURTHER READING
Classic Miniature Vehicles: Made in Germany,
Edward Force, Millbank Books, Schiffer
Publishing Ltd.
Matchbox and Lledo Toys, Edward Force,
Millbank Books, Schiffer Publishing Ltd.

Disney

A selection of Mickey Mouse figures, 1960s and 70s.
£5-10 each *COB*

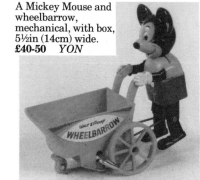

A Mickey Mouse, c1930, 6in (15cm) high.
£450-500 *YON*

A Mickey Mouse and wheelbarrow, mechanical, with box, 5½in (14cm) wide.
£40-50 *YON*

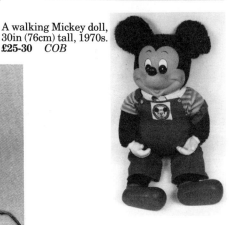

A fat Minnie with moving legs, 3½in (9cm) high.
£12-18 *YON*

A walking Mickey doll, 30in (76cm) tall, 1970s.
£25-30 *COB*

An early Mickey Mouse radiator grille ornament, the brass figure with painted black ears, torso and legs, paint flaking, c1934, 6in (15cm) high.
£400-500 *S*

Two Mickey Mouse toys, c1930, 7in (18cm) high.
£200-250 each *YON*

Paper and cardboard figures of Mickey Mouse, 4in (10cm) high, 1980s.
£2-3 each *COB*

A Disney castle and figures set, 1970.
£15-20   *COB*

A tinplate Mickey Mouse musical Organ Grinder with Minnie dancing on top, paint worn and one of Mickey's arms missing, c1930, 8in (20cm) high.
£1,320-1,500   *SWO*

Disney wax candles, 1960s, 4in (10cm) high.
£10-15 each   *COB*

A set of Christmas tree lights, 1950, in original box.
£35-40   *COB*

Three Disney tins:
Round, 7in (18cm) diam.
£18-20
2 pencil tins, 1970s, 6in (15cm) long.
£5-7 each   *COB*

Cross Reference
Tins

A jelly mould, early 1930s, 4in (10cm) high.
£15-20   *COB*

Disney 'Band Aids' in tin, 1980s.
£3-5   *COB*

A Disney lampshade, 1960s.
£5-8   *COB*

A bagatelle game, 1940s,
30in (76cm) long.
£35-40 *COB*

Mickey Mouse Annual,
1979, and Donald Duck
Annual, 1978.
£3-5 each *COB*

Minnie with pram,
plastic, 3in
(7.5cm) long.
£15-20 *YON*

Mickey Mouse sand
buckets:
Large, 5in (12.5cm).
£35-40
Small, 3in (7.5cm).
£20-25 each *RTT*

Annuals, 1959 and 1960.
£10-12 each *COB*

A selection of magnets.
£1-3 each *COB*

Mickey Mouse Annuals,
1942 and 1943.
£35-40 each
COB

A Mickey clock, 8½in
(21.5cm) high.
£10-20 *YON*

Disney sand buckets.
£20-35 each *COB*

A set of Disney thimbles, 1980s.
£10-15 *COB*

A plastic money bank, 1960s, 12in (30.5cm) high.
£15-20
A tin money bank, 1980s, 6in (15cm) high.
£10-12 *COB*

A metal lunch box, early 1960s, 12in (30.5cm) long.
£35-45 *COB*

l. A plastic beaker, 1960s.
£5-7
c. A Mickey 60 years tin, 1988.
£3-5
r. A mug, 1980s.
£2-3 *COB*

A Disney television set, 5in (12.5cm) high.
£100-115 *YON*

A friction drive Mickey and racing kart, with box, 5in (12.5cm) wide.
£25-35 *YON*

A musical jewellery box, 1970s.
£8-10 *COB*

An Ingersoll Mickey Mouse pocket watch, American, 1930s, 2in (5cm) diam, and an Ingersoll Mickey Mouse mantel clock, casing worn, 4in (10cm) high.
£300-350 *S*

Mickey Mouse telephone,
1960s, 22in (55.5cm)
high.
£45-50   *COB*

l. A quartz watch, 1988.
£20-30
r. A plastic watch, 1960s.
£20-25   *COB*

Donald Duck.
£3-5   *CT*

A water sprayer for
gardens, 1970s, 6in
(15cm) tall.
£10-15   *COB*

An alarm clock radio,
1960s, 9in (22.5cm) high.
£35-40   *COB*

Mickey Mouse spinning
top, c1950.
£25-35   *COB*

Model Figures
& Soldiers

Britain

The Gloucestershire
Regiment, No. 119, in
tropical dress, with
original box, card liner
and tissue paper.
£200-250   *WAL*

13th Duke of Connaughts
Own Lancers, No. 66,
including mounted
trumpeter and troopers
with lances, in original
box with liner.
£110-130   *WAL*

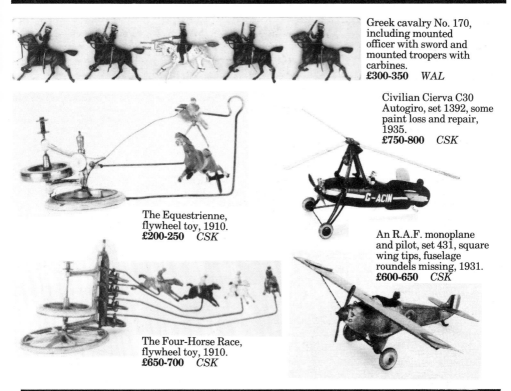

Greek cavalry No. 170, including mounted officer with sword and mounted troopers with carbines.
£300-350   *WAL*

The Equestrienne, flywheel toy, 1910.
£200-250   *CSK*

The Four-Horse Race, flywheel toy, 1910.
£650-700   *CSK*

Civilian Cierva C30 Autogiro, set 1392, some paint loss and repair, 1935.
£750-800   *CSK*

An R.A.F. monoplane and pilot, set 431, square wing tips, fuselage roundels missing, 1931.
£600-650   *CSK*

General

A collection of Elastolin
WWI infantry figures,
German, and a Britains
cannon.
£300-350 *S(C)*

Six carved and painted
wooden cavalry soldiers,
mounted on green
painted stands with wire
springs, damaged,
Thuringen, mid-19thC,
4½in (11.5cm) high.
£200-250 *CSK*

A collection of semi-flat
figures, in original
paintwork, German, late
19thC.
£200-220 *C*

A Charben's No. 222
Jack's Band.
£400-450 *CSK*

Lead soldiers, unpainted
collectors' models bought
to paint in whatever
uniform they chose.
40-60p each *COL*

A boxed set of Cupperly,
Blondel & Gerbeau lead
soldiers, French, in
original box bearing
printed label, with

5 large size Britains
Bikinir Camel Corps,
4 lacking arms, early
20thC.
£150-200 *S(C)*

A Taylor and Barrett
Coster Series
Greengrocery, complete
with donkey and barrow,
in original box; with a
similar donkey, barrow
and basket.
£90-100 *HSS*

A British made cold
painted lead Nigger Jazz
Band, in original box,
and a British made cold
painted lead 'Musical
Trio', in original box.
£180-220 *HSS*

Model Railways

General

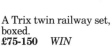

Two white metal paperweights, a Britain's Canadian National Railways 4–8–2; and a L.N.E.R. Flying Scotsman, 5½in (14cm) long.
£50-80 *C*

A Trix twin railway set, boxed.
£75-150 *WIN*

A Bowman Pacific.
£150-250
WIN

A Marx battery operated tin locomotive, 1960.
£40-50 *WIN*

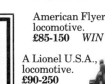

American Flyer locomotive.
£85-150 *WIN*

A Lionel U.S.A., locomotive.
£90-250
WIN

A J.E.P. clockwork train set, comprising: PLM style 4–4–0 locomotive and tender, 2 passenger coaches and 1 brake van, with Paris station, destination indicator, telegraph pole and signal parts, a quantity of track, all contained in International Express box, some re-painting and box lid damaged, c1912.
£1,000-1,200 *C*

Wilag: a PLM Lits-Salon/Salon coach, with fitted interior and opening doors, 27in (68.5cm) long, and a German full brake in Märklin style, with opening doors and external details, c1970, 22½in (57cm) long.
£500-550 *C*

A Schoenner 75mm gauge 2–2–2 steam locomotive, with 2 handpainted tinplate coaches, with circle of original tinplate track, some retouching, roofs and some details missing, c1885.
£750-800 *C*

A three-rail electric model of the K Lines 2–6–0 locomotive and tender, No. 326, Manstead Foundry No. 105, built by Leeds Model Coy., 17½in (44.5cm) long.
£300-350   *C*

A 3in gauge display model of an S.N.C.F. 2nd Couchettes twin-bogie corridor coach, with cut-away section to reveal day and night accommodation, and with some external detailing, 46in (116.5cm) long.
£220-250   *CSK*

An Ernst Plank, 2½in gauge live-steam, spirit fired, brass and tinplate 2–2–0 Vulkan locomotive, some alterations and possibly restored, 7in (17.5cm) long.
£200-250   *Bon*

American Flyer, electric locomotive.
£45-75   *WIN*

A Triang wooden train set, 1936.
£45-50   *COB*

A pre-war clockwork DL7 tank G.W.R. 6699, boxed.
£200-300   *C*

A detailed model of the Metropolitan Vickers 1200 h.p. electric locomotive, No. 5, John Hampden, the display base and track with lighting, control unit and other details, 20in (50.5cm) long.
£800-900   *C*

An advertising display model of the Trans Europ Express TEE-DB, 27in (68.5cm) long.
£80-100   *CSK*

A fine model of a flat wagon carrying an Albion omnibus, 18in (45.5cm) long.
£1,500-1,700   *C*

A German tinplate station building, incomplete, 23in (58.5cm) long.
£80-100   *Bon*

Scale Model Locomotives

A 5in gauge model of the G.W.R. 15XX Class 0–6–0 pannier tank locomotive No. 1501, built by C. H. Cockayne, 1964, 35in (89cm) long.
£3,500-4,000   *CSK*

A 7¼in gauge model of the B.R. 0–4–0 side tank locomotive Midge, 36½in (93cm) long.
£1,200-1,500   *C*

A 3½in gauge model of the Buffalo and Susquehanna Rail Road Brooks 4–6–0 wood burning locomotive and tender No. 8, built by C. W. Brooks, Poundstock, 49½in (126cm) long.
£3,500-4,000   *CSK*

A 3½in gauge model of the L.M.S. 4–6–0 locomotive and tender No. 6100 Royal Scot, built by H. W. Webb, Oxshott, 49½in (126cm) long.
£2,000-2,500   *CSK*

A 3½in gauge model of the B. & S.R.R. Baldwin 2–4–4 narrow gauge locomotive No. 7, built to the design of Lucky Seven by D. Young, by A. D. Eves, Manchester, 59in (149.5cm) long.
£4,000-4,500   *C*

A 7¼in gauge model of the G.C.R. Director Class 4–4–0 locomotive and tender Princess Mary, built by J. S. Beeson, recently checked and re-painted by Severn Lamb Ltd., c1938, 88in (223.5cm) long.
£6,500-7,000   *CSK*

A 5in gauge model of the L.S.W.R. Adams 4–4–0 locomotive and tender, No. 677, 60½in (153cm) long.
£3,000-3,500   *C*

A 2½in gauge spirit-fired model of the L.M.S. 2–6–0 locomotive and tender, No. 2971, 31½in (80cm) long.
£650-750   *CSK*

Hornby

Hornby Dublo 3-rail electric EDG7 LNER tank goods set, black locomotive No. 9596, c1948.
£400-450   *CSK*

A Hornby 20-volt electric E420 SR Schools Class Eton, No. 900, and No. 2 special tender, in L.M.S. tender boxes, locomotive box taped, c1937.
£1,500-2,000   *C*

A Hornby O gauge locomotive, post-war.
£20-80   *WIN*

Hornby O gauge signal box and station.
Signal box. **£25-45**
Station. **£45-85**   *WIN*

A Hornby 20-volt electric E220 Special L.N.E.R. Bramham Moor, No. 201, and No. 2 special tender, in original box, one set of cab hand-irons missing.
£900-1,000   *C*

A Hornby O gauge passenger set.
£35-65   *WIN*

A Hornby gauge O electric LMS 4–6–2 Princess Elizabeth, in presentation box.
£3,000-4,000   *FEN*

Hornby Dublo, The Princess Royal.
£20-65   *WIN*

Two Hornby milk tank wagons, United Dairies and Nestlés Milk, c1936.
£450-500 *C*

A Hornby LNER E320 Flying Scotsman passenger train set, in original box, with transformer and circuit breaker, box lid and illustration torn, c1938.
£2,000-2,500 *C*

A Hornby O gauge passenger set, post-war.
£50-175 *WIN*

A Hornby 3½in gauge live steam Stephenson's Rocket, boxed.
£150-200 *WIN*

A Hornby clockwork L & NER No. 2 4–4–4 tank locomotive, in grey Hornby box, box poor, c1924.
£250-350 *C*

A gauge 'O' electric L.M.S. goods set, including a 4–4–2 tank locomotive, No. 2180, minor damage to locomotive, box lid damaged.
£350-400 *S(S)*

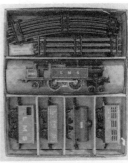

Hornby O gauge goods trucks and a set of signals, boxed, post-war.
£15-75 each *WIN*

A Hornby series LMS 70, EPM6 special tank locomotive, red, electric, boxed.
£550-600 *FEN*

Bing

A Bing for Bassett-Lowke
steam LNWR 4–4–0
freelance steam
locomotive, No. 1902,
original paintwork,
original wooden box,
slight damage to tender,
c1928.
£650-700   *C*

A Bing painted tinplate
clockwork Continental
type 4–4–0 locomotive
and painted 6-wheel
tender, front lamp,
buffers and coupling
missing, c1905.
£200-300
C

A Bing for
Bassett-Lowke
clockwork painted
tinplate LSWR 0–4–4
M7 tank locomotive,
c1912.
£1,000-1,500   *C*

A Bing clockwork
lithographed tinplate
4–6–0 Royal Scot and
matching 6-wheel
tender, c1928.
£300-400   *C*

A clockwork Southern
0–6–0 goods locomotive
and tender, c1930.
£300-350   *CSK*

A Bing for Bassett-Lowke
3-rail electric GNR Ivatt
Atlantic with 6-wheel
tender, some paint
flaking to tender, c1912.
£1,000-1,200   *C*

A Bing for Bassett-Lowke
clockwork LB&SCR
4–4–2 Marsh tank
locomotive, rear buffer
beam damaged, c1921.
£650-700   *C*

A gauge III spirit-fired
live steam LSWR 4–4–0
locomotive, No. 593, part
refinished, some
restoration, together
with a hand made
replacement tender.
£1,800-2,000   *S(S)*

Bassett-Lowke

A Bassett-Lowke gauge O electric 4–4–0 locomotive Prince Charles, No. 62453, in original box, with Bassett-Lowke 3-rail track and a Bassett-Lowke transformer, c1955.
£500-550   *S*

A Märklin for Bassett-Lowke clockwork S.R. 4–4–0 Schools Class locomotive and tender, No. 910 Merchant Taylors, with key, tender with B.R. transfers overlaid, couplings altered, c1933.
£1,000-1,500   *C*

A Bassett-Lowke 2½in gauge live steam spirit-fired M.R. 0–6–0 tank locomotive No. 207, finished in maroon livery with straw lining, c1923.
£600-700   *C*

A Bassett-Lowke 3-rail electric model of the L.M.S. 5XP Class 4–6–0 locomotive and tender No. 5712 Victory, in original paintwork and box.
£2,200-2,500   *C*

A 3-rail electric model of the S.R. Merchant Navy class 4–6–2 locomotive and tender, No. 21C1 Channel Packet, in original paintwork, built by an employee of Bassett-Lowke for them.
£1,000-1,200   *C*

A Bassett-Lowke 3-rail electric model of the G.W.R. Castle Class 4–6–0 locomotive and tender No. 4079 Pendennis Castle, in original paintwork.
£3,500-4,000   *C*

A Bassett-Lowke gauge O Post Office mail van, with pick-up apparatus, in L.M.S. livery, slight marks and scratches to lithography, c1925.
£130-180   *S*

A Trix for Bassett-Lowke Princess set, including LMS 4–6–2 Princess locomotive and tender, with controller, in original case, pre-war.
£400-450   *C*

FURTHER READING
The Bassett-Lowke Story, Roland Fuller.

Märklin

A pair of Märklin wagon lits teak finished coaches, a sleeping car and a dining car, with fitted interiors, c1921.
£2,200-2,500 *C*

A Märklin gauge 1 3-rail electric model of a Continental 4–4–0 locomotive and tender No. E13041, lacks bulbs, 1920s.
£500-550 *CSK*

A Märklin gauge electric 4–6–2 PLM locomotive, slight chips and rubbing to paint in places, c1912.
£2,500-3,000 *S*

A Märklin hand painted station, with candle-holders and opening doors, c1910, 10½in (26cm) wide.
£650-750 *C*

A Märklin painted tinplate engine shed No. 2112R, with 2 sets of double doors, in original paintwork, slightly chipped, c1908, 14in (36cm) long.
£90-120 *C*

A Märklin 4–4–0 Continental electric locomotive, with correct mechanism, now removed but complete, c1904, fitted with 1920s low voltage mechanism, with an incorrect tender, c1914.
£1,200-1,500 *C*

A Märklin clockwork MR 2–4–4 Flatiron side-tank locomotive, No. 2000, some corrosion, in original box.
£700-800 *C*

A Märklin E 800 L.M.S. Compound locomotive and tender, with tinplate and diecast body, 20 volt 3-rail.
£15,000-18,000 *C*

One of the rarest Märklin models of its period, this was imported into the U.K. briefly during 1938.

Robots

A mechanical soldier on parade, 6½in (16.5cm) high.
£60-80 *YON*

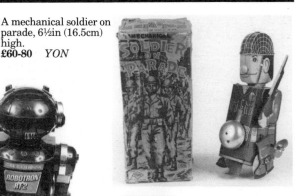

A clockwork robot, made in Japan, 4½in (11.5cm) high.
£70-100 *BY*

A Robotron RT-2, made in Hong Kong, 16in (40.5cm) high.
£15-20 *BY*

A printed and painted tinplate battery operated Attacking Martian, by Horikawa, 1960s, G.
£100-150 *CAm*

A clockwork Sparking Robot, clockwork mechanism, driving with sparks visible through transparent chest, with box, by Sconosciuto, Japanese, 1950s, 6½in (16cm) high, M, box E, and clockwork Mechanical Robot, Greek copy of above, with same functions, with box, marked M in circle, 1970s, G, box E.
£70-100 *CAm*

A printed and painted tinplate Piston Robot, battery operated, with 8 moving pistons in transparent head with flashing light, with box, by Horikawa, Japanese, 1960s, 10½in (26cm) high, G, box G.
£150-200 *CAm*

A printed and painted tinplate and plastic battery operated Mr. Xerox, by Horikawa, 1960s, G.
£250-350 *CAm*

A Robot, made in Hong Kong, 12in (30.5cm) high.
£15-20 *BY*

A battery operated Dalek, incomplete, Hong Kong, 6in (15cm) high.
£15-20 *BY*

T.V. Toys

Noddy

Noddy crayons.
£3-6 *YON*

A friction drive
aeroplane, with box,
7½in (19cm) long.
£20-30 *YON*

A rubber Noddy, in box,
5in (12.5cm) high.
£3-6 *YON*

General

A Mr. Men bendy toy,
10½in (26.5cm) high.
£8-12 *BY*

Felix the Cat, c1930,
13in (33cm) high.
£340-380 *YON*

A Celluloid Popeye,
c1930, 9in (22.5cm) high.
£180-200 *YON*

Batman

Batman purses, 4½in
(11.5cm) long.
£25-35 *YON*

A Batmobile, 6½in
(16.5cm) high.
£70-80 *YON*

A Batman figure, 13in
(33.5cm) high.
£10-12 *BY*

Rocking Horses

A rocking horse on shaped wooden platform, with 4 metal wheels attached to half moon wooden rockers, English, considerable damage, late 19thC, 33½in (85cm) high.
£450-500 *S*

A carved wooden rocking horse, painted dapple grey, on safety rockers, 47in (119cm) wide.
£200-250 *C*

A rocking horse on oak trestle stand, English, repainted and some wear, c1910, 44in (111.5cm) long.
£450-500 *S*

A dapple grey carved wooden rocking horse, on curved rockers, G. & J. Lines, c1910, 84in (213cm) wide.
£1,200-1,500 *C*

A wooden horse, c1900.
£45-60 *COB*

MAKE THE MOST OF MILLER'S
Price ranges in this book reflect what one should expect to *pay* for a similar example. When selling, however, one should expect to receive a lower figure. This will fluctuate according to a dealer's stock, saleability at a particular time, etc. It is always advisable, when selling, to approach a reputable specialist dealer or an auction house which has specialist sales.

Teddy Bears

A Steiff blond teddy bear, with button in ear, worn, pads replaced, c1908, 20in (50.5cm) high.
£750-850   *S*

A Steiff central seam golden plush covered teddy bear, pads replaced, some wear, growler inoperative, c1905, 20in (50.5cm) high.
£1,000-1,200   *C*

A rare set of 3 Clifford Berryman hand-drawn pencil sketches of bears, each signed C.K. Berryman, one entitled Sleepy Hollow, New York, c1920, 6½ by 5in (16.5 by 12.5cm).
£1,800-2,000   *S*

Clifford Berryman was the political cartoonist who started his career in 1889 for the Washington Post, and from 1908 for the Washington Star. One of his sketches in 1902 became famous, depicting Theodore Roosevelt refusing to shoot a small bear while settling a boundary dispute between the States of Louisiana and Mississippi. Berryman adopted the little bear as a symbol and the Teddy Bear is believed to have originated from this story. These sketches were a gift for the present owner whose aunt and uncle, William and Mary Knight, were close friends of Mr. Berryman.

A Steiff beige plush covered teddy bear, with button in ear, c1903, 10in (25cm) high.
£550-650   *CSK*

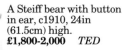

A Steiff bear with button in ear, c1910, 24in (61.5cm) high.
£1,800-2,000   *TED*

A Laughing Roosevelt teddy bear, the opening mouth with pull bellows growler, by Columbia Teddy Bears Manufacturers, pads replaced, composition teeth detached, c1907, 23in (58.5cm) high.
£1,000-1,300   *CSK*

A Celluloid headed teddy doll, with plush covered body, beige felt hands and feet, moulded hair and painted features, c1908, 16in (40.5cm) high.
£100-150   *C*

A Steiff brown mohair bear, original black boot button eyes, button in ear removed, pads replaced.
£250-300   *TED*

A clockwork mechanical bear, mouth opening and closing, with key, probably Roullet & Descamps, c1900, 9½in (24cm) long, in remnants of original box.
£350-400   *S(C)*

A Steiff blond plush teddy bear, 14½in (37cm) high, and a blond plush teddy bear, early 20thC, 12in (30cm) high.
£150-200 *HSS*

A Steiff gold plush teddy bear, button removed, some wear and repairs, c1908, 10in (25cm) high.
£450-500 *S*

A Steiff teddy bear on wheels, button in left ear, c1910, 9in (22.5cm) long.
£450-500 *S(C)*

A Steiff apricot plush teddy bear, button removed, pads replaced, re-stitched, plush worn, c1908, 21in (53.5cm) high.
£600-700 *S*

A German blond plush teddy bear, early 20thC, 13in (33cm) high.
£300-400 *HSS*

A pale golden plush covered teddy bear, Steiff button in ear, paws worn, growler inoperative, c1911, 28in (71.5cm) high, on a Thonet bent wood armchair, 26in (66cm) high.
£2,000-3,000 *CSK*

FURTHER READING
Teddy Bears Past And Present, Linda Mullins, Hobby House, 1986.

'TEDDY BEARS'
of Witney

In May, 1989, Ian Pout of 'Teddy Bears' gave £12,100 (then a world record price), for Alfonzo, a wonderful and rare red Steiff Bear, once owned by a Russian princess. This was an exceptional price for an exceptional item.

We always want to buy old bears, especially by Steiff, Schuco, Merrythought, Farnells, Deans, Chiltern and Chad Valley.

We also want to buy any items relating to Teddy Bears – old postcards, jewellery, china items. Old copies of Pooh and Rupert, drawings, etc.

Please contact Ian Pout at:

'Teddy Bears'
99 High Street
Witney
Oxfordshire
OX8 6LY

Tel: Witney
(0993) 702616

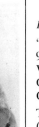

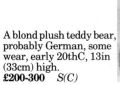

A blond plush teddy bear, probably German, some wear, early 20thC, 13in (33cm) high.
£200-300 *S(C)*

A Steiff roly poly bear, stuffed with wood wool, c1910, 7in (17.5cm) high.
£500-600 *TED*

An English mohair bear in a dress, with American cloth pads, c1930, 14in (35.5cm) high.
£60-80 *TED*

An English pink bear, filled with wood wool, 24in (61.5cm) high.
£10-15 *TED*

An English teddy bear pyjama case, 1930s, 18in (45.5cm) high.
£70-80 *TED*

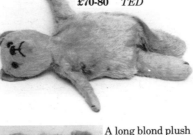

A straw filled teddy bear, c1920, 24in (61.5cm) high.
£100-125 *COB*

A long blond plush musical teddy bear, one pad holed, probably German, 1920s, 19in (48.5cm) high.
£220-250 *S(C)*

An English much loved teddy bear, extremely worn, eyes restitched, 15in (38cm) high.
£15-20 *TED*

A koala bear, 1950s, 11in (28cm) high.
£8-12 *TED*

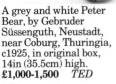

A grey and white Peter Bear, by Gebruder Süssenguth, Neustadt, near Coburg, Thuringia, c1925, in original box, 14in (35.5cm) high.
£1,000-1,500 *TED*

This is now a rare toy as few were made because his fierce expression was unpopular.

A Steiff baby teddy bear, with button in ear and remnant of orange tag, c1930, 13in (33cm) high.
£500-600 *TED*

DID YOU KNOW?

Hugglets Teddy Bear Club has been formed to encourage contacts amongst teddy bear collectors and to promote teddy bear events around the country.

If you would like to become a member, contact: Hugglets, P.O. Box 290, Brighton, England.

An unjointed panda bear, probably Chiltern, 1950s, 9½in (24cm) high.
£15-20 *TED*

A dark golden plush covered teddy handbag, pads replaced, possibly Schuco, 8in (20cm) high.
£700-750 *CSK*

A black bear, with squeaker when turned over, German, 1940s, 30in (76.5cm) high.
£120-150 *TED*

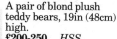

A pair of blond plush teddy bears, 19in (48cm) high.
£200-250 *HSS*

An English mohair bear, very much loved, 1940s, 14in (35.5cm) high.
£10-20 *TED*

A white straw filled teddy bear, in Cunard cap, c1937, 36in (91.5cm) high.
£100-120
Cunard cap **£5-10**
COB

A battery operated teddy, made in Japan, 1950s, 8in (20cm) high.
£110-115 *COB*

A Chad Valley gold plush bear, with label, 1950s, 16in (40.5cm) high.
£80-90 *TED*

A Chad Valley Sooty hand puppet, c1960, 8in (20cm) high.
£10-15   *TED*

A mohair Chiltern bear, 1950s, 20in (50.5cm) high.
£110-130   *TED*

A Chad Valley bear, as used for shop window displays by Bear Brand, 1950s, 41in (104cm) high.
£700-800   *TED*

A mechanical teddy bear, 1960.
£40-45   *COB*

An English cotton plush bear, maker unknown, c1960, 29in (73.5cm) high.
£40-50
TED

A Chiltern Rupert Bear on tricycle, c1955, 10in (25cm) high.
£100-120   *TED*

A mohair Deans ragbook bear, with characterful expression.
£130-150   *TED*

A golden curly plush covered teddy bear, with original Chad Valley swing twicket and label on pad, 21in (53.5cm) high.
£250-350   *CSK*

A cotton plush Sooty bear, maker unknown, 1950s.
£25-35   *TED*

An English teddy bear, with original outfit, 8in (20cm) high.
£90-110   *TED*

Bears

Bears were collected by the Victorians long before the 'Teddy Bear' evolved. This selection is typical of the carved bear figures that are available in a variety of guises.

A bear ashtray, 5in (13cm) wide.
£20-25 *SP*

A bear ashtray, 6in (15cm) wide.
£30-40 *SP*

A European carved bear, 6in (15cm) high.
£20-30 *SP*

Used for holding pens, thimbles, etc., and many were ashtrays.

A carved wooden bear, 3in (8cm) wide.
£10-12 *CA*

A musical bear, 10in (25cm) high.
£25-30 *SP*

A European souvenir, pre-war, with original box, 3in (7.5cm).
£30-60 *SP*

A pair of miniature carved wooden bears, 1in (2.5cm) high.
£5-10 each *SP*

Tinplate Toys

A mechanical cat and
ball, with box, Japanese,
5in (13cm) long.
£50-60 *YON*

A Wolverine Sunny
Andy Fun Fair, in
damaged box, 14in
(36cm) long.
£250-300 *CNY*

A Martin clockwork
tinplate and cloth
climbing polar bear, with
tinplate climbing pole,
pole 20in (51cm) high.
£500-550 *C*

A Ring-A-Ling Circus,
8in (20cm) high.
£400-450 *CNY*

A tinplate frog.
£14-16 *COL*

A Bing painted tinplate
clockwork 3-funnel liner,
pennants missing, c1925,
16in (41cm) long.
£500-600 *C*

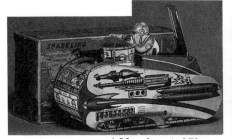

A Marx keywind Planet
Patrol space tank, with
pop-up soldier and
sparking action in
original box, 10in (25cm)
long.
£200-250 *CNY*

A Hornby clockwork
speedboat, with box,
c1930.
£250-350 *BY*

A German keywind
tinplate cockfight toy,
when wound the roosters
roll and bend forward
pecking each other, 10in
(25cm) long.
£250-300 *CNY*

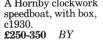

A Marx Buck Rogers
Rocket Police Patrol,
c1934, 12in (31cm) high.
£600-650 *CNY*

Motorcycles

A selection of tinplate motorcycles.
£8-30 each   *YON*

A clockwork Police
Patrol motorcycle,
English, c1930, 7½in
(19cm) long.
£200-250   *RTT*

An Arnold lithographed
tinplate Mac 700
motorcycle and rider, in
original box, c1948.
£450-500   *C*

A Mettoy tinplate
clockwork Speed King
Mechanical Motor Cycle,
in original box.
£300-350   *C*

A Mettoy tinplate Big
Chief Mechanical
Clockwork Motor Cycle,
in original box.
£450-500   *C*

Motor Vehicles

A Roadmaster battery
powered car, Eastern
European, with box,
c1950, 7½in (19cm) long.
£50-75   *RTT*

A police car, Empire
made, 1950, 6in (15cm)
long.
£40-50   *RTT*

A Chad Valley lithographed tinplate clockwork Delivery Van, in original box, 1940s, 10in (25cm) long.
£650-850   *C*

A CIJ clockwork painted tinplate P2 Alfa Romeo, with 12-spoke Michelin pneumatic wheels, Made in France stamped on base, c1927, 20½in (52cm) long.
£2,200-2,500   *Bon*

A friction drive tin car, 1960s.
£10-12   *COB*

An Oro lithographed tinplate clockwork limousine with opening doors, 1 side light missing, c1914, 8in (20cm) long.
£350-400   *C*

A clockwork tinplate St John's Ambulance, c1919, 6in (15cm) long.
£120-130   *COB*

A clockwork tinplate racing car, c1929, 10in (25cm) long.
£130-140   *COB*

A clockwork tin racing car, c1920.
£100-125   *COB*

A Triang tin tipper lorry, 1936.
£50-60   *COB*

Two Gunthermann clockwork record cars, in original boxes, Kay Don's Sunbeam Silver Bullet, printed tinplate, 22in (56cm) long, and Captain Campbell's Bluebird, painted tinplate, 20in (51cm) long.
£1,300-1,700 each   *C*

Toys & Games

Arks

A Bavarian painted wooden Noah's Ark, containing approximately 275 carved and painted animals, some damage, c1880, 23in (59cm) long.
£700-750 *S*

A German carved wooden Noah's Ark, with 22 pairs of carved wooden animals and 2 members of the Noah family, c1880.
£650-750 *C*

Games

A birch cribbage board with fixed brass pegs, 19thC, 11in (28cm) long.
£220-240 *BS*

A Playboy Playmate puzzle with centre fold, c1967, 5½in (14cm) high.
£12-18 *BY*

Treen bezique marker, 6in (15cm) long.
£15-18 *CA*

A Chad Valley Robin Hood badge, c1960.
£18-22 *BY*

A Bayko Building Outfit, 1950.
£12-18 *COL*

A pack of Animal Grab playing cards, with instructions, c1930.
£5-10 *COL*

Blow Football, 1960.
£5-10 *COL*

A Gyroscope, in box, 3in (8cm) high.
£5-7 *BY*

A Superman game, 2½in (6cm) diam.
£12-15 *YON*

A No. 3 Meccano Outfit, with instruction manual, in original box, Italian, c1928.
£150-200   *CSK*

A No. 2 Meccano Motor Car Constructor Outfit, assembled as a sports tourer, with instructions, c1932, 12in (30cm) long.
£600-650   *CSK*

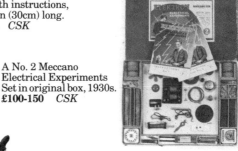

A No. 2 Meccano Electrical Experiments Set in original box, 1930s.
£100-150   *CSK*

A Mechanics Made Easy first set, in original tin box, with remains of instruction manual which is believed to be the only copy in existence, c1901.
£950-1,000   *CSK*

General

Two 00 gauge electric tramcar models finished in Blackpool Corporation livery, by H. Piltz, Wilmslow, c1930.
£650-700   *C*

A French toy theatre with scene of Mors Car racing a locomotive, 50½in (128cm) high.
£550-650   *ONS*

A musical birdcage, 1960s.
£30-35   *COB*

A model steam engine.
£30-40   *COL*

Tinplate sewing machine Black, 1930.
£25-30
COL

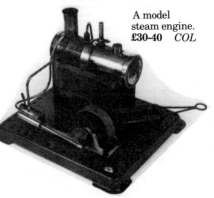

A toy dog, 1930s, 12in (31cm) high.
£10-15 *SP*

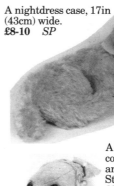

A nightdress case, 17in (43cm) wide.
£8-10 *SP*

A blond long plush covered dog with felt face and legs, ears torn, by Steiff, c1908.
£250-300 *CSK*

A Father Christmas cake decoration, 2½in (6cm) high.
£30-40 *LEW*

A snow baby cake decoration, 2in (5cm) long.
£30-40 *LEW*

A Merrythought rabbit, post-war, 13in (33cm) high.
£8-10 *SP*

A collection of papier mâché toy animals, c1880, average length 6in (15cm).
£130-200 *CSK*

A Roullet et Descamps rabbit automaton, with key wind movement, c1900, 14in (36cm).
£1,000-1,300 *S(S)*

A Steiff white plush tumbling elephant, with button in the ear, one tusk broken, c1913, 13½in (34cm).
£550-650 *S*

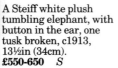

A South American marionette, the clothes made from scraps, 20thC.
£45-55 *SWN*

Treen

Treen is the generic term for small wooden artefacts made from wood. Native woods were used primarily, but from the 18thC onwards imported exotic timbers, e.g. ebony, lignum vitae, mahogany and teak were used.

See Miller's Collectables Price Guide Volume I, pages 465-480, for an extensive selection.

A Welsh love token spoon, 8in (20cm) long.
£85-95 *SBA*

Two wooden children's seaside spades, c1950, 18in (46cm) long.
£10-14 each *UC*

A lignum vitae string holder.
£140-160 *SWN*

There is a cutting blade inset in the top.

A Welsh love token spoon, 8in (20cm) long.
£125-150 *SBA*

A carved wooden scoop, 7in (18cm) long.
£25-30 *SBA*

A sycamore love token spoon, carved E.A with a heart, 18thC.
£40-50 *SWN*

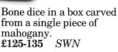

A bird scarer, c1860.
£25-30 *HUN*

Bone dice in a box carved from a single piece of mahogany.
£125-135 *SWN*

Probably the work of a sailor.

A fruitwood mortar, carved ES & TM and dated 1719, probably to commemorate a marriage, 4in (10cm) high.
£250-350 *SWN*

A 19thC mouse trap.
£115-125 *SWN*

Three English hand
carved wooden pigeon
decoys, retaining
original paint.
£150-250 each *RYA*

A painted wooden
mallard decoy, minor
wear, 11½in (29cm).
£8-12 *WAL*

Four wooden eggs:
l. Mauchline needle
container.
l.c. Screw top, containing
thimble, needle and
thread.
r.c. Painted.
r. Carved, with nut
inside.
£25-35 each *CA*

A wooden box, decorated
with a print, to hold
cotton in various sizes,
made for Coates and
Clarkes, c1900.
£40-60 *PC*

Glove stretchers, 8½in
(21cm) long.
£10-12 *CA*

A miniature cabin trunk,
8in (20cm) wide.
£500-550 *C(S)*

A set of 8 Victorian decoy
ducks, 12in (31cm) long.
£350-375 *HUN*

Mauchline Ware Tartan Ware

Mauchline Ware (pronounced Mochlin)
was produced in Mauchline, Ayr, these
very collectable examples all feature
Scottish geographical or literary scenes.
The prices vary depending on size,
condition, quality of printing and subject
matter.
£30-80 each *C(S)*

During the 1840s the Smith family, who
pioneered the photographic process used
on Mauchline Ware, designed a machine
that was capable of producing a tartan
pattern using a series of coloured pens. It
was very time consuming to produce, but
extremely popular with customers.
£30-80 each *C(S)*

Walking Sticks

See Miller's Collectables Price Guide
Volume I, pages 481-483 and Volume II,
pages 478-479 for further extensive
selections of walking sticks.

An 18thC scrimshaw
walking cane, repaired,
36in (92cm) long.
£300-350 *LAY*

A carved ivory walking
stick or parasol handle in
the form of a dog's head.
£130-150 *DEN*

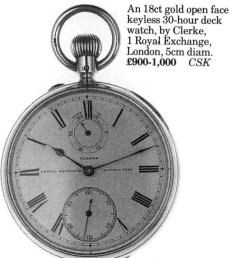

An 18ct gold open face
keyless 30-hour deck
watch, by Clerke,
1 Royal Exchange,
London, 5cm diam.
£900-1,000 *CSK*

A gold keyless open face
pocket watch, by Patek
Philippe & Co., Geneve,
c1880, 4.6cm diam.
£800-900 *CSK*

Watches
Pocket Watches

A silver cased lever
pocket watch by Ilbery,
London, for the Chinese
market, 6cm diam.
£300-400 *CSK*

A silver open face
cylinder and date pocket
watch, by Eardley
Norton, No. 8556,
hallmarked London
1796, 6.2cm diam.
£450-550 *CSK*

A pink gold keyless
hunter pocket watch, by
Uhrenfabrik Union,
Glasshutte bei Dresden,
5.3cm diam.
£1,500-2,000 *CSK*

An 18ct gold quarter
repeating chronograph
hunter pocket watch, by
Longines, 5.3cm diam.
£1,700-2,000 *CSK*

Wristwatches

A Cyma gentleman's stainless steel watch, with original receipt.
£25-30   *COB*

A stainless steel automatic alarm wristwatch by Jaeger-le Coultre, Memovox model, 3.6cm diam.
£320-400   *CSK*

A Mickey Mouse novelty watch, by Ingersoll, 3.4cm long.
£300-400   *CSK*

> **Cross Reference**
> Disney

A lady's gold and multi-coloured enamel Art Nouveau wristwatch, signed Luor Factory C.F. Co., Geneva, 3.7cm long.
£450-500   *CSK*

A gold/steel Cartier Santos automatic and date wristwatch, 3cm diam.
£850-950   *CSK*

An early Omega waterproof wristwatch, 3.5cm long.
£850-1,000   *CSK*

An 18ct pink gold jump hour wristwatch by Patek Philippe, Geneve, made for the 150th anniversary of the Company, 3.8cm long.
£26,000-30,000   *CSK*

This watch is accompanied by certificate of origin, dated 25th January 1990, and Attestation stating that only 450 of these watches were made in pink gold and 50 in platinum and giving the movement number of the watch, presentation medal commemorating the 150th anniversary of the Company, booklet of instructions, list of distributors, a register of Patek Philippe owners, red leather wallet and presentation packaging.

A gold wristwatch by Zenith for Favre-Leuba & Co., 4cm long.
£800-900   *CSK*

A gentleman's gold wristwatch by Gubelin, Geneve.
£300-500   *CSK*

The back of the watch is engraved W.E. Hutton, III.

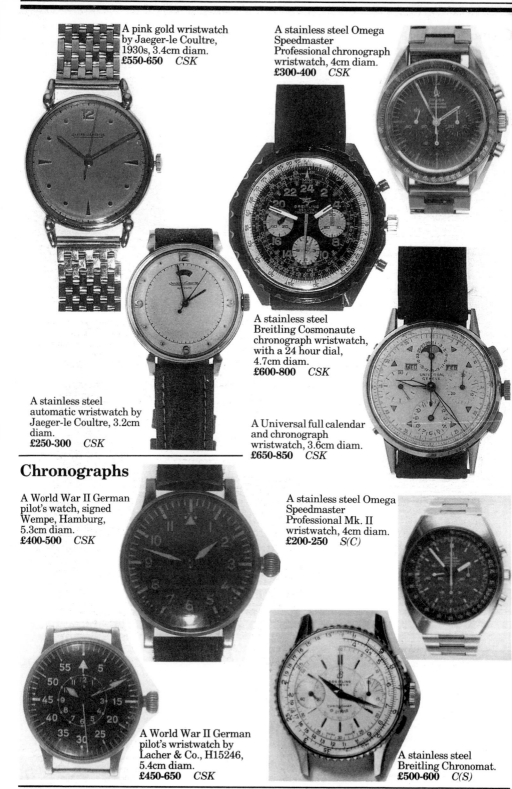

A pink gold wristwatch by Jaeger-le Coultre, 1930s, 3.4cm diam.
£550-650 *CSK*

A stainless steel Omega Speedmaster Professional chronograph wristwatch, 4cm diam.
£300-400 *CSK*

A stainless steel Breitling Cosmonaute chronograph wristwatch, with a 24 hour dial, 4.7cm diam.
£600-800 *CSK*

A stainless steel automatic wristwatch by Jaeger-le Coultre, 3.2cm diam.
£250-300 *CSK*

A Universal full calendar and chronograph wristwatch, 3.6cm diam.
£650-850 *CSK*

Chronographs

A World War II German pilot's watch, signed Wempe, Hamburg, 5.3cm diam.
£400-500 *CSK*

A stainless steel Omega Speedmaster Professional Mk. II wristwatch, 4cm diam.
£200-250 *S(C)*

A World War II German pilot's wristwatch by Lacher & Co., H15246, 5.4cm diam.
£450-650 *CSK*

A stainless steel Breitling Chronomat.
£500-600 *C(S)*

General

An early 9ct gold wristwatch with Prima movement, 3.5cm long.
£1,000-1,500 *CSK*

A stainless steel Oyster Perpetual Datejust chronometer wristwatch, No. D39708 with Rolex steel bracelet, 3.3cm diam.
£350-400 *CSK*

A stainless steel Oyster Perpetual chronometer bubble back wristwatch, the signed movement numbered 52084, 3.1cm diam.
£600-700 *CSK*

A stainless steel Oyster Perpetual Date chronometer wristwatch, 3.5cm diam.
£500-550 *CSK*

A stainless steel Oyster Perpetual Date chronometer wristwatch, 3.4cm diam.
£450-500 *CSK*

A stainless steel Oyster Perpetual Datejust chronometer wristwatch, with Rolex steel bracelet, 3.5cm diam.
£400-450 *CSK*

A stainless steel Oyster Quartz Datejust wristwatch, with Rolex flexible steel bracelet, green Rolex tag numbered 5576443 and presentation case, 3.5cm diam.
£500-600 *CSK*

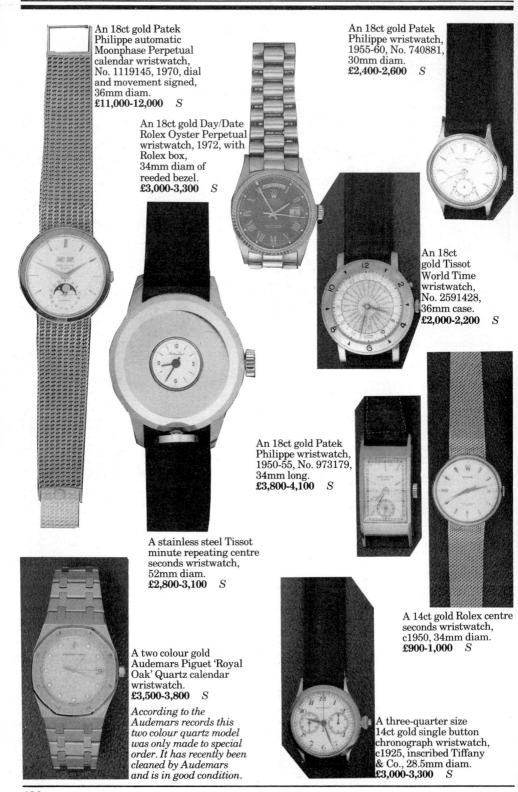

An 18ct gold Patek Philippe automatic Moonphase Perpetual calendar wristwatch, No. 1119145, 1970, dial and movement signed, 36mm diam.
£11,000-12,000 *S*

An 18ct gold Day/Date Rolex Oyster Perpetual wristwatch, 1972, with Rolex box, 34mm diam of reeded bezel.
£3,000-3,300 *S*

An 18ct gold Patek Philippe wristwatch, 1955-60, No. 740881, 30mm diam.
£2,400-2,600 *S*

An 18ct gold Tissot World Time wristwatch, No. 2591428, 36mm case.
£2,000-2,200 *S*

An 18ct gold Patek Philippe wristwatch, 1950-55, No. 973179, 34mm long.
£3,800-4,100 *S*

A stainless steel Tissot minute repeating centre seconds wristwatch, 52mm diam.
£2,800-3,100 *S*

A 14ct gold Rolex centre seconds wristwatch, c1950, 34mm diam.
£900-1,000 *S*

A two colour gold Audemars Piguet 'Royal Oak' Quartz calendar wristwatch.
£3,500-3,800 *S*

According to the Audemars records this two colour quartz model was only made to special order. It has recently been cleaned by Audemars and is in good condition.

A three-quarter size 14ct gold single button chronograph wristwatch, c1925, inscribed Tiffany & Co., 28.5mm diam.
£3,000-3,300 *S*

An 18ct pink gold Rolex Oyster chronograph wristwatch, c1947, 39mm diam.
£7,500-10,000 *Bon*

An 18ct gold Omega wristwatch, with import marks for London 1928, 37 by 27mm.
£650-850 *Bon*

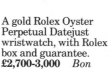

A 9ct gold Rolex Prince wristwatch, with import marks for 1937, 39 by 21mm.
£3,000-3,300 *Bon*

A gold Rolex Oyster Perpetual Datejust wristwatch, with Rolex box and guarantee.
£2,700-3,000 *Bon*

An 18ct gold Rolex GMT-Master Oyster Perpetual wristwatch, 1976, in original leather covered box in card case with guarantee, 39mm diam of bezel.
£3,800-4,000 *S*

A 9ct gold Rolex curved case wristwatch, 1929, with Dublin import mark, 35mm long.
£600-750 *S*

An 18ct pink gold Cartier centre seconds alarm watch, c1945, signed, 35mm diam.
£1,000-1,200 *S*

An 18ct gold Rolex Day/Date Oyster Perpetual wristwatch, 34mm diam of bezel.
£3,500-3,800 *S*

A stainless steel Audemars Piguet automatic 'Royal Oak' wristwatch, No. B 1619.
£900-1,000 *S*

A stainless steel Rolex gilt centre seconds precision wristwatch, 25mm square.
£750-850 *S*

A stainless steel Tissot centre seconds World Time Navigator wristwatch, 1950, 36mm diam.
£850-1,000 *S*

Wales

The following pages consist of collectables with the common theme of Wales.

It is always very interesting to see the diversity of the items as well as the quality and interest of individual pieces.

A Llanelli pottery mug, with inscription and date.
£80-100 *RP*

A Swansea Cambrian pottery dish, painted by Thomas Pardoe, c1810.
£400-450 *RP*

A Ewenny pottery cat, c1900, 15in (38cm) high.
£250-300 *RP*

A Swansea Glamorgan pottery mug, transfer decorated in 2 colours.
£80-100 *RP*

A Swansea pottery jug, c1870.
£30-40 *RP*

A Swansea pottery ribbon plate, c1820.
£80-120 *RP*

A Swansea pottery chemist's mixing bowl, c1840.
£200-300 *RP*

A Llanelli pottery cockerel plate, c1910.
£150-200 *RP*

A Llanelli pottery cow creamer, c1850.
£300-400 *RP*

A Swansea Glamorgan pottery jug, c1830.
£80-100 *RP*

A Swansea pottery ship plate, marked Dillwyn, c1830.
£100-130 *RP*

A Swansea Glamorgan pottery sheet pattern jug, c1825.
£50-70 *RP*

A Swansea Glamorgan pottery jug, with inscription, dated 1832.
£100-140 *RP*

A Ewenny pottery pig, c1900, 7in (18cm) long.
£80-100 *RP*

A Swansea Cambrian pottery plate.
£120-140 *RP*

A Swansea copper lustre jug, c1820.
£180-200 *RP*

A Swansea Glamorgan pottery hand decorated jug, c1830.
£60-80 *RP*

MAKE THE MOST OF MILLERS

Condition is absolutely vital when assessing the value of any item. Damaged pieces appreciate much less than perfect examples. However, a rare, desirable piece may command a high price even when damaged.

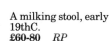

A milking stool, early 19thC.
£60-80 *RP*

A cast iron doorstop by Jones, Carmarthen.
£40-60 *RP*

Two Buckley pottery dishes, c1880.
£180-200 each *RP*

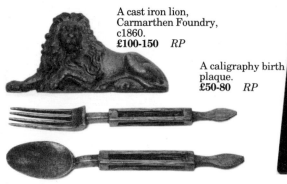

A cast iron lion, Carmarthen Foundry, c1860.
£100-150   *RP*

A caligraphy birth plaque.
£50-80   *RP*

A pair of treen love tokens, c1860.
£200-250   *RP*

A very rare mutton bone love token, c1850.
£150-200   *RP*

A butter print with cow and farm name.
£60-80   *RP*

A rare sycamore butter scoop and marker, mid-19thC.
£120-140   *RP*

A collection of miners' tobacco boxes, c1900.
£25-35 each   *RP*

Whistles

A brass bosun's whistle, 4in (10cm) long.
£25-30   *CA*

A selection of whistles.
£4-6 each   *AL*

l. An ARP whistle.
£40-50
c. An old patent Metropolitan Police whistle, numbered 315, with key and chain.
£20-25
r. A current Metropolitan Police whistle and chain.
£5-8   *MIT*

Writing Accessories

Travelling inkwells,
c1840, 1in (2.5cm) high.
£50-60   *EHA*

A Typhoo Tea blotter, 8in
(20cm) wide.
£8-10   *CA*

A cast iron pencil
sharpener, 19thC, 4½in
(11.5cm) high.
£220-250   *BS*

A late Victorian ebonised
and brass mounted quill
pen sharpening knife, by
Wade Wingfield &
Rowbotham of Sheffield,
4in (10cm) long.
£30-40   *DDM*

A brass horseshoe pen
holder, c1873.
£65-75   *BS*

A letterhead press,
Jordans and Son, c1920,
9in (22.5cm) high.
£100-120   *BS*

A cast iron and glass
snail inkwell/pen stand,
c1900, 5½in (13.5cm)
wide.
£110-130   *BS*

A brass paper weight,
19thC, 5in (12.5cm) long.
£65-75   *BS*

A brass letter clip, c1872,
3½in (8.5cm) long.
£85-95   *BS*

Typewriter ribbon tins,
1950s, 2in (5cm) square.
£4-5 each   *COL*

485

Pens & Pencils

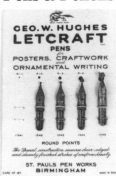

Letcraft nibs, c1940.
£3-5 *COL*

A German propelling
pencil, c1950.
£3-6 *COL*

A red Parker Lucky
Curve Duofold Senior,
twin cap bands, fitted
with Arrow nib, c1929.
£100-120 *Bon*

A diamond, sapphire and
gem set extending pencil.
£300-350 *CSK*

A retractable base metal
pencil, with glass top,
c1920.
£5-8 *COL*

A black/pearl Waterman
Patrician, with nickel
trim and large Patrician
nib, with Waterman
service box, lacks clip,
c1929.
£70-90 *Bon*

A black chased hard
rubber Weidlich eye
dropper pen, with
2 chased gold plated
bands, and fitted with
Weidlich No. 2 nib,
probably c1915.
£60-70 *Bon*

An early Parker pencil,
c1920.
£3-6 *COL*

A black Parker Lucky
Curve Duofold Special,
twin cap bands, fitted
with Duofold C nib,
c1928.
£50-70 *Bon*

A Waterman Patrician desk pen, fitted with
Waterman yellow nib, c1928.
£60-80 *Bon*

FURTHER READING
Collecting Writing Instruments, Dietmar Geyer,
Millbank Books, Schiffer Publishing Ltd.
*Fountain Pens & Pencils: The Golden Age of
Writing Instruments,* George Fischler and
Stuart Schneider, Millbank Books, Schiffer
Publishing Ltd.

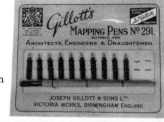

A mapping pen
and nibs,
on card, 1940.
£6-10 *COL*

A red Parker Lucky Curve Senior Duofold, twin cap bands, fitted with Duofold Canada F nib, c1928.
£300-350 *Bon*

A turquoise Waterman Patrician pen, fitted with Patrician nib, lacks clip, c1929.
£250-300 *Bon*

An Italian snorkel fill fountain pen, with gold nib, c1960.
£6-10 *COL*

A jade Parker Lucky Curve Lady Duofold, 3 cap bands, ribbon ring, fitted with Canadian Duofold A nib, c1928.
£35-45 *Bon*

A chased black rubber Sheaffer pen, lever filled with broad gold plated cap band, fitted with Sheaffer No. 3 nib, c1915.
£70-90 *Bon*

A limited edition Parker 105 Royal Wedding pen, issued to commemorate the wedding of H.R.H. the Prince of Wales to The Lady Diana Spencer, the cap with Prince of Wales feathers, the barrel with date 29th July 1981, the end individually numbered 0111, complete with presentation box, certificate of authenticity, instructions and outer box.
£250-350 *Bon*

Edition limited to 1,000 pens.

DIRECTORY OF SPECIALISTS

This directory is in no way complete. If you wish to be included in next year's directory or if you have a change of address or telephone number, please could you inform us by December 31st 1991. Entries will be repeated in subsequent editions unless we are requested otherwise. Finally we would advise readers to make contact by telephone before a visit, therefore avoiding a wasted journey, which nowadays is both time consuming and expensive.

DEALERS SPECIALISING IN COLLECTABLES

AERONAUTICA

London
Alfie's Antique Market,
13-25 Church Street, London,
NW8
Tel: 071-723 6066

Hampshire
Cobwebs,
78 Northam Road, Southampton
Tel: (0703) 227458

AUTOMOBILIA

London
Grays Antique Market,
AAA Stand 121, 58 Davies
Street, London, W1
Tel: 071-629 7034

Sarah Baddiel,
S.12 Grays Mews, London, W1
Tel: 071-408 1239/081-452 7243

Brian R. Verrall & Co,
20 Tooting Bec Road, London,
SW17
Tel: 081-672 1144

Kent
Falstaff Antiques Motor
Museum,
63-67 High Street, Rolvenden,
Nr Cranbrook
Tel: (0580) 241234

Hampshire
Cobwebs,
78 Northam Road, Southampton
Tel: (0703) 227458

Lincolnshire
The Complete Automobilist
Dept 1, The Old Rectory,
Greatford, Nr Stamford
Tel: (077 836) 312

West Midlands
Walton & Hipkiss,
194A Worcester Road, Hagley,
Stourbridge
Tel: (0562) 885555/883426

Cotswold Motor Museum,
The Old Mill, Bourton on the
Water, Gloucestershire
Tel: (0451) 21255

South Yorkshire
Bardwell Antiques,
919 Abbeydale Road, Sheffield
Tel: (0742) 584669

ART DECO

Scotland
Millars,
9-11 Castle Street,
Kirkcudbright
Tel: (0557) 30236

BAROMETERS

London
Patrick Capon,
350 Upper Street, Islington, N1
Tel: 071-354 0487/081-467 5722

Barometer Fair, at
Cartographia Ltd,
Pied Bull Yard, Bury Place,
Bloomsbury, WC1
Tel: 071-404 4521/4050

Avon
Barometer Shop,
3 Lower Park Row, Bristol
Tel: (0272) 272565

Cheshire
Derek Rayment Antiques,
Orchard House, Barton Road,
Barton, Nr Malpas
Tel: (0829) 270429

Essex
It's About Time,
863 London Road,
Westcliff-on-Sea
Tel: (0702) 72574

Hereford & Worcs
Barometer Shop,
New Street, Leominster
Tel: (0568) 3652

Somerset
Bernard G. House
(Mitre Antiques),
Market Place, Wells
Tel: (0749) 72607

BAXTER PRINTS

Cambridgeshire
Cambridge Fine Art Ltd,
Priest House, 33 Church Street,
Little Shelford
Tel: (0223) 842866/843537

Leicestershire
Charnwood Antiques,
Coalville, Leicester
Tel: (0530) 38530

BOTTLES

London
Rob Gee,
Flea Market, Camden Passage,
London, N1
Tel: 071-226 6627

Georgian Village – 1st Floor,
Islington Green, London, N1
Tel: 071-226 1571/5393

Isle of Wight
Kollectarama,
Old Railway Station,
Horringford, Arreton
Tel: (0983) 865306

Staffordshire
Gordon The 'Ole Bottleman,
25 Stapenhill Road, Burton-on-
Trent
Tel: (0283) 67213

BOXES

London
Barham Antiques,
83 Portobello Road, London,
W11
Tel: 071-727 3845

Avon
Gloria Gibson,
2 Beaufort West, London Road,
Bath BA1 6QB
Tel: (0225) 446646

Berkshire
Boxes From Derek McIntosh,
10 Wickham Road, Stockcross,
Newbury
Tel: (0488) 38295

Mostly Boxes,
92 & 52B High Street, Eton,
Windsor
Tel: (0753) 858470

Yorkshire
Danby Antiques,
65 Heworth Road, York
Tel: (0904) 415280

BUCKLES

London
Moderne,
Stand 5, Georgian Village,
Camden Passage, N1

Monica Jaertelius, The Mall,
Camden Passage, N1
Tel: 081-546 2807

Avon
Jessie's Button Box,
Great Western Antique Centre,
Bartlett Street, Bath
Tel: (0272) 299065

BUTTONS

London
The Button Queen,
19 Marylebone Lane, W1
Tel: 071-935 1505

Avon
Jessie's Button Box,
Great Western Antique Centre,
Bartlett Street, Bath
Tel: (0272) 299065

Dorset
The Old Button Shop,
Lytchett Minster
Tel: (0202) 622169

BUTTON HOOKS

London
David Hogg,
S.141 Grays Antique Market,
58 Davies Street, W1
Tel: 071-493 0208

Noelle Antiques,
S.26 Chelsea Antiques Market,
253 Kings Road, SW3
Tel: 071-352 5581

Kent
The Variety Box,
16 Chapel Place, Tunbridge
Wells
Tel: (0892) 31868/21589

North Wales
Paul Gibbs,
25 Castle Street, Conwy
Tel: (0492) 593429

CAMERAS

London
Jessops,
65 Great Russell Street, WC1
Tel: 071-831 3640

Vintage Cameras Ltd,
254 & 256 Kirkdale, Sydenham,
SE26
Tel: 081-778 5416/5841

London & Essex

Cliff Latford Photography,
G006, Aflie's Antique Market,
13-25 Church Street, London,
NW8
and Colchester, Essex
Tel: 071-724 5650/
(0206) 564474

Hertfordshire

P. Coombs,
87 Gills Hill Lane, Radlett
Tel: (0923) 856949

Warwickshire

Fred Topping,
Warwick Antique Centre,
20 High Street, Warwick
Tel: (0926) 499078

West Yorkshire

The Camera House,
Oakworth Hall, Colne Road,
Oakworth
Tel: (0535) 42333

CARD CASES
London

Eureka Antiques,
105 Portobello Road, W11
(Saturdays)

Grays Antique Market,
58 Davies Street, W1
Tel: 071-629 7034

Avon

Carr Linford,
10-11 Walcot Buildings, London
Road, Bath
Tel: (0225) 317516

Cheshire

Eureka Antiques,
18 Northenden Road, Sale
Tel: (061 962) 5629

Shropshire

F. C. Manser & Son Ltd,
53 Wyle Cop, Shrewsbury
Tel: (0743) 51120

CERAMICS
ART DECO
London

A.J. Partners (Shelley),
S.133/114, Alfies Antique
Market, 13-25 Church Street,
NW8
Tel: 071-258 3602

Beverley,
30 Church Street, Marylebone,
NW8
Tel: 071-262 1576

Bloomsbury Antiques,
58-60 Kensington Church
Street, W8
Tel: 071-376 2810

Dimech,
248 Camden High Street,
London, NW1
Tel: 071-485 8072

Jag
248 Camden High Street,
London, NW1
Tel: 071-485 8072

Monty & Anita,
Stand V14-V15 Antiquarius,
135-141 Kings Road, SW3
Tel: 071-351 5382

Past & Present,
York Arcade, Unit 5, Camden
Passage, N1
Tel: 071-833 2640

Patrician Antiques,
1st Floor Georgian Village,
Camden Passage, N1
Tel: 071-359 4560/071-435 3159

Rotation Antiques,
Pierrepont Row Fleamarket,
Camden Passage, London, N1
Tel: 071-226 8211

Sailor Ceramics,
Camden Lock Antique Centre,
248 Camden High Street,
London, NW1
Tel: 081-981 1180

Berkshire

Lupin Antiques,
134 Peascod Street, Windsor
Tel: (0753) 856244

Essex

A. Waine,
Tweedale, Rye Mill Lane,
Feering, Colchester

Hampshire

The Art Deco China Centre,
62 Murray Road, Horndean
Tel: (0705) 597440

Kent

Manor Antiques (Radford Ware)
2A High Street, Westerham
Tel: (0959) 64810

Lancashire

A.S. Antiques,
26 Broad Street, Pendleton,
Salford
Tel: 061-737 5938

Norfolk

Neville Pundole,
1 White House Lane,
Attleborough
Tel: (0953) 454106

Shropshire

Antiques on the Square,
2 Sandford Court, Church
Stretton
Tel: (0694) 724111

Expressions,
17 Princess Street, Shrewsbury
Tel: (0743) 51731

Somerset

Decoration,
Taunton Antique Centre, Silver
Street, Taunton
Tel: (0460) 40958

Surrey

Church Street Antiques,
15 Church Street, Godalming
Tel: (0483) 860894

East Sussex

Le Jazz Hot,
14 Prince Albert Street,
Brighton
Tel: (0273) 206091

Tyne & Wear

Ian Sharp Antiques (Maling
Ware),
23 Front Street, Tynemouth
Tel: 091-296 0656

Wiltshire

Clem Harwood,
The Old Bakery, Keevil, Nr
Trowbridge
Tel: (0380) 870463

Wales

Paul Gibbs Antiques,
25 Castle Street, Conwy
Tel: (0492) 593429

Warwickshire

Rich Designs,
Sheep Street Antique Centre,
Stratford-upon-Avon
Tel: (0789) 772111

Art Deco Ceramics,
The Ocsbury, 10 Mill Street,
Warwick
Tel: (0926) 498068

Jazz,
Civic Hall, Rother Street,
Stratford-on-Avon
Tel: (0789) 298362

East Yorkshire

Tim Barnett,
Carlton Gallery, 60A Middle
Street, Driffield
Tel: (0482) 443954

West Yorkshire

Muir Hewitt,
Halifax Antiques Centre,
Queens Road/Gibbet Street,
Halifax
Tel: (0442) 366657/366657

DOULTON
London

Britannia,
Stand 101, Grays Antique
Market, 58 Davies Street, W1
Tel: 071-629 6772

The Collector,
Alfie's Antique Market,
13-25 Church Street, NW8
Tel: 081-883 0024/071-706 4586

Doug Pinchin,
Dixons Antique Centre,
471 Upper Richmond Road
West, East Sheen, SW14
Tel: 081-878 6788/081-948 1029

Leicester

Janice Williamson,
9 Coverdale Road, Meadows
Wiston, Leicester
Tel: (0533) 812926

COMMEMORATIVE
London

Britannia,
Stand 101, Grays Antique
Market, 58 Davies Street, W1
Tel: 071-629 6772

British Commemoratives,
1st Floor, Georgian Village,
Camden Passage, N1
Tel: 071-359 4560

Surrey

Church Street Antiques,
15 Church Street, Godalming
Tel: (0483) 860894

East Sussex

Leonard Russell,
21 Kings Avenue, Mount
Pleasant, Newhaven
Tel: (0273) 515153

Warwickshire

Midlands Goss &
Commemoratives,
Warwick Antique Centre,
22 High Street, Warwick
Tel: (0926) 495704

GOSS & CRESTED
CHINA
London

British Commemoratives,
1st Floor, Georgian Village,
Camden Passage, N1
Tel: 071-359 4560

Hampshire

Goss & Crested China Ltd,
62 Murray Road, Horndean
Tel: (0705) 597440

Kent

The Variety Box,
16 Chapel Place, Tunbridge
Wells
Tel: (0892) 31868/21589

Warwickshire

Midlands Goss &
Commemoratives,
Warwick Antique Centre,
22 High Street, Warwick
Tel: (0926) 495704

East Yorkshire

The Crested China Company,
Station House, Driffield
Tel: (0377) 47042

STAFFORDSHIRE
London

Gerald Clark Antiques,
1 High Street, Mill Hill Village,
NW7
Tel: 081-906 0342

Jacqueline Oosthuizen,
1st Floor, Georgian Village,
Camden Passage, N1
Tel: 071-226 5393/071-352 5581
and
Chelsea Antique Market,
Unit 30, 253 Kings Road, SW3
Tel: 071-352 6071/5581

Jonathan Horne,
66B & C Kensington Church
Street, W8
Tel: 071-221 5658

Kent
Beaubush House Antiques,
95 High Street, Sandgate,
Folkestone
Tel: (0303) 49099

Lancashire
Roy W. Bunn Antiques,
34-36 Church Street,
Barnuldswick, Colne
Tel: (0282) 813703

Suffolk
Crafers Antiques,
The Hill, Wickham Market
Tel: (0728) 747347

West Sussex
Ray & Diane Ginns,
PO Box 129,
East Grinstead
Tel: (0342) 326041

Wiltshire
Bratton Antiques,
Market Place, Westbury
Tel: (0373) 823021

Wiltshire
Bratton Antiques,
Market Place, Westbury
Tel: (0373) 823021

TORQUAY POTTERY
London
Jacqueline Oosthuizen,
1st Floor, Georgian Village,
Camden Passage, N1
Tel: 071-226 5393/071-359 4560
and
Chelsea Antique Market,
Unit 30, 253 Kings Road, SW3
Tel: 071-352 6071/5581

POT LIDS
London
Rob Gee,
Flea Market, Camden Passage,
N1
Tel: 071-226 6627

East Sussex
Ron Beech,
Brambledean Road, Portslade,
Brighton
Tel: (0273) 423355

Warwickshire
Burman Antiques,
5A Chapel Street, Stratford-on-
Avon
Tel: (0789) 293917

POTTERY
London
Robert Young Antiques,
68 Battersea Bridge Road, SW11
Tel: 071-228 7847

Valerie Howard,
131E Kensington Church
Street, London, W8
Tel: 071-792 9702

Avon
Robert Pugh,
2 Beaufort Mews, St Saviours
Road, Larkhall, Bath
Tel: (0225) 314713

Hampshire
Millers of Chelsea Ltd,
Netherbrook House,
Christchurch Road, Ringwood
Tel: (0425) 472062

Kent
Angela Page Antiques,
Tunbridge Wells
Tel: (0892) 22217

Wales
Islwyn Watkins,
1 High Street/29 Market Street,
Knighton, Powys
Tel: (0547) 520145/528940

Howards Antiques,
10 Alexandra Road,
Aberystwyth, Dyfed
Tel: (0970) 624973

Warwickshire
Janice Paull,
125 Warwick Road, Kenilworth
Tel: (0926) 55253

Yorkshire
In Retrospect,
2 Pavement, Pocklinton, York
Tel: (0759) 304894

VICTORIAN CERAMICS
London
Sue Norman,
Stand L4 Antiquarius,
135 Kings Road, London, SW3
Tel: 071-352 7217

Avon
Scott's,
Stand 24, Great Western
Antique Centre, Bartlett Street,
Bath
Tel: (0225) 310388

Buckinghamshire
Gillian A. Neale,
The Old Post Office, Wendover
Tel: (0296) 625335

Gloucestershire
Acorn Antiques,
Sheep Street, Stow-on-the-Wold
Tel: (0451) 31519

Nottinghamshire
Breck Antiques,
726 Mansfield Road,
Nottingham
Tel: (0602) 605263

Tyne & Wear
Ian Sharp Antiques (Sunderland
Lustre),
23 Front Street, Tynemouth
Tel: 091-296 0656

Warwickshire
Fan Attic,
Stratford Antique Centre, Ely
Street, Stratford-on-Avon
Tel: (0789) 297496

Bow Cottage Antiques,
Stratford Antique Arcade,
Sheep Street, Stratford-on-Avon
Tel: (0789) 297249

COLLECTABLES
Kent
Collectables,
335 High Street, Rochester
Tel: (0634) 828767

East Sussex
Rin Tin Tin,
34 North Road, Brighton
Tel: (0273) 672424/733689

West Sussex
Bygones, Collectors Shop,
123 South Street, Lancing
Tel: (0903) 750051/763470

CORKSCREWS
London
David,
141 Grays Antique Market,
Davies Street, W1
Tel: 071-493 0208

Patricia Harbottle,
Geoffrey Vann Arcade,
107 Portobello Road, W11
(Saturdays)
Tel: 071-731 1972

Bedfordshire
Christopher Sykes Antiques,
The Old Parsonage, Woburn
Tel: (0525) 290259

Cumbria
Bacchus Antiques,
Longlands at Cartmel
Tel: (044 854) 475

East Sussex
Chateaubriand Antiques
Centre,
High Street, Burwash
Tel: (0435) 882535

DOLLS
London
Antique Dolls,
Stand L14 Grays Mews,
1-7 Davies Mews, W1
Tel: 071-499 6600

Brenda Gerwat-Clark,
Alfie's Antique Market, 13-25
Church Street, London, NW8
Tel: 071-706 4699

Chelsea Lion Dolls,
Chenil Galleries, 181-183 Kings
Road, London, SW3
Tel: 071-351 9338

Childhood Memories,
Teapot Arcade, Portobello,
London, W11

The Doll Cupboard,
Portwine Galleries, Unit No. 17,
175 Portobello Road, London,
W11
Tel: 071-727 4681/(0378) 76848

Dollyland,
864 Green Lanes, Winchmore
Hill, London, N21
Tel: 081-360 1053

Pat Walker,
Georgian Village, Camden
Passage, N1
Tel: 071-359 4560/071-435 3159

Yesterday Child,
24 The Mall, Camden Passage,
N1
Tel: 071-354 1601/
(0908) 583403

Avon
Bath Dolls' Hospital and Teddy
Bear Clinic,
2 Grosvenor Place, London
Road, Bath
Tel: (0225) 319668

The China Doll,
31 Walcot Street, Bath
Tel: (0225) 465849

Cheshire
Dollectable,
53 Lower Bridge Street, Chester
Tel: (0244) 44888/679195

Gloucestershire
Lillian Middleton's Antique
Dolls Shop,
Days Stable, Sheep Street,
Stow-on-the-Wold
Tel: (0451) 31542

Parkhouse Antiques,
Park Street, Stow-on-the-Wold
Tel: (0451) 30159

Hampshire
Toys Through Time,
Fareham
Tel: (0329) 288678

Past & Present Crafts,
19 Ditton Close, Stubbington
Tel: (0329) 661377

Hertfordshire

Carrousel,
59 High Street, Hemel
Hempstead
Tel: (0442) 219772/42518

Kent

Amelia Dolls,
Pantiles Spa Antiques, The
Pantiles, Tunbridge Wells
Tel: (0892) 541377/(0342)
713223

Dolly Daydreams,
Unit B3, Copers Cope Road,
Beckenham
Tel: 081-663 3506

Hadlow Antiques,
No. 1 The Pantiles, Tunbridge
Wells
Tel: (0892) 29858

The Magpie's Nest,
14 Palace Street, Canterbury
Tel: (0227) 764883

Surrey

Dorking Dolls House Gallery,
23 West Street, Dorking
Tel: (0306) 885785

Victoriana Dolls,
Reigate
Tel: (0737) 249525

East Sussex

Dolls Hospital,
17 George Street, Hastings
Tel: (0424) 444117/422758

Sue Pearson,
13½ Prince Albert Street,
Brighton
Tel: (0273) 29247

West Sussex

Recollect Studios,
Dept M, The Old School, London
Road, Sayers Common
Tel: (0273) 833314

DOLLS HOUSE FURNITURE

Avon

The China Doll,
31 Walcot Street, Bath
Tel: (0225) 465849

Essex

Blackwells of Hawkwell,
733 London Road,
Westcliff-on-Sea
Tel: (0702) 72248

Kent

The Magpie's Nest,
14 Palace Street, Canterbury
Tel: (0227) 764883

TEDDY BEARS
London

Heather's Teddys,
World Famous Arcade,
177 Portobello Road, London,
W11
Tel: 081-204 0106

Pam Hebbs,
5 The Annexe, Camden
Passage, Islington, N1

Past and Present Toys,
862 Green Lanes, Winchmore
Hill, London N21
Tel: 081-364 1370

Berkshire

Asquiths of Windsor,
10 George V Place, Thames
Avenue, Windsor
Tel: (0753) 854954/831200

Gloucestershire

Park House Antiques,
Park Street, Stow-on-the-Wold
Tel: (0451) 30159

Oxfordshire

Teddy Bears,
99 High Street, Witney
Tel: (0993) 702616

East Sussex

Sue Pearson,
13½ Prince Albert Street,
Brighton
Tel: (0273) 29247

West Midlands

Mr Morgan,
F11 Swincross Road, Old
Swinford, Stourbridge
Tel: (0384) 397033

West Yorkshire

Memory Lane,
69 Wakefield Road, Sowerby
Bridge
Tel: (0422) 833223

COCKTAIL/ DRINKING
London

Beverley,
30 Church Street, Marylebone,
NW8
Tel: 071-262 1576

J.A.G. Applied Arts,
248 Camden High Street, NW1
Tel: 071-485 8072

EPHEMERA
CIGARETTE CARDS
London

Murray Cards (International)
Ltd,
51 Watford Way, Hendon
Central, NW4
Tel: 081-202 5688

Avon

Winstone Stamp Company,
S.82 Great Western Antiques
Centre, Bartlett Street, Bath
Tel: (0225) 310388

Middlesex

Albert's Cigarette Card
Specialists,
113 London Road, Twickenham
Tel: 081-891 3067

Somerset

The London Cigarette Card Co
Ltd,
Sutton Road, Somerton
Tel: (0458) 73452

Suffolk

W. L. Hoad,
9 St Peter's Road, Kirkley,
Lowestoft
Tel: (0502) 587758

COMICS
London

Forbidden Planet,
71 New Oxford Street, W1
Tel: 071-379 6042

Gosh Comics,
39 Great Russell Street, WC1
Tel: 071-636 1011

Somerset

Yesterday's Paper,
40 South View, Holcombe
Rogus, Wellington
Tel: (0823) 672774

GREETINGS CARDS
London

Judy A. Bebber,
Stand L14, Grays Mews,
1-7 Davies Street, W1
Tel: 071-499 6600

Pleasures of Past Times,
11 Cecil Court, Charing Cross
Road, WC2
Tel: 071-836 1142

MATCHBOXES
Kent

Kollectomania,
4 Catherine Street, Rochester
Tel: (0634) 45099

POSTCARDS
London

Memories,
18 Bell Lane, Hendon, NW4
Tel: 081-203 1772/081-202 9080

Cheshire

Avalon,
1 City Walls, Northgate Street,
Chester
Tel: (0244) 318406

Derbyshire

Norman King,
24 Dinting Road, Glossop
Tel: (045 74) 2946

Essex

R.F. Postcards,
17 Hilary Crescent, Rayleigh
Tel: (0268) 743222

Gloucestershire

Specialised Postcard Auctions,
25 Gloucester Street,
Cirencester
Tel: (0285) 659057

Hampshire

Garnet Langton Auctions,
Burlington Arcade,
Bournemouth
Tel: (0202) 552352

Kent

Mike Sturge,
39 Union Street, Maidstone
Tel: (0622) 54702

West Midlands

George Sawyer,
11 Frayne Avenue,
Kingswinford
Tel: (0384) 273847

Norfolk

Bluebird Arts,
1 Mount Street, Cromer
Tel: (0263) 512384/78487

Northamptonshire

Shelron,
9 Brackley Road, Towcester
Tel: (0327) 50242

Nottinghamshire

Reflections of a Bygone Age,
15 Debdale Lane, Keyworth
Tel: (06077) 4079

T. Vennett Smith,
11 Nottingham Road, Gotham
Tel: (0602) 830541

East Sussex

John & Mary Bartholomew,
The Mint Arcade, 71 The Mint,
Rye
Tel: (0797) 225952

South Eastern Auctions,
39 High Street, Hastings
Tel: (0424) 434220

West Sussex

Bygones, Collectors Shop,
123 South Street, Lancing
Tel: (0903) 750051/763470

Wiltshire

David Wells,
Salisbury Antique & Collectors
Market, 37 Catherine Street,
Salisbury
Tel: (0425) 476899

BEER MATS
West Midlands

Roger Summers,
92 Nursery Road, Edgbaston,
Birmingham

PLAYING CARDS

London

Intercol (Yasha Beresiner),
1A Camden Walk, Islington
Green, N1
Tel: 071-354 2599

SCRIPOPHILY

London

The Scripophily Shop,
Britannia House, Grosvenor
Square, W1
Tel: 071-495 0580

Essex

G.K.R. Bonds Ltd.,
PO Box 1, Kelvedon
Tel: (0376) 71711

FANS

Kent

The Variety Box,
16 Chapel Place, Tunbridge
Wells
Tel: (0892) 31868/21589

Shropshire

F. C. Manser & Son Ltd,
53-54 Wyle Cop, Shrewsbury
Tel: (0743) 51120

FISHING

Dorset

Yesterday's Tackle & Books,
42 Clingan Road, Southbourne
Tel: (0202) 476586

Shropshire

Vintage Fishing Tackle Shop
and Angling Art Gallery,
103 Longden Coleham,
Shrewsbury
Tel: (0743) 69373

Scotland

Jamie Maxtone Graham,
Lyne Haugh, Lyne Station,
Peebles
Tel: (072 14) 304

Jess Miller,
PO Box 1, Birnam, Dunkeld,
Perthshire
Tel: (03502) 522

Wales

Brindley John Ayers,
45 St. Anne's Road, Hakin,
Milford Haven, Pembrokeshire
Tel: (06462) 78359

GOLFING

London

Sarah Baddiel,
The Book Gallery, B.12 Grays
Mews, 1-7 Davies Mews, W1
Tel: 071-408 1239/081-452 7243

King & Country,
Unit 46, Alfie's Antique
Market, 13-25 Church Street,
NW8
Tel: 071-724 3439

Oxfordshire

Manfred Schotten,
Crypt Antiques, 109 High
Street, Burford
Tel: (099 382) 2302

Warwickshire

Smith Street Antique Centre,
7 Smith Street, Warwick
Tel: (0926) 497864

GLASS – EARLY 18thC/19thC

London

Christine Bridge,
78 Castelnau, SW13
Tel: 081-741 5501

East Gates Antiques,
Stand G006, Alfies Antique
Market, 13-25 Church Street,
NW8
Tel: 071-724 5650

Pryce & Brise,
79 Moore Park Road, Fulham,
SW6
Tel: 081-736 1864

Mark J. West – Cobb Antiques,
39B High Street, Wimbledon
Village, SW19
Tel: 081-946 2811/081-540 7982

Avon

Somervale Antiques,
6 Radstock Road, Midsomer
Norton, Bath
Tel: (0761) 412686

Essex

East Gates Antiques,
91a East Hill, Colchester
Tel: (0206) 564474

Kent

Variety Box,
16 Chapel Place, Tunbridge
Wells
Tel: (0892) 31868/21589

Warwickshire

Sharon Ball,
Stratford-on-Avon Antique
Centre, Ely Street, Stratford-on-
Avon
Tel: (0789) 204180

GLASS – 20thC

London

Frank Andrews – Monart
and Vasart,
10 Vincent Road, London, N22
Tel: 081-881 0658 (Home)

Beverley – Cloud Glass, Jobling,
30 Church Street, NW8
Tel: 071-262 1576

The Scottish Connection,
Alfie's Antique Market,
13-25 Church Street, NW8
Tel: 071-723 6066

Stephen Watson – Powell,
Alfie's Antique Market,
13-25 Church Street, NW8
Tel: 071-723 0678

HAIRDRESSING/ HAT PINS

London

Ursula,
P16, 15 & 14 Antiquarius,
135 Kings Road, SW3
Tel: 071-352 2203

Kent

The Lace Basket,
1A East Cross, Tenterden
Tel: (05806) 3923

Variety Box,
16 Chapel Place, Tunbridge
Wells
Tel: (0892) 31868/21589

INKWELLS

London

Patrician,
1st Floor, Georgian Village,
Camden Passage, N1
Tel: 071-359 4560/071-435 3159

Berkshire

Mostly Boxes,
92 & 52B High Street, Eton,
Windsor
Tel: (0753) 858470

Kent

Ann Lingard,
Ropewalk Antiques, Rye
Tel: (0797) 223486

JEWELLERY

VICTORIAN/ EDWARDIAN

Gloucestershire

Lynn Greenwold,
Digbeth Street,
Stow-on-the-Wold
Tel: (0451) 30398

Kent

Old Saddlers Antiques,
Church Road, Goudhurst,
Cranbrook
Tel: (0580) 211458

Norfolk

Peter Howkins,
39, 40 and 135 King Street,
Great Yarmouth
Tel: (0493) 844639

ART DECO

London

Pierre De Fresne 'Beaux Bijoux',
Q 9/10 Antiquarius, 135 Kings
Road, SW3
Tel: 071-352 8882

Abstract,
Kensington Church Street
Antique Centre,
58-60 Kensington Church
Street, W8
Tel: 071-376 2652

JUKE BOXES

London

Anything American,
33-35 Duddenhill Lane, NW10
Tel: 081-451 0320

Hertfordshire

Connexions (UK) plc
Unit 3, South Mimms
Distribution Centre, Huggins
Lane, Welham Green
Tel: (07072) 72091

Dorset

The Chicago Sound Company,
Northmoor House, Colesbrook,
Gillingham
Tel: (0747) 824338

Surrey

Nostalgia Amusements,
73 Angus Close, Chessington
Tel: 081-397 6867

KITCHENALIA

London

David,
141 Grays Antique Market,
Davies Street, W1
Tel: 071-493 0208

Relic Antiques,
248 Camden High Street,
London, NW1
Tel: 071-485 8072

Hampshire

Millers of Chelsea Ltd,
Netherbrook House,
Christchurch Road, Ringwood
Tel: (0425) 472062

Lancashire

The Old Bakery,
36 Inglewhite Road, Longridge,
Nr. Preston
Tel: (0772) 785411

Kent

Penny Lampard,
28 High Street, Headcorn
Tel: (0622) 890682

Up Country,
Old Corn Stores, 68 St John's
Road, Tunbridge Wells
Tel: (0892) 23341

Shropshire

Scot Hay House Antiques,
7 Nantwich Road, Woore
Tel: (063 081) 7118

Tiffany Antiques,
Unit 15, Shrewsbury Antique
Market, Frankwell Quay
Warehouse, Shrewsbury
Tel: (0743) 50916/(0270) 225425
and
Unit 5, Telford Antique Centre,
High Street, Wellington, Telford
Tel: (0952) 56450

Surrey
Wych House Antiques,
Wych Hill, Woking
Tel: (04862) 64636

East Sussex
Ann Lingard,
Rope Walk Antiques, Rye
Tel: (0797) 223486

West Midlands
The Doghouse,
309 Bloxwich Road, Walsall
Tel: (0922) 30829

LE BLOND PRINTS
Warwickshire
Janice Paull,
125 Warwick Road, Kenilworth
Tel: (0926) 55253

LOCKS & KEYS
Nottinghamshire
The Keyhole,
Dragonwyck, Far Back Lane,
Farnsfield, Newark
Tel: (0623) 882590

LUGGAGE
London
Stanhope Bowery,
Grays Antique Market, Davies
Street, W1
Tel: 071-629 6194

METALWARE
London
Christopher Bangs,
SW11
Tel: 071-223 5676

Jack Casimir Ltd,
The Brass Shop, 23 Pembridge
Road, W11
Tel: 071-727 8643

Avon
Nick Marchant,
13 Orwell Drive, Keynsham,
Bristol
Tel: (0272) 865182

Bedfordshire
Christopher Sykes,
The Old Parsonage, Woburn
Tel: (0525) 290259

Derbyshire
Spurrier-Smith Antiques,
28b, 39-41 Church Street,
Ashbourne
Tel: (0335) 43669/42198

Kent
Old Saddlers Antiques,
Church Road, Goudhurst,
Cranbrook
Tel: (0580) 211458

Oxfordshire
Key Antiques,
11 Horse Fair, Chipping Norton
Tel: (0608) 3777

MILITARIA
MEDALS
Hampshire
Charles Antiques,
101 The Hundred, Romsey
Tel: (0794) 512885

Scotland
Edinburgh Coin Shop,
2 Powarth Crescent, Edinburgh
Tel: 031-229 3007/2915

East Sussex
Wallis & Wallis,
West Street Auction Galleries,
Lewes
Tel: (0273) 480208

ARMS & ARMOUR
London
Michael German,
38B Kensington Church Street,
W8
Tel: 071-937 2771

East Sussex
George Weiner,
2 Market Street, The Lanes,
Brighton
Tel: (0273) 729948

West Yorks
Andrew Spencer Bottomley,
The Coach House,
Thongsbridge, Holmfirth
Tel: (0484) 685234

ARMS & MILITARIA
London
Pieter G. K. Oosthuizen,
16 Britten Street, London, SW3
Tel: 071-352 1094/071-352 1493

Hampshire
Romsey Medal Centre,
5 Bell Street, Romsey
Tel: (0794) 512069

Kent
Keith & Veronica Reeves,
Burgate Antiques, 10c Burgate,
Canterbury
Tel: (0227) 456500/(0634)
375098

Surrey
West Street Antiques,
63 West Street, Dorking
Tel: (0306) 883487

East Sussex
V.A.G. & Co,
Possingworth Craft Centre,
Brownings Farm, Blackboys,
Uckfield
Tel: (0323) 507488

Wallis & Wallis,
West Street Auction Galleries,
Lewes
Tel: (0273) 480208

Warwickshire
Arbour Antiques Ltd,
Poet's Arbour, Sheep Street,
Stratford-upon-Avon
Tel: (0789) 293453

Scotland
Edinburgh Coin Shop,
2 Polwarth Crescent, Edinburgh
Tel: 031-229 2915/3007

ORIENTAL
London
Ormonde Gallery,
156 Portobello Road, W11
Tel: 071-229 9800/(042482) 226

Dorset
Lionel Geneen Ltd,
781 Christchurch Road,
Boscombe, Bournemouth
Tel: (0202) 422961

East Sussex
Chateaubriand Antique Centre,
High Street, Burwash
Tel: (0435) 882535

Scotland
Koto Buki,
The Milestone, Balmedie,
Aberdeen
Tel: (0358) 42414

PAPIER MÂCHÉ
London
Sue Simpson,
The Original Chelsea Antique
Market, Stand 28, 245-263
King's Road, London, SW3
Tel: 071-352 5581

Kent
Antiques & Interiors,
22 Ashford Road, Tenterden
Tel: (05806) 5422

PERFUME BOTTLES
London
Patrician Antiques,
1st Floor, Georgian Village,
Camden Passage, N1
Tel: 071-359 4560/071-435 3159

Trio (Theresa Clayton),
Grays Mews, 1-7 Davies Mews,
W1
Tel: 071-629 1184

Avon
Somervale Antiques,
6 Radstock Road, Midsomer
Norton, Bath
Tel: (0761) 412686

POLICE MEMORABILIA
London
David,
141 Grays Antique Market,
Davies Street, W1
Tel: 071-493 0208

Dorset
Mervyn A. Mitton,
161 The Albany, Manor Road,
Bournemouth
Tel: (0202) 293767

RADIOS
London
The Originals,
Stand 37, Alfie's Antique
Market, 13-25 Church Street,
NW8
Tel: 071-724 3439

Devon
Jonathan Hill,
2-4 Brook Street, Bampton
Tel: (0398) 31310

Hereford & Worcs
Radiocraft,
56 Main Street, Sedgeberrow,
Nr Evesham
Tel: (0386) 881988

RAILWAYS
Avon
Winstone Stamp Co,
Great Western Antique Market,
Bartlett Street, Bath
Tel: (0225) 310388

West Midlands
Railwayana Collectors Journal,
7 Ascot Road, Moseley,
Birmingham

Yorkshire
National Railway Museum,
Leeman Road, York
Tel: (0904) 621261

SCIENTIFIC & MEDICAL INSTRUMENTS
London
David Weston Ltd,
44 Duke Street, St James's, SW1
Tel: 071-839 1051/2/3

Bedfordshire
Christopher Sykes,
The Old Parsonage, Woburn
Tel: (0525) 290259

Surrey
David Burns,
116 Chestnut Grove, New
Malden
Tel: 081-949 7356

SEWING
London
The Thimble Society of London,
The Bees, S134 Grays Antique
Market, 58 Davies Street, W1
Tel: 071-493 0560

Kent

The Variety Box,
16 Chapel Place, Tunbridge
Wells
Tel: (0892) 31868/21589

Suffolk

Crafers Antiques,
The Hill, Wickham Market
Tel: (0728) 747347

SHIPPING

Hampshire

Cobwebs,
78 Northam Road, Southampton
Tel: (0703) 227458

SILVER

London

Donohoe,
L25/7 M10/12 Grays Mews,
1-7 Davies Mews, W1
Tel: 071-629 5633/081-455 5507

Goldsmith & Perris,
Stand 327, Alfie's Antique
Market, 13-25 Church Street,
NW8
Tel: 071-724 7051

The London Silver Vaults,
Chancery House, 53-65
Chancery Lane, WC2
Tel: 071-242 3844

Kent

The Variety Box,
16 Chapel Place, Tunbridge
Wells
Tel: (0892) 31868/21589

Oxfordshire

Thames Gallery,
Thameside, Henley-on-Thames
Tel: (0491) 572449

Shropshire

F. C. Manser & Son Ltd,
53-54 Wyle Cop, Shrewsbury
Tel: (0743) 51120

SPORT –
FOOTBALL

London

Final Whistle,
50, 61-63 Alfie's Antique
Market, 13-25 Church Street,
London, NW8
Tel: 071-262 3423

TARTANWARE

London

Eureka Antiques,
Geoffrey Vanns Arcade,
105 Portobello Road, W11
(Saturdays)

Grays Antique Market,
58 Davies Street, W1
Tel: 071-629 7034

Cheshire

Eureka Antiques,
18 Northenden Road, Sale
Tel: 061-962 5629

TELEPHONES

Devon

Bampton Telephone & General
Museum of Communication and
Domestic History,
4 Brook Street, Bampton

Kent

Candlestick & Bakelite,
3 Amherst Drive, St. Mary
Cray, Orpington
Tel: (0689) 23448/01-445 1100

Scotland

Now & Then Classic Telephones,
7/9 Crosscauseway, Edinburgh
Tel: 031-668 2927/(0592) 890235

TEXTILES
SAMPLERS

London

Sophia Blanchard,
Alfie's Antique Market, Church
Street, NW8
Tel: 071-723 5731

Matthew Adams Antiques,
69 Portobello Road, W11
Tel: 081-579 5560

*QUILTS,
PATCHWORK,
COSTUME*

London

The Antique Textile Company,
100 Portland Road, Holland
Park, W11
Tel: 071-221 7730

The Gallery of Antique Costume
& Textiles,
2 Church Street, Marylebone,
NW8
Tel: 071-723 9981

Lincolnshire

20th Century Frocks,
Lincolnshire Art Centre, Bridge
Street, Horncastle
Tel: (06582) 7794/(06588) 3638

West Yorkshire

Echoes,
650A Halifax Road, Eastwood,
Todmorden
Tel: (0706) 817505

LINEN & LACE
London

Act One Hire Ltd,
2A Scampston Mews,
Cambridge Gardens, London,
W10
Tel: 081-960 1456/1494

Antiquarius,
135-141 Kings Road, SW3
Tel: 071-351 5353

Audrey Field,
Alfie's Antique Market,
13-25 Church Street, NW8
Tel: 071-723 6066

Devon

Honiton Lace Shop,
44 High Street, Honiton
Tel: (0404) 42416

Kent

Antiques & Interiors,
22 Ashford Road, Tenterden
Tel: (05806) 5462

The Lace Basket,
1A East Cross, Tenterden
Tel: (05806) 3923

East Sussex

Celia Charlotte's,
7 Malling Street, Lewes
Tel: (0273) 473303

Chateaubriand Antique Centre,
High Street, Burwash
Tel: (0435) 882535

TILES
London

Ilse Antiques,
30-32 The Vaults, The Georgian
Village, Islington, N1

East Sussex

Ann Lingard,
Rope Walk Antiques, Rye
Tel: (0797) 223486

The Old Mint House,
Pevensey
Tel: (0323) 762337

Wales

Paul Gibbs Antiques,
25 Castle Street, Conwy
Tel: (0492) 593429

Victorian Fireplaces
(Simon Priestley),
Ground Floor, Cardiff Antique
Centre, 69/71 St Mary Street,
Cardiff
Tel: (0222) 30970/226049

TINS & METAL
SIGNS

London

Keith, Old Advertising,
Unit 14, 155A Northcote Road,
Battersea, SW11
Tel: 071-228 0741/6850

Avon

Michael & Jo Saffell,
3 Walcot Buildings, London
Road, Bath
Tel: (0225) 315857

Oxfordshire

R.A.T.S.,
Unit 16, Telford Road, Bicester
Tel: (0869) 242161/40842

East Sussex

Rin Tin Tin,
34 North Road, Brighton
Tel: (0273) 672424/
(0273) 733689 (Eves)

Wiltshire

Relic Antiques, Lea,
Malmesbury
Tel: (0666) 822332

TOYS

MECHANICAL

London

Stuart Cropper,
Grays Mews, 1-7 Davies Mews,
W1
Tel: 071-629 7034

Yonna Cohen,
B19 Grays Mews, 1-7 Davies
Mews, London, W1
Tel: 071-629 3644

Avon

Great Western Toys, Great
Western Antique Centre,
Bartlett Street, Bath

DIECAST MODELS

London

Colin Baddiel,
Grays Mews, 1-7 Davies Mews,
W1
Tel: 071-408 1239/081-452 7243

Mint & Boxed,
110 High Street, Edgware,
Middx
Tel: 081-952 2002

Past Present Toys,
862 Green Lanes, Winchmore
Hill, London N21
Tel: 081-364 1370

Buckinghamshire

Cars Only,
4 Granville Square, Willen
Local Centre, Willen, Milton
Keynes
Tel: (0908) 690024

Cornwall

Model Garage (Redruth) Ltd,
Lanner Hill, Redruth
Tel: (0209) 215589/211311

Isle of Wight

Nostalgia Toy Museum,
High Street, Godshill
Tel: (0983) 730055

Norfolk

Trains & Olde Tyme Toys,
Aylsham Road, Norwich
Tel: (0603) 413585

Shropshire

Stretton Models,
12 Beaumont Road, Church
Stretton
Tel: (0694) 723737

East Sussex

Clockwork and Steam,
35 Western Street, Brighton
Tel: (0273) 203290

Wallis & Wallis,
West Street Auction Galleries,
Lewes
Tel: (0273) 480208

West Sussex

Trains,
67 London Road, Bognor Regis
Tel: (0243) 864727

Warwickshire

Time Machine,
Paul M. Kennelly, 198 Holbrook
Lane, Coventry
Tel: (0203) 663557

West Midlands

Moseley Railwayana Museum,
Birmingham
Tel: 021-449 9707

Wiltshire

David Wells,
Salisbury Antique & Collectors
Market, 37 Catherine Street,
Salisbury
Tel: (0425) 476899

Yorkshire

Andrew Clarke,
42 Pollard Lane, Bradford
Tel: (0274) 636042

John & Simon Haley,
89 Northgate, Halifax
Tel: (0422) 822148

Wales

Corgi Toys Ltd,
Kingsway, Swansea Industrial
Estate, Swansea
Tel: (0792) 586223

MONEY BOXES

Yorkshire

John Haley,
89 Northgate, Halifax
Tel: (0422) 822148

GAMES

London

Donay,
35 Camden Passage, N1
Tel: 071-359 1880

ROCKING HORSES

Cornwall

The Millcraft Rocking Horse Co,
Lower Trannack Mill, Coverack
Bridges, Helston
Tel: (0326) 573316

Wales

Stuart & Pam MacPherson,
A.P.E.S.,
Ty Isaf, Pont Y Gwyddel,
Llanfair T.H., Abergele, Clwyd
Tel: (074 579) 365

TREEN

London

Simon Castle,
38B Kensington Church Street,
W8
Tel: 081-892 2840

Wynyards Antiques,
5 Ladbroke Road, W11
Tel: 071-221 7936

Buckinghamshire

A. & E. Foster,
Little Heysham, Forge Road,
Naphill
Tel: (024 024) 2024

TUNBRIDGEWARE

Berks

Mostly Boxes,
52B High Street, Eton
Tel: (0753) 858470

Kent

Strawsons Antiques
33, 39 & 41 The Pantiles,
Tunbridge Wells
Tel: (0892) 30607

The Variety Box,
16 Chapel Place, Tunbridge
Wells
Tel: (0892) 31868/21589

East Sussex

Barclay Antiques,
7 Village Mews, Little Common,
Bexhill-on-Sea
Tel: (0797) 222734

WALKING STICKS

London

Cekay Antiques,
Grays Antique Market,
58 Davies Street, W1
Tel: 071-629 5130

Michael German,
38B Kensington Church Street,
W8
Tel: 071-937 2771

WATCHES

London

Pieces of Time, Grays Mews,
1-7 Davies Street, W1
Tel: 071-629 2422

WRITING

London

Jasmin Cameron,
Stand J6 Antiquarius,
131-141 Kings Road, SW3
Tel: 071-351 4154

CALENDAR OF FAIRS from April 1991

This calendar is in no way complete. If you wish your event to be included in next year's edition or if you have a change of address or telephone number, please could you inform us by December 1st 1991. Finally we would advise readers to make contact by telephone before a visit, therefore avoiding a wasted journey, which nowadays is both time consuming and expensive.

London

APRIL

The London International
Antique Dolls, Toys, Miniatures
& Teddy Bear Fair, Granny's
Goodies, PO Box 734, SE23
Tel: 081-693 5432

Mon 8th-9th
Little Chelsea Antiques Fair,
Old Town Hall, Kings Road,
SW3
Ravenscott Fairs.
Tel: 071-727 5045

Thurs 25th-28th
Westminster Antiques Fair,
Horticultural Old Hall, SW1
Penman Antiques Fairs.
Tel: (0444) 482514

Thurs 6th-16th
Fine Arts & Antiques Fair,
Olympia, W14
Tel: 071-370 8211

JUNE

The London International
Antique Dolls, Toys, Miniatures
& Teddy Bear Fair, Granny's

Goodies, PO Box 734, SE23
Tel: 081-693 5432

Wed 12th-22nd
Grosvenor House Antiques
Fair, Park Lane, W1
Tel: (0799) 26699

Fri 14th-16th
London Ceramics Fair,
Cumberland Hotel, Marble
Arch, Wakefield Fairs.
Tel: (0634) 723461

Fri 14th-17th
International Ceramics Fair,
Park Lane Hotel, Piccadilly, W1
Tel: 071-734 5491

AUGUST

Thurs 15th-18th
West London Antiques Fair,
Kensington Town Hall, W8
Penman Antiques Fairs.
Tel: (0444) 482514

SEPTEMBER

The London International
Antique Dolls, Toys, Miniatures
& Teddy Bear Fair, Granny's

Goodies, PO Box 734, SE23
Tel: 081-693 5432

Tues 3rd-8th
London Antique Dealers' Fairs,
Cafe Royal, Regent Street
Jane Sumner. Tel: (0799) 23611

Tues 10th-21st
Chelsea Antiques Fair, Old
Town Hall, King's Road, SW3
Penman Antiques Fairs.
Tel: (0444) 482514

Fri 20th-21st
Arms Fair, The Ramada Inn,
Lillie Road, SW6
Tel: 071-405 7933

Wed 25th-29th
20th Century British Art Fair,
The Royal College of Art,
Kensington Gore, SW7
Tel: 071-371 1703

Mon 30th-1st Oct
Little Chelsea Antiques Fair,
Old Town Hall, Kings Road,
SW3
Ravenscott Fairs.
Tel: 071-727 5045

OCTOBER

Bi-annual Antique Doll &
Juvenilia Fair, The Cumberland
Hotel, Marble Arch, W1
Tel: 081-398 5324

Wed 2nd-7th
The Park Lane Antiques Fair,
The Park lane Hotel,
Piccadilly, W1
Tel: 071-603 0165

Tues 8th-13th
Fine Art & Antiques Fair,
Olympia, W14
Tel: 071-370 8211

Wed 16th-20th
The LAPADA Show, Royal
College of Art, Kensington
Gore, SW7
Penman Antiques Fairs.
Tel: (0444) 482514

NOVEMBER

Tues 5th-10th
40th Kensington Antiques Fair,
Town Hall, Kensington, W8
Cultural Exhibitions.
Tel: (04868) 22562

Wed 20th-25th
City of London Antiques Fair,
Barbican
Tel: 081-441 8940

DECEMBER
Mon 2nd-3rd
Little Chelsea Antiques Fair,
Old Town Hall, Kings Road,
SW3
Ravenscott Fairs.
Tel: 071-727 5045

Avon

APRIL
Symes Promotions,
93 Charleton Mead Drive,
Westbury on Trym, Bristol
Tel: (0272) 501074

Sat 6th-7th
Spring Antiques, Collectors &
Book Fair, Bristol Exhibitions
Centre
West Country Antiques &
Collectors Fairs.
Tel: (0364) 52182

Thurs 25th-27th
4th Annual Bath Guildhall
Antiques Fair, Guildhall, Bath
Antiques in Britain Fairs.
Tel: (0273) 423355

MAY
Tues 14th-18th
West of England Antiques Fair,
Assembly Rooms, Bath
Tel: (0225) 463727

Wed 15th-18th
Bath Decorative Fair,
The Pavilion
Robert Bailey.
Tel: (0277) 362662

JULY
Thurs 18th-20th
Ceramics Fair, Assembly
Rooms, Bath
Wakefield Fairs.
Tel: (0634) 723461

AUGUST
Tues 6th-7th
Summer Antiques, Collectors &
Book Fair, Guildhall, Bath
West Country Antiques &
Collectors Fairs.
Tel: (0364) 52182

SEPTEMBER
Wed 25th-28th
City of Bath Antiques Fair,
The Pavilion
Robert Bailey.
Tel: (0277) 362662

OCTOBER
Sat 5th-6th
Antiques & Decorative Arts
Fair, Bristol Exhibition Centre
Tel: (0934) 624854

Sat 26th-27th
Autumn Antiques & Collectors
Fair, Exhibition Centre, Bristol
West Country Antiques &
Collectors Fairs
Tel: (0364) 52182

DECEMBER
Fri 13th-14th
Bath Christmas Antiques,
Collectors & Book Fair,
Guildhall
West Country Antiques &
Collectors Fairs.
Tel: (0364) 52182

Bedfordshire

OCTOBER
Mon 14th-15th
32nd Luton Antiques Fair,
Chiltern Hotel, Dunstable
Road, Luton
Tel: (0462) 434525

Buckinghamshire

MAY
Sun 26th-27th
Fine Arts & Antiques Fair,
Bellhouse Hotel, Beaconsfield
Midas Fairs. Tel: (0753) 886993

JULY
Fri 19th-21st
Decorative Interiors Fair, Stowe
School
Robert Bailey.
Tel: (0277) 362662

OCTOBER
Thurs 31st-Sat Nov 2nd
High Wycombe Autumn
Antiques Fair, Royal Grammar
School
Tel: (0494) 6734674

Cambridgeshire

JUNE
Wed 5th
Antiques & Collectors Fair,
Fisher Hall, Cambridge
Charlin Fairs.
Tel: (0787) 237138

Wed 19th
Antiques & Collectors Fair,
Fisher Hall, Cambridge
Charlin Fairs.
Tel: (0787) 237138

Sat 22nd-23rd
Antiques Fair, East of England
Showground, Peterborough
Four in One Promotions.
Tel: (0533) 712589

JULY
Wed 3rd
Antiques & Collectors Fair,
Fisher Hall, Cambridge
Charlin Fairs.
Tel: (0787) 237138

Wed 17th
Antiques & Collectors Fair,
Fisher Hall, Cambridge
Charlin Fairs.
Tel: (0787) 237138

AUGUST
Wed 3rd
Antiques & Collectors Fair,
Fisher Hall, Cambridge
Charlin Fairs.
Tel: (0787) 237138

Wed 17th
Antiques & Collectors Fair,
Fisher Hall, Cambridge
Charlin Fairs.
Tel: (0787) 237138

SEPTEMBER
Wed 4th
Antiques & Collectors Fair,
Fisher Hall, Cambridge
Charlin Fairs.
Tel: (0787) 237138

Wed 18th
Antiques & Collectors Fair,
Fisher Hall, Cambridge
Charlin Fairs.
Tel: (0787) 237138

Sat 28th-29th
Antiques Fair, East of England
Showground, Peterborough
Four in One Promotions.
Tel: (0533) 712580

OCTOBER
Wed 2nd
Antiques & Collectors Fair,
Fisher Hall, Cambridge
Charlin Fairs.
Tel: (0787) 237138

Wed 16th
Antiques & Collectors Fair,
Fisher Hall, Cambridge
Charlin Fairs.
Tel: (0787) 237138

NOVEMBER
Wed 6th
Antiques & Collectors Fair,
Fisher Hall, Cambridge
Charlin Fairs.
Tel: (0787) 237138

Wed 20th
Antiques & Collectors Fair,
Fisher Hall, Cambridge
Charlin Fairs.
Tel: (0787) 237138

DECEMBER
Wed 4th
Antiques & Collectors Fair,
Fisher Hall, Cambridge
Charlin Fairs.
Tel: (0787) 237138

Wed 18th
Antiques & Collectors Fair,
Fisher Hall, Cambridge
Charlin Fairs.
Tel: (0787) 237138

Cheshire

JULY
Fri 12th-14th
Fine Art Fair, Tatton Park
Robert Bailey.
Tel: (0277) 362662

SEPTEMBER
Wed 11th-15th
Tatton Park Antiques Fair
Robert Bailey.
Tel: (0277) 362662

NOVEMBER
Fri 8th-10th
Antiques Fair, Peckforton
Castle
Robert Bailey.
Tel: (0277) 362662

Christleton Country Club,
Plough Lane, Christleton
Tel: 051-327 3853
The last Sunday of every month
10am-5pm

Cornwall

APRIL
Fri 19th-20th
Spring Antiques & Collectors
Fair, City Hall, Truro
West Country Antiques &
Collectors Fairs.
Tel: (0364) 52182

AUGUST
Fri 16th-17th
Antiques, Collectors & Book
Fair, City Hall, Truro
West Country Antiques &
Collectors Fairs.
Tel: (0364) 52182

DECEMBER
Fri 6th-7th
Truro Christmas Antiques &
Collectors Fair, City Hall
West Country Antiques &
Collectors Fairs.
Tel: (0364) 52182

Cumbria

NOVEMBER
Fri 15th-17th
Antiques Fair, Holker Hall
Robert Bailey.
Tel: (0277) 362662

Derbyshire

MAY
Sat 11th-18th
27th Buxton Antiques Fair,
Pavilion Gardens, Buxton
Cultural Exhibitions.
Tel: (04868) 22562

JUNE
Sat 1st-2nd
The Pavilion Gardens, Buxton
Unicorn Fairs.
Tel: (061 773) 7001

JULY
Sat 13th-14th
The Pavilion Gardens, Buxton
Unicorn Fairs.
Tel: (061 773) 7001

AUGUST
Sat 24th-25th
The Pavilion Gardens, Buxton
Unicorn Fairs.
Tel: (061 773) 7001

SEPTEMBER
Sat 7th-8th
Ceramics Fair, Royal Crown
Derby Museum, Derby
Wakefield Fairs.
Tel: (0634) 723461

Sat 28th-29th
The Pavilion Gardens, Buxton
Unicorn Fairs.
Tel: (061 773) 7001

NOVEMBER
Sat 9th-10th
The Pavilion Gardens, Buxton
Unicorn Fairs.
Tel: (061 773) 7001

DECEMBER
Sat 28th-29th
The Pavilion Gardens, Buxton
Unicorn Fairs.
Tel: (061 773) 7001

Devon
APRIL
Sat 6th-7th
Westpoint Exhibition Centre,
Exeter
Devon County Antiques Fairs.
Tel: (0363) 82571
Thurs 11th-12th
External Annual Spring
Antiques Fair, Imperial Hotel,
Exeter
West Country Antiques &
Collectors Fairs.
Tel: (0364) 52182
MAY
Sat 4th
New Exeter Livestock Centre,
Exeter
Devon County Antiques Fairs.
Tel: (0363) 82571
Thurs 30th-31st
North Devon Antique Dealers'
Fair, Queens Hall, Barnstaple
West Country Antiques &
Collectors Fairs.
Tel: (0364) 52182
JUNE
Wed 5th-6th
Giant Antiques, Collectors &
Book Fair, Racecourse, Newton
Abbot
West Country Antiques &
Collectors Fairs.
Tel: (0364) 52182
Sat 8th-9th
Westpoint Exhibition Centre,
Exeter
Devo County Antiques Fairs.
Tel: (0363) 82571
JULY
Sat 6th
New Exeter Livestock Centre,
Exeter
Devon County Antiques Fairs.
Tel: (0363) 82571
Sat 20th-21st
South Devon & Dartmoor
Antiques & Collectors Fair,
Moorland Hotel, Haytor
West Country Antiques &
Collectors Fairs.
Tel: (0364) 52182
Sat 20th-21st
Blundell's School, Tiverton
Devon County Antiques Fairs.
Tel: (0363) 82571
AUGUST
Sat 3rd
New Exeter Livestock Centre,
Exeter
Devon County Antiques Fairs.
Tel: (0363) 82571
SEPTEMBER
Sat 7th
New Exeter Livestock Centre,
Exeter

Devon County Antiques Fairs.
Tel: (0363) 82571
Wed 11th-12th
Giant Antiques, Collectors &
Book Fair, Racecourse, Newton
Abbot
West Country Antiques &
Collectors Fairs.
Tel: (0364) 52182
Thurs 26th-27th
Exeter Annual Autumn
Antiques Fair, Imperial Hotel,
Exeter
West Country Antiques &
Collectors Fairs.
Tel: (0364) 52182
OCTOBER
Fri 4th-5th
Autumn Antiques & Collectors
Fair, Imperial Hotel, Exeter
West Country Antiques &
Collectors Fairs.
Tel: (0364) 52182
Sat 12th-13th
Westpoint Exhibition Centre,
Exeter
Devon County Antiques Fairs.
Tel: (0363) 82571
NOVEMBER
Sat 9th
New Exeter Livestock Centre,
Exeter
Devon County Antiques Fairs.
Tel: (0363) 82571
Sat 9th-10th
South Devon & Dartmoor
Autumn Antiques & Collectors
Fair, Moorland Hotel, Haytor
West Country Antiques &
Collectors Fairs.
Tel: (0364) 52182
Sat 30th-Sun Dec 1st
Giant Christmas Antiques,
Collectors & Book Fair,
Racecourse, Newton Abbot
West Country Antiques &
Collectors Fairs.
Tel: (0364) 52182
DECEMBER
Thurs 12th-13th
Barnstaple Annual Christmas
Antiques & Collectors Fair,
Queens Hall
West Country Antiques &
Collectors Fairs.
Tel: (0364) 52182

Dorset
APRIL
Fri 5th-7th
The Dales Antique Dealers'
Fair, Canford Magna, Nr
Wimborne
Castle Fairs. Tel: (0937) 845829

OCTOBER
Sat 5th-6th
4th Annual Autumn Antiques
Fair, Coach House Inn,
Tricketts Cross, Ferndown
Antiques in Britain Fairs.
Tel: (0273) 423355

Gloucestershire

APRIL
Thurs 11th-13th
Ceramics Fair, Pittville Pump Rooms, Cheltenham
Wakefield Fairs.
Tel: (0634) 723461

Wed 24th-27th
Cotswolds Antiques Fair, Pittville Pump Rooms, Cheltenham
Robert Bailey.
Tel: (0277) 362662

OCTOBER
Wed 30th-Sat Nov 2nd
Cotswold Antiques Fair, Pittville Pump Rooms, Cheltenham
Robert Bailey.
Tel: (0277) 362662

Hampshire

JUNE
Thurs 6th-8th
Petersfield Antiques Fair, Town Hall, Petersfield
Gamlin Exhibition Services.
Tel: (0452) 862557

AUGUST
Fri 23rd-26th
The Hampshire Antique Dealers' Fair, Royal College of Maritime Studies, Warsash
Castle Fairs. Tel: (0937) 845829

SEPTEMBER
Thurs 5th-7th
Petersfield Antiques Fair, Town Hall, Petersfield
Gamlin Exhibition Services.
Tel: (0452) 862557

Fri 13th-15th
Antiques Fair, Guildhall, Winchester
Wakefield Fairs.
Tel: (0634) 723461

Hereford & Worcs

OCTOBER
Tues 8th-10th
21st Annual Hereford & Worcestershire Antiques Fair, Bank House Hotel, Bransford, Nr Worcester
Antiques in Britain Fairs.
Tel: (0273) 423355

Sat 19th-20th
Ceramics Fairs, Dyson Perrins Museum, Worcester
Wakefield Fairs.
Tel: (0634) 723461

Hertfordshire

JULY
Sat 13th-14th
Antiques Fair, Rhodes Centre, Bishops Stortford
Britannia Antiques Fair.
Tel: (0984) 31668

SEPTEMBER
Fri 6th-8th
Antiques Fair, Hatfield House
Robert Bailey.
Tel: (0277) 362662

OCTOBER
Sat 19th-20th
Rhodes Centre, Bishops Stortford
Britannia Antiques Fairs.
Tel: (0984) 31668

Kent

MAY
Sun 26th-27th
Antiques Fair, Cobham Hall, Cobham
Wakefield Fairs.
Tel: (0634) 723461

NOVEMBER
Sat 2nd-3rd
Antiques Fair, Cobham Hall, Cobham
Wakefield Fairs.
Tel: (0634) 723461

Lancashire

OCTOBER
Fri 25th-27th
The Lancashire Antique Dealers' Fair, Stonyhurst, Nr Whalley
Castle Fairs. Tel: (0937) 845829

NOVEMBER
Fri 22nd-24th
Antiques Fair, Hoghton Tower, Preston
Robert Bailey.
Tel: (0277) 362662

Leicestershire

MAY
Fri 3rd-6th
Antiques Fair, Beaumanor Hall
Robert Bailey.
Tel: (0277) 362662

Lincolnshire

MAY
Sat 4th-6th
Tolethorpe Hall Antiques Fair, Nr Stamford
Tel: (0603) 623326

Fri 24th-27th
Antiques Fair, Harlaxton Manor, Grantham
Robert Bailey.
Tel: (0277) 362662

SEPTEMBER
Sat 14th-15th
Tolethorpe Hall Antiques Fair, Nr Stamford
Tel: (0603) 623326

OCTOBER
Fri 4th-6th
Antiques Fair, Harlaxton Manor, Grantham
Robert Bailey.
Tel: (0277) 362662

Northumberland

JUNE
Fri 7th-9th
Border Antique Dealers' Fair, Alnwick Castle
Castle Fairs. Tel: (0937) 845829

Nottinghamshire

JUNE
Fri 21st-23rd
The Thoresby Antiques Fair, Nr Ollerton
Whittington Exhibitions.
Tel: 081-644 9327

SEPTEMBER
Fri 20th-22nd
The Thoresby Antiques Fair, Nr Ollerton
Whittington Exhibitions.
Tel: 081-644 9327

OCTOBER
Fri 25th-27th
Ceramics Fair, Worksop College, Worksop
Wakefield Fairs.
Tel: (0634) 723461

Oxfordshire

AUGUST
Sat 3rd-4th
4th Annual Radley College Antiques Fair & Staffordshire Figures Fair, Radley College, Nr Abingdon
Antiques in Britain Fairs.
Tel: (0273) 423355

OCTOBER
Fri 11th-12th
Ceramics Fair, Town Hall, Henley-on-Thames
Wakefield Fairs.
Tel: (0634) 723461

Shropshire

JULY
Tues 9th-11th
Shropshire Summer Antiques Fair, Lion Hotel, Shrewsbury
Antiques in Britain Fairs.
Tel: (0273) 423355

Somerset

MAY
Sat 25th-26th
Millfield School, Street
Devon County Antiques Fairs.
Tel: (0363) 82571

OCTOBER
Fri 11th-12th
Taunton Annual Antiques & Collectors Fair, County Cricket Ground
West Country Antiques & Collectors Fairs.
Tel: (0364) 52182

NOVEMBER
Fri 1st-2nd
Wells Annual Autumn Antiques Fair, Bishops Palace
West Country Antiques & Collectors Fairs.
Tel: (0364) 52182

DECEMBER
Sat 14th-15th
Millfield School, Street
Devon County Antiques Fairs.
Tel: (0363) 82571

Staffordshire

JUNE
Fri 21st-23rd
Giant Antique Fair, Bingley Hall, County Showground
Bowman Fairs.
Tel: (0532) 843333

AUGUST
Fri 16th-18th
Giant Antique Fair, Bingley Hall, County Showground
Bowman Fairs.
Tel: (0532) 843333

OCTOBER
Fri 4th-6th
Giant Antique Fair, Bingley Hall, County Showground
Bowman Fairs.
Tel: (0532) 843333

DECEMBER
Fri 13th-15th
Giant Antique Fair, Bingley Hall, County Showground
Bowman Fairs.
Tel: (0532) 843333

Suffolk

JULY
Thurs 25th-28th
25th Annual Snape Antiques Fair, The Maltings, Snape
Anglian Arts & Antiques.
Tel: (0986) 872368

SEPTEMBER
Thurs 5th-7th
25th Annual East Anglia Antiques Fair, Athenaeum, Bury St Edmunds
Antiques in Britain Fairs.
Tel: (0273) 423355

OCTOBER
Thurs 31st-Sat Nov 2nd
20th Annual St Edmunds Antiques Fair, Athenaeum, Bury
Anglian Arts & Antiques.
Tel: (0986) 872368

Surrey

MAY
Sun 26th-27th
Antiques Fair, Cobham Hall, Cobham
Wakefield Fairs.
Tel: (0634) 723461

AUGUST
Fri 2nd-4th
Antiques Fair, Charterhouse School, Godalming
Robert Bailey.
Tel: (0277) 362662

Sat 24th-26th
Antiques Fair, Cranleigh School
Wakefield Fairs.
Tel: (0634) 723641

Sun 25th-26th
Antiques Fair, Dorking Hall, Dorking
Tel: 081-874 3622

OCTOBER
Fri 4th-8th
24th Surrey Antiques Fair,
Civic Hall, Guildhall
Cultural Exhibitions.
Tel: (04868) 22562

NOVEMBER
Sat 2nd-3rd
Antiques Fair, Cobham Hall,
Cobham
Wakefield Fairs.
Tel: (0634) 723461

Thurs 7th-9th
Farnham Antiques Fair,
Church House, Farnham
Gamlin Exhibition Services.
Tel: (0452) 862557

East Sussex
APRIL
Fri 5th-7th
Petworth Antiques Fair,
Seaford College
Robert Bailey.
Tel: (0277) 362662

JUNE
Fri 14th-16th
The Summer South East
Counties Antiques Dealers'
Fair, Goodwood House
Castle Fairs. Tel: (0937) 845829

AUGUST
Fri 30th-Sun Sept 1st
Petworth Antiques Fair,
Seaford College
Robert Bailey.
Tel: (0277) 362662

NOVEMBER
Fri 1st-3rd
Antiques & Decorative Arts at
Parham, Parham Park
Castle Fairs. Tel: (0937) 845829

Fri 22nd-24th
The Christmas South East
Counties Antique Dealers' Fair,
Goodwood House
Castle Fairs. Tel: (0937) 845829

DECEMBER
Sat 28th-31st
Petworth Antiques Fair,
Seaford College
Robert Bailey.
Tel: (0277) 362662

West Sussex
MAY
5th-6th
Ceramics Fair, Felbridge Hotel,
East Grinstead
Wakefield Fairs.
Tel: (0634) 723461

Sat 18th-19th
3rd Spring Antiques Fair,
Village Hall, Wivelsfield Green
Antiques in Britain Fairs.
Tel: (0273) 423355

AUGUST
Fri 23rd-24th
24th Annual Lindfield Antiques
Fair, King Edward Hall,
Lindfield
Antiques in Britain Fairs.
Tel: (0273) 423355

SEPTEMBER
Sat 21st-22nd
Ceramics Fair, Felbridge Hotel,
East Grinstead
Wakefield Fairs.
Tel: (0634) 723461

OCTOBER
Fri 25th-27th
Antiques Fair, Lancing College,
Worthing
Robert Bailey.
Tel: (0277) 362662

Sat 26th-27th
3rd Annual Autumn Antiques
Fair, Wivelsfield Green Village
Hall
Antiques in Britain Fairs.
Tel: (0273) 423355

Warwickshire

OCTOBER
Tues 22nd-26th
Kenilworth Antiques Fair,
Chesford Grange, Kenilworth
Jane Sumner.
Tel: (0799) 23611

NOVEMBER
Fri 29th-Sun Dec 1st
Antiques Fair, Ragley Hall,
Alcester
Wakefield Fairs.
Tel: (0634) 723461

West Midlands

APRIL
Thurs 4th-10th
British International Antiques
Fair, National Exhibition
Centre, Birmingham
Tel: 021-780 4141

Fri 19th-21st
Antiques Fair, Hagley Hall,
Stourbridge
Wakefield Fairs.
Tel: (0634) 723461

AUGUST
Thurs 8th-11th
NEC Fair, National Exhibition
Centre, Birmingham
Tel: 021-780 4141

SEPTEMBER
Thurs 26th-28th
33rd Warwickshire County
Antiques Fair, Cricket Ground,
Edgbaston, Birmingham
Tel: 021-743 2259

NOVEMBER
Thurs 7th-9th
34th Warwickshire County
Antiques Fair, Cricket Ground,
Edgbaston, Birmingham
Tel: 021-743 2259

Scotland
APRIL
Thurs 4th-6th
The Scottish Antiques Fair
1991, Roxburghe Hotel,
Charlotte Square

JUNE
Fri 28th-30th
Grampian Antiques &
Decorative Arts Fair, Bridge of
Don, Aberdeen
Castle Fairs. Tel: (0937) 845829

JULY
Tues 23rd-25th
20th Edinburgh Antiques Fair,
Roxburghe Hotel, Charlotte
Square, Edinburgh
Antiques in Britain Fairs.
Tel: (0273) 423355

OCTOBER
Fri 11th-13th
The Antiques Dealers' Fair of
Scotland, Hopetoun House,
South Queensferry
Castle Fairs. Tel: (0937) 845829

NOVEMBER
Fri 15th-17th
14th Annual Edinburgh Winter
Antiques Fair, Roxburghe
Hotel, Charlotte Square,
Edinburgh
Antiques in Britain.
Tel: (0273) 423355

Wales

MAY
Thurs 2nd-4th
11th Annual Brecon Antiques
Fair, Castle of Brecon Hotel,
Brecon, Powys
Antiques in Britain Fairs.
Tel: (0273) 423355

Fri 24th-27th
Antique Dealers' Fair of Wales,
Margam Castle, Nr Swansea
Castle Fairs. Tel: (0937) 845829

JUNE
Sat 1st-2nd
North Wales Antiques Fair,
Bodelwyddan Castle, Clwyd
Antiques in Britain Fairs.
Tel: (0273) 423355

SEPTEMBER
Thurs 12th-14th
22nd Annual Welsh Antiques
Fair, Castle of Brecon Hotel,
Brecon, Powys
Antiques in Britain Fairs.
Tel: (0273) 423355

Wiltshire

NOVEMBER
Fri 22nd-24th
Ceramics Fair, Michael Herbert
Hall, Wilton
Wakefield Fairs.
Tel: (0634) 723461

Yorkshire

MAY
Fri 24th-25th
York Antiques & Book Fair,
De Grey Rooms, Exhibition
Square

West Country Antiques &
Collectors Fairs.
Tel: (0364) 52182

JULY
Fri 26th-28th
Antiques Fair, Granby Hotel,
Harrogate
Robert Bailey.
Tel: (0277) 362662

AUGUST
Fri 23rd-26th
Antiques Fair, Kings Hall,
Ilkley
Robert Bailey.
Tel: (0277) 362662

SEPTEMBER
Fri 13th-15th
Antiques Eurofair, Hazelwood
Castle, Nr Tadcaster
Tel: (0937) 845829

Thurs 26th-Wed Oct 2nd
41st Northern Antiques Fair,
Royal Baths, Harrogate
Tel: (0799) 26699

Fri 27th-29th
Antiques & Decorative Arts at
Settrington, The Orangery,
Settrington, Nr Malton
Castle Fairs. Tel: (0937) 845829

OCTOBER
Fri 18th-19th
York Annual Antiques & Book
Fair, De Grey Rooms
West Country Antiques &
Collectors Fairs.
Tel: (0364) 52182

NOVEMBER
Fri 8th-10th
Antiques & Decorative Arts at
Rudding, Rudding House,
Harrogate
Castle Fairs. Tel: (0937) 845829

Fri 15th-17th
Ceramics Fair, Cairn Hotel,
Harrogate
Wakefield Fairs.
Tel: (0634) 723461

Wed 27th-Sun Dec 1st
Antiques Fair, Castle Howard
Robert Bailey.
Tel: (0277) 362662

DIRECTORY OF MARKETS & CENTRES

This directory is in no way complete. If you wish to be included in next year's directory or if you have a change of address or telephone number, please could you inform us by December 31st 1991. Entries will be repeated in subsequent editions unless we are requested otherwise.

London

Alfies Antique Market,
13-25 Church Street, NW8
Tel: 071-723 6066
Tues-Sat 10-6pm

Angel Arcade,
116-118 Islington High Street,
Camden Passage, N1
Open Wed & Sat

Antiquarius Antique Market,
135/141 Kings Road, Chelsea, SW3
Tel: 071-351 5353
Open Mon-Sat 10-6pm

Antiques & Collectors Corner,
North Piazza, Covent Garden,
WC2
Tel: 071-240 7405
Open 9-5pm every day

Bermondsey Antiques Market,
corner of Long Lane and
Bermondsey Street, London, SE1
Tel: 071-351 5353
Friday 5am-2pm

Bermondsey Antique Warehouse,
173 Bermondsey Street, SE1
Tel: 071-407 2040/4250
Open 9.30-5.30pm, Thurs 9.30-8pm,
Fri 7-5.30pm. Closed Sat and Sun

Bond Street Antiques Centre,
124 New Bond Street, W1
Tel: 071-351 5353
Open Mon-Fri 10-5.45pm,
Sat 10-4pm

Camden Antiques Market,
Corner of Camden High Street,
and Buck Street, Camden Town,
NW1
Thurs 7-4pm

Camden Passage Antique Centre,
12 Camden Passage, Islington, N1
Tel: 071-359 0190
Stalls open Wed 8-3pm (Thurs
Books 9-4pm), Sat 9-5pm

Chapel Street Market,
Jubilee Shopping Hall,
65-67 Chapel Market, Islington,
N1
Tel: 071-278 9942
Open Wed, Fri, Sat & Sun

Chelsea Antiques Market,
245-253 Kings Road, SW3
Tel: 071-352 5689/9695/1424
Open 10-6pm

Chenil Galleries,
181-183 Kings Road, SW3
Tel: 071-351 5353
Mon-Sat 10-6pm

**Corner Portobello Antiques
Supermarket,**
282, 284, 288, 290 Westbourne
Grove, W11
Tel: 071-727 2027
Open Fri 12-4pm, Sat 7-6pm

Covent Garden Antiques Market,
Jubilee Market, Covent Garden
Piazza, WC2
Tel: 071-240 7405
Mon only 6-4pm

Cutler Street Antiques Market,
Goulston Street, near Aldgate
End, E1
Sun 7-2pm

Crystal Palace Collectors Market,
Jasper Road, Westow Hill, Crystal
Palace, SE19
Tel: 081-761 3735
Open Wed 9-4pm, Fri 9-5pm,
Sat 9-4pm, Sun 11-4pm

Dixons Antique Centre,
471 Upper Richmond Road West,
East Sheen, SW14
Tel: 081-878 6788
Open 10-5.3pm, Sun 1.30-5.30pm,
Closed Wed

**Franklin's Camberwell Antiques
Market,**
161 Camberwell Road, SE5
Tel: 071-703 8089
Open 10-6pm, Sun 1-6pm.

**Georgian Village Antiques
Market,**
100 Wood Street, Walthamstow,
E17
Tel: (0304) 853418
Open 10-5pm. Closed Thurs

Georgian Village,
Islington Green, N1
Tel: 071-226 1571
Open Wed 10-4pm, Sat 7-5pm

Good Fairy Open Market,
100 Portobello Road, W11
Tel: 071-351 5950/071-221 8977 ·
Sats only
Open Sat 5-5pm

Grays Antique Market,
58 Davies Street, W1
Tel: 071-629 7034
Open Mon-Fri 10-6pm

Grays Mews,
1-7 Davies Street, W1
Tel: 071-629 7034
Open Mon-Fri 10-6pm

Grays Portobello,
138 Portobello Road, W11
Tel: 071-221 3069
Open Sat 7-4pm

Greenwich Crafts Market,
Burney Street Car Park,
Greenwich, SE10
Tel: 071-240 7405/6
Open Sat (& Sun Summer)

Greenwich Flea Market,
Burney Street Car Park,
Greenwich, SE10
Tel: 071-240 7405/6
Open Sat & Sun

Hampstead Antique Emporium,
12 Heath Street, Hampstead, NW3
Tel: 071-794 3297
Open 10-6pm. Closed Mon & Sun

Jubilee Market,
Covent Garden, WC2
Tel: 081-836 2139
Open Mon

L'Aiglon Galleries,
220 Westbourne Grove, W11
Tel: 071-727 6596

The London Silver Vaults,
Chancery House,
53-65 Chancery Lane, WC2
Tel: 071-242 3844
Open 9-5.30pm, Sat 9-12.30pm

The Mall Antiques Arcade,
Camden Passage, Islington, N1
Tues, Thurs, Fri 10-5pm,
Wed 7.30-5pm, Sat 9-6pm

Northcote Road Antiques Market,
155A Northcote Road, Battersea,
SW11
Tel: 071-228 6850
Open Mon-Sat 10-6pm,
Sun 12-5pm

Old Church Galleries,
320 Kings Road, SW3
Tel: 071-351 4649
Open Mon-Sat 10-6pm
Closed Sun & Bank Holidays

Peckham Indoor Market,
Rye Lane Bargain Centre,
48 Rye Lane, Peckham, SE15
Tel: 081-639 2463
Open Tues-Sat

Pierrepoint Arcade,
Camden Passage, N1
Tel: 071-359 0190
Open Wed & Sat

Portobello Road Market,
London, W11
Open Sat 5.30-5pm

Roger's Antiques Gallery,
65 Portobello Road, W11
Tel: 071-351 5353
Open Sat 7-4pm

Rochefort Antique Gallery,
32/34 The Green, Winchmore Hill,
London, N21

Steptoes Yard
52A Goldhawk Road, W12
Tel: 071-240 7405
Open Sat & Sun 6-5pm

**Streatham Traders & Shippers
Market,**
United Reform Church Hall,
Streatham High Street, SW16
Tel: 071-764 3602
Open Tues 8-3pm

Wimbledon Market, Car Park,
Wimbledon Greyhound Stadium,
Plough Lane, SW19
Tel (0774) 258115

Willesden Market, Car Park,
White Hart Public House,
Willesden, NW10
Tel: 071-240 7405/6
Open Wed & Sat

World Famous Portobello Market
177 Portobello Road and
1-3 Elgin Crescent, W11
Tel: 071-221 7638/229 4010
Open Sat 5-6pm

York Arcade,
80 Islington High Street, N1
Tel: 071-837 8768
Open Wed & Sat 8-5pm, Tues,
Thurs, Fri 11-3pm

Greater London

Antiques Arcade,
22 Richmond Hill, Richmond,
Surrey
Tel: 081-940 2035
Open Tues, Thurs, Fri 10.30-5.30,
Sun 2-5.30pm

Avon

Great Western Antique Centre,
Bartlett Street, Bath
Tel: 081-886 4779/081-363 0910
Open 10-6pm, Closed Wed & Fri
Tel: (0225) 424243/42873/310388
Open Mon-Sat 10-5pm
Wed 8.30-5pm

Bath Antiques Market,
Guinea Lane, off Lansdown Road,
Bath
Open Wed 6.30-2.30pm

Bristol Antique Market,
St Nicholas Markets,
The Exchange, Corn Street
Tel: (0272) 260021
Open Thurs & Fri 9-4pm

Clifton Antiques Market,
26/28 The Mall, Clifton, Bristol
Tel: (0272) 741627
Open 10-6pm. Closed Mon

Bedfordshire

**The Woburn Abbey Antiques
Centre,**
Woburn
Tel: (0525) 290350
Open every day 11-5pm Nov to
Easter. 10-5.30pm Easter to Oct

Reading Emporium,
1A Merchant Place (off Friar
Street), Reading
Tel: (0734) 590290
Open 10-5pm

Berkshire

Hungerford Arcade,
High Street, Hungerford
Tel: (0488) 683701
Open 9.30-5.30pm, Sun 10-6pm

500

Twyford Antiques Centre,
1 High Street, Twyford
Tel: (0734) 342161
Open Mon-Sat 9.30-5.30pm,
Sun 10.30-5pm, Closed Wed

Buckinghamshire

Amersham Antique Collectors
Centre, 20-22 Whieldon Street,
Old Amersham
Tel: (0494) 431282
Open Mon-Sat 9.30-5.30pm

Antiques at Wendover,
The Old Post Office, Wendover
Tel: (0296) 625335
Open Mon-Sat 10-5.30pm,
Sun 11-5.30pm

Olney Antiques Centre,
Rose Court, Olney
Tel: (0234) 712172
Open 10-5.30pm, Sun 12-5.30pm

Bell Street Antiques Centre,
20/22 Bell Street, Princes
Risborough
Tel: (084 44) 3034
Open 9.30-5.30pm, Sun 12-5pm

Tingewick Antiques Centre,
Main Street, Tingewick
Tel: (0280) 848219
Open 10.30-5 inc. Sun

Market Square Antiques,
20 Market Place, Olney
Tel: (0234) 712172
Open Mon-Sat 10-5.30pm,
Sun 2-5.30pm

Cambridgeshire

Collectors Market,
Dales Brewery, Gwydir Street
(off Mill Road), Cambridge
Open 9.30-5pm

Willingham Antiques & Collectors
Market,
25-29 Green Street, Willingham
Tel: (0954) 60283
Open 10-5pm. Closed Thurs

Cheshire

Davenham Antique Centre,
Northwick
Tel: (0606) 44350
Open Mon-Sat 10-5pm,
Closed Wed

Stancie Cutler Antique &
Collectors Fairs,
Nantwich Civic Hall, Nantwich
Tel: (0270) 624288
Open 1st Thurs each month
12-9pm except May — 1st Wed,
Bank Hol Mons & New Year's
Date 10-6pm, 3rd Sat of each
month 9-4pm

Nantwich Antique Centre,
The Old Police Station, Welsh
Row, Nantwich
Tel: (0270) 624035
Open 10-5.30pm. Closed Wed

Melody's Antique Galleries,
32 City Road, Chester (towards
railway station)
Tel: (0244) 341818/328968
Open Mon-Sat 10-5.30pm

Cornwall

Waterfront Antique Complex,
1st Floor, 4 Quay Street, Falmouth
Tel: (0326) 311491
Open 9-5pm

New Generation Antique Market,
61/62 Chapel Street, Penzance
Tel: (0736) 63267
Open 9.30-5pm

Cumbria

Carlisle Antique & Craft Centre,
Cecil Hall, Cecil Street, Carlisle
Tel: (0228) 21970
Open Mon-Sat 9-5pm

Cockermouth Antiques Market,
Courthouse, Main Street,
Cockermouth
Tel: (0900) 824346
Open 10-5pm

Devon

Dartmoor Antiques Centre,
Off West Street, Ashburton
Tel: (0364) 52182
Open Tues 9-4pm

The Antique Centre on the Quay,
The Quay, Exeter
Tel: (0392) 214180
Open 10-5pm, Sun 11-5pm

The Antique Centre,
Abingdon House, 136 High Street,
Honiton
Tel: (0404) 42108
Open Mon-Sat 10-5pm

Newton Abbot Antiques Centre,
55 East Street, Newton Abbot
Tel: (0626) 54074
Open Tues 9-3pm

Barbican Antiques Market,
82-84 Vauxhall Street, Barbican,
Plymouth
Tel: (0752) 266927
Open 9.30-5pm

Dorset

Bridport Antique Antique Centre,
5 West Allington, Bridport
Tel: (0308) 25885
Open 9.30-5pm

The Antique Centre,
837-839 Christchurch Road,
Boscombe East, Bournemouth
Tel: (0202) 421052
Six days a week 9.30-5.30

Gold Hill Antiques & Collectables,
3 Gold Hill Parade, Gold Hill,
Shaftesbury
Tel: (0747) 54050

Sherborne Antique Arcade,
Mattar Arcade, 17 Newlands,
Sherborne
Tel: (0935) 813464
Open 9-5pm

The Antique Centre,
Boscombe East, 837/839
Christchurch Road, Bournemouth
Tel: (0202) 421052
Open Mon-Sat 9.30-5.30pm

Barnes House Antiques Centre,
West Row, Wimborne Minster
Tel: (0202) 886275
Open 10-5pm

Wimborne Antique Centre,
Newborough Road, Wimborne
Tel: (0202) 841251
Open Thurs 10-4pm, Fri 8.30-5pm,
Sat 10-5pm, Sun 9.30-5pm

Essex

Battlesbridge Antiques Centre,
The Green, Chelmsford Road,
Battlesbridge, Nr Wickford
Tel: (0268) 764197
Open all weekend & most
weekdays

Kelvedon Antiques Centre,
139 High Street, Kelvedon
Tel: (0376) 70896
Open Mon-Sat 10-5pm

Trinity Antiques Centre,
7 Trinity Street, Colchester
Tel: (0206) 577775
Open 9.30-5pm

Gloucestershire

Cirencester Antique Market,
Market Place, Cirencester
Tel: 071-240 0428
Open Fri

Gloucester Antiques Centre,
Severn Road, Gloucester
Tel: (0452) 29716
Open Mon-Fri 9.30-5pm,
Sat 9.30-4.30pm, Sun 1-5.30pm

Hampshire

Folly Antiques Centre,
College Street, Petersfield
Tel: (0730) 64816
Open 9.30-5pm, Thurs 9.30-1pm

Hereford & Worcester

Leominster Antiques Market,
14 Broad Street, Leominster
Tel: (0568) 2189
Open Mon-Sat 10-5pm

Hertfordshire

St Albans Antique Market,
Town Hall, Chequer Street,
St Albans
Tel: (0727) 50427
Open Mon 9.30-4pm

By George! Antiques Centre,
23 George Street, St Albans
Tel: (0727) 53032
Open 10-5pm

The Herts & Essex Antique Centre,
The Maltings, Station Road,
Sawbridgeworth
Tel: (0279) 722044
Tues-Fri 10-5pm, Sat & Sun
10.30-6pm, Closed Mon

Humberside

New Pocklington Antiques Centre,
26 George Street, Pocklington
near York
Tel: (0759) 303032
Open Mon-Sat 10-5pm

Kent

Burgate Antiques,
10 Burgate, Canterbury
Tel: (0227) 456500
Open Mon-Sat 9.30-5.30pm

Folkestone Market,
Rotunda Amusement Park,
Marine Parade, Folkestone
Tel: 081-981 0797/081-278 9942
Open Sun

Malthouse Arcade,
High Street, Hythe
Tel: (0303) 260103
Open Fri & Sat 10-6pm

Hythe Antique Centre,
5 High Street, Hythe
Tel: (0303) 269643
Open 10-4, Sat 10-5pm, Closed
Wed & Sun

Rochester Antiques & Flea
Market,
Corporation Street, Rochester
Tel: 071-240 0428
Open Sat 9-2pm

Sandgate Antiques Centre,
61-63 High Street, Sandgate
Tel: (0303) 48987
Open 10-6pm, Sun 11-6pm

The Antiques Centre,
120 London Road, Sevenoaks
Tel: (0732) 452104
Open 9-1pm, 2-5.30pm

Tudor Cottage Antiques Centre,
22-23 Shipbourne Road, Tonbridge
Tel: (0732) 351719
Open 10-5.30pm

Noah's Ark Antiques,
5 King Street, Sandwich
Tel: (0304) 611144
Open 10-4.30pm, Closed Wed &
Sun

Tunbridge Wells Antique Centre,
Union Square, The Pantiles,
Tunbridge Wells
Tel: (0892) 33708
Open Mon-Sat 9.30-5.30pm

Castle Antiques Centre,
1 London Road, Westerham
Tel: (0959) 62492
Open Mon-Sat 10-5pm

Lancashire

Last Drop Antique & Collectors
Club,
Last Drop Hotel, Bromley Cross,
Bolton
Open Sun 11-4pm

Bygone Times Antiques,
Eccleston (6 mins from J27, M6)
Tel: (0257) 453780
Open 7 days a week 8-6pm

Levenshulme Antiques
Hypermarket,
Levenshulme Town Hall,
965 Stockport Road, Levenshulme,
Manchester
Tel: 061-224 2410
Open 10-5pm

Preston Antique Centre,
The Mill, New Hall Lane, Preston
Tel: (0772) 794498
Fax: (0772) 651694
Open Mon-Fri 8.30-5.30pm,
Sat 10-4pm, Sun 9-4pm or by
appointment

Royal Exchange Shopping Centre,
Antiques Gallery, St Ann's
Square, Manchester
Tel: 061-834 3731/834 1427
Open Mon-Sat 9.30-5.30pm

Walter Aspinall Antiques,
Pendle Antique Centre, Union
Mill, Watt Street, Sabden near
Blackburn
Tel: (0282) 76311
Open Mon-Thurs Summer 9-8pm,
Winter 9-6pm
All year Fri 9-5pm, Sat 10-5pm,
Sun 11-4pm

Leicestershire

The Antiques Complex,
St Nicholas Place, Leicester
Tel: (0533) 533343
Open 9.30-5.30pm

Oxford Street Antiques Centre Ltd,
16-26 Oxford Street, Leicester
Tel: (0533) 553006
Open Mon-Fri 10-5.30pm,
Sat 10-5pm, Sun 2-5pm

Lincolnshire

Boston Antiques Centre,
12 West Street, Boston
Tel: (0205) 361510
Open 9-5.30pm

Hemswell Antique Centre,
Caenby Corner Estate, Hemswell
Cliff near Gainsborough
Tel: (042 773) 389
Open 10-5pm 7 days-a-week

The Lincolnshire Antiques Centre,
26 Bridge Street, Horncastle
Tel: (0507) 527794
Open Mon-Sat 9-5pm

Talisman Antiques,
51 North Street, Horncastle
Tel: (0507) 526893
Open 10.30-5pm. Closed Mon

Talisman Antiques,
Regent House, 12 South Market,
Alford
Tel: (0507) 463441
Open 10.30-4.30pm, Closed Thurs

Norfolk

Coltishall Antiques Centre,
High Street, Coltishall
Tel: (0603) 738306
Open 10-5pm

Fakenham Antique Centre,
Old Congregational Chapel,
14 Norwich Road, Fakenham
Tel: (0328) 862941
Open 10-5pm, Thurs 9-5pm

The Old Granary Antique &
Collectors Centre,
King Staithe Lane,
(off Queens Street), King's Lynn
Tel: (0553) 775509
Open Mon-Sat 10-5pm

Cloisters Antiques Fair,
St Andrew's & Blackfriars Hall,
St Andrew's Plain, Norwich
Tel: (0603) 628477
Open Wed 9.30-3.30pm

Norwich Antiques & Collectors
Centre,
Quayside, Fye Bridge, Norwich
Tel: (0603) 612582
Open 10-5pm

Antique & Collectors Centre,
St Michael at Plea, Bank Plain,
Norwich
Tel: (0603) 619129
Open 9.30-5.00

Angel Antique Centre,
Pansthorn Farmhouse, Redgrave
Road, South Lopham, near Diss
Tel: (037 988) 317
Open 9.30-6pm inc Sun

Wymondham Antique Centre,
No 1 Town Green, Wymondham
Tel: (0953) 604817
Open 10-5pm

Northamptonshire

The Village Antique Market,
62 High Street, Weedon
Tel: (0327) 42015
Open 9.30-5.30pm,
Sun 10.30-5.30pm

Antiques & Bric-a-Brac Market,
Market Square, Town Centre,
Wellingborough
Tel: (0905) 611321
Open Tues 9-4pm

Northumberland

Colmans of Hexham,
15 St Mary's Chare, Hexham
Tel: (0434) 603811/2
Open Mon-Sat 9-5pm

Nottinghamshire

Castle Gate Antiques Centre,
55 Castle Gate, Newark
Tel: (0636) 700076
Open 9-5.30pm

Newark Antiques Centre,
Lombard Street,
Newark-on-Trent,
Tel: (0636) 605504
Open 9.30-5pm

Newark Antique Warehouse,
Kelham Road, Newark
Tel: (0636) 74869
Open 9-5.30pm

Nottingham Antique Centre,
British Rail Goods Yard, London
Road, Nottingham
Tel: (0602) 504504/505548
Open 9-5pm. Closed Sat

Top Hat Antiques Centre,
66-72 Derby Road, Nottingham
Tel: (0602) 419143
Open 9.30-5pm

Oxfordshire

Burford Antiques Centre
(at the roundabout), Cheltenham
Road, Burford
Tel: (099 382) 3227
Open 10-6pm 7 days a week

Cotswold Gateway Antique
Centre,
Cheltenham Road, Burford
Roundabout, Burford
Tel: (099 382) 3678
Open 10-5.30pm, Sun 2pm-5.30pm

Chipping Norton Antique Centre,
Ivy House, Middle Row, Chipping
Norton
Tel: (0608) 644212
Open 10-5pm inc Sun

Deddington Antique Centre,
Laurel House, Bull Ring, Market
Square, Deddington
Tel: (0869) 38968
Open Mon-Sat 10-5pm

Oxford Antiques Centre,
The Jam Factory, Oxford Antiques
Centre, 27 Park End Street,
Oxford (opp the station)
Tel: (0865) 251075
Open Mon-Sat 10-5pm & 1st Sun
every month

Antique & Collectors Market,
Town Hall, Thame
Tel: (0844) 28205
Open 8.30-3.30pm. Second Tues
each month

The Lamb Arcade,
High Street, Wallingford
Tel: (0491) 35166
Open 10-5pm, Sat 9.30-5pm,
Wed 10-4pm

Span Antiques,
6 Market Place, Woodstock
Tel: (0993) 811332
Open 10-1pm, 2-5pm. Closed Wed

Shropshire
Stretton Antiques Market,
36 Sandford Avenue, Church
Stretton
Tel: (0694) 723718
Open Mon-Sat 9.30-5.30pm,
Sun 10.30-4.30pm

Ironbridge Antique Centre,
Dale End, Ironbridge
Tel: (0952) 433784
Open 10-5pm, Sun 2-5pm

Pepper Lane Antique Centre,
Pepper Lane, Ludlow
Tel: (0584) 876494
Open Mon-Sat 9.30-5pm

St Leonards Antiques,
Corve Street, Ludlow
Tel: (0584) 875573
Open Mon-Sat 9-5pm

Shrewsbury Antique Centre,
15 Princess House, The Square,
Shrewsbury
Tel: (0743) 247704
Open Mon-Sat 9.30-5pm

Shrewsbury Antique Market,
Frankwell Quay Warehouse,
Shrewsbury
Tel: (0743) 50916
Open 10-5.30pm, Sun 12-5pm

Telford Antique Centre,
High Street, Wellington, Telford
Tel: (0952) 56450
Open Mon-Sat 10-5pm,
Sun 2-5pm

Somerset
Guildhall Antique Market,
The Guildhall, Chard
Open Thurs 8-4pm

Dulverton Antique Centre,
Lower Town Hall, Dulverton
Tel: (0398) 23522
Open Mon-Sat 9.30-5pm

County Antiques Centre,
21/23 West Street, Ilminster
Tel: (0460) 54151
Open 10-5pm

Taunton Silver Street Antiques
Centre,
27/29 Silver Street, Taunton
Tel: 071-351 5353
Open Mon 9-4pm

Staffordshire
Rugeley Antique Centre,
161/3 Main Road, Brereton near
Rugeley
Tel: (08894) 77166
Open 10-5pm

The Antique Centre,
128 High Street, Kinver
Tel: (0384) 877441
Open 10-5.30pm

Antique Market,
The Stones, Newcastle-under-
Lyme
Tel: (088 97) 527
Open Tues 7-2pm

Barclay House Antiques,
14-16 Howard Place, Shelton,
Stoke-on-Trent
Tel: (0782) 274747
Open Mon-Sat 9.30-6pm

Tutbury Mill Antiques,
6 Lower High Street, Tutbury near
Burton-on-Trent
Tel: (0283) 815999
Open 7 days 9-6pm

Suffolk
Waveney Antiques Centre,
Peddars Lane, Beccles
Tel: (0502) 716147
Open Mon-Sat 10-5pm

Debenham Antique Centre,
The Forresters Hall, High Street,
Debenham
Tel: (0728) 860777
Open 9.30-5.30pm

Long Melford Antiques Centre,
The Chapel Maltings, Long
Melford
Tel: (0787) 79287
Open Mon-Sat 9.30-5.30pm,
Closed Bank Holidays

Old Town Hall Antiques Centre,
High Street, Needham Market
Tel: (0449) 720773
Open 10-5pm

The Barn,
Risby, Bury St Edmunds
Tel: (0284) 811126
Open 7 days-a-week

Surrey
Antiques & Interiors,
34 Station Road East, Oxted
Tel: (0883) 712806
Open Mon-Sat 9.30-5.30pm

Victoria & Edward Antiques
Centre,
61 West Street, Dorking
Tel: (0306) 889645
Open Mon-Sat 9.30-5.3pm

Surrey Antiques Centre,
10 Windsor Street, Chertsey
Tel: (0932) 563313
Open 10-5pm

The Antiques Arcade,
77 Bridge Road, East Molesey
Tel: 081-979 7954
Open 10-5pm

Maltings Monthly Market,
Bridge Square, Farnham
Tel: (0252) 726234
First Sat monthly

The Antiques Centre,
22 Haydon Place
corner of Martyr
Road, Guildford
Tel: (0483) 67817
Open 10-5pm. Closed Mon, Wed

Wood's Wharf Antiques Bazaar,
56 High Street, Haslemere
Tel: (0428) 642125
Open Mon-Sat 9.30-5pm

The Old Smithy
Antique Centre,
7 High Street, Merstham
Tel: (073 74) 2306
Open 10-5pm

Reigate Antiques Arcade,
57 High Street, Reigate
Tel: (0737) 222654
Open 10-5.30pm

Sutton Market,
West Street, Sutton
Tel: 01-661 1245
Open Tues & Sat

Fern Cottage Antique Centre,
28/30 High Street,
Thames Ditton,
Tel: 081-398 2281
Open 10-5.30pm

Sussex East
Bexhill Antiques Centre,
Quakers Mill, Old Town, Bexhill
Tel: (0424) 210182/221940
Open 6 days, 10-5.30pm

Brighton Antiques Gallery,
41 Meeting House Lane,
Brighton
Tel: (0273) 26693/21059
Open 10-5.30pm

Brighton Market,
Jubilee Shopping Hall,
44-47 Gardner Street, Brighton
Tel: (0273) 600574
Open Mon-Sat

Kollect-O-Mania,
25 Trafalgar Street, Brighton
Tel: (0273) 694229
Open 10-5pm

Prinnys Antique Gallery,
3 Meeting House Lane, Brighton
Tel: (0273) 204554
Open Mon-Sat 9.30-5pm

Chateaubriand Antiques Centre,
High Street, Burwash
Tel: (0435) 882535
Open 10-5pm, Sun 2-5pm

Lewes Antique Centre,
20 Cliffe High Street, Lewes
Tel: (0273) 476148
Open 10-5pm

Newhaven Flea Market,
28 South Way, Newhaven
Tel: (0273) 517207/516065
Open every day

Mint Arcade,
71 The Mint, Rye
Tel: (0797) 225952
Open 10-5pm every day

Seaford's "Barn Collectors"
Market & Studio Book Shop,
The Barn, Church Lane, Seaford
Tel: (0323) 890010
Open Tues, Thurs
& Sat 10-4.30pm

Sussex West
Antiques & Collectors Market,
Old Orchard Building, Old House,
Adversane near Billingshurst

Copthorne Group Antiques,
Copthorne Bank, Crawley
Tel: (0342) 712802
Open Mon-Sat 10-5pm

Eagle House Antiques Centre,
Market Square, Midhurst
Tel: (0730) 812718
Open daily except Sun

Mamie's Antiques Market,
5 River Road, Arundel
Tel: (0903) 882012
Open Sat 9-5pm

Midhurst Antiques Market,
Knockhundred Row, Midhurst
Tel: (0730) 814231
Open 9.30-5.30pm (winter 5pm)

Shirley, Mostyns Antique Centre,
64 Brighton Road, Lancing
Tel: (0903) 752961
Open Mon-Fri 10-5pm or by
appointment

Petworth Antique Market,
East Street, Petworth
Tel: (0798) 42073
Open 10-5.30pm

Tyne & Wear
Vine Lane Antique Market,
17 Vine Lane, Newcastle-upon-
Tyne
Tel: 091-261 2963/232 9832
Open 10-5.30pm

Antique Centre Newcastle,
8 St Mary Place East, Newcastle-
upon-Tyne (opp Civic Centre)
Tel: 091-232 9832
Open Tues-Sat 10-5pm

Warwickshire
The Antiques Centre,
High Street, Bidford-on-Avon
Tel: (0789) 773680
Open 10-5pm, Sun 2-5.30pm.
Closed Mon

Dunchurch Antique Centre,
16/16A Daventry Road,
Dunchurch near Rugby
Tel: (0788) 817147
Open 7 days 10-5pm

Spa Antiques Market,
4 Windsor Street,
Leamington Spa
Tel: (0926) 22927
Open 9.30-5.30pm

Antiques Etc,
22 Railway Terrace, Rugby
Open 10-5pm.
Closed Tues & Wed

The Antique Arcade,
4 Sheep Street, Stratford-upon-
Avon
Tel: (0789) 297249
Open 10-5.30pm

Stratford Antiques Centre,
60 Ely Street,
Statford-upon-Avon
Tel: Mike Conway (0789) 204180
Open 10-5.30 every day

Smith Street Antiques Centre,
7 Smith Street, Warwick
Tel: (0926) 497864
Open 10-5.30pm

Vintage Antique Market,
36 Market Place, Warwick
Tel: (0926) 491527
Open 10-5.30pm

Warwick Antique Centre,
20-22 High Street, Warwick
Tel: (0926) 495704
Open 6 days-a-week

West Midlands
Birmingham Antique Centre,
141 Bromsgrove Street,
Birmingham
Tel: 021-692 1414/622 2145
Open every Thurs from 9am
The City of Birmingham Antique
Market,
St Martins Market, Edgbaston
Street, Birmingham
Tel: 021-267 4636
Open Mon 7-2pm

Stancie Cutler Antique &
Collectors Fair,
Town Hall, Sutton Coldfield
Tel: (0270) 624288
Open Wed monthly 11-8pm

Walsall Antiques Centre,
7a The (Digbeth) Arcade, Walsall
Tel: (0922) 725163/5

Wiltshire
London House Antique Centre,
High Street, Marlborough
Tel: (0672) 52331
Open Mon-Sat 9.30-5.30pm

The Marlborough Parade
Antiques Centre,
The Parade, Marlborough
Tel: (0672) 55331
Open 10-5pm

Antique Market,
37 Catherine Street, Salisbury
Tel: (0722) 26033
Open 9-6pm

The Avon Bridge Antiques &
Collectors Market,
United Reformed Church Hall,
Fisherton Street, Salisbury
Open Tues 9-4pm

Mr Micawber's Attic,
73 Fisherton Street, Salisbury
Tel: (0722) 337822
Open 9.30-5pm. Closed Wed

Yorkshire North
The Ginnel,
Harrogate Antique Centre
(off Parliament Street), Harrogate
Tel: (0423) 508857
Open 9.30-5.30pm

Grove Collectors Centre,
Grove Road, Harrogate
Tel: (0423) 61680
Open 10-5pm

Montpelier Mews Antique Market,
Montpelier Street, Harrogate
Tel: (0423) 530484
Open 9.30-5.30pm

West Park Antiques Pavilion,
20 West Park, Harrogate
Tel: (0423) 61758
Open 10-5pm. Closed Mon

Micklegate Antiques Market,
73 Micklegate, York
Tel: (0904) 644438
Open Wed & Sat 10-5.30pm

York Antique Centre,
2 Lendal, York
Tel: Peter Banks (0904) 641445
Open Mon-Sat Winter 10-5pm,
Summer 9.30-5.30pm

Yorkshire South
Treasure House Antiques Centre,
4-10 Swan Street, Bawtry near
Doncaster
Tel: (0302) 710621
Open 10-5pm inc Sun

Yorkshire West
Halifax Antiques Centre,
Queens Road/Gibbet Street,
Halifax
Tel: (0422) 366657

Scotland
Bath Street Antique Galleries,
203 Bath Street, Glasgow
Open 10-5pm, Sat 10-1pm

Corner House Antiques,
217 St Vincent Street, Glasgow
Tel: 041-248 2560
Open 10-5pm

The Victorian Village,
53 & 57 West Regent Street,
Glasgow
Tel: 041-332 0808
Open 10-5pm

Wales
Pembroke Antique Centre,
The Hall, Hamilton Terrace,
Pembroke
Tel: (0646) 687017
Open 10-5pm

Cardiff Antique Centre,
69-71 St Mary Street, Cardiff
Tel: (0222) 30970

Jacobs Antique Centre,
West Canal Wharf, Cardiff
Tel: (0222) 390939
Open Thurs & Sat 9.30-5pm

Offa's Dyke Antiques Centre,
4 High Street, Knighton, Powys
Tel: (0547) 528634/528940
Open Mon-Sat 10-1pm, 2-5pm,
Wed 10-1pm

Swansea Antique Centre,
21 Oxford Street, Swansea
Tel: (0792) 466854

Crew Market,
Crew Airfield on A477
(Carmarthen to Pembroke Road),
Port Talbot
Tel: (0639) 884834
Open Sun

Port Talbot Market,
Jubilee Shopping Hall,
64-66 Station Road, Port Talbot,
Glamorgan
Tel (0639) 883184
Open Mon-Sat

Channel Islands
Union Street Antique Market,
8 Union Street, St Helier, Jersey
Tel: (0534) 73805/22475
Open 9-6pm

DID YOU KNOW?
Miller's Collectables
Price Guide is
designed to build up,
year by year, into the
most comprehensive
reference system
available.

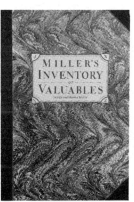

INDEX

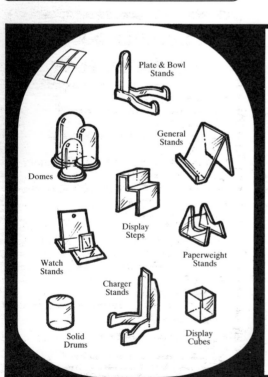